"Welcome, Holy Spirit should be welcome in the libraries of all Christians interested in the Charismatic Renewal. Written by and for Lutherans, it will nevertheless constitute a standard theological work for Pentecostals and Charismatics in all of the churches.

"The publication of this foundational volume marks a milestone in the development of the charismatic movement in our time. Well written and researched, it gives well-balanced answers to most of the questions usually raised about the modern Pentecostal/Charismatic Movement."

> —*Vinson Synan*
> *North American Renewal Service Committee*

"This book makes it clear that the renewal is not Gospel tinsel, a peripheral adornment, a passing enthusiasm of the religious adolescent. *Welcome, Holy Spirit* is an ecumenically sensitive presentation of what God has been doing in the charismatic renewal in Lutheran churches. To the process of theological discernment the international team brings academic credentials, pastoral experience, and a worldwide contact with the Lutheran renewal. From this global perspective it faces the issues of justification, the cross, Christ alone, grace alone, faith alone, scripture alone."

> —*Kilian McDonnell*
> *St. John's University*

"We've waited for years for someone to chronicle the acts of the Holy Spirit in this generation. This is history, systematic theology, and inspiration combined in a practical, 'how to' volume."

> —*Jamie Buckingham*

WELCOME, HOLY SPIRIT

A Study of Charismatic Renewal in the Church

LARRY CHRISTENSON, editor

AUGSBURG Publishing House • Minneapolis

WELCOME, HOLY SPIRIT
A Study of Charismatic Renewal in the Church

Scripture quotations unless otherwise noted are from the Revised Standard Version of the Bible, copyright 1946, 1952, and 1971 by the Division of Christian Education of the National Council of Churches.

Scripture quotations marked NIV are from the Holy Bible: New International Version. Copyright 1978 by the New York International Bible Society. Used by permission of Zondervan Bible Publishers.

Scripture quotations marked KJV are from the (Authorized) King James Version.

Library of Congress Cataloging-in-Publication Data

WELCOME, HOLY SPIRIT.

Based on papers originally presented at the
International Lutheran Charismatic Theological
Consultation held outside Helsinki, Finland, in
the summer of 1981.
    Bibliography: p.
    Includes index.
    1. Pentecostalism—Lutheran Church—Congresses.
2. Lutheran Church—Doctrines—Congresses.
I. Christenson, Larry, 1928–   II. International
Lutheran Charismatic Theological Consultation (1981 :
Helsinki, Finland)
BX8065.5.W45   1987   284.1   87-14565
ISBN 0-8066-2273-3

Manufactured in the U.S.A.   APH 10-7021

2   3   4   5   6   7   8   9   0   1   2   3   4   5   6   7   8   9

Being therefore exalted at the right hand of God, and having received from the Father the promise of the Holy Spirit, Jesus has poured out this which you see and hear.
                                                                    Acts 2:33

CONTENTS

INTRODUCTION

A VIEW FROM WITHIN

The charismatic renewal has been around for more than a quarter of a century. It has evoked a variety of reactions, and still does. Some people personally identify with the movement and talk about the blessings they have received. Others point out problems that the movement has caused, and raise critical questions. The movement has been the occasion for considerable controversy in the church.

Yet the charismatic renewal has not become a breakaway movement. It has generally remained in the churches. This is a special grace of God. In the past, the encounter between renewal movements and the church has often resulted in separation. One thing that can help prevent separation is for members to speak honestly and openly with each other, and to continue to listen to one another.

This book is an invitation to think together about charismatic renewal in the church, and with particular reference to the Lutheran church. It is not an official position of the church. *It is a statement on behalf of a group within the church, those members whom we have come to call "charismatics."* In a sense, it is a response to such oft-repeated questions as: "Who are these charismatics, anyway? What do they believe?"

This book is the product of a consultation that was initiated at an International Lutheran Charismatic Renewal Leaders' Conference held in Finland in the summer of 1981, with about 100 people from 12 different countries in attendance. Members of the consultation were chosen on the basis of long-term pastoral experience and theological training in the Lutheran tradition. In addition, they represented a broad range of firsthand experience in the charismatic renewal.

In 1981–1982, several members prepared papers based on an overall outline of the projected work. The group held its first meeting at Schloss Craheim in Bavaria, July 15-22, 1982. The prepared papers were thoroughly discussed. Generous time was also given to prayer, worship, and fellowship; this was felt to be an essential aspect of the undertaking.

Further writing assignments were handed out to members of the consultation. Larry Christenson was asked to be overall editor of the work. A second meeting was held at Løgumkloster Refugium in Denmark, October 6-13, 1983. The format of the meeting was similar to the first one: discussion of the document, prayer, worship, fellowship. In addition, a considerable amount of new material, drawn from the broad experience of the group, was introduced and discussed.

Overall evaluation of the work continued during the following three years, as subsequent drafts of the work were sent to members of the consultation. Although various members contributed first drafts for major sections of the book, the final work is the product of the group as a whole, working together with one another in the fellowship of the Holy Spirit.

The meetings and correspondence were lively. Members exchanged views freely, and they were not always in agreement with one another. Indeed, the final result—the book now before you—would probably still evoke some good discussions, including some disagreements, if the consultation were to meet again.

This book is presented with the prayer that the Lord may use it to help strengthen and unify his body, the church, so that it may better accomplish his purposes in the world.

PARTICIPANTS IN THE INTERNATIONAL LUTHERAN CHARISMATIC THEOLOGICAL CONSULTATION

Austria
Gerhard Grosse

Denmark
Jan Bjerregaard
Svend Boysen
Ole Skjerbaek Madsen
Per Mollerup

Federal Republic of Germany
Lorenz Hein
Gerhard Kelber
Wolfram Kopfermann

German Democratic Republic
Gottfried Rebner
Paul Toaspern

Finland
Kirsti Löytty
Seppo Löytty
Gunnar Weckström

Norway
Tormod Engelsviken
Jens-Petter Jørgensen
Johan Østerhus
Asbjørn Simonnes

Pakistan
Arne Rudvin
Geir Valle

Sweden
Fredrik Brosché
Per Eckerdal
Helge Fosseus
Bengt Holmberg
Per-Olof Söderpalm
Carl Gustav Stenbäck

United States
Larry Christenson
Theodore Jungkuntz
Herbert Mirly
W. Dennis Pederson
Morris Vaagenes
Arthur Vincent

A brief description of each participant's background and ministry is provided in Appendix 2.

PART ONE

RENEWED BY THE SPIRIT
The Presence and Purpose of the Charismatic Renewal

He saved us, not because of deeds done by us in righteousness, but in virtue of his own mercy, by the washing of regeneration and renewal in the Holy Spirit, which he poured out upon us richly through Jesus Christ our Savior, so that we might be justified by his grace and become heirs in hope of eternal life. The saying is sure.

Titus 3:5-8

CHAPTER 1

THE SCOPE OF THE
CHARISMATIC RENEWAL

A brief perspective

The charismatic renewal is a religious phenomenon that began around 1960. In the span of less than two decades the movement spread to every continent of the globe and into every major Christian denomination. No other movement in the history of Christianity has spread so fast and so extensively.[1]

Like most religious movements, the charismatic renewal has a distinguishing characteristic: as the Protestant Reformation focused on justification, or Wesleyanism on sanctification, the charismatic renewal has emphasized the person and work and gifts of the Holy Spirit. It has similarities to the classical Pentecostal movement, though it is historically distinct from it. It includes the practice of some spiritual gifts that have not been commonly experienced in mainline churches, but that have been a part of classical Pentecostal spirituality, notably, speaking in tongues, prophecy, and healing.[2] A major thrust of the movement, especially as it moved into its third decade, has been on world evangelization in the power of the Holy Spirit.

The emphasis on spiritual gifts has given the movement its distinctive name: *charismatic* comes from the Greek word *charis* ("grace") and its derivative *charismatic* ("gifts of grace" or, more commonly, "spiritual gifts"). According to Scripture, every Christian could be called a "charismatic" (see Rom. 6:23; 1 Cor. 12:7). However, that is not what most people mean when they use the word today.

The dictionary definition of a *charismatic* is simply "a member of a charismatic religious group or movement." It is primarily in this practical sense that we will be using the term. When we speak about charismatics, we mean people who participate in the experience and meetings and fellowship of the charismatic renewal; who generally tell other people what it has meant in their lives; who listen to the teachings, read the literature, and share the sense of mission of this widespread renewal movement. In short, charismatics are people who personally identify with the charismatic renewal. This is what most people mean when they use the word.

In less than 20 years: worldwide, churchwide

Many factors contribute to the occurrence and growth of religious movements. Before they surface as identifiable movements, their shape and direction is already being affected by many forces. Yet movements are often dated from a particular event that symbolizes the meaning of the movement and its outbreak into the public arena. We usually date the Reformation from the day Luther nailed his *95 Theses* to the door of the castle church in Wittenberg in 1517, or Methodism from the meeting in Aldersgate Street in 1738 when John Wesley's heart was "strangely warmed." The present-day charismatic renewal is usually dated from the Sunday morning in 1959 when Dennis Bennett announced to his Episcopalian congregation in Van Nuys, California, that he had been baptized in the Holy Spirit and spoke in tongues.

In little more than a year, similar events were occurring in a variety of Protestant congregations in the United States—Baptist, Church of Christ, Methodist, Presbyterian. Lutherans in California, Montana, and Minnesota began testifying to charismatic experiences in 1961–1962. (See Appendix 1 for a country-by-country overview of the development of the charismatic renewal among Lutherans.) As early as 1970, the religion editor of *The New York Times* referred to it as the most vital movement in American religion.[3] By 1980, nearly one-fifth of the adult population of the United States, more than 29 million people, were calling themselves Pentecostal or charismatic Christians.[4]

From its beginning in the Episcopal church in the United States, the movement spread to most parts of the worldwide Anglican communion in less than 10 years. At the quarter-century mark, 1984, no less than 47 percent of the world's Anglican bishops were openly identified with the charismatic renewal.[5]

Within two years of its beginnings in the United States, the phenomenon was spreading to mainline Protestant churches in other countries. By 1970 the movement was present and growing on every continent. Every major denomination numbered charismatics among its members. "There is nothing quite like it in the history of the church," said Presbyterian pastor and historian Robert Whitaker. "Earlier renewal movements have been limited geographically and denominationally. This one has penetrated every denomination and is present on every continent of the globe—and all within a space of about 15 years."[6]

In 1967 the renewal movement broke out in the Roman Catholic Church in the United States, where it experienced its most remarkable growth. By the 1980s Catholics in 120 countries were actively involved. Asked about the number of charismatic prayer groups in Colombia, one priest said, "Maybe ten thousand—maybe a hundred thousand. They're everywhere." In Poland, charismatic prayer groups were described as "springing up like mushrooms after the rain." The International Catholic Charismatic Renewal Office in Rome was in touch with more than 100 charismatic prayer groups in the city of Budapest. By the mid-1980s, Roman Catholic participants in the charismatic renewal, worldwide, were conservatively estimated at twenty million, and the movement showed no signs of abating.[7]

According to projections made by the World Council of Churches, by the year 2000, over 50% of all Christians in the world will be: (1) nonwhite, (2) from the southern hemisphere, and (3) of the pentecostal or charismatic variety.[8]

How are we to understand a movement of such evident scope and dynamism? What effect is it having throughout the church? What does it portend for the future of Christianity?

In the mid-1980s, it is too early to compose a definitive study of the charismatic movement. It is still growing and changing. The following chapters are not offered as a comprehensive or exhaustive study of the charismatic renewal; they present an "underway perspective" by an international consultation of 31 Lutheran charismatic leaders and theologians, who worked on this project over a period of five years. It is our hope that this work may contribute to a greater understanding of things that are taking place throughout the church today and that will affect the lives of believers in Christ for years to come.

CHAPTER 2

THE QUESTIONS
AND THE QUEST
OF THE CHARISMATIC
RENEWAL

Martin Luther's basic question was, "How can I find a gracious God?" In an earlier century, Francis of Assisi asked how the church of Christ, which had fallen into corruption, could be restored. In the 18th century, John Wesley's quest was for holiness of life.

What kind of questions are people asking in the latter half of the 20th century?

When the Lutheran World Federation met in Helsinki, Finland, in 1963 under the theme "Christ Today," they recognized that people today are asking different questions:

> The man of today no longer asks, "How can I find a gracious God?" His question is more radical, more elementary: he asks about God as such, "Where is God?" He suffers not from God's wrath, but from the impression of his absence; not from sin, but from the meaninglessness of his existence; he asks not about a gracious God, but whether God really exists.[1]

A young missionary, reflecting on his seminary training, described his own experience, and his frustration, in rather similar terms:

> Luther's question was not my question at all. For myself there was the question of meaning and direction in life. I was active in confirmation and the church's youth group, but other than the fun times with friends who gave me a lot of social support (which shouldn't be underestimated) there was no real spiritual seeking within the context of that group.

"Is God real?" was one of the questions that I struggled with. Another question that was on my mind was, "What difference does it make whether I believe in God or not?" The answer for me became clear when God revealed himself as being personally concerned for me. *The central issue of my quest was that of personal experience.* The meaning of my existence was thoroughly wrapped up in the question of God's existence and his concern for me as an individual. You can imagine the kind of problems that arose when I came up against astute theologians who were skeptical of personal experience. For which reason, of course, I became skeptical of all theological activity, formally speaking. It all seemed totally irrelevant. The basic problem was that their questions were not my questions and my questions were not their questions, and there was no sensitivity on either side for the questions of the other. So all they could offer me was answers to questions that I never asked.[2]

People today *are* asking different questions than were asked in earlier centuries. Behind this difference, however, is a common quest: the desire to relate to God.

Luther's question about a gracious God was not an abstract theological inquiry. It was a personal quest. The reformers of the 16th century recognized that people looking on from the outside regarded "justification by faith" with contempt as a mere teaching; but for the reformers themselves it was a profound experience of God.[3]

The same concern motivates people today. When they ask whether God is real, it is not to satisfy intellectual curiosity. They want to know whether there is a God to whom they can relate and respond.

The questions that people ask change precisely because the quest remains the same. Experience tends to evolve into tradition. The questions and answers of one generation become the doctrine of later generations. This can enrich the church's understanding of the faith, but it also runs the danger of blunting the quest for a genuine relationship with God. People may learn about God and talk about God, rehearsing the traditions of the past, without experiencing the reality of a relationship with God today. Recitation of truth, even heartfelt acceptance of a doctrine, does not necessarily involve a personal relationship with God. That is a gift of God, and it often comes only as people wrestle with the particular questions that God sets before their generation.

In 1985, the International Lutheran Renewal Center in St. Paul, Minnesota, conducted a survey of people with varying degrees of involvement in the charismatic renewal, to determine the nature of their spiritual quest and the kind of basic religious questions that they were asking. The survey indicated that these people were not asking the modern question, "Does God exist?" Nor were they asking, "How can I find a gracious God?" For them, the existence of God and the mercy of God were not in question. The reality of spiritual life was in a sense taken for granted. Their questions dealt rather with the quality of their life as Christians. They expressed discontent with a merely perfunctory expression of faith. They asked practical questions about living the Christian life more effectively.

A pastor from Minnesota wrote: "The question is not, 'Is God real?' but rather, 'How can I be real to God?' "

The relationship between church membership and spiritual life was the concern of a woman from Iowa: "Is there spiritual life beyond church membership? If you educate the mind, does this have the same result as spiritual conversion? I want to know the fullness of God in my life."

The response of a man from Canada was typical of a number of people who noted the lack of correspondence between church ritual and genuine spiritual life in their own experience: "I was brought up in a Lutheran church, baptized as an infant, and confirmed at age 14, but had never received Jesus as my Lord and Savior. I believed in God and knew about Jesus but had never experienced his love, until I surrendered my life to him. I was filled with the Holy Spirit, and my new life began. Since my life began, God has opened many doors of ministry to me."

A pastor in Norway expressed concern about the apathy of many church members: "There is so little joy in the churches and prayer fellowships. People know the right doctrine of salvation, but it doesn't show in their lives. One of the main things that the charismatic renewal has to offer, it seems to me, is to give people *joy* in their faith."

Side by side with testimonies of revitalized faith came questions about the daily struggle to live more effectively as Christians. Their understanding of experience was not static, but involved a continuing response to the initiatives of the Spirit.

"The Lord seems to be prodding me to witness. I want to be a more effective witness, but how?"

"How can I pray more effectively?"

"How do I develop relationships with others in the body of Christ so that I move and work in unity and harmony in the body? We have stepped into the charismatic dimension and the infilling of the Holy Spirit with all the accompanying gifts of the Spirit, but where is the power? Why do we make such a limited impact on the non-Christian world? Why are we [the church] seemingly so powerless over the powers of sin, sickness, satanic tyranny, godless thinking in high places throughout the land? The non-Christians seem to make all the noise, draw big crowds, make more decisive moves, and influence the world and society more than the church does. How come? Where is the power?"

"How can I hear the Lord's voice more clearly? Many times I have experienced his guidance specifically and many other times I see it in hindsight. Still I long for more."

The charismatic renewal has raised the question of personal religious experience, but it has given particular shape to the question: it has moved the central focus from the human individual to the Holy Spirit—from psychology to pneumatology. Personal religious experience is rooted primarily in what the Holy Spirit says and does; the human response is secondary and derivative. This is a fundamental conviction that lies behind what is presented in this book. The charismatic renewal has arisen in response to a sovereign move of the Spirit of God in the latter half of the 20th century. No examination of the movement that ignores God's sovereign initiative will come to a balanced understanding of its true significance.

This does not mean that everything associated with charismatic renewal should be approved and accepted out of hand. Human response to an initiative of God often involves a mixture of flesh and Spirit. We need to be as attentive to any word that the Spirit would address *to* the charismatic renewal as we are to the word that he wants to speak *through* the renewal. Where criticism or correction of the charismatic renewal is needed, we shall call attention to it. A renewal that is truly of the Spirit can only be strengthened when it honestly faces its own weaknesses and failures. Indeed, this is a simple necessity if a renewal is to be taken seriously and fulfill God's purpose.

CHAPTER 3

THE MEANING OF CHARISMATIC EXPERIENCE

The reason for charismatic experience

The charismatic renewal understands itself as a renewal of biblical faith and experience. Its central feature is a profound encounter with the triune God who has revealed himself in the Scriptures, his inspired Word. Thus charismatic experience in a real sense stems from the Word of the Lord. It has this Word both as its basic impulse and as its final norm. It is from this perspective that we speak of charismatic experiences.

If Scripture is the plumb line for understanding and evaluating charismatic experience, the plumb bob itself is *the lordship of Jesus Christ*. Every aspect of the charismatic renewal must be seen in relationship to Christ's lordship—over his church first and foremost, then also over the world and all creation.

The charismatic renewal has not been called into being by the Holy Spirit simply to promote an experience, or spiritual gifts, or particular doctrines. It stands in the midst of this generation as a particular witness to the lordship of Christ.

If we speak about charismatic experiences, it is because we understand that this is something Christ wants said in his church (cf. 1 Peter 4:10-11). If we call for a more radical dependence on the Holy Spirit, it is because we understand that Jesus himself, perhaps for a variety of reasons, wants to honor and call attention to the ministry of the Holy Spirit.

If we have emphasized certain parts of Scripture, such as those dealing with spiritual gifts, it is because we understand this to be a present priority of the Lord. The charismatic renewal has sometimes been dubbed a "tongues movement," as though that designation fully accounted for its significance. This would be like dismissing Israel as a "silent marching people" because that was a feature of their behavior at the battle of Jericho. We know, however, that behind the marching was a command of the Lord, who wanted his people to carry out a particular strategy. The reality of his lordship, not a technique of marching in silence, was the central issue. If the charismatic renewal gives particular attention to spiritual gifts, it is because we believe that the restoration of the full spectrum of spiritual gifts to the church is part of the Lord's present strategy.

The lordship of Christ is the central issue that the charismatic renewal raises in the church, and it is by this issue that it wishes to be judged (2 Cor. 4:5).

The focus of charismatic experience

Religious experience has often been equated with subjectivity, or, even more narrowly, with interiority or feelings.[1] It is understood merely in terms of what goes on inside a person's consciousness.

In the charismatic renewal there exists a broader and more objective understanding of experience. It is a comprehensive term embracing every aspect of an action of God that touches a person and creates in him or her a consciousness of God's reality. *Experience is thus a conscious encounter with God himself or with an action of God, initiated by God, and having observable results in the natural world or in the lives of individuals and communities.*

Authentic charismatic experience is God-given evidence of God's reality and power. This does not mean that it is scientifically verifiable, for science is not its frame of reference. Verification of empirical data must be appropriate to a particular frame of reference: verification of temperatures requires different instruments and procedures than verification of musical pitch; the density of a physical object is not verified in the same way as the speed of a projectile; actuarial tables are tested differently than the findings of a psychological study; yet all are based on empirical data. *The data of charismatic experience must be tested and verified within the framework of God's Word and the community of faith.*

Scripture instructs us to confirm prophetic words or experience, test the spirits, prove all things, beware of false visions, and distinguish between spirits (Acts 13:3; 16:10; 1 John 1:4; 1 Thess. 5:21; Col. 2:18; 1 Cor. 12:10). This kind of instruction is not aimed at developing psychological profiles of people who have had religious experiences, but at verifying the objective truth or falsity of their reports.

When charismatics talk about "experience," they may have in mind something visible and concrete, such as a healing. They would draw no significant distinction between this and an inner perception or change of attitude; both would be attributed to the intervention and working of the Spirit, the only difference being that one took place publicly and the other took place in the privacy of the inner life. The focus is on the empirical reality behind the experience—the intervention of God—not simply on one's subjective response.[2]

Charismatic experience may affect a person's inner life, or the world he or she lives in, or both. In the charismatic renewal, people refer as readily to the objective action of God as to their own subjective response. To illustrate: "The Lord healed her. . . . The Spirit guided us. . . . God forgave me" are as common as, "I felt his love and forgiveness. . . . I knew a joy I had never known before. . . . I sensed his presence." Whichever the focus, the experience arises out of something that God has done. The action of God is objective and primary; human response is derivative and secondary.

Two aspects of charismatic experience

In the charismatic renewal, experience does not follow a rigidly uniform pattern. One sees some diversity both at the individual and the corporate level. Nevertheless, millions of Christians who identify with the charismatic renewal (Lutherans among them) tend to speak of their encounter with God in two major ways.

First, this encounter usually represents an initiation into a new dimension of Christian living. This is true whether it occurs at the beginning of a person's life as a consciously committed Christian, or at a later stage. As an initiating experience, it is often called "baptism with the Holy Spirit" or "spiritual renewal." Second, such experience has far-reaching consequences for most aspects of one's Christian life. The continuing dimension is frequently called "life in the Spirit" or a "renewed life."

Most people who enter into charismatic experience associate it with an initiating event, though this is not always the case. Some people who have had no clearly identifiable initiatory experience may become deeply involved in the renewal and move into a life of ongoing charismatic spirituality.

In the early years of the charismatic movement, "baptism with the Holy Spirit," as an initiatory event, captured major attention for the simple reason that many Protestants and Catholics were at the level of initiates in regard to charismatic experience. By the mid-1960s, however, the overall emphasis had already begun to shift more toward the value of charismatic experience for ministry, spiritual growth, and the formation of Christian community. The emphasis on initiatory experience remains an integral part of the renewal, for the movement continues to draw in new people, but it has less overall prominence than it did when the movement first broke on the scene.

What remains at the center of the renewal, however, is the conviction that charismatic experience is a normal, indeed an indispensable, part of Christian life—which is simply another way of saying that God's intervention in our lives, according to the pattern and teaching of Scripture, is an objective reality. Without it our witness will be weak and impoverished.

CHAPTER 4

THE CONTENT OF CHARISMATIC EXPERIENCE

How do people actually come into charismatic experience? How does it affect their faith?

Although charismatic experience is essentially personal, it is not an individualistic experience. Sometimes people come into charismatic experience in the quiet of their own devotions, but usually there is, or there follows, communal relationships; the prayer group or the praying community play a distinctive role in the charismatic renewal. The groups may vary considerably in size—from two or three to thousands. They form a fellowship with social and spiritual functions that are interrelated.

The group provides a loving, caring, and praying fellowship in which one may learn about charismatic experience and in which charismatic experience can be sustained and deepened. In this community, through observation and instruction, one often acquires a certain biblical and doctrinal framework that makes charismatic experience more meaningful and serves as a guideline for the individual's own search and experience. One then goes on to actually desire such experience in expectant faith.

Opening up to charismatic experience may include such things as confession and the receiving of forgiveness; setting aside theological and emotional passivity; active, personal prayer for the Holy Spirit; and a readiness to yield to the exercise of charismatic gifts as a result of the experience.

The charismatic community provides a framework for such experience. It also serves as a supportive fellowship, praying for the seeker to receive an expanded awareness and experience of the Spirit. Frequently this happens through the laying on of hands by some who have had a charismatic experience and who exercise their gifts within the fellowship.

The fellowship is the setting where the spiritual gifts are used, and where charismatic worship and spirituality are encouraged and practiced. Charismatic fellowships are strongly oriented toward personal participation and individual freedom of religious expression, though in a structured way under responsible leadership. In the charismatic renewal, freedom and authority do not appear as contradictory terms. Both find expression in charismatic fellowships.

Charismatic experience has several aspects to it. *Primarily it is an encounter with Christ that results in a person being filled with the Holy Spirit.* It involves a heightened confidence in the Spirit's continuous presence. The underlying essence of people's diverse experience seems to be a conscious awareness that the indwelling Holy Spirit is affecting the whole person. It may or may not be an instantaneous experience, but it seems to set the recipient on a fresh course, with a spiritual orientation of conscious dependence on the presence and activity of the Holy Spirit.

A businessman described his experience in this way:

> The Lord has blessed me with a renewal of the Holy Spirit. Many of the blessings are not yet completed, but only in the process, and many of the blessings I am probably still unaware of. However, I do have the confidence that I am growing in the Spirit and in God's will.
>
> The gift of speaking in tongues came to me only after I had witnessed the effect it was having on my wife. It then was given to me after I had sought it in confession, prayer, and release. The gift came to me in song, and I still most often express it in this way.
>
> Of course spiritual renewal and conformity to God's will are possible without the gift of speaking in tongues. They can be fruit of a dedicated Christian life. However, I must confess that until I experienced this gift they were not very evident in my life. I was, and had been, active in church activities, and undoubtedly many would have said that I was living a truly Christian life. I can assure you I was trying, but there was something missing: *I* was trying to do God's work. There is now within me a new joy, a new vitality, a new desire and urgency. It is not *I* but Christ in me. I am aware of this continually, and I thank God for it in prayers of tongues and in prayers of my understanding.
>
> As to the overall effect, I would say this renewal of the Holy Spirit has awakened within me an awareness to the true blessing of Christ: his ministry, his death, his resurrection—our salvation. I have found a new desire to read God's Word, new understanding as I read and hear it preached. I have found a greater conviction of sin—mine and others. I have felt much more the urge to witness to others, and the ability to do so seems to be increasing. I believe that more and more my desire is to put God's work first and to be truly dedicated to Christ.[1]

Charismatic experience is signally a revelation of *God*. The individual Christian has a perception of being directly and personally faced with divine reality. God is encountered both in his majestic power and in his loving nearness. God is *real, present,* and *personal*. The intense and positive awareness of God's immediate presence brings a "here and now" quality into one's personal testimony of faith.

Frequently the experience has a pronounced *trinitarian* structure as it unfolds in a person's life, involving each of the persons of the Godhead in a particular way.

Jesus is experienced primarily as the living Lord, present with his people, to be loved and obeyed. This realization may involve an awareness of his saving power, a deep knowledge of redemption from sin and deliverance from the power of Satan that is experienced presently and personally by the believer. But the continuing experience tends to focus more on the effective lordship of Christ, both in terms of one's own life and the establishment of God's kingdom. In its fundamental structure, charismatic experience is thus as Christ-centered as it is Spirit-centered.

The Holy Spirit is experienced as a distinct person who grants supernatural power, equipping the believer both for ministry and for holy living. Another way of putting it is that the Holy Spirit brings the living, redeeming, ministering presence of Christ into vital union with the believer. The experience of the Spirit is not simply equated with the person of Christ and his saving work. The focus of charismatic experience is different from an initial experience of conversion and salvation, though the two may occur at the same time. Charismatic experience brings a more conscious awareness of the presence and work of the Spirit that enables Christ to express his life in the life of a believer.

Finally, God is experienced as the loving, caring Father. The experience of being a loved child of God is often related to the first person of the Trinity. The encounter with God the Father, who in charismatic experience meets us so personally and immediately, often brings with it a sense of being overwhelmed by love and grace.

At the concluding service of a charismatic conference in Germany, one of the participants stood up and said, "All my life I have known Jesus as my Savior. By God's grace I have led many people to personal and saving faith in Christ. But in these days, for the first time in my life, I have been able to say, *Lieber Vater* (my beloved Father)."[2]

CHAPTER 5

THE EFFECTS OF CHARISMATIC EXPERIENCE

Charismatic experience as such is greater than any of its effects. In a certain sense the subjective effects are secondary to the content of the experience as described in the previous chapters. A distinction must be maintained between the *God* who is experienced and the *effects* of this experience in the lives of individuals and communities. Yet the results of an experience do contribute to our understanding of its purpose and add vitality to our Christian witness.

Assurance and power

For many, a desire for greater spiritual power, enabling them to live and serve more effectively as Christians, has led them to seek charismatic experience. The encounter with God in charismatic experience frequently brings about a keen sense of assurance, both with regard to the objective reality of God and the more personal question of one's salvation and ministry, for there is a close connection between experiencing the power of God and experiencing the presence of God. The power that is received through charismatic experience heightens one's awareness of God's presence; such awareness renews the spiritual life both in its ethical and in its ministry dimensions. Knowledge made alive through objective experience produces a personal and profound certainty not arrived at through teaching alone.

The power received in connection with charismatic experience equips one to live more effectively as a Christian. Since the commencement of the classical Pentecostal movement at the beginning of this century, a major reason for seeking charismatic experience seems to have been the quest for spiritual power, effectiveness, and authenticity. Evidence continues to mount, particularly in the Third World, that charismatic power is a necessary ingredient for effective evangelism.[1]

Both biblically and experientially, the outpouring of the Holy Spirit's power produces noticeable results. For example, Christians gain a deeper personal conviction that God's Word is truth, a heightened awareness of the Spirit's indwelling presence, a boldness to proclaim the gospel even in the face of widespread indifference or stiff opposition, a divine confirmation of the spoken message through "signs and wonders," and greater results from evangelistic ministry, as people are convinced and convicted through confrontation with charismatically empowered ministry.

This power is not simply the power that accompanies and is contained in the gospel itself; it is a power given to persons, anointing and equipping them for ministry. It is not something added to their life in Christ. It is a release of the power of that life through the Holy Spirit, working actively in and through them for the salvation and upbuilding of others.

Use of spiritual gifts

When we focus on the dynamics and power of the Holy Spirit, we see another essential characteristic of charismatic experience: the gifts of the Spirit, or the *charisms,* come into active use. As the Spirit fills believers, bringing home to them the reality and presence of the triune God, the Spirit is manifested in the individual and in the community. One way that this is experienced is in the variety of charisms.

The charisms have played such a prominent role in the movement that they have provided it with its most widely accepted name, "charismatic." Practical and realistic emphasis on the charisms is a prominent characteristic of the charismatic movement. On theological grounds one may affirm that there is no basic difference between those inside and outside the movement: "every Christian is a charismatic," as the saying goes.[2] What one encounters in the charismatic movement, however, is a more conscious expectation and experience of the entire range of spiritual gifts that we find in Scripture. The gifts are earnestly desired and sought after (see 1 Cor. 14:1). They are seen as indispensable for the building up of the body of Christ, the church.

The conviction that the Spirit manifests his divine presence through observable gifts underlies charismatic experience. The charisms are seen as vehicles through which the Spirit comes to visibility in the body of Christ. The heightened awareness of God's presence that one finds in the charismatic renewal contributes decisively to the operation of the gifts. Although all the charisms may not be evident in the life of a given community, there is open-ness, expectation, and a seeking after a full range of spiritual gifts.

Recognition of the supernatural

Closely related to the awareness of God's concern for all areas of human life is an increased appreciation of the biblical worldview, especially the recognition of the supernatural dimension.[3] A common result of charismatic experience is an awakening to the spiritual dimensions of the universe such as the "powers of the age to come" (Heb. 6:5), the existence of Satan and evil spirits, the reality of spiritual warfare (including expulsion of evil spirits)—in general, the reality of the supernatural realm, which modern Western culture has largely dismissed.[4]

Worship and prayer

In response to God's manifestation in Word and deed, charismatic fellow-ships break forth in expressions of Spirit-inspired *praise* and *worship*. New songs, spontaneous speech (prayer, tongues, prophecy, testimony), and ex-pressive bodily actions (upraised hands, clapping, kneeling, prostration, dance) have come to characterize gatherings in the charismatic renewal.

Together with the emphasis on praise and worship, there is also an enhanced awareness of the value and necessity of prayer. The charismatic experience opens up depths of freedom in prayer and intercession. For many, prayer ceases to be a heavy obligation and becomes a joyous and refreshing event.

The impact of the Bible as the authoritative Word of God is strengthened. Traditional doctrines may take on fresh meaning and become relevant in unexpected ways. One example of this would be the teaching and practice surrounding confirmation.[5]

Ethics and attitudes

Although more difficult to measure, charismatic experience does produce noticeable ethical effects. People frequently testify that the experience of God's love kindles in them a love for God and for others. This is evidenced in the charismatic movement by close, deeply committed relationships between peo-ple, by a sense of oneness and unity within the fellowship, by a genuine appreciation for Christians of other denominations, and by social ministries that reach out to the suffering and deprived, both through proclamation of the gospel and attention to human needs.[6]

Along with love, charismatic experience often enhances the sense of joy and peace, both individually and corporately. Joy may be expressed in exu-berant praise, or in peaceful contentedness that waits quietly on the Lord.

An assembled worshiping community may break into loud praise or remain in prolonged periods of expectant silence. The popular image of charismatic meetings is more associated with praise than with silence. Where the renewal matures, however, the value of silent waiting on the Lord is increasingly appreciated.

Charismatic experience tends to have a broad rather than a narrow impact on a person's life. Where one experiences a release of power and effectiveness in ministry, more than likely there will be noticeable changes in attitude and behavior that affect daily life. Charismatic experience is consistent with the Spirit's purpose and strategy, which is to vitalize and make effective the fullness of the life of Christ which has been given us.

CHAPTER 6

THE THREEFOLD TASK OF THE CHARISMATIC RENEWAL

For the most part, the charismatic movement has been a renewal movement occurring within historic denominations. It is both similar and dissimilar to previous renewal movements. It is similar in its emphasis on a personal relationship with Jesus Christ, personal piety, Scripture study, prayer, worship, and evangelistic fervor. It has a distinctive emphasis on the Holy Spirit, which it partly shares with Pentecostalism. But it is unique in the history of the church by virtue of its worldwide scope and its penetration of virtually every denomination of the Christian church.

The apologetic task

As is true for all movements within the church that claim to be initiated by the Holy Spirit, the teachings and practices of those who speak for the movement must be tested. They must be examined relative to the whole of the biblical message, the ecumenical creeds, historic theological understanding, and church tradition. Thus there is an apologetic task required of leaders and theologians within a renewal movement in answer to the question, Are the teachings and practices of this movement consistent with the historic Christian faith?

This is one part of our task in this book: we wish to present and evaluate the charismatic renewal in the light of the historic Christian faith, and with particular reference to the Lutheran tradition.

The prophetic task

But there is also a prophetic task historically characteristic of renewal movements initiated by the Holy Spirit. In its prophetic role a renewal movement must challenge, correct, redirect, and perhaps even help redefine the church's character and mission. By definition, God-initiated renewal breaks in to challenge prevailing practices in the church, to cause reassessment of traditional expressions of the gospel, to renew loyalties to essential doctrines, and to foster the kind of change necessary to accomplish in the present time the unvarying purpose of the Spirit: to bring people into relationship with the living Christ, and to extend his kingdom. Seen from this perspective, a renewal movement does not bring something "new" in an absolute sense. On the contrary, it seeks to bring the church in line with a truth older than that by which it is presently living. It addresses unchanging truth to a changed time. It is a corrective, not a new norm.

Periodically the church must redefine itself in contrast to non-Christian values and practices that have crept into the church, or with reference to forces outside the church against which the church must stand in judgment. Here, too, renewal movements may exercise a prophetic role.

As a prophetic presence within the church, the charismatic renewal must pose some timely and straightforward questions:

- Is the church in the 20th century charismatic in a practical, realistic sense? Is the charismatic power of the Holy Spirit evident in the church today, or has a doctrine of the third person of the Trinity replaced him as a living reality?
- Does prevailing Western biblical interpretation—exegetical and hermeneutical methodology—strengthen or weaken belief in the living God who is presented in Scripture?
- Why does an emphasis on the Word sometimes give people an intellectual belief system rather than a living faith?
- How clearly is the biblical call to holy living being sounded in the church today?
- Does traditional teaching on certain biblical themes need to be restated and, where necessary, expanded for our day (for example, justification, sanctification, the nature and government of the church, demonology, the ministry of the laity, and the doctrine of the means of grace)?
- Are the Lutheran Confessions generally used to limit or to release the full dynamic of the biblical revelation?
- Is the Spirit redirecting the church, including the charismatic renewal, to greater dependence on the Spirit—to brokenness, humility, and servanthood rather than to power, organization, and program?

The theological task

Almost from the outset, Lutherans addressed themselves to some of the theological questions raised by the renewal. This found expression in articles and books written by Lutherans who had become personally involved in the renewal. To begin with, these centered on certain distinctives that the renewal shared with classical Pentecostalism: personal experience of the Holy Spirit and the catalog of spiritual gifts in 1 Corinthians 12. Then other issues began to be addressed, for example, family and congregational life, social issues, spiritual formation and pastoral care, and world evangelization.

Beginning in 1962, Lutheran church bodies began to produce theological statements, position papers, study documents, and pastoral guidelines that sought to deal with the charismatic renewal.[1] Looked at as a whole, they present a moderate stance toward the charismatic renewal—not as negative as the Southern Baptist Convention in the USA,[2] not as positive as the Roman Catholic Church.[3] For the most part, these documents were written by people not personally involved in the charismatic renewal. While this offered the advantage of some measure of objectivity, it also had certain built-in limitations. It is hard to get a truly objective view of a widespread renewal movement from the outside. It is like attempting to write a mission report without the participation of any missionaries.

The study by an international group of Lutheran charismatic leaders and theologians that led to this book reflects not only knowledge and training in Lutheran theological tradition but also a broad range of firsthand experience in the charismatic renewal. It is written with charismatics in mind—to help them articulate as accurately as possible the meaning and importance of their experience, so that they can share it more effectively with others. It is written for those who want to gain a better understanding of what God is saying through this renewal. Scholarly and technical information is generally placed in the notes. This book is written with the "priesthood of all believers" in mind—the ministers who sit in the pews as well as those who stand in the pulpits.

A renewal must take seriously its responsibility to be faithful and consistent with regard to the historic teaching of the church. It must have ears to hear what the church has said and is saying. That is the apologetic task.

The other part of the task, the prophetic, is equally important, and here the church also must exercise responsibility: it must set aside defensiveness and have ears to hear a word that calls for change, a word that calls it to break free from bondages and enter into the freedom of the Spirit. In an age that makes much of human technology and achievement, the church must hear a word calling for radical dependence on the Holy Spirit in every area of its life and mission. If this were not needed, the Lord would not have graced the churches with the Spirit's demonstrative, unsettling presence in our day.

PART TWO

INSPIRED BY THE SPIRIT
Biblical Foundations

All scripture is inspired by God and profitable for teaching, for reproof, for correction, and for training in righteousness.

2 Timothy 3:16

CHAPTER 7

BIBLICAL INTERPRETATION IN THE CHARISMATIC RENEWAL

In preceding chapters we have maintained that charismatic experience grows out of an encounter with the triune God according to God's self-revelation in Scripture. It is true, however, that although various denominational expressions of the worldwide charismatic movement see the Bible as the primary source and norm for the interpretation of their experience, biblical interpretations vary, depending on one's biblical methodology and theological tradition.

No interpretation of the Scriptures takes place in a historical vacuum. We come to the study of Scripture from our own personal backgrounds, often with strong denominational and theological traditions, in the midst of a contemporary situation that to a considerable degree determines the impetus and framework for our study. Those who have prepared this study stand in a Lutheran tradition, with certain presuppositions, emphases, and concerns that belong to our Lutheran heritage. We treasure this heritage. We recognize its value for our theological endeavor. At the same time, we recognize the Spirit's call to humility. No one tradition in the body of Christ has a monopoly on understanding. While we, as Lutherans, have gifts to share, we must also have the humility to receive and learn from others. Above all, we must be willing to be taught and led by the Spirit as he[1] sheds light on the Word of God.

A charismatic hermeneutic

Hermeneutics (principles and methodology of biblical interpretation), like everything else in the Christian life, depends on the Holy Spirit if it is to produce good fruit. Lutheran charismatics build their hermeneutic outward, from the center of Scripture, which is *the lordship of Christ,* preeminently revealed through the redemptive work of his death, resurrection, ascension, and session at the right hand of the Father.

Lutheran hermeneutics distinguishes between two basic motifs of Scripture's redemptive message: *law* (what God demands) and *gospel* (what God gives). It does not assume, however, that distinguishing between law and gospel is a simple matter of categorizing texts of Scripture. Here, too, one is totally dependent upon the working of the Spirit.

> To distinguish between law and gospel is no dialectic art, but it is only possible in the experience realized by the Spirit. It is easy enough logically (*formali causa*) to distinguish between law and gospel as the demanding and the giving word. But in practice (*material causa*) when the question is: what is demanded of me in the individual moment, it is not easy to differentiate. Then the gospel easily becomes a law. *For everything is law and demand outside the reality of the Holy Spirit.* The real distinction between law and gospel is not made in theology, but in the experience of the Holy Spirit himself [italics added].[2]

In the charismatic renewal, hermeneutics has served primarily the task of practical or applied theology. In regard to systematic theology, it has adopted essentially the traditional or conservative position within each of the confessions in which the renewal has found expression. As a movement it has not yet developed a comprehensive or unique systematic theology of its own.

Its distinctive contribution has been a lively sense of how the Holy Spirit applies Scripture to present situations. It views hermeneutics as a dynamic interplay of believers, Scripture, and the Holy Spirit. A high view of scriptural authority is thus linked to a hermeneutic that calls for considerable flexibility in terms of application.

Exegetical and doctrinal work in the renewal

Exegetical work in the charismatic renewal tends to reflect the range and diversity of the movement itself. Men like Arnold Bittlinger, Stephen Clark, Tormod Engelsviken, and George Montague have produced competent exegetical work, using the basic skills of scholarly exegesis.[3] Most of the speaking and writing in the renewal, however, has taken place in conferences and publications aimed at the broad cross section of a grass roots movement; it has been pitched at a popular rather than an academic level, with a strong

emphasis on practical application. This is not to say that exegesis and interpretation in the renewal is inadequate or poorly grounded, but simply that it
has been pressed more into the service of proclamation than of scholarly
writing.[4] Therefore the groundwork for biblical interpretation tends to be more
implicit than explicit in the writing and speaking that the renewal has produced.

The fruit of biblical interpretation in the charismatic movement cannot be
reduced to a catalog of doctrinal conclusions; the movement is too broad and
diverse. Among those who identify with the charismatic renewal, interpretation of the Bible still varies considerably on a number of issues, such as
Baptism, Eucharist, eschatology, church order and government, the roles of
men and women—even on things that are part of the particular focus or
emphasis of the renewal, such as baptism with the Holy Spirit, speaking in
tongues, exorcism, or prophecy.[5] Biblical interpretation in the charismatic
renewal has not led to a quick, detailed, doctrinal consensus.

The point of concurrence: worldview

The charismatic renewal does not raise major questions in the field of
hermeneutics at the point of methodology or research. Charismatic biblical
students, like everyone else, must use sound scholarship to help get at the
original sense of the text. Full weight must be given to the context, to differences in literary form and style; allegorical interpretations or generalizations
must be drawn with caution. All of this is part of the task of the Spirit-led
interpreter of Scripture.

The place where a charismatic hermeneutic raises questions is at the point
of *presuppositions.* At this point the charismatic renewal has involved an
intellectual renewal for many people. What one sees throughout the renewal
is a certain *Weltanschauung,* a worldview that has both been produced by
Scripture and in turn affects one's approach to Scripture. One aspect of this
has been to question the assumptions of naturalism and to take a more realistic
stance toward what is generally termed "supernatural." This has practical
implications for biblical interpretation when we deal with the question of
epistemology, that is, How do we arrive at accurate knowledge? In effect, a
new epistemology is being developed which is significantly at variance with
the accepted wisdom of our time, and which has been variously characterized
as "biblical realism," "radical orthodoxy," or "supernaturalism."[6]

The effect of this epistemological shift is that one begins to treat the biblical
material more realistically. Miraculous events are no longer embarrassing
"myths" that must somehow be explained (away!) before modern men and

women will take the Bible seriously. Prophetic passages that contain a predictive element do not need to be historically repositioned in order to be taken
seriously. Moral standards and practical instructions for the community of
faith are not lightly dismissed as mere cultural transmissions or accretions; a
heightened sense of the transcendent appears to carry with it a sense also for
that which is transcultural, perhaps because it is accompanied by awe.

The churches have made some attempt to address themselves to the experience and spirituality of the charismatic renewal, but another challenge,
one that has scarcely been recognized, much less addressed, is the substantial
intellectual challenge that this movement presents to the church. It poses a
challenge to the naturalism and rationalism that dominate much of the contemporary theological scene, in practice if not wholly in theory, by presenting
the church with a vital, worldwide movement in which biblical presuppositions
consciously shape theological methodology and practical ministry.[7]

Historical-critical studies

Luther was decisively a biblical theologian. On the one hand, he held the
traditional view that everything in the Bible was the Word of God, including
its cosmological and historical presuppositions.[8] On the other hand, he did
not equate the Bible and God's Word in a simplistic way. The purpose of the
Bible, and that which governs the interpretation of it, is that it promotes Christ
and his gospel.[9] Luther replied pointedly to Erasmus of Rotterdam, "Take
Christ out of the Scriptures and you will not find much else in them."[10] He
provoked his opponents among the Anabaptists by stating, "When opponents
set the Scriptures against Christ, so we set Christ against the Scriptures."[11]

Rightly used, the Scriptures are God's intended instrument for the proclamation of Christ. Luther asserted with vigor: "And what is the New Testament but a public sermon and proclamation of Christ?"[12] With regard to
the Old Testament, he wrote in the Prolog of 1523: "Here you will find the
manger and swaddling cloths in which Christ lies . . . meager raiment it is,
but precious is Christ, the Treasure which lies within."[13] With this sentence
Luther staked out his perimeter for "biblical criticism." Biblical criticism has
to do with "the manger" and "the sort of material it is made of." Most critical
for the reader and hearer of biblical texts, however, is whether he or she has
personally gained access to Christ and is ready to worship him as did the
Wise Men from the East.

Charismatics would insist on the classic understanding and use of the historical-critical method of biblical interpretation, that is, the attempt to interpret
Scripture according to the way it was meant by those who wrote it, and the
way it was understood by those to whom it was addressed. They are critical

of the tendency to impose present-day presuppositions or concerns on the text. In terms of formal exegetical methodology they come fairly close to the Swedish school of "biblical realism," though for somewhat different reasons: charismatics take seriously the truth claims, and therefore the authority, of biblical presuppositions; the focus of the biblical realism school is more on scholarly objectivity:

> In its purest scientific form this historical realism is utterly indifferent to our needs and our questions. It is even consciously suspicious of them, since they threaten to lead to anachronistic distinctions—as, for example, between healing miracles (as conceivable in the light of psychosomatic medicine) and nature miracles (inconceivable by reason of "the laws of nature") or between "Jesus' simple teaching" and the eschatology and Christology of the early church. When a saying or action is said to have essential significance, then that can only signify that it seems to have had such for Jesus or Paul or for any other of the "authors" of the New Testament.[14]

While charismatics and some historical-critical scholars would essentially agree on what Scripture says, they might apply it in quite different ways. Charismatics would probably accord more cross-cultural significance to the Bible than some historical-critical scholars. They would be less likely to relativize a teaching of Scripture simply because it comes out of another culture. Beneath obvious differences in culture and ways of thinking, they would be more inclined to see themes and truth that are independent of culture, true for all time.

Charismatics might be more tentative about historical judgments than some historical-critical scholars. Historical research from literary sources does not yield the kind of objective and verifiable data that we normally associate with the word *science*. In the nature of the case there is little empirical data to substantiate the notion that we can think our way back into the culture and mental processes of an earlier culture with great precision. We encounter no little difficulty understanding accurately what people in our own time think and mean—to say nothing of thinking our way back into a culture separated from us by 2000 years—as C. S. Lewis so clearly demonstrated in his essay, "Modern Theology and Biblical Criticism."[15] That fact alone should instill in us some humility when we attempt to reconstruct the thought world of the New Testament. Our attempt to be "historically realistic" must be seen as just that, an attempt. In this intellectually demanding enterprise, too, we must look to the Holy Spirit to guide us.

What charismatics most strongly take issue with in historical-critical studies, however, is not its methodology as such, but precisely an *un*critical use of this method, whereby one imposes on the text a presupposition, such as an antisupernatural bias, that is basically alien to the biblical world.

A typical example of the way in which the so-called historical-critical method imposes an antisupernatural bias on a text is the following commentary on Mark 6:45-52, which tells about Jesus coming to his disciples walking on the water. The explanation of this text concludes:

> We must conclude that homiletical and doctrinal interests have left their mark upon an original tradition coloured from the first, in which the action of Jesus in *wading through the surf near the hidden shore* was interpreted as a triumphant progress across the waters [italics added].[16]

This kind of interpretation would be widely discounted in the charismatic renewal—not because charismatics are wooden literalists or antiintellectual, nor because they are simply credulous, but rather because they have a fundamentally different *Weltanschauung,* or worldview. Aside from the patent absurdity of the disciples mistaking a hidden shore for deep water on a lake which they had plied for years as professional fishermen, the interpretation does not realistically consider the possibility that the point the story means to convey—that Jesus exercised supernatural powers—was in fact true. That possibility is ruled out *a priori,* and a naturalistic interpretation is laid on the text under the guise of "scientific exegesis." Charismatics would approach the text more realistically, not because they hold to a particular theory of biblical inspiration (there would be some variety on this point among charismatics), but rather because the event, while unusual, is not fundamentally incredible within the framework of their worldview.

Generally speaking, charismatics are also leery of attempts to read present-day ideologies back into the New Testament: casting Jesus, for instance, in the role of a political revolutionary, or pressing apostolic testimony into the service of the latest fad in social reform.

Practical application of Scripture

It is a frequent experience in the charismatic renewal to have new light shed on well-known biblical passages or to have neglected and forgotten passages come alive with present-day meaning. A charismatic hermeneutic takes seriously both the historical character of the Scriptures and their present relevance and application, for the other side of understanding Scripture in its historical setting is applying it in the present situation.

The scholarly study of Scripture does not exclude a personal, edifying use of Scripture as the Holy Spirit lets the words speak into a person's contemporary situation, though this will not necessarily become a basis for general teaching.

The Holy Spirit is the source of Scripture (2 Tim. 3:16) and he is also the source of sound interpretation (2 Peter 1:20-21). Prayer for the fullness of the Spirit is the indispensable accomplishment to serious Bible study. Belief in the Bible, separated from the active intervention of the Holy Spirit, withers into mere formalism. "What makes a theologian," said Luther, "is prayer, meditation, and temptation." [17] Only the Spirit can bring into us the living, redemptive presence of Christ whereby we "have the mind of Christ" and are able therefore to "understand the gifts bestowed on us by God" (1 Cor. 2:12-16).

Lutheran theological heritage

A Lutheran perspective on charismatic experience involves two points of reference: the biblical revelation and the theological confessions and traditions of the Lutheran church.

Scripture is the norm by which all experiences must be evaluated. It is the source for understanding Christian doctrine and life. This is a fundamental Reformation principle. Contemporary charismatic experience must be shown to lie within the boundaries of Scripture, consistent with the experience and doctrine of the Holy Spirit set forth in the Word.

The Lutheran Confessions are in essence an interpretation of Scripture. Our attempt to evaluate charismatic experience from a particular place in the body of Christ called "Lutheran," therefore, is not being undertaken in a narrow, sectarian spirit. Rather, it is our response to a worldwide visitation of the Spirit that sets before every body of Christians the apostolic injunction, "test everything; hold fast what is good" (1 Thess. 5:21). In this we want humbly to heed the wisdom and instruction that the Lord brings through our Lutheran heritage, yet also boldly challenge Lutheran tradition or contemporary practice when these would lead us to distort or restrict the Spirit's work.

The prominent features of charismatic experience that we have described in previous chapters are certainly laden with biblical and theological content. Yet charismatic Christians from different denominations have not reached biblical consensus concerning all aspects of biblical interpretation and validation of charismatic experience. This means, among other things, that charismatic experience is not self-validating or self-explanatory.

We shall outline the fundamental biblical message that pertains to charismatic thought and experiences. Although this can only be a summary statement, it is based on accepted principles of biblical interpretation and reflects both scholarly historical and contemporary biblical scholarship. The Bible in its plain, historical sense gives a clear and adequate basis for establishing the validity of charismatic experience. Upon reflection it also shows the efficacy of a movement of charismatic renewal in the Lutheran church today.

Interpreting the biblical witness

The books of the Old and New Testament are normative for the church. This does not mean that one can directly apply every part of Scripture to present-day life. Certain Old Testament practices and doctrines have been superseded in the New Testament as a result of the progressive character of salvation history. There is also development within the New Testament itself, as the events of salvation history unfold. What happened in the life of Jesus may not necessarily be transferred to the era of the church. Certain events of salvation history are unique, such as the birth and baptism of Jesus, his death and resurrection, his ascension, and the sending of the Spirit on the day of Pentecost. What is repeatable in history and what is not can only be determined by a thorough analysis of the texts themselves.

Classical Pentecostal theology draws heavily on Luke-Acts for its interpretation of charismatic experience. Without denying the central role of Luke-Acts in interpreting and validating charismatic experience, we would emphasize the totality of the biblical witness. On the other hand, we must be on guard against the tendency to let our reading of other New Testament writers, primarily Paul and John, color our reading of Luke. Some interpreters downgrade the theological significance of Luke's material, asserting that "the purpose of God in Scripture should be sought in its *didactic,* rather than its *historical* parts."[18] This kind of distinction, however, is alien to the thought world of the New Testament. Luke stands in the tradition of Old Testament historiography that sees divine revelation imbedded in the understanding of historical events.[19] The biblical message expressed in narrative form is an indispensable part of the scriptural revelation, with profound significance for the church today.[20] While narrated events may not be repeatable, nor meant as invariable patterns for the church today, their theological significance and meaning are still normative.

Biblical doctrine that is valid and normative for the charismatic movement within the Lutheran church today is set forth in a simple and general way in the chapters that follow.

CHAPTER 8

THE SPIRIT IN CREATION AND REDEMPTION

THE SPIRIT IN CREATION

The concept of "spirit," most often rendered by the Hebrew term *ruach* in the Old Testament and by the Greek term *pneuma* in the New Testament, is not easily defined or described. In its concrete connotations it denotes air in motion: wind and breath. On the more abstract level it denotes breath of life, the human spirit, good or evil spirits, and, finally, God's Spirit. Even in its abstract use it may frequently have very concrete connotations, as the use of the imagery of wind and breath indicates (see Ezek. 37:9,10,14; John 3:8; 20:22).

The common distinction in Western thought between visible and invisible reality, between the material and the spiritual realm, does reflect a biblical viewpoint (see, for example, 2 Kings 6:15-17; 2 Cor. 4:18; Eph. 6:10-12). Yet if we think of the Holy Spirit simply in relation to the "spiritual realm," we miss the essential point in the biblical understanding of the Spirit. Throughout the Bible the Spirit is God as he is personally and powerfully present in the world, mysterious and inexplicable in rational terms, yet having tangible and visible effects in the created world, both in human experience and in nature. Although the Spirit is present in the world as God's power, he is wholly transcendent and beyond the control of human beings. He expresses the *sovereignty* of God. Any attempt to limit or control the freedom of the Spirit, which is the freedom of God himself, is futile. "The wind blows where it wills" (John 3:8).

Although the term *spirit* may be used in several different senses in the Scriptures, God's Spirit is fundamentally different from all that may be called "spirit" in the world. The weakness of human beings and the created order stands in contrast to the creative power of the Spirit of God (Isa. 31:3). The Spirit of God as the breath of God is the life-giving force granting to men and women their existence as human beings (Gen. 2:7; Job 33:4).

This life-giving reality, however, is not limited to human beings, but permeates the whole creation, "living things both small and great" (Ps. 33:6; 104:25). The creation, preservation, and renewal of all life depends on the activity of the Spirit of God. "When thou sendest forth thy Spirit, they are created; and thou renewest the face of the ground" (Ps. 104:30; also Job 34:14-15). Life comes from God and remains God's. As depicted in the creation story, the Spirit is God's agent in creating and ordering the universe (Gen. 1:2).

Humanity has come into being and received life by the power of the Spirit of God. We are dependent on God in all areas of life. And God has reserved his divine right to revoke this gift of life (Gen. 6:3; 2:17).

This is the universal aspect of the Spirit's work. All people without distinction, whether they know it or not, are dependent on the Spirit of God for their physical life. The natural mysteries of human conception, birth, growth, strengthening in weakness, and healing in sickness are in a profound sense attributable to the power of God's Spirit.

The work of the creative, life-giving Spirit is also seen in the promise of spiritual renewal and rebirth of the people of God. "I will put my Spirit within you, and you shall live" (Ezek. 37:14; also Isa. 32:15-20; 44:3-5). What had been lost in the fall would be restored.

THE SPIRIT IN REDEMPTION

The Old Testament promises of a perfect kingdom, an eschatological time of salvation, center equally on the pouring out of the Spirit of God and the coming of the anointed Davidic king, the Messiah. King David was anointed with the Spirit (1 Sam. 16:13; also 10:1,10) and thus equipped for his kingly reign. Likewise, the Messiah will usher in a time of divine blessings comparable to the first creation, because the Spirit of God rests permanently on him. "And the Spirit of the Lord shall rest on him, the spirit of wisdom and understanding, the spirit of counsel and might, the spirit of knowledge and the fear of the Lord" (Isa. 11:2).

The Messiah and the Spirit

The Messiah's endowment with the Spirit is related to his authority as a righteous judge. He punishes the guilty and saves the suffering (Isa. 11:3b-4a); he is a king who knows and fears God (Isa. 11:2b-3). The effects of the

Spirit of God resting on the Messiah will be felt in all areas of human life, in the religious and ethical as well as in the political and social spheres (Isa. 11:4-9).

In the "Songs of the Servant of the Lord," the coming one is depicted as a prophet endowed with the Spirit of God. The servant has a universal role to fulfill: as one sent by God, he has a missionary assignment to be a new covenant and a light to the nations (Isa. 42:6-7). The Spirit is here understood both as a means of inspiration and as power for carrying out this great task: "I have put my Spirit on him, he will bring forth justice to the nations" (Isa. 42:1).

In the New Testament, the promises concerning the Messiah and the Spirit come to fulfillment in the divine person and the redemptive ministry of Jesus Christ. The incarnation of the Son of God is the result of a direct intervention by the Spirit of God. Jesus' human existence is derived from a unique, creative act by God through the Spirit: "The Holy Spirit will come on you, and the power of the Most High will overshadow you; therefore the child to be born will be called holy, the Son of God" (Luke 1:35; also Matt. 1:18-23).

The birth narratives not only describe the Spirit in terms of the Old Testament concept as the creative force of God, they also address themselves to the question of the relationship between Jesus and the Spirit. Jesus' uniqueness as the Son of God and Savior from sin are closely associated with his miraculous conception: Jesus was the Son of God incarnate by his miraculous conception by the Spirit and birth of a virgin. He did not later become the Son of God, by his endowment with the Spirit at his baptism in the Jordan or by his resurrection from the dead, though these events did serve to designate or reveal him as such (Matt. 3:17; Rom. 1:4).

Jesus' Spirit-filled ministry

Jesus proclaimed and manifested the kingdom of God in the power of the Holy Spirit. He brought to visibility the powers of the age to come. He overcame the power of Satan and his demons. He extended to people forgiveness of sins, deliverance, healing, and fullness of life. He was anointed with the Spirit at his baptism. He was permanently filled with the Spirit and exercised his ministry in word and deed by the power of the Spirit. In every sense of the word, Jesus was a charismatic person.

1. The unique God-man. Of course, Jesus was more than a charismatic prophet and healer; some Old Testament figures would also be included in that category. He was also the Son of God who came from the bosom of the Father and made him known (John 1:18). He was more than a charismatic, more than a prophet. He is divine and human, the God-man. He transcends all human categories.

A Christology that interprets Jesus' earthly ministry solely in terms of his deity on the one hand, or solely in terms of his endowment with the Spirit on the other hand, is an unbiblical theology. Jesus did not act sometimes as the divine Son of God, and at other times as a human being empowered by the Spirit. He did everything as the unique God-man. He spoke and acted in his capacity as the Son of God and in the power of the Spirit. Jesus' charismatic ministry was meant to be an encouragement to his disciples; with the coming of the Spirit they would do the same kind of things (John 14:12). Yet, being one with the Father, Jesus' relationship to the Spirit is unique.

2. Anointed at Jordan. According to the unanimous testimony of the four Gospels, Jesus did not begin his public ministry until after he had been baptized by John the Baptist. Two important elements conspicuously distinguished Jesus' baptism from the "baptism of repentance" that John administered to others: the voice from heaven and the descent of the Holy Spirit. The heavenly voice identified Jesus as the divine Son of God (Matt. 3:17; Mark 1:11; Luke 3:22); closely related was his identification as the Lamb of God who, by his sacrificial death, "takes away the sins of the world" (John 1:29). The descent of the Spirit as a dove testified to Jesus' messianic calling (cf. Luke 3:16-17); by his permanent possession of the Spirit he is authorized and endowed by God to carry out his mission.

3. Conflict with Satan. Jesus' endowment with the Spirit brought him into conflict with the enemy, Satan. Immediately after he was empowered by the Spirit, Jesus was led or driven by the Spirit into a confrontation with Satan (Matt. 4:1; Mark 1:12; Luke 4:1), but he overcame the temptations, defeated the enemy, and returned to his ministry "in the power of the Spirit" (Luke 4:14).

It is noteworthy that the Spirit-filled Christ used the Word of God recorded in the Old Testament as he struggled against Satan. At every point Jesus took his stand on Scripture. According to the view of the biblical authors, the Scriptures are inspired by the Holy Spirit (2 Tim. 3:16; 1 Peter 1:11; 2 Peter 1:21), and as such they are also a vehicle for the Spirit. This comes to the fore both in the proclamation of the gospel, which often is tied to Old Testament texts, and preeminently in the conflict with Satan: "And take . . . the sword of the Spirit, which is the word of God" (Eph. 6:17).

Another feature of Jesus' response to temptation is important: he submitted absolutely to the will of God. The redemptive work of Christ involved the way of obedience to the Father's will, even to death on a cross (Phil. 2:8; Heb. 2:14-15). The temptation in the desert and the struggle in Gethsemane (Matt. 26:30-46)—in which Jesus obeyed the Father, though it meant suffering and death—stand as a constant reminder that suffering and death lie along the pathway of obedience. Although Jesus himself bore the sins of the world, his disciples cannot claim a life free from suffering. Their destiny is bound up with that of the Master (Phil. 3:10-11).

Another aspect of Jesus' victory over Satan is seen in his deliverance of those oppressed by demons. The expulsions of evil spirits by Jesus are not isolated events. They belong to the bedrock of the gospel tradition and are a central part of Jesus' ministry. They have eschatological significance: "But if it is by the Spirit of God that I cast out demons, then the kingdom of God has come upon you" (Matt. 12:28).

Deliverance from bondage to Satan is one of the gifts granted to all who enter the kingdom of God. The vanquishing of Satan and the freeing of those who are oppressed by demons are signs that the time of salvation has come. The driving out of evil spirits also shows who Jesus is: the Son of God, the one who is "stronger than he" (Luke 11:22).

The healing of people suffering from physical and psychological illness, though different from deliverance, also stems from the power of the Spirit (Matt. 12:15-21). Both the healings and the deliverances make the kingdom of God visible and are meant to be so understood. In Matthew, the word about sinning against the Holy Spirit is set in the context of Jesus' miracles. It is a warning to those who render prejudiced and cynical judgments against his miracles, attributing to Satan that which is the work of the Spirit; it implies a hardening of the heart against the evident work of the Spirit (Matt. 12:24, 31-32).

Both the authority to expel demons and to heal was given by Jesus to his disciples (Matt. 10:1; Luke 9:1). However, there was a significant difference between the healing ministry of Jesus and that of his disciples: Jesus healed on his own authority; he was himself the healer. The disciples healed and expelled demons in the name of Jesus. Jesus was the author both of his own healings and of those of his disciples (Luke 10:17; Acts 3:6). Jesus rejoiced in the Spirit when his disciples returned from a successful healing mission, and he specifically related their success to the authority that he had given them and which they had successfully exercised (Luke 10:19).

The Spirit empowered Jesus' ministry with divine authority. This is evident in Jesus' words and in his acts (Luke 4:18-21; John 14:11); in the Bible the Spirit of God manifests himself in both word and deed. Jesus spoke with a fullness of authority because he was full of the Spirit: "For he whom God has sent utters the words of God, for it is not by measure that he gives the Spirit" (John 3:34). In his conflict with Satan, the decisive issue was not simply power, but *authority* (Mark 1:27).

The promise of the Spirit to Jesus' followers

Jesus' own anointing with the Spirit at his baptism in the Jordan has paradigmatic significance: he is the one who baptizes with the Holy Spirit (John 1:33). God has sent his Son, his Messiah, and equipped him with the Spirit according to the Old Testament promises. The Spirit of God, which had been quenched for hundreds of years, was poured out on the Messiah. This was a unique event of salvation history, a change of times. The time of salvation was at hand, the eschatological era had begun. The anointing of the Messiah ("the anointed one") marked the beginning of his ministry (Acts 10:36-38), a ministry that would be shared by his followers, on whom he would pour out the Spirit.

Both in the wonder of the incarnation and in the events associated with the baptism of Jesus, God the Father, God the Son, and God the Holy Spirit are seen carrying out the redemption of humanity through their divine interrelationship: the Father sent the Son to serve and save; the Spirit conceived him; the Father testified to him and endowed him with the Spirit.

During his earthly ministry, Jesus was the sole bearer of the fullness of the Spirit. In the power of the Spirit he proclaimed the dawn of the kingdom of God (Luke 4:18-19). When he ascended back to the Father, he poured out the Spirit on his followers, as he had promised (Acts 1:5; 2:33).

Jesus' uniqueness as the incarnate Son of God does not rule out continuity between his ministry and that of the post-Easter Christian community. Jesus is not only the unique bearer of the Spirit; he is also the Lord who gives the Spirit (Luke 3:16; John 16:7; 20:22).

After the exaltation of Jesus, his followers continued his ministry of healing, deliverance, prophecy, and powerful proclamation of the gospel. The ministry of Jesus has paradigmatic significance for the ministry of the church; it serves as an example and a pattern. The Spirit who at Jesus' baptism descended on him and empowered him for his ministry is the same Spirit who later was given as a gift to the disciples. The continuity between the Spirit's work in the earthly ministry of Jesus and the ministry of the post-Easter community is part of the scriptural validation of the present-day charismatic renewal in the church.

A STRATEGIC VIEW OF THE COMING OF THE SPIRIT

In considering the coming and the working of the Holy Spirit in the post-Pentecost Christian community, it can be instructive to study the New Testament, especially the historical sections, from a perspective of the Spirit's *strategy*. There are a number of basic factors or elements that Scripture links to the coming of the Spirit. The way that they occur, however, suggests a discriminating and varied use of the different factors—sovereign and often surprising *strategies*—that the Holy Spirit employs to accomplish particular objectives. This approach offers a fresh way of looking not only at the biblical material but also at some of the traditional systematic approaches to the topic.

Three systematic approaches to the coming of the Spirit are prominent in the church today: the *sacramental,* the *evangelical,* and the *Pentecostal.* Simply stated, the sacramental approach teaches that the Holy Spirit is given in Baptism. The evangelical approach links the gift of the Spirit to regeneration; you receive the Holy Spirit when you are born again. The Pentecostal approach distinguishes between a reception of the Spirit in regard to regeneration, and baptism with the Spirit, understood as a charismatic reception of the Spirit that empowers one for witness and ministry, and which happens subsequent to regeneration. Although these three approaches involve some overlap and do not altogether exclude one another, they nevertheless stand in considerable contention. Historically, they have been sources of controversy and division.

We are proposing neither an alternative systematic, nor a critique of existing systems, but simply a different way of looking at the reality of the Spirit's coming—a way that gives perhaps greater attention to the sovereign strategy of the Spirit in varying situations.

Certainly the Holy Spirit is not unsystematic, in the sense of being sloppy and disorganized. But in his coming and working he has not bound himself to one particular way of doing things. He is goal-oriented, like a brilliant field commander who comes up with unexpected strategies to deal with particular situations. Serving under that kind of a commander can be unsettling: he keeps you constantly on your toes. But the other side of it is that you keep the enemy off balance and continue to advance.

The Spirit is concerned with advancing the cause of Christ. Whether that satisfies our preconceived theological expectations is not the Spirit's major concern. He wants to communicate not merely correct ideas about Christ but the very life of Christ in all its fullness. That requires more than a clear and accurate statement of truth. It requires application of the truth that is appropriate to a given situation—a strategy that can move successfully against powers that actively oppose the life and kingdom of Christ.

A strategic approach to the coming of the Spirit is consistent with the realistic way in which the New Testament presents the kingdom of God and the kingdom of this world in conflict with one another. It helps identify fundamental truths in the scriptural revelation, yet recognizes that the Spirit is sovereign in applying these truths to specific situations.

A strategic approach can help us make sense of both the consistencies and the seeming irregularities that we observe in the early church's experience of the Holy Spirit. And because the same Spirit is still at work today, it may also help us understand and open up to present strategies that the Spirit wants to employ in our own lives, or in the lives of fellow believers.

In the next 10 chapters we will look at a variety of actions or concepts that the New Testament links closely to the coming of the Holy Spirit—basic factors that we must take into account if we are to understand his coming and working among us. At the same time we want to acknowledge the Spirit's sovereignty in applying these factors to life situations, whether in Scripture or in the ongoing life of the church.

CHAPTER 9

THE PROMISE
OF THE SPIRIT

In the New Testament, the promise of a coming of the Holy Spirit in power was prophesied by John the Baptist and reiterated by Jesus.

John the Baptist administered a baptism of repentance. He contrasted this with the ministry that Jesus would perform: "I have baptized you with water; but he will baptize you with the Holy Spirit" (Mark 1:8; also Matt. 3:11; Luke 3:16; John 1:33).

Jesus returned to this promise before his ascension: "I send the promise of my Father upon you; but stay in the city, until you are clothed with power from on high" (Luke 24:49); "John baptized with water, but before many days you shall be baptized with the Holy Spirit" (Acts 1:4-5). Jesus had taught his disciples to pray for the Holy Spirit (Luke 11:13). Between Jesus' ascension and Pentecost the disciples were gathered together in prayer, waiting for the fulfillment of the promise (Luke 24:53; Acts 1:14; also Luke 3:16).

The coming of the Spirit

On the day of Pentecost, Jesus kept the promise: his followers were filled with the Holy Spirit (Acts 2:4). What the disciples experienced was the manifest fulfillment of "the promise of my Father" (Luke 24:49; Acts 1:5).

The early church was not concerned with creating a watertight theology about the coming of the Holy Spirit. What was immediately important to the disciples was that every believer receive and experience the full reality of the Holy Spirit, and recognize that in this the Lord was fulfilling his promise to the church.

Although the historical event of Pentecost was not repeated, the personal experience of being filled with the Spirit was. The personal experience of believers being filled or empowered with the Spirit is recorded repeatedly throughout Acts. Often this is in connection with their coming to faith and being baptized (Acts 2:38-39; 10:44; 19:5-6). The gift of the Spirit was not intended for the first disciples alone. It is a reality promised to everyone who hears, believes, and is baptized in the name of Jesus for the forgiveness of sins (see Acts 2:39).

Forgiveness, Baptism, and the gift of the Spirit

The apostle Peter's exhortation and promise at the close of his sermon on the day of Pentecost gives us insight into how the early church experienced and understood the coming of the Spirit. It sets a pattern for the relationship between various aspects of Christian initiation:

> Now when they heard this they were cut to the heart, and said to Peter and the rest of the apostles, "Brethren, what shall we do?" And Peter said to them, "Repent, and be baptized every one of you in the name of Jesus Christ for the forgiveness of your sins; and you shall receive the gift of the Holy Spirit" (Acts 2:37-38).

In this passage of Scripture the promise of the gift of the Spirit is connected to the preceding part of Peter's statement by a consecutive "and." This "and" is important because it shows that what Luke meant by the gift of the Spirit cannot be simply equated either with the forgiveness of sins or with Baptism. The gift of the Spirit is not identical with receiving forgiveness of sins, though it is related. Likewise, Baptism in water is not identical with baptism in the Spirit, though the two may occur simultaneously.

Of course, the Spirit is active in bringing people to repentance and salvation. Throughout Scripture, the giving of the Spirit is linked to cleansing from sin (see, for example, Ezek. 36:25; Ps. 51:7-12; Eph. 1:7,13); this understanding is evident also in Acts (see, for example, 11:18). However, this is not identical with what Luke means by the gift of the Spirit. His focus is more precisely on the power of the Holy Spirit for mission.

Manifest demonstrations of the Spirit

Acts emphasizes another significant aspect of receiving the gift of the Holy Spirit: it is normally accompanied by a visible or audible manifestation of the Spirit. Acts tells about believers in various circumstances and with various backgrounds who received the gift of the Spirit with demonstrable manifestations.

1. The household of Cornelius. A crucial step in the Christian mission was taken, under the evident guidance of the Spirit, when Gentiles in the household of Cornelius were received into the church without the obligation of circumcision or adherence to the Mosaic Law (Acts 10:1—11:18). It was the Gentiles' demonstrable reception of the Spirit that forced Peter and the other apostles to accept them as fellow believers. The exceptional circumstances under which this took place do not detract from the narrative's enduring theological significance.

In the case of Cornelius and his household, the pattern of the day of Pentecost was followed with an important variation. The word of salvation through Christ was preached, and forgiveness of sins was offered (Acts 11:4-18; 10:43). Cornelius and his household repented, believed, and on believing received forgiveness of sins and eternal life (Acts 11:17-18; 15:9). What was outwardly noticeable to Peter and the other Jews, however, was not their faith, but the effects of their reception of the Spirit: "They heard them speaking in tongues and extolling God" (Acts 10:46).

The irregular aspect of the event was the fact that the Gentiles were not baptized before they received the Spirit. Peter commanded that they be baptized, thereby providing for their full inclusion in the church (Acts 10:47-48; cf. 11:18). Although in Acts, Baptism in water normally precedes baptism with the Spirit, in this instance baptism with the Spirit occurred prior to Baptism with water, when Cornelius and his household received the gospel in faith. The Cornelius case may not be as unique as is sometimes imagined. The missionary experience of the church testifies to similar occurrences.[1]

2. *The Samaritans.* The narrative of the Samaritans' reception of the Spirit (Acts 8:4-25) seems to present an opposite kind of situation. The Samaritans heard the gospel preached by Philip in the power of the Spirit. They believed and were baptized. Yet the Holy Spirit did not fall on any of them. They received the Spirit at a later time, when Peter and John came down from Jerusalem and prayed for them and laid hands on them.

As we have seen, where the Spirit is mentioned in Acts, the focus is on manifest demonstrations of his presence. It was this dimension of the Spirit's working that was not apparent in the initiation of the new converts in Samaria. The fact that the apostles came down from Jerusalem to pray for them suggests that the situation was somewhat irregular. The normal experience in the apostolic community was that new converts would receive and manifest the Holy Spirit. When this did not happen, the apostles took special steps to rectify the situation.

3. *The Ephesians.* In Ephesus the apostle Paul encountered a situation that at first glance seemed to resemble what had happened in Samaria. He found some disciples and asked them, "Did you receive the Holy Spirit when you believed?" (Acts 19:2). As it turned out, they were disciples of John the Baptist and had not yet received Christian instruction or Christian Baptism.

The way that Paul questioned them, however, clearly entertained the possibility that they might have believed and been baptized without experiencing a manifest outpouring of the Holy Spirit. What had happened in Samaria could well have become common knowledge in the early church, and Paul may have suspected that he was encountering a similar situation in Ephesus.

The importance of Luke as a theologian

Luke the historian has sometimes been downgraded as a theologian. Prominent expositors of Scripture have said that in shaping our doctrine of the Holy Spirit, we must look to the Epistles, not to Acts.[2] The Epistles tend to highlight the Holy Spirit's work of bringing people to faith and salvation. Paul, for example, testified to the fact that every Christian is indwelt by the Spirit: "But you are not in the flesh, you are in the Spirit, if the Spirit of God really dwells in you. Any one who does not have the Spirit of Christ does not belong to him" (Rom. 8:9). In writing to the Corinthian church, Paul presupposed that all the believers had received the Holy Spirit (1 Cor. 12:13; also Gal. 3:2). John, likewise, spoke of receiving the Spirit in the context of salvation (John 7:37-39).

Lately, however, there are signs of renewed appreciation for Luke as a theologian of the Holy Spirit in his own right.[3] He did not contradict what was taught by Paul or John; he built on it. He added a significant dimension to our understanding of the work of the Holy Spirit with his emphasis on receiving the Spirit in terms of *power for mission*. This may open the way for dealing more effectively with some of the nettlesome disagreements that have plagued discussions about receiving the Holy Spirit.

The danger of reading Luke through Pauline glasses was pointed out by Larry Christenson in one of his contributions to the book *Practical Christianity:*

> The New Testament writers spoke of receiving the Holy Spirit in different contexts. Paul talked about receiving the Spirit of adoption into God's family: "for you did not receive a spirit that makes you a slave. . . . but you received the Spirit of sonship" (Rom. 8:15.) Luke, on the other hand, spoke about receiving or being filled with the Holy Spirit primarily in terms of power for ministry: "You will receive power when the Holy Spirit comes on you" (Acts 1:8).
>
> We do this same kind of thing in everyday speech. Depending on context, the same word can have different connotations. For example, "He's cool!" may refer to the temperature of a man's skin, or it may describe a certain behavior style, or it may reveal how the speaker feels about the man.
>
> Luke used the word *receive* in a particular way when he referred to the coming of the Holy Spirit. We should not attempt to impose Paul's usage on the writings of Luke. That would distort the meaning, and it would rob us of the unique emphasis the Spirit wants to bring through Luke.

Is receiving the Spirit different from receiving Christ? In Paul's writings these concepts run very close to each other, yet the element of the Spirit's charismatic manifestation is not absent. In Gal. 3:1-5, he spoke of the Holy Spirit coming in power, complete with miracles. He asked, "Did you receive the Spirit by observing the law, or by believing what you heard? . . . Does God give his Spirit and work miracles among you because you observe the law, or because you believe what you heard?" The Galatians had experienced the power of the Spirit in miraculous manifestations, and Paul pointed to this as confirming the reality of the saving faith by which they received Christ. In Luke, however, the focus is somewhat different. Receiving the Holy Spirit is the way that those who already believe in Christ are empowered to serve him.

People receive the Holy Spirit, in Luke's meaning of the term, in different ways. Some people receive the Spirit more or less spontaneously, while for others the response is quite conscious and deliberate; some experience dramatic manifestations of the Spirit, while with others the manifestations are more subdued. The way in which people receive the Spirit will be determined, to some extent, by the situation and by the person (his or her personality type, age, station in life, church environment). More important than the particular way that we receive the Spirit, however, is what we do after having received.

It's like the difference between a big church wedding and a small family wedding. The kind of wedding you have doesn't determine the kind of marriage you'll have. What's important is how you live out the reality of married life.

It's important that we receive the power of the Spirit for living the Christian life: Luke's message needs to come through loud and clear. But when it comes to the question of *how*, it's more important to focus on how one lives the Spirit-filled life than on a rigid formula for receiving it.

Receiving the Spirit in the Lukan sense is not a one-time event, but an ongoing way of life. It is needed every day; some occasions may call for a special filling of the Spirit (see Acts 4:31; 7:55). The effects of the Spirit's filling may be dramatic, accompanied by supernatural signs; they may open up a new area of witness or ministry; they may issue in a quiet growth of the fruit of the Spirit. When the Spirit controls us, we are moved to accomplish God's will in God's way.

Luke's emphasis on receiving the Spirit to empower us for ministry is a needed emphasis today, when one thinks of the enormous missionary challenge facing the church—three billion people who haven't heard the gospel. We need to move beyond past misunderstandings and get on with the task![4]

In Acts, several expressions are used to describe the manifest coming of the Spirit. The expression, "to be baptized with the Spirit" is used on two occasions; in both, it is an initial reception and manifestation of the Spirit that is in view (Acts 1:5; 11:16). The phrase, "filled with the Spirit" is used both of initial and subsequent experiences of the Spirit's coming (Acts 2:4; 4:31). On occasion, several expressions can be used more or less interchangeably to denote nuances of the same experiential reality: "the Holy Spirit fell on" (Acts 10:44; 11:15), "the gift of the Holy Spirit was poured out or given" (10:45; 11:17), "these people have received the Holy Spirit" (10:47), "[they were] baptized with the Holy Spirit" (11:16).

A careful exegetical study shows that "Luke gives pride of place to the term filled with the Holy Spirit."[5] Other terms add nuance, but his foundational term for describing the coming of the Spirit is "filled." Luke's preference for this term is important for understanding his theology of the Holy Spirit: it puts the primary focus not on a single, initiatory experience of receiving the Spirit, but on a coming of the Spirit that may be repeated from time to time in a believer's life.

Jesus had promised his disciples that the Holy Spirit would come and be with them forever, would indwell them (John 14:15-17). For the disciples, this did not stand in contradiction to previous or subsequent comings of the Spirit. According to John, the disciples received the Holy Spirit on Easter evening, when Jesus breathed on them (John 20:22). According to Acts, Jesus baptized them with the Holy Spirit on Pentecost, 50 days later (Acts 1:5; 2:4). Some time later they were again filled with the Holy Spirit (Acts 4:31).

Stephen provides a particularly vivid example of a believer in whom the abiding, indwelling presence of the Spirit was clearly evident. He is introduced to us as a man "full of faith and of the Holy Spirit . . . full of grace and power" (Acts 6:5,8). Yet at his martyrdom he is described as full of the Holy Spirit, "not in the sense of an abiding endowment, as in Acts 6:3-8, but as a rapture granted at that moment" by which he saw Jesus standing at the right hand of God (Acts 7:55-56).[6]

The community of believers that grew up around the disciples, filled individually and corporately by the Holy Spirit, expected fresh anointings of the Spirit. They looked for the manifest presence of the Spirit to be seen in new converts (Acts 8:16; 19:2). Believers continued to experience new infillings of the Spirit (Acts 4:31; 13:9-11,52; 4:8)—a renewing of the gift of the Holy Spirit (Acts 5:32)—as they faced new difficulties and challenges.

CHAPTER 10

THE SPIRIT
AND THE WORD

From the day of Pentecost onward, the coming of the Spirit has been inseparably linked with telling people what God has done, is doing, and will do through Christ and the giving of the Holy Spirit. The spreading of the Word and the activity of the Spirit are so intimately linked with one another that theologians speak about the Word as a "means of grace," that is, a God-appointed vehicle through which his grace enters into a person's life.

There is some danger if we conceive of this in a simplistic, casual sense, whereby the recitation of the Word becomes the cause and the giving of the Spirit an invariable result. That would run the danger of making the New Testament a book of word-magic: if we simply recite or teach the right words, we will get an assured result. This assumption can easily creep into theological and catechetical traditions.

Charismatics hold to a high view of the power and authority of Scripture (this is dealt with in greater detail in Chapter 36), but they take issue with any doctrine or use of Scripture that does not recognize the sovereignty of the Spirit. It is one thing to recognize the "means of grace" (the Word and the sacraments) as the Lord's gracious provision for coming to his people. It is something else to think of the means of grace as something that we can use or control to obtain the Spirit, or to teach the doctrine in a way that dismisses any working of the Spirit that is not immediately linked with hearing the Word or receiving the sacraments. A theology of the Word that is not linked to a profound sense of dependence on the Holy Spirit can end up ministering death rather than life. Both Scripture and experience confirm the Spirit's sovereign authority to come when and where and how he pleases—

never at variance with the Word, but also sovereign over the Word and our proclamation of it.

The Spirit works through the Word

Nevertheless, the relationship between the Word and the coming of the Spirit is extremely close and must be seen as a key feature of the Spirit's sovereign strategy. The Spirit exercises creative and redemptive power through the Word.

Already in the Old Testament, God the Father sovereignly created by his Spirit and with his Word. While this connection is implicit in the creation story (Gen. 1:2-26), it is explicit elsewhere: "By the word of the Lord the heavens were made, and all their host by the breath of his mouth" (Ps. 33:6). In the prophecy of Ezekiel, the Word and the Spirit bring new life to the dry bones. The Spirit of God will renew the people religiously and ethically through the Word of God (Ezek. 37:1-14). Words spoken in the Spirit of God are effective words, words of power (Num. 23:19-20; 24:2-4,16).

The notion of the Spirit using the Word as an instrument to accomplish God's purpose is carried over into the New Testament. The gospel of John, especially, emphasizes that the life-giving quality of Jesus' words is due to the Spirit: "The words that I have spoken to you are spirit and life" (John 6:63b). In commissioning his disciples to spread the gospel, Jesus laid strong emphasis on the proclamation of the Word: "Go into all the world and preach the gospel" (Mark 16:15).

The Spirit brings salvation through the proclamation of the Word

On the day of Pentecost, 3000 people came to salvation (Acts 2:41). Prior to their Baptism and inclusion in the church, Peter preached the gospel to them. His words, spoken in the power of the Spirit, convicted them of their sin and convinced them of the messiahship and lordship of Jesus. On the one hand, the Spirit empowered and inspired the messenger. On the other hand, the Spirit worked through the Word to bring the hearers to repentance and faith.

The apostle Paul also taught that saving faith comes through hearing the gospel (Rom. 10:17). The Spirit inspires and reveals the words that are to be spoken, making them effective for salvation in the hearers. The Word is the Spirit's instrument in creating faith. Paul made much the same point in writing to the Corinthians: "My speech and my message were not in plausible words of wisdom, but in demonstration of the Spirit and power, that your faith might not rest in the wisdom of men but in the power of God" (1 Cor. 2:4-5).

The Spirit makes the Word effective

The Spirit is the power behind the proclaimed Word. When we speak about the Word as a means of grace, we mean that the Spirit uses the Word as a vehicle of his presence and power. Spirit and Word must be understood in relation to one another. Especially in relation to the missionary situation, Paul emphasized how the Spirit and the Word are united in bringing about saving faith: "God chose you from the beginning to be saved, through sanctification by the Spirit and belief in the truth. To this he called you through our gospel" (2 Thess. 2:13-14; also 1 Thess. 1:4-6).

Paul's own apostolic ministry to the Gentiles illustrates this in a special way. In his "priestly service of the gospel of God . . . the offering of the Gentiles . . . is sanctified by the Holy Spirit." It is Christ himself who, through the ministry of Paul, has won obedience from the Gentiles "by word and deed, by the power of signs and wonders, by the power of the Holy Spirit" (Rom. 15:16-19).

The Spirit inspires the message ("words not taught by human wisdom but taught by the Spirit" [1 Cor. 2:13]), and through our hearing of this message the Spirit creates faith that receives salvation (Eph. 3:5; 2:8).

The Spirit uses the Word to apply Christ's redemptive work to the individual

The objective basis of salvation, Christ's redemptive work carried out in history, has universal validity. Christ's incarnation, earthly ministry, passion and death, and resurrection and ascension all belong to the events of salvation once for all carried out in history almost 2000 years ago. "He has appeared once for all at the end of the age to put away sin by the sacrifice of himself" (Heb. 9:26). All of humanity was included in Christ's redemptive work. He died for all, that all might rise with him (2 Cor. 5:14-15).

God has made Jesus Lord and Christ (Acts 2:36). That is the fundamental truth. However, only the Holy Spirit can make this truth a personal confession: "No one can say 'Jesus is Lord' except by the Holy Spirit" (1 Cor. 12:3). The Spirit applies to individuals what Christ has secured for all. But the Spirit does not do this by divine fiat. He does it in such a way that one may freely respond. He makes this application through the Word.

According to the strategy of the Spirit, the fruit of redemption—forgiveness of sins and eternal life—shall be appropriated personally by each individual through the Spirit's working. It is the unanimous testimony of the New Testament that the Spirit uses the proclamation of the gospel to accomplish this. Personal faith, the subjective side for salvation, is created by the Spirit in connection with the proclamation of the gospel.

The Spirit is sovereign in using the Word

The link between the Word and the coming of the Spirit cannot be locked into one predictable pattern. Nevertheless, the happening of Pentecost does provide something of a paradigm, for throughout the New Testament the proclamation of the gospel is the primary means by which the Holy Spirit initiates people into new life in Christ (for example, see Rom. 1:16-17; 10:17; 1 Cor. 1:17-18). In the book of Acts, wherever the Spirit is received for the first time, the preaching of the gospel precedes it (Acts 2:14-36; 8:5,14-15; 10:34-43; 19:4-5).

Furthermore, the Spirit is linked to an ongoing revelation of God's purpose in Christ. The apostle Paul prayed that God may give "a spirit of wisdom and of revelation in the knowledge of him, having the eyes of your hearts enlightened, that you may know what is the hope to which he has called you, what are the riches of his glorious inheritance in the saints, and what is the immeasurable greatness of his power in us who believe" (Eph. 1:17-19; also Col. 1:9; Phil. 1:9; John 15:15). When he comes, the Spirit inspires a proclamation of the Word in order that people's experience of Christ will be accompanied by clear and ever-growing knowledge and understanding.

The Spirit inspires prophecy

The Word is sometimes oriented toward the future, through prophetic utterance. This accords with Jesus' promise: "When the Spirit of truth comes, he will guide you into all the truth; for he will not speak on his own authority, but whatever he hears he will speak, and he will declare to you the things that are to come" (John 16:13).

This statement by Jesus indicates that the Spirit will inspire predictive prophecy in the church. At the same time, the words provide a safeguard from aberration by emphasizing that the Spirit speaks on Christ's authority; he speaks only what he hears, and his aim is to glorify Christ (John 16:14).

In the three basic revelatory functions of the Spirit—witnessing, teaching, and prophesying—we see the intimate connection between the Spirit and the Word.

The Word is the keystone in the strategy of the Spirit

Those who seek or desire the Spirit must recognize that he links himself to the proclamation of the Word. We should be wary of any alleged experience of the Spirit that is not rooted in the Word. This does not mean that the Word will in every case precede an activity of the Spirit, in a simplistic causal sense.

People were often initially drawn to the New Testament community by the demonstration of supernatural power, as Emil Brunner correctly pointed out:

> People draw near to the Christian community because they are irresistibly attracted by its supernatural power. They would like to share in this new dimension of life and power, and they enter the zone in which the Spirit operates before they have heard a word about what lies behind it as an ultimate transcendent-immanent cause. There is a sort of fascination which is exercised mostly without any reference to the Word, comparable rather to the attractive force of a magnet or the spread of an infectious disease.[1]

When the apostle Paul was put ashore on the island of Malta, people were moved by a demonstration of the Spirit's power before there was any proclamation of the Word (Acts 28:3-6). The Spirit is sovereign; he moves when and where he pleases (cf. John 3:8). Whether the Word precedes, coincides with, or occurs subsequent to an action of the Spirit is a matter of his particular determination. Yet it is his settled strategy to act in concert with the Word.

Where the Word is neglected, we may infer that the activity of the Spirit will be thwarted, for in neglecting the Word we grieve the Spirit who has strategically linked himself to the Word. For the same reason, where some part of the scriptural revelation is neglected, the Spirit's activity in that area of truth will be diminished. The Spirit's strategy may then call for special attention to that neglected area. Renewal often comes at a point where the Spirit stirs up response to some aspect of truth that has been neglected.

Many people in the charismatic movement testify to a more vital experience of the Holy Spirit than they have ever known before. This has been accompanied by widespread teaching on the subject of receiving the Holy Spirit and his gifts—what one writer has called "the charismatic work of the Spirit"[2]— and for many this has been a new thing. More than superficial charismatic enthusiasm lies behind the statement, "We never *heard* about this in our church!" It says something about the non-place that the Holy Spirit has traditionally held in our everyday expressions of the faith. In many sacramental churches and evangelical circles there has been less, and sometimes no, specific teaching on receiving the Holy Spirit and his gifts. Other truths have been emphasized, but not this one.

This raises an important question about the strategy of the Spirit: *Does the Spirit come with his gifts on the basis of a doctrinal position that assumes his coming without our specifically proclaiming it?* The sacramental tradition says, "You receive the Holy Spirit when you are grafted into Christ in Baptism." Evangelicals say, "You receive the Holy Spirit when you are born again." Assuming that both of these traditions teach something important about receiving the Spirit, to what degree will a charismatic work of the Spirit actually happen, if a clear word about receiving the Spirit in this sense is not part of the proclamation and teaching? Is the Holy Spirit's word-strategy linked to proclamation that is specific? Would people, for example, experience the reality of forgiveness even though the word of forgiveness were not specifically proclaimed? For example, if God were presented and believed in merely as Creator? Will people experience guidance, healing, or spiritual gifts if these are seldom even mentioned? Will people be empowered as witnesses by the Spirit if they are never told that such a thing is possible?

Each of the three positions—sacramental, evangelical, and Pentecostal—has something to teach the others about the coming of the Spirit; their doctrinal differences are not irreconcilable. But it is not likely that people will be led into a charismatic experience of the Holy Spirit and his gifts without a clear and energetic proclamation of this particular biblical truth. The Spirit comes where the Word is clearly presented. It's part of his strategy.

CHAPTER 11

FAITH, REPENTANCE, AND OBEDIENCE

FAITH

The Spirit's objective is to unite the lives of human beings with the life of Christ. Faith involves making this connection—bringing about and maintaining the union of Christ's life and our life.

Two aspects of faith: gift and response

Faith describes the whole action by which the Holy Spirit brings the living, redeeming presence of Christ into a living union with a human being. The initiative and the power to accomplish this lies with the Spirit. In this sense, faith is a gift. That is the understanding that lies behind the comment by Peter in regard to the coming of the Spirit to the Gentiles: "God who knows the heart bore witness to [the Gentiles], giving them the Holy Spirit just as he did to us; and he made no distinction between us and them, but cleansed their hearts by faith" (Acts 15:8-9). Faith, in this context, was an action accomplished by God that was clearly manifested by the coming of the Spirit.

Faith, however, also involves a human response, and Scripture usually views it from this perspective: ". . . that whoever *believes* in [Jesus] should not perish but have eternal life. . . . He who *believes* and is baptized will be saved. . . . Those who *received [Peter's] word* were baptized, and there were added that day about three thousand souls. . . . Many of those who heard the word *believed;* and the number of men came to about five thousand. . . . They *believed* Philip as he preached good news about the kingdom of God and the name of Jesus Christ. . . . We have heard of *your faith* in Christ Jesus" (John 3:16; Mark 16:16; Acts 2:41; 4:4; 8:12; Col. 1:4 [italics added]).

In Scripture, the grammar of faith is weighted overwhelmingly toward the side of human response. "Believe" is something we are told to *do;* "faith" is something we are exhorted to *have.*

The emphasis on human response, however, is set in the context of divine action: the Word has been proclaimed; God has cleansed their hearts; God has granted them repentance unto life. Both the context and the emphasis make sense in the light of the Spirit's strategy. God wants to effect a living union between Christ and us not by coercion, but after the model of marriage—freely offered and freely received (Eph. 5:32). The Spirit takes the initiative, presents the proposal, demonstrates that the basis for new life in Christ has been established by God, and removes any obstacles to union. The Spirit creates the context in which human response can take place.

Even though God's initiative and action are primary in the matter of faith, Scripture gives more emphasis to the side of human response. God's will in the matter is already a settled issue. He does not need to be convinced. The strategy of the Spirit is aimed at eliciting a response from us. He holds aloft the invitation to enter into a life of faith, to receive what God has prepared and now offers.

In establishing faith, the strategy of the Spirit will vary from one individual to another. For one person he may create the reality of faith through a message that is preached. Another person may come to faith as the result of a personal testimony that someone has shared. Faith may be sparked by something that is read, by an act of kindness, by an exhortation to believe, by a struggle of conscience, by a charismatic demonstration of the Spirit.

The entire action of establishing and maintaining a living union between Christ and the believer is included in the biblical meaning of faith, both the side of God's gift and the side of human response. In individual cases, however, the Spirit may focus strategically on one side or the other. If we labor under the notion that faith is a "work" that we ourselves must "do," he may point out that faith is a gift. If we turn faith into an intellectual belief system, he may turn our attention to the practical results of a life of faith: works of love. If he has amply demonstrated God's provision for life in Christ, he may command us to believe with such vehemence that the whole issue of faith seems to hang on our decision.

Receiving the Spirit by faith

In Ephesus the apostle Paul met a small group of disciples and asked them, "Did you receive the Holy Spirit when you believed?" (Acts 19:2). The shape of his question illustrates the fact that, in the early church, believing in Jesus was closely linked to receiving the Holy Spirit, though the two were not identical. Their answer showed that the problem, in this case, stemmed not from a lack of faith but from a deficient proclamation: "We have never even heard that there is a Holy Spirit." When Paul corrected the matter, they promptly responded with faith and received the Spirit. The episode began with an inquiry about faith and ended with a demonstration of faith.

This incident illustrates that faith is always faith *in Jesus*. It is a manifestation of the living union between Jesus and the believer. But it also illustrates the fact that faith, because it manifests life, is a growing thing. The challenge to receive and be filled with the Holy Spirit is not something added to one's faith in Jesus, as though Jesus were not enough. It is, rather, a manifestation of one's life in Jesus, which, like every manifestation of that life, calls for a response of faith.

REPENTANCE UNTO LIFE

Repentance is the negative side of faith: it involves that which we *cease* to believe and do. In repentance we turn away from that which prevents us from entering into living union with Christ. The groundwork for repentance, like that of faith, is laid by the Spirit. It is the coming of the Spirit that makes repentance possible and opens the gateway to redemption.

The Spirit of God was a redemptive power in the history of Israel. It was prophesied that the Spirit would be instrumental in the future salvation of the people as well, as a means of judgment and cleansing. A purified and sanctified people would remain when the Spirit had carried out his work: "And he who is left in Zion and remains in Jerusalem will be called holy" (Isa. 4:3).

Gateway to eternal life

John presents salvation in terms of "life"—life in the kingdom of God (John 3:3); abundant life (10:10); eternal life, which is life lived in communion with the Father and the Son (14:6; 17:3). Jesus sent his disciples, in the power of the Holy Spirit, to proclaim this salvation and the forgiveness by which one enters into it (20:20-23).

Repentance unto life lies at the very heart of the Spirit's strategy. In order to bring us into a living union with Christ, he must lead us through repentance, for "all have sinned and fall short of the glory of God" (Rom. 3:23). This is his most notable work, but it is not always his most noticed work.

When the Spirit came on the Gentiles in the household of Cornelius, there were some dramatic manifestations of his presence: speaking in tongues and prophecy. The central issue for the apostles, however, was that of life. When Peter reported the incident back in Jerusalem, their comment was telling: "Then to the Gentiles also God has granted repentance unto life" (Acts 11:18).

Sometime later Peter again referred to this incident, and with the same emphasis: God "cleansed their hearts by faith" (Acts 15:9).

It is a mark of wisdom and maturity to give first importance to the issue of *life,* even though it may be less noticeable than other workings of the Spirit. Jesus said to his disciples, "Do not rejoice in this, that the spirits are subject to you; but rejoice that your names are written in heaven" (Luke 10:20).

Evangelical Christianity has given first importance to the issue of life, and that has given strength and endurance to its witness. Evangelicals have recognized that repentance unto life is basic to the strategy of the Spirit. It is important to keep this in mind as we consider certain other aspects of the Spirit's strategy that may be more dramatic.

Repentance and faith

The preached gospel is always either being received or rejected by its hearers. The basic call to those who receive it is the call to repentance. In his call for repentance Peter stood in the tradition of the Old Testament prophets, John the Baptist, and Jesus himself (see, for example, Ezek. 14:6; Matt. 3:1-2; 4:17).

The term *repentance* denotes a complete change of relationship to God with serious ethical consequences. It consists of a twofold movement: a turning away from one's unbelief and sins and a turning to God in faith and obedience.

Repentance and faith in God are two sides of the same coin. Turning from sin is always a turning to Christ (Acts 2:40-41; 26:18; 20:21). Wherever repentance is called for, faith is implied, and vice versa. Peter, therefore, in a situation similar to that of Pentecost, could call for faith without mentioning repentance (Acts 10:43; 11:18).

Although the motivation to repent is a result of the working of God's Spirit, repentance is nevertheless a person's own response. We are the subject of the action and the ones who are commanded to repent (Acts 17:30). Thus repentance is a person's first step in becoming a Christian. There can be no salvation without repentance and faith.

OBEDIENCE

Peter said that God gives the Holy Spirit to those who obey him (Acts 5:32). Paul said that his ministry was aimed at producing the obedience of faith (Rom. 1:5; 16:26). Obedience to the Spirit, the obedience of faith, involves more than adherence to general principles. It means paying heed to the specific directions of the Spirit; it means following the initiatives of the indwelling Christ, with whom we are united through faith. Obedience expresses itself not only in our belief concerning the basic truths of the gospel, but also in our readiness to heed the Spirit's specific strategy for implementing the will of God.

But this obedience is not attainable by human beings. It involves not only obedience *to* the Spirit but obedience *in* the Spirit. It is the result of the Spirit's own work in our lives (Rom. 8:4; Phil. 2:13; 2 Cor. 3:5).

Pentecostal Christianity is sometimes faulted for emphasizing the Holy Spirit at the expense of Christ or of the Father. It is a fair question whether the emphasis does not in fact restore balance, especially in some of the churches of the Reformation that have virtually developed a unitarianism of the Son. Jesus spoke at some length with his disciples about the coming of the Holy Spirit. It was important not only that the Spirit would come, but that they would *know* he was coming, and would then recognize and welcome him when he came.

When Christ is preached and people are urged to "believe," what results all too often is an acceptance of an intellectual belief system followed by moral striving rather than a living faith. Too often we aim merely at getting people to accept a theology and then dedicate their own energies to serving God. "To believe" is understood simply in human terms, something people must do in order to be saved. They may get a well-packaged, orthodox warning to avoid any attempt at "works-righteousness," but they pitch headlong into "belief-righteousness": agree with right teaching and you will be saved. Then they have a good try at living the Christian life in their own strength. Or, if that becomes too arduous, they fall back into a well-memorized doctrine of forgiveness. And this they call Christianity. It's a religion of the flesh, dependent on human achievement from first to last.

It is precisely a dependence on the Holy Spirit that helps keep faith and obedience from becoming an exercise in human achievement. The Holy Spirit is Scripture's counterpoise to the Word of God that is impossible to obey. I behold that Word, impossibly beyond my grasp, and pray, "Come, Holy Spirit! Make Christ to be my wisdom, my righteousness and sanctification and redemption" (1 Cor. 1:30).

No believer can bypass the fundamental of obedience: the strategy of the Spirit makes no provision for cheap grace. Yet neither can one undertake obedience apart from the Spirit: his strategy just as rigorously rules out sanctification by self-effort. Any preaching of holy obedience without dependence on the Holy Spirit will miss the mark. It will veer left into Antinomianism, or right into legalism. Obedience is not a product of my own effort: it is a gift of grace. Its appropriate accompaniment is not human willpower, but loving and thankful confidence in a Holy Spirit who unites my life with the life of Christ, who obeys the Father in all things.

CHAPTER 12

THE INDWELLING
OF THE SPIRIT

The strategy of the Spirit is to come and dwell within the believer. This was laid down in prophecy: "I will put my spirit within you, and cause you to walk in my statutes" (Ezek. 36:27). Jesus promised the fulfillment of the prophecy when he said, "I will pray the Father, and he will give you another Counselor, to be with you for ever, even the Spirit of truth, whom the world cannot receive, because it neither sees him nor knows him; you know him, for he dwells with you, and will be in you" (John 14:16-17).

The coming of the Spirit must always be understood as a strategy for establishing or strengthening his indwelling. The whole redemptive plan of God comes to reality only when the Holy Spirit brings the living, redeeming presence of Christ to indwell the life of a believer, and from that indwelling proceeds to work out God's purpose in and through the indwelt believer.

The Spirit as down payment on life in the kingdom

The Spirit indwells the person who has been forgiven and justified by faith (Gal. 2:16; 3:2,5,14). He comes to those who have been adopted into divine sonship. The internal testimony of the Spirit gives assurance of this sonship and of the fatherhood of God. "And because you are sons, God has sent the Spirit of his Son into our hearts, crying 'Abba! Father!' " (Gal. 4:6). "When we cry 'Abba! Father!' it is the Spirit himself bearing witness with our spirit that we are children of God" (Rom. 8:15-16). Our divine sonship is completed in eternity (Rom. 8:21-23); in the meantime, the Spirit serves as the guarantee or down payment on the coming salvation.

Closely associated with the inner testimony of the Spirit is what Scripture calls "sealing" with the Holy Spirit. "In him you also, who have heard the word of truth, the gospel of your salvation, and have believed in him, were sealed with the promised Spirit, which is the guarantee of our inheritance" (Eph. 1:13; also 2 Cor. 1:22).

The biblical terms *seal, guarantee,* or *earnest* (2 Cor. 1:22; 5:5; Eph. 1:14), and *first fruits* (Rom. 8:23) all denote the Spirit as both experiential and eschatological—as a present and a future reality; in the life of faith we experience him now, and in the life of the coming kingdom we shall experience him even more fully. The experiential possession of the Spirit in the present is a guarantee that the Christian will also have the full future salvation (see Rom. 5:5).

Orthodox theology, together with the early church fathers, identifies "sealing" with the practice of chrismation following Baptism; this parallels later Roman Catholic confirmation practice.[1] It is closely identified with the scriptural precedent of baptism with the Holy Spirit on the day of Pentecost, described by Peter as a promise "to you and to your children and to all that are far off, every one whom the Lord our God calls to him" (Acts 2:39).

Union with Christ

What does it actually mean to be indwelt by the Spirit? We see something close to it in Christ himself. By his incarnation, Christ walked as a unique man on the earth: in him two natures, the human and the divine, lived in perfect union. His preeminence is directly attributed to the fact that his human nature was indwelt by the divine nature: "He is before all things, and in him all things hold together. He is the head of the body, the church; he is the beginning, the first-born from the dead, that in everything he might be preeminent. For in him all the fulness of God was pleased to dwell" (Col. 1:17-19).

Something analogous to this is true of the Christian. A Christian's uniqueness lies in the fact that he or she is indwelt by the living Christ through the working of the Holy Spirit. This is a reality so dizzying that the human tongue stutters to express it: "I am crucified with Christ: nevertheless I live; yet not I, but Christ liveth in me: and the life which I now live in the flesh I live by the faith of the Son of God, who loved me and gave himself for me" (Gal. 2:20 KJV). It is no patching up of the old creation, but a new beginning. Human life is superseded by eternal life: "If any one is in Christ, he is a new creation" (2 Cor. 5:17). The newness lies not simply in the fact that human nature has been forgiven and cleansed. That is, in a sense, preparation. The newness goes deeper: a person now lives in union with the risen Christ. That which has been created, the "new creation," is precisely this reality of the indwelling Spirit establishing and maintaining the risen Christ and the believer in a living union.

Every believer must experience the reality of the indwelling Christ (Rom. 8:9). And, in the strategy of the Spirit, it is a truth that must be rehearsed again and again—not least by those who have experienced dramatic manifestations of the Spirit in the midst of a charismatic renewal movement. A steady and consistent spiritual walk does not happen automatically.

When we ask the practical question—How then is this life of indwelling sustained?—the apostle Paul points to the relationship between what we *do* and what we *think:* "Those who *live* according to the flesh *set their minds* on the things of the flesh, but those who *live* according to the Spirit *set their minds* on the things of the Spirit" (Rom. 8:5; also Col. 3:2; Eph. 5:10-11; Rom. 12:2; Phil. 4:8-9; Eph. 5:17-20 [italics added]). The mind is custodian of the environment on which life in the Spirit depends.

The outpouring of the Spirit

The Spirit indwells believers in order that Christ may live his life through them. The outpouring of the Spirit may be broadly understood as a means to that end. The Spirit is poured out in order that the indwelling presence of Christ might be established, strengthened, or released in power and ministry.

Pentecostals have laid special stress on the outpouring of the Spirit, and in this they have assessed accurately a strategy of the Spirit: *a signal outpouring of the Spirit may be necessary when the indwelling of Christ is at low ebb among his people, or when they face formidable opposition.* It will not do simply to reemphasize the truth of his indwelling if the Lord has prepared a strategic outpouring. That would be like a company of soldiers plodding straight ahead when their commander has ordered a quick, flanking movement. Mainline churches have frequently made the mistake of pitting a theology of indwelling, with an emphasis on gradual growth, against a theology of outpouring accompanied by signs, as though the two were in competition, or one obviated any need for the other.

Francis Sullivan, a Jesuit scholar, makes the interesting observation that St. Thomas Aquinas saw the two motifs rather as complementary to one another:

> St. Thomas asks the question whether one can speak of a sending of the Holy Spirit to a person in whom he is already dwelling, and if so, how this is to be understood. His answer is as follows: "There is an invisible sending of the Divine Person not only in the initial gift of grace but also with respect to an advance in virtue or an increase of grace . . . as for example when a person moves forward into the grace of working miracles, or prophecy."[2]

Discussions between different segments of the body of Christ have sometimes become a sterile restatement of positions when they have focused simply on the question, How do you receive the Holy Spirit? We may make more progress by shifting the ground of the question and asking, What is the strategy of the Spirit? How is he employing these two basic truths—indwelling and outpouring—in the present situation?

CHAPTER 13

THE SPIRIT
AND BAPTISM

In the early church, the initial coming of the Spirit to an individual was closely associated with Baptism. It was a basic component of the Spirit's strategy, which the apostles remembered from Jesus' instructions (Matt. 28:19; Mark 16:16), and which they recognized in the Spirit-led life of the witnessing community. When the Spirit fell on those who heard the Word in the household of Cornelius, Peter's first thought was for their Baptism (Acts 10:47). When Paul spoke with some believers in Ephesus and discovered that they had not even heard about the Holy Spirit, the first thing he inquired about was their Baptism (Acts 19:3).

Apostolic teaching makes a strong link between Baptism and the believer's union with Christ (Rom. 6:4; Gal. 3:27). The Western mind has a hard time thinking in any terms other than an almost mechanical sense of cause and effect, and this may be part of the problem when we consider the sacramental tradition. The Western mind-set drives sacramentalists toward a virtually automatic view of Baptism: the rite of Baptism is the cause, union with Christ is the result. The same thinking drives those on the other end of the spectrum toward a purely symbolic view of Baptism: since faith is the efficient cause of spiritual life, Baptism can be allowed no higher role than that of a symbol or confirming witness.

A strategic view would approach Baptism from another direction: the Holy Spirit himself is responsible for spiritual life. Baptism is an indispensable part of his strategy for uniting a believer with Christ. Attempting to identify Baptism as the cause, or something other than the cause, of spiritual life is a little like asking whether weapons cause military victories. They are an indispensable part of a commander's strategy. By themselves they do not guarantee victory, but victory can scarcely be conceived of apart from them.

The Spirit's activity in Baptism

The activity of the Spirit in the work of salvation has a particular focus in Jesus' words to Nicodemus: "unless one is born of water and the Spirit, he cannot enter the kingdom of God" (John 3:5). This evident allusion to Christian Baptism indicates that Baptism has a prominent place in the Spirit's work of bringing about the new birth, which is necessary for entering the kingdom of God. It is an integral part of the Spirit's strategy for bringing salvation.

A similar understanding of Baptism is found in the Pauline writings: "[God] saved us . . . in virtue of his own mercy, by the washing of regeneration and renewal in the Holy Spirit" (Titus 3:5). "You were washed, you were sanctified, you were justified in the name of the Lord Jesus Christ and in the Spirit of our God" (1 Cor. 6:11).

The "washing" of Baptism in these texts is linked to regeneration, justification, and sanctification, by the working of the Spirit. This does not mean that the performance of the baptismal rite of itself brings about salvation. Baptism cannot be viewed apart from the activity of the Spirit himself, and the response that he works in the heart of the individual. It does mean, however, that in a sovereign way the Holy Spirit links new life with the waters of Baptism. Baptism is used by the Spirit in regeneration.

To avoid the impression that Baptism works automatically, simply by virtue of being performed, it is necessary to point out that the New Testament also links regeneration to *faith:* "But to all who received him, who believed in his name, he gave power to become children of God; who were born, not of blood nor of the will of the flesh nor of the will of man, but of God" (John 1:12-13). Going through the ritual of Baptism does not in itself guarantee salvation unless there is a corresponding reception of Jesus by faith (Col. 2:12). The Holy Spirit makes the necessary connection between the outer means (Baptism, the Word) and the inner reception (faith).

In Baptism the Spirit unites the believer with Christ

Those who have heard the gospel, repented of their sins, and believed in Jesus as their Savior and Lord (Acts 2:21,36) are exhorted to be baptized (2:38). Baptism is integral to the Spirit's work of uniting a new believer with Christ. Scripture links the promise of life in Christ to the event of Baptism (for example, Acts 22:16; 1 Cor. 6:11; Col. 2:12-14; Titus 3:5; Mark 16:16; John 3:5; 1 Peter 3:21).

The ministry of baptizing, like that of proclamation, is carried out by human agents, and those being baptized submit voluntarily to Baptism. Nevertheless, as in the proclamation of the Word, the Spirit is at work. Baptism is not simply a rite entered into by a man or woman in order to express their faith and commitment. It is a means that the Spirit uses, together with the gospel message, to unite the believer with Christ (Rom. 6:3-4; Gal. 3:26-27).

Mere water and ritual could never grant the blessings that Scripture promises in connection with Baptism. Jesus himself acts in Baptism, for it is carried out in his name, that is, in his authority and power. When the New Testament community prayed and acted in the name of Jesus, the crucified and risen Savior—now the living and exalted Lord—was present in power among his people. As surely as they expected the Spirit to come in charismatic power, they expected him to move powerfully through the waters of Baptism.

CHAPTER 14

BAPTISM WITH
THE HOLY SPIRIT

John the Baptist prophesied that Jesus would baptize his followers with the Holy Spirit. Jesus confirmed it. Believers in the early church experienced it. The phrase "baptized with the Holy Spirit" is used in reference to two events in Acts: Pentecost and the outpouring of the Spirit in the household of Cornelius.

Systematic explanations of the coming of the Spirit come to sharp disagreement here. The Pentecostal view sees baptism with the Spirit as a "second blessing" by which someone who has already received salvation is empowered for service.. The sacramental and evangelical views both take exception to this interpretation. They hold that baptism with the Spirit is either identical with or invariably happens along with Baptism or salvation. Thus every believer has been baptized with the Spirit.

On purely exegetical grounds, the case is hard to resolve: neither in the Gospels, where it is used prophetically, nor in Acts where it is used descriptively, is baptism with the Holy Spirit precisely defined; and its use in Acts is somewhat ambiguous. It is difficult to make Pentecost out to be a salvation event for the disciples. Jesus' words to them in Acts 1:4-8 speak not in terms of salvation but rather in terms of power for witness. Jesus' expression, "You shall be baptized with the Holy Spirit" (Acts 1:5) was not a reference to Baptism with water, since the disciples were not baptized at Pentecost when the promise was fulfilled. It was rather a metaphorical expression denoting the experience that the disciples would have of being filled with the Holy Spirit and manifesting that reality in a demonstrable way. That was exactly what happened to those who were gathered together on Pentecost: "And they were all filled with the Holy Spirit and began to speak in other tongues, as the Spirit gave them utterance" (Acts 2:4). On the other hand, the primary interpretation that the apostles in Jerusalem put on the occurrence in the household of Cornelius was that it was a salvation event (Acts 11:18).

Despite its presence in the New Testament, "baptized with the Holy Spirit" is terminology that was little used in the history of the church until the advent of the Holiness and Pentecostal movements. Even in the later writings of the New Testament it does not occur. Luke himself, as we noted earlier, gives greater weight to the phrase "filled with the Spirit."

In our own century, however, through the Pentecostal and charismatic movements, the term "baptism with the Holy Spirit" has broken on the scene with dramatic results. To give disproportionate emphasis to a teaching or a term that has relatively little biblical or historical weight could lead to distortion. However, this does not mean that we should altogether abandon or neglect the term "baptism with the Holy Spirit." We should seek to understand it more clearly.

It has been fashionable in some mainline churches with venerable theological traditions to acknowledge the vitality and growth of Pentecostal Christianity while at the same time belittling its exegesis and theology in general and its doctrine of baptism with the Spirit in particular. It is possible, of course, that the Spirit could enliven the life and worship and witness of Pentecostals, prosper their missionary endeavors in an unprecedented way, yet make little headway with them in regard to their understanding of Scripture and their theology. Authentic experience can be inaccurately assessed and explained. To make such a judgment, however, in regard to a movement with the scope and significance and history of worldwide Pentecostalism takes some cheek. It might be that the Spirit wants to correct some aspects of Pentecostal teaching; a second wave of Pentecostalism in our century, the charismatic movement, may be the Spirit's occasion for addressing some new questions to Pentecostal theology. But it may equally be the Spirit's occasion for Catholics and Protestants to give more respectful consideration to the exegesis and theology of Pentecostals.

If we consider baptism with the Spirit strategically, it seems to answer to the need for an outpouring of the Spirit's power to initiate or renew witness and ministry. In the book of Acts, both times the term occurs it describes a dramatic initial outpouring of the Spirit. The history of the Pentecostal and charismatic movements tends to echo this: a key factor in the spread of the movements has been the widely shared personal experience of an outpouring of the Spirit. For many, perhaps most, this has initiated a new sense of the Spirit's presence and power for life and ministry.

The experience of baptism with the Holy Spirit has commonly been accompanied by a manifest demonstration of the Spirit's presence through charismatic gifts, and this is also consistent with the scriptural witness. In the theology of Luke, the experience of being filled with the Holy Spirit consistently results in a manifest demonstration of the Spirit's presence, usually in the form of exalted speech—they spoke in tongues (Acts 2:4; 10:46; 19:6), prophesied (Acts 19:6), extolled God (Acts 10:46), and spoke the Word of God with boldness (Acts 4:31); or it was accompanied by a supernatural sign—a healing (Acts 9:17-18), a divine judgment (Acts 13:9-11), or a rapturous vision (Acts 7:55).

To state that such an event, or such charisms, are "not necessary" in terms of systematic theology is to miss the point. It goes without saying that a specific outpouring of the Spirit with the manifestation of spiritual gifts is not "necessary" either for salvation or for fruitful ministry. One could argue the case both from Scripture and history—systematically. (One has but to mention a handful of prominent and universally respected movements or believers outside the Pentecostal tradition to make the point.) But that would be like saying, "It is not necessary that an air strike precede an infantry engagement in order for a battle to be won." However, if the commander has planned things that way, then another kind of necessity comes into play: the necessity of paying heed to his strategy. An argument among the troops or junior officers on the necessity or nonnecessity of air strikes would miss the point. The question, rather, is what strategy the commander wants to use in this situation.

Given the worldwide spread and witness of the Pentecostal and charismatic movements since the beginning of the 20th century, the church as a whole must consider questions not only of exegesis and systematic theology but also of the Spirit's strategy. This emphasis on a personal Pentecost—an outpouring of the Holy Spirit in one's life, a baptism with the Holy Spirit—how are we to understand it? Its key role in the amazing spread of Pentecostal and charismatic Christianity is well documented, but what are we to make of it? Is it a human doctrine, and an erroneous one at that? Or does it reflect a strategy of the Spirit for our day?

It may be that Pentecostals and charismatics have oversystematized their own perception and experience of the Holy Spirit. If so, that would be an understandable response to other systematizations that have produced deficient results in their own lives. Any attempt to systematize the working of the Holy Spirit, however, will be a helpful approximation at best. We may not agree with some aspects of the Pentecostal way of explaining the coming of the Spirit, but we will not be far off if we acknowledge that they have accurately perceived the Spirit's strategy: he is calling believers to receive a personal outpouring of the Holy Spirit; he is calling them to be filled with the Holy Spirit in a way and to a degree that they have not done before.

One of the great misconceptions that circulates around discussions of the Holy Spirit is the notion that we *have* everything that we state in our doctrines.

That is like claiming a victory on the battlefield because you have a textbook on military strategy. The strategy of the Spirit is calling the church to experience more of what the doctrines talk about—to go beyond an intellectual belief in the third person of the Trinity to a demonstration of the Spirit and his power (see 1 Cor. 2:4), to extend our expectation of the Spirit's working to the horizons of Scripture. This will not happen simply by asserting doctrines of the Holy Spirit. It calls for an obedient response to the strategy of the Spirit: a personal encounter with Jesus, who fills his followers with the Holy Spirit.

Whether one understands this as an appropriation of something already received (sacramental, evangelical) or a reception of something promised (Pentecostal), the strategy of the Spirit will be served: the Spirit will be poured out; believers will talk about the Holy Spirit with a new sense of reality; they will walk in a new dimension of reality and power; and the Lord's people will register gains against the powers that oppose the gospel.

CHAPTER 15

PRAYING FOR THE SPIRIT

The promise of Jesus

Jesus taught his disciples that the Father would give the Holy Spirit in response to prayer (Luke 11:13). The outpouring of the Spirit on the day of Pentecost, and elsewhere in the book of Acts, took place in the context of prayer.

Kilian McDonnell, a leading Roman Catholic authority on charismatic renewal, has observed that, seen from the outsider, the charismatic renewal could almost be mistaken for a prayer movement. Especially in the early years of the movement, the prayer meeting was the major gathering place for the nurture and spread of the renewal. Over and over the pattern was repeated: a handful of people would decide to gather for prayer, and the word would get around. Soon people would be coming from miles away to study the Bible together, hear a speaker, and pray. Prayer groups sprang up all over. In metropolitan areas one could find prayer groups to visit almost any time of day, every day of the week. It was a springtime of prayer, Bible study, and personal experience of the Holy Spirit. Some of the prayer groups continued a few months or years; others were still going on when the movement entered its third decade.

Here we come very close to the practical center of the Holy Spirit's basic strategy, vividly described in the New Testament and fulfilling the promise of Christ himself. Prayer is the activity par excellence that bridges the gap between an intellectual belief system and a living faith. In prayer we move from talking *about* God to talking *to* God. When prayer ceases to be a ritual formality and becomes a genuine encounter with God, then the central focus of life begins to shift from self back to God.

This fits the strategy of the Spirit: he is coming against an entrenched humanism, a religion that has planted the autonomous human being firmly at the center of all things. The Spirit knows that an alternative belief system, be it ever so biblical and orthodox, will not break the grip of secular humanism. The strategy of the Spirit is to equip believers to demonstrate a life that proceeds in every regard from a radical dependence on God; for that, prayer is indispensable.

Laying on of hands

In the book of Acts, the Spirit is sometimes given through the laying on of hands; or, to state it negatively, the Spirit is not given until hands have been laid on (Acts 8:17). In these cases it functioned as part of initiation, performed in close relationship to Baptism. Laying on of hands is also used in other contexts: in the healing of the sick (Matt. 9:18; Mark 6:5; Acts 9:12; 28:8; also Acts 5:12; 19:11-12), in the blessing of children (Matt. 19:13-15), in dedicating people to special ministries (Acts 6:6; 13:3). Charisms were given through laying on of hands (1 Tim. 4:14; 2 Tim. 1:6). Only in one place, however, is a promise directly tied to laying on of hands: "They will lay their hands on the sick, and they will recover" (Mark 16:18).

There are no promises that the gift of the Holy Spirit will be granted, or granted exclusively, through the laying on of hands. The promise of the gift of the Spirit, as we have seen in Chapter 9, is linked quite simply to becoming a Christian.

Jesus did, however, promise the Spirit to those who pray (Luke 11:13). This is the essential significance of laying on of hands. It is a form of prayer, and, as such, it is of great significance. God's promises are tied to prayer. Prayer is faith in action: it reaches out for what is promised. In this sense laying on of hands is an act of faith. It should be seen in the light of passages like Matt. 18:19-20: "If two of you agree on earth about anything they ask, it will be done for them by my Father in heaven."

We cannot exclude the possibility that the act of laying on of hands serves as a channel for God's power, but we cannot tie God to this act. There are cases in which God grants his Spirit without laying on of hands (Acts 2:4; 10:44). However, according to the biblical testimony, laying on of hands seems to be used quite regularly in connection with Christian initiation and dedication of individual Christians for special ministries. Being filled with the Spirit and manifesting the gifts of the Spirit are sometimes associated with this action. It may therefore be used with expectation as a form of earnest prayer. Through laying on of hands the Christian church prays concretely and personally that a particular individual may receive the gifts that God wants to grant in a particular situation. There are no "rules" for laying on of hands, except the warning, "Do not be hasty in the laying on of hands" (1 Tim. 5:22).

Somewhat akin to the laying on of hands would be the practice of anointing with oil. In Eastern Orthodox churches, as well as Roman Catholic confirmation, this is done with reference to the biblical concept of being "sealed" with the Holy Spirit (2 Cor. 1:22; Eph. 1:13).[1] The use of oil in connection with prayers for healing, based on James 5:14, is found in both ancient and contemporary liturgies of the church.

Paradoxically, radical dependence on the Spirit goes hand in hand with a high regard for such external means as the laying on of hands or anointing with oil. Believers are so anointed by the Spirit that "you have no need that any one should teach you; as his anointing teaches you about everything" (1 John 2:27). Nevertheless they are told to "teach and admonish one another in all wisdom" (Col. 3:16); and elders who labor in preaching and teaching are considered worthy of double honor (1 Tim. 5:17). Lest we become spiritually self-sufficient, or fail to recognize the significance of the body of Christ—or when faith needs special encouragement—the Spirit may call us to humble ourselves and receive his outpouring of his gifts through such special ministrations as the prayers of fellow believers, including laying on of hands or anointing with oil.

CHAPTER 16

MANIFESTATIONS OF THE SPIRIT

In the book of Acts, the coming of the Spirit was demonstrable. In writing a report of these early days in the church, Luke observed that the strategy of the Spirit apparently did not include any coming so quiet and unobserved that one would not know for certain whether he had come or not. If new believers did not experience a manifest outpouring, the Spirit took further initiatives to correct the matter.

This is a point at which a strategic approach to the coming of the Spirit may help us avoid unprofitable arguments about who "has" the Holy Spirit. When the apostles heard that Samaria had received the Word of God (Acts 8:14), they did not initiate a detailed theological discussion to determine how, whether, or in what degree these new believers had the Holy Spirit. They made a practical observation: "The Holy Spirit had not yet fallen on any of them" (Acts 8:16). There had been no manifestations of the Spirit, though this normally happened when the Spirit came to new believers.

What the apostles did, and how Luke reported it, is best understood in relation not to the question of eternal life, but to the more focused issue of the Spirit's strategy in this particular situation: "They laid their hands on them and they received the Holy Spirit" (Acts 8:17). The strategy of the Spirit called for manifestations. The new believers needed to receive the Spirit in that specific sense, and the apostles took steps to bring it about.

If the strategy of the Spirit calls for manifest demonstrations of his presence, then we need to talk about "receiving" him in this specific sense with the simplicity and directness that Scripture itself employs. Discussions about having or receiving the Spirit in terms of eternal life are important in themselves, but if they intrude into this context, they could blunt the strategy of the Spirit.

Pentecostals and charismatics have been faulted for making too much of spiritual gifts, especially the gift of tongues. If an emphasis on particular manifestations of the Spirit is implicitly linked to the issue of salvation or to one's status as a believer, the criticism is needed and helpful. But if the strategy of the Spirit is the point at issue, then an emphasis on manifestations of the Spirit was probably long overdue. Pentecostals and charismatics are coming up to the front lines, bearing a clear, even a stern, communique: "Do not neglect the gifts! God has provided them for a purpose. Learn about them, pray for them, use them." Manifestations of the Spirit are not options. They are equipment that every soldier is expected to receive and use—an integral part of the strategy of the Spirit for advancing the cause of Christ.

Spirit-empowered ministry

The outpourings of the Spirit in Acts focus on the Spirit as an endowment for Christian life and ministry, granted to Christians as a gift. It is the manifest demonstration of the Spirit which is primarily in view, rather than his work of bringing people to salvation.[1] The strong missionary emphasis of Acts (Acts 1:8) brings to special focus the Spirit's work of empowering believers for ministry.

One sees this clearly in the story of Philip and the Ethiopian eunuch (Acts 8:26-39). The Spirit's working is not mentioned in direct connection with the eunuch's conversion. It is simply recorded that the eunuch requests Baptism; some manuscripts include also his profession of faith. The references to the Spirit focus not on his working with the eunuch, but rather on his charismatic manifestations in Philip: the Spirit gives specific guidance that brings Philip in contact with the eunuch, and when the task is accomplished he literally "Spirits" Philip away.

It is the special concern of Acts to present the Spirit as the one who is poured out on believers to empower them for their missionary task. Jesus said this clearly: "You shall receive power when the Holy Spirit has come upon you" (Acts 1:8). When Acts speaks of "receiving the Holy Spirit," "being baptized with the Holy Spirit," "being filled with the Holy Spirit," "receiving the gift of the Holy Spirit"—when Paul asks, "Did you receive the Holy Spirit when you believed?"—the issue being addressed is not whether these people are saved, but whether they have been empowered for ministry.

The witness of Paul

An important question at this point is whether the way that Acts presents the coming of the Spirit finds confirming evidence in the Pauline epistles.

Do letters such as Galatians and Romans, the rich soil out of which the Reformation experience grew, provide corroborating or contradictory material?

Galatians 3:1-5 provides helpful insight into Paul's teaching and ministry concerning Christian initiation and the Spirit as gift. In the verses immediately preceding (2:15-21), Paul revealed his self-understanding as a Christian and what conversion meant in his own experience. Contrary to the assertions of the legalists, Paul knew that justification comes through faith in Christ. By the work of the indwelling Holy Spirit (Gal. 5:18; Rom. 8:10), Paul experienced an altogether new kind of existence: "Christ . . . lives in me" (Gal. 2:20). Therefore he realized that he was a new creation before God and a new being in the reality of this world, even though the reality was "hid with Christ in God" (Col. 3:3).

Paul went on in Galatians to develop his argument for justification by faith: it was through listening and believing the gospel that they had experienced a specific, clear, and undeniable change. What is interesting to note, however, is that he pointed to the gift of the Holy Spirit, coming in power to the Galatian Christians, replete with miracles, and the confirmation of his argument against living by the law.[2]

> You foolish Galatians! Who has bewitched you? Before your very eyes Jesus Christ was clearly portrayed as crucified. I would like to learn just one thing from you: Did you receive the Spirit by observing the law, or by believing what you heard? Are you so foolish? After beginning with the Spirit, are you now trying to attain your goal by human effort? Have you suffered so much for nothing if it really was for nothing? Does God give you his Spirit and work miracles among you because you observe the law, or because you believe what you heard? (Gal. 3:1-5 NIV).

Historically, Paul's argument for justification has won the day. Justification by faith is the secure foundation stone of the Reformation heritage. The way that Paul built his case, however, reveals an understanding of the Spirit that is similar to what we find in Acts. He pointed to manifest demonstrations of the Spirit, coming not through keeping the law but in response to faith, as confirming evidence for the doctrine of justification by faith. The experience of being empowered by the Spirit, including miraculous manifestations, provided an instructive parallel for understanding justification.

Any attempt to set an objective doctrine of justification against a subjective experience of the Spirit as gift and power would be unthinkable for the apostle Paul. For him, the experience of the Spirit, received by faith, was a confirmation of the preaching of the cross. Furthermore, the gift of the Holy Spirit is absolutely necessary to live out the new existence as Christians (Gal. 5:16, 18). The parallelism of Gal. 3:8 and 3:14 is telling: the coin on which is stamped *justification by faith* has on its other side *the gift of the Holy Spirit.*

CHAPTER 17

THE FULLNESS
OF THE SPIRIT

In the New Testament, believers in a variety of situations are described as being "filled with the Spirit." Believers are exhorted to be filled with the Spirit (Eph. 5:18). The strategy of the Spirit calls for Spirit-filled believers.

"Filled" is essentially a quantitative concept. The exhortation to be filled makes sense only if the one spoken to is less than full. Here we see clearly that the strategy of the Spirit is a dynamic, rather than a static, concept. It does not focus primarily on what we are. In a sense that is taken for granted, a given: we are disciples of Christ. The strategy of the Spirit looks rather to where we are going and how we are to get there. When that comes into focus, the coming of the Spirit will be more than a piece of systematic theology, something to look back on: it will be an expectation of what is yet to be.

Life in the Spirit

The new life is characterized by the fulfillment of the law of God (Rom. 8:4). Power for ethical living comes through the Spirit's indwelling. Although keenly aware of his or her own weakness and sinfulness (2 Cor. 4:7; 12:9-10; Rom. 7:18), the believer experiences with Paul the power of the Spirit, giving both a new desire and a new ability to live according to the will of God (Phil. 2:13). Those who are indwelt by the Spirit are enabled to go on to lead lives of active holiness and effective ministry (1 Cor. 6:11; 1 Thess. 4:3-8; 2 Cor. 3:5).

Since the Spirit is the Spirit of Jesus, the Spirit by his indwelling conforms the Christian to the image of Christ. Conformity to Christ is the goal of the transforming work of the Spirit (Rom. 8:29; 2 Cor. 3:17-18).

The Spirit, however, does not change the lives of Christians into holiness and conformity to Christ against their own wills. Believers must respond to the Spirit, and are encouraged and exhorted to do so. As they do this, Christ communicates his heart and will so that they may fulfill the commandments of God (Phil. 2:13; Rom. 8:4; 12:1-2).

This does not mean that the Christian is perfect or sinless. He or she is involved in a deep conflict between the flesh (the old sinful nature) and the Spirit. According to the flesh one is a sinner, but according to the Spirit, a new and righteous creation (Rom. 7:13-25; Gal. 5:16-25).

The Christian is called to side with the Spirit and live accordingly: "But I say, walk by the Spirit, and do not gratify the desires of the flesh . . . . If we live by the Spirit, let us also walk by the Spirit" (Gal. 5:16,25; also Rom. 8:2-4,12-14). The Christian is called by the power of the Spirit to become in actual life what he or she is in Christ.

The expression "fruit of the Spirit" can be seen as a comprehensive designation of how the Spirit's indwelling affects the believer's relationship both to God and to other people: "But the fruit of the Spirit is love, joy, peace, patience, kindness, goodness, faithfulness, gentleness, self-control; against such there is no law" (Gal. 5:22; also Col. 1:9-10).

First and foremost among the fruit is love, which is "poured into our hearts through the Holy Spirit which has been given to us" (Rom. 5:5). Both in terms of one's personal Christian life and in carrying out one's ministry, love is seen as the highest expression of the Spirit's work in a believer, the "more excellent way" (1 Cor. 12:31; 13:13).

This love is united with joy and peace. Although these concepts do have a psychological dimension, they should not be limited to expressing merely emotional experiences. Joy may exist in the midst of sorrow and afflictions (2 Cor. 6:10; Col. 1:24; 1 Thess. 1:6). It is a quality of existence in the kingdom of God. So also is the peace of God: "For the kingdom of God does not mean food and drink but righteousness and peace and joy in the Holy Spirit" (Rom. 14:17).

It is really a foretaste of the salvation to come, granting an assured hope of salvation: "May the God of hope fill you with all joy and peace in believing, so that by the power of the Holy Spirit you may abound in hope" (Rom. 15:13).

Living in the fullness of the Spirit

We have already pointed out that the term "to be filled with the Spirit" may denote either an initial, manifest reception of the Spirit or subsequent receptions of the Spirit in the lives of Christians.

Although all Christians are indwelt by the Spirit, there is a place in the Christian life for experiences of being filled with the Spirit. This may happen to individual Christians or to Christian communities. Some Christians may be characterized as "full of the Spirit," in obvious contrast to others who are less subject to the influence of the Spirit in their lives and ministry.

The fullness of the Spirit may come about as the result of experiences in which he is poured out (Acts 4:8,31; 13:9,52). The relation between the Spirit indwelling and the Spirit outpoured may be explained by reference to the nature of the Spirit himself. The Spirit who indwells believers is a divine person, alive and active. He is never at our disposal, as if owned or controlled by us. His indwelling presence is effective only as we give ourselves ever anew to the Spirit's leading (Rom. 8:13-14). The Spirit may be sinned against (Acts 5:3; 1 Thess. 4:8) and withdraw. There is no guarantee that Christians, who are the temple of the Spirit (1 Cor. 3:16; 6:19), will continue to live and serve in the Spirit. Therefore Paul warned against grieving or quenching the Spirit and encouraged Christians to be filled with the Spirit (Eph. 4:30; 5:18; 1 Thess. 5:19).

According to the New Testament, the Christian life should be one of expectancy, openness, preparedness, and prayer for the repeated and continuous coming of the Holy Spirit (Luke 11:13). There are no significant differences in the testimony of the Scripture between the effects of the Spirit's first outpouring on a believer and his later comings. The term "filled with the Spirit" may be used in either case. The experiential reality is essentially the same.

CHAPTER 18

WITNESSING IN THE POWER OF THE SPIRIT

As we have seen, one strand of biblical testimony presents the creative and life-giving activity of the Spirit: the Spirit is the agent who accomplishes God's work of creation and redemption. Another major strand presents the Spirit as gift, the one whom believers receive in a concrete and personal way. We have called this a *charismatic work of the Spirit;* scholars, even apart from the charismatic movement, commonly denote this second activity of the Spirit as charismatic. It is this charismatic endowment by the Spirit that is primarily in view when we consider the Spirit's work of empowering the church for its mission. Luke is the principal New Testament spokesman in this regard, and he stands in a well-established Old Testament tradition.

Charismatic endowment in the Old Testament

In the Old Testament, the charismatic Spirit came on select individuals for specific tasks of service among the people of God. These tasks included military, political, and religious leadership through powerful words and deeds. Outstanding leaders such as Moses, Joshua, the judges, Samuel, Saul, and David were all equipped for their tasks by the possession of the Spirit of God (Num. 11:16-30; Deut. 34:9; Judg. 3:10; 6:34; 1 Sam. 10:5-7, 10-11; 16:13).

The reception of the Spirit was often sudden and unexpected, even violent and irresistible (for example, 1 Sam. 10:10). It was never merited, often contrary to human expectations or qualifications, always a free gift (Judg. 6:15, 34).

The charismatic Spirit granted power and courage to carry out heroic feats and to perform miracles. Through the words and deeds of charismatically equipped leaders, the people were directly confronted with the power of God.

The visible and tangible effects of the possession of the charismatic Spirit served as a divine confirmation of leadership and ministry among the people.

The outward evidence of the presence of the Spirit could be prophecy, miracles, or some form of trance. However, spirit possession in itself was no unambiguous proof of the presence of God's Spirit. Since there were also other spirits and false prophecy, the Spirit of God would be recognized on the basis of the truth of the word spoken and the correspondence of the ministry of the prophet to the will of God revealed in the covenant (Deut. 18:22; 1 Kings 22:21-25). The claims of the charismatic person had to be backed up by the genuineness of his or her message and integrity of life.

Closely related to the charismatic Spirit is the prophetic Spirit. In the prophets the charismatic endowment with the Spirit of God served primarily their ministries of proclaiming the Word of God with power. However, powerful deeds accompanied the ministries of the prophets and supported their prophetic calling (for example, 1 Kings 18:25-40).

In the Psalms and the Chronicles, the priests and the Levites are included among the charismatically equipped leadership, leading the congregation of Israel in worship and praise (1 Chron. 25:1; 2 Chron. 20:14; 24:20).

In Psalm 51 we meet an Old Testament man of God, a man who had committed adultery, murder, and falsehood (2 Samuel 11–12), but who confessed his sin and asked forgiveness (Ps. 51:3-11). Following the reestablishment of a right relationship to God, the author asked for a renewal of his human spirit: "Create in me a clean heart, O God, and put a new and right spirit within me" (v. 10). Then he prayed that he might remain in God's gracious presence and that the Holy Spirit might remain with him. The result of the Holy Spirit's sanctifying work in the penitent sinner's heart was a restoration of the joy of salvation, a willing spirit, and the desire to teach other sinners repentance and faith (vv. 12-13). Prayer for the Holy Spirit thus had its place also in the lives of Old Testament saints, although the fullness of the gift of the Spirit had not yet been given.

The promise of a future outpouring of the Spirit

The Spirit of God was never granted in the Old Testament as a gift to the people as a whole. It was limited to select individuals or groups. However, there was a vision of a future, general outpouring of the Spirit on all the people of God. The charismatic, prophetic Spirit, characterized by prophetic revelation in dreams and visions, would be poured out on all the people. They would have direct access to the Lord. He would put his words in their mouths, words of witness to the saving acts of God in history (Joel 2:28-29; Isa. 59:21). God's blessing would rest on his people, resulting in ethical and religious transformation (Isa. 44:3-5; 32:15-17). They would receive a new heart that would make them God's people and cause them to live according to his will (Ezek. 36:26-28).

The Spirit makes witnesses who glorify Christ

The Christocentric nature of the Spirit's ministry is particularly noticeable in Jesus' farewell discourse: the Father would send the Spirit in response to Jesus' prayer (John 14:16) and in Jesus' name (John 14:26), or Jesus would send him from the Father (John 15:26; 16:7). The Spirit thus proceeds from the Father and the Son. The Holy Spirit carries the features of Jesus. When a believer experiences the Spirit, he or she encounters Christ. Therefore, the Holy Spirit represents the glorified Christ on earth, both in relation to the church and to the world. He communicates Jesus' message, he mediates salvation by creating faith and giving new life to believers, and he makes believers into credible witnesses who glorify Christ through their life and ministry.

Jesus' prophecy of the Paraclete

In Jesus' farewell discourse to his disciples, he taught them concerning the work of the Holy Spirit, the "Paraclete" or Counselor (John 14:15-17, 25-26; 15:26-27; 16:5-15). Here the Spirit's work is seen with regard to the *disciples* and with regard to the *world*.

With regard to the disciples, he is the Spirit of truth who would reveal to them the things of Christ. It would not be a new revelation, but rather a revelation of Christ, who himself is the truth (John 14:6). The Spirit would be witness, teacher, and prophet to them.

As a witness, the Spirit is a witness to Christ: "But when the Counselor comes . . . even the Spirit of truth . . . he will bear witness to me; and you also are witnesses, because you have been with me from the beginning" (John 15:26-27).

Concretely, the testimony of the Spirit takes place in and through the testimony of the disciples. The content of the witness is not only the historical facts of Jesus' earthly ministry, death, and resurrection, but also who Jesus was and the significance of his work for our redemption. The testimony aims at showing that "God gave us eternal life, and this life is in his Son" (1 John 5:11). The content of the testimony that the Spirit gives the disciples is precisely this inner awareness of who Christ is and what he has done. Because he is the Son of God, become flesh, his death and resurrection have saving significance. Through this testimony the Spirit brings about faith: "And the Spirit is the witness, because the Spirit is the truth. There are three witnesses, the Spirit, the water, and the blood; and these three agree. . . . He who believes in the Son of God has the testimony in himself" (1 John 5:7,8,10a). This inner testimony, this personal application and appropriation of the gospel, is the aim of the Spirit's testimony.

The teaching ministry of the Spirit will enable the disciples to grasp the full significance of Jesus' own teaching: "But the Counselor, the Holy Spirit, whom the Father will send in my name, he will teach you all things, and bring to your remembrance all that I have said to you" (John 14:26). He makes the words of Jesus clear, relevant, and personal.

Sent into the world

Through the disciples' ministry, the Holy Spirit also confronts the world. The role of the Spirit in this respect is that of a prosecuting attorney. "And when he comes, he will convince the world of sin and of righteousness and of judgment: of sin, because they do not believe in me; of righteousness, because I go to the Father, and you will see me no more; of judgment, because the ruler of this world is judged" (John 16:8-11).

The Spirit is not given to the world, but he confronts the world through the testimony of Jesus' disciples. Here the Spirit's work is to convict, showing the world its sin and calling it to repentance. The concept of conviction does not necessarily include the notion that the world actually turns to God. Some people do; others do not. The basic sin that the Spirit exposes is unbelief, rejection of Christ. The righteousness that the Spirit testifies to is God's justification of Christ by raising him from the dead. The judgment is Jesus' defeat of Satan.

The Spirit as power behind the proclaimed Word

The era of the church is the era of mission to the end of the earth. As the Father sent the Son, Jesus sent the disciples (John 20:21). The Spirit was given in order to enable them to carry out the missionary task (John 20:22; Acts 1:4-5, 8).

Wherever missionary proclamation of the gospel takes place, it also provokes opposition and persecution. The Spirit is the strength of Christians in inner temptations, but he also gives them power and words to resist and conquer external pressure, opposition, and persecution. In his eschatological discourses Jesus said that Christians should expect persecution in connection with the missionary task. He encouraged them to trust in the presence and inspiration of the Spirit: "And the gospel must first be preached to all nations. And when they bring you to trial and deliver you up, do not be anxious beforehand what you are to say; but say whatever is given you in that hour, for it is not you who speak, but the Holy Spirit" (Mark 13:10-11).

The fulfillment of this promise is seen in the early church (Acts 4:8; 7:54-56; 13:9), and in the lives of Christian martyrs down through the history of the church. In the early church, martyrs were seen as possessing a special charism that gave their words additional authority.

It is inherent in the universal scope of the redemption wrought by Christ that the good news of this redemption be proclaimed to people everywhere. Because Christ died and rose to bring forgiveness of sins and righteousness to all, the salvation message must be brought within reach of all. The Holy Spirit gives believers power and boldness in proclaiming the gospel. He equips and empowers them in such a way that the gospel will be heard and believed in all the earth, and a people of God from all nations will be established (Matt. 28:18-20; Acts 15:14). Thus the oral proclamation of the gospel— through various methods such as preaching, debate, conversation, legal defense, and teaching—carries with it the convincing and convicting power of the Spirit.

The importance of signs and wonders

A basic characteristic of the Spirit both in the Old Testament and in the New Testament is that of divine power that makes possible inspired witness and miraculous deeds. With the gift of the Spirit comes divine power. It is in terms of power that Jesus promised the coming of the Spirit: "But you shall receive power when the Holy Spirit has come on you; and you shall be my witnesses in Jerusalem and in all Judea and Samaria and to the end of the earth" (Acts 1:8; also Luke 24:49).

In addition to the oral proclamation, the wonders and signs that were performed served to confirm the spoken message and contributed decisively to the growth of the early church (Acts 5:12-16; 4:30; 8:6; 13:9-11; 15:12). These signs were mainly signs of healing and deliverance from evil spirits. But there were also occurrences of visions (Acts 10:9-20; 11:28), discernment of secret thoughts (Acts 13:9-11; 5:3,9), divine guidance in the work of missionaries (Acts 8:29; 11:12,17; 13:2-3; 16:6-10; 15:8-9,28), and direct insight into God's will and purpose (Acts 10:19-20).

The importance of miraculous events can hardly be overestimated in looking at the mission of the early church. They are testified and alluded to in all parts of the New Testament (for example: John 20:30-31; Gal. 3:5; 1 Cor.

12:8-11; 1 Thess. 1:5; Heb. 2:4). The ministry of the apostles was confirmed with the "signs of a true apostle," including "signs and wonders and mighty works" (2 Cor. 12:12). Paul described his own ministry comprehensively in the following terms: "For I will not venture to speak of anything except what Christ has wrought through me to win obedience from the Gentiles, by word and deed, by the power of signs and wonders, by the power of the Holy Spirit, so that from Jerusalem and as far round as Illyricum I have fully preached the gospel of Christ" (Rom. 15:18-19). There is no evidence that these signs were limited to the apostles. They also confirmed the ministry of others in the early church (see Acts 8:6-7; 9:17-18; Mark 16:14-20).

This combination of words and works, of proclamation and demonstration, confronting people with the power of God, is a crucial dimension in the missionary efforts of the apostles and the early church. There is no indication in the Scriptures that this aspect of missionary work was to cease with the passing of the apostles (see Mark 16:17-18; John 14:12). Today, the missionary purpose and the missionary power of the church must again be seen in connection with the exercise of spiritual gifts.

Strategy is a term appropriate to warfare or contest. One employs strategy with a view to an *opponent*. When we speak about the strategy of the Spirit, we need to think also about the opponent. Too often we have made opponents of one another; differing theological perspectives on the coming of the Spirit have become a basis for warfare and division within the body of Christ.

The strategy of the Spirit is indeed devised with a view to an opponent. But "we are not contending against flesh and blood, but against the principalities, against the powers, against the world rulers of this present darkness, against the spiritual hosts of wickedness in the heavenly places" (Eph. 6:12). The strategy of the Spirit is devised with a view to how the kingdom of God opposes the kingdom of Satan. His strategy unites us with Christ and with one another; it fills us with the Holy Spirit, so that together we may move forward in the cause of Christ.

This book is written in the conviction that the Holy Spirit has a strategy for our day, and that he is ready and willing for us to learn about it and become involved in it. This book is not intended to be a systematic and exhaustive presentation of the doctrine of the Holy Spirit, yet neither is it an uncritical acceptance of all present-day experience. It is an attempt to discern as accurately as possible the strategy of the Spirit, which means that firsthand experiences and practical observations will be tested in the light of Scripture and theological reflection.

Our hope and prayer is that the ways of God may not only be considered and understood, but also accomplished in the life of God's people, for that is surely the goal of the Spirit's strategy.

PART THREE

DECLARED BY THE SPIRIT
A Lutheran Theological Perspective

He will glorify me, for he will take what is mine and declare
it to you.

John 16:14

SOLUS CHRISTUS— CHRIST ALONE

INTERPRETING THE CENTRAL TEACHINGS OF SCRIPTURE

The most important contribution that the Lutheran Confessions could make to the development of a charismatic theology is a hermeneutic, that is, a basic approach to biblical interpretation that hews to the center of the scriptural revelation. In previous chapters we have seen how the charismatic renewal has affected some of the *presuppositions* of biblical interpretation, especially as they relate to the question of a worldview. In the next five chapters we want to consider charismatic experience in relation to those central teachings of Scripture that were particularly brought to light in the Lutheran Reformation.

Biblical interpretation in the Lutheran tradition

The Lutheran Confessions reflect criteria that one can use to test an interpretation of Scripture. The two basic criteria could be shaped in question form as follows:

1. *Does this teaching magnify the honor of Christ?* Does it present the biblical subject matter in such a way that Christ's honor is in no way diminished, but rather extolled because it prompts people to declare his lordship?
2. *Does this teaching have a saving effect on people?* Does it present subject matter in such a way that sinners are not left to despair, but rather find godly comfort as they are liberated from the destructive power of sin, death, and Satan?

A Lutheran hermeneutic would test any doctrine, or theology as a whole, against these two basic and interrelated criteria.[1] They would not be applied only now and then, but consistently and to Scripture as a whole.[2] The authority of Scripture would not be reduced to these two categories narrowly conceived, yet they would stand as sentinels over the whole enterprise of interpretation. It is in this way that the Lutheran Confessions contend for the *apostolicity* ("Jesus Christ is the same . . .") and the *catholicity* (". . . yesterday and today and forever") of its teaching.

The Lutheran Confessions and the charismatic renewal

When Lutheran theology approaches a phenomenon such as the charismatic movement, it must evaluate it on the basis of the entirety of Scripture, interpreting the texts according to the principle stated above. It is not sufficient merely to quote a series of "proof texts" that seem to confirm the existence of a "charismatic dimension" in Scripture; nor is it adequate to have a correct principle of interpretation, but fail to apply it to the entirety of Scripture. If a hermeneutical principle has validity, it can be applied to all of Scripture— including, for example, 1 Corinthians 12–14.[3]

Using this approach, we will consider a variety of subjects to help develop an understanding of the charismatic renewal that is based on Scripture and reflects the wisdom that the Spirit gave to the church through the Lutheran reformers.

The Lutheran Confessions bring key theological concerns to a focus through a strategic use of the word *alone*. For example: Christ alone, grace alone, faith alone, Scripture alone. They do not use this term in an absolute sense. That would distort its intended meaning. Rather, *alone* is used to qualify a term in a specific sense. Thus, for example, "grace alone" is directed against any attempt to earn salvation by one's own effort, not against good works or the sacraments or prayer; "Scripture alone" is directed against anything that sets another authority above the Bible, not against ecclesiastical authority or tradition as such. It is in this same sense that we employ this helpful literary form in what follows.

"SOLUS CHRISTUS"—CHRIST ALONE

The charismatic movement places a fresh emphasis on the person and work of the Holy Spirit. This does not lead to a lack of emphasis on the Son and the Father, a "unitarianism of the Spirit," as some critics have charged. On the contrary, a consistent witness to Jesus as our only Savior and Lord and a high regard for the structures of creation as given and preserved by the "Father almighty, maker of heaven and earth," have been typical of the many Lutherans involved in the charismatic movement.[4]

Christ alone: not antitrinitarian

When we interpret Scripture so as to illumine and magnify the honor of Christ, we do not contradict or detract from the honor that is due the Trinity. Rather, in doing this we interpret our trinitarian faith. When Christ is not properly honored, neither is the Father, who "gave his only Son" (John 3:16), nor the Spirit, who "will glorify me" (John 16:14).

For example, a charismatic theology of healing, if it is to honor Christ, will be trinitarian. It will respect what Luther recognized as the Father's provision for health and healing in creation, as it has been studied by medical science and observed by common sense.[5] It will recognize the significant role that healing played in the ministry of Jesus, which was then carried on by his disciples (Acts 3:7; 4:30; 5:12; 9:18; 14:10; also Matt. 10:1; 28:20; Mark 16:20).[6] It will honor the provision for healing that the Holy Spirit brings through gifts of healing (1 Cor. 12:9), and by the quickening of faith and prayer among God's people.

Luther wrote:

> Since the devil is not only a liar but also a murderer, he incessantly seeks our life and vents his anger by causing accidents and injury to our bodies. . . . Thus you see how God wants us to pray to him for everything that affects our bodily welfare and directs us to seek and expect help from no one but him.[7]

An approach that unites the work of Father, Son, and Holy Spirit magnifies the honor of Christ. His compassion and healing grace thus continue to reach out to touch broken and suffering lives, even as during his earthly ministry.

Christ alone: not antihuman

Charismatics are presently struggling to express themselves critically against a secular-humanist mentality that puts the autonomous, self-sufficient human being at the center of all things. On the other hand, they do not want to fall into the trap of overstating the doctrine of God to the point of obliterating human responsibility. They sense the necessity of maintaining an appropriate tension between the results of the fall (Gen. 2:17) and the effects of the new creation (2 Cor. 5:17).

Secular humanism teaches a doctrine of humankind that is something like the free-will theology that the Formula of Concord opposes. Free-will theology does not reckon realistically with the continuing limitations that the Creator places on those created in his own image; nor does it truthfully acknowledge the results of the curse that God pronounced on human disobedience. The Creator is thereby effectively exiled to a position of irrelevance, and his creatures are supposedly "free" to live as practical atheists.[8] Today's secular humanists are a close parallel.

The Formula of Concord, in effect, asserts the impossibility of the secular-humanist position: our free will is limited both by the fall and by the sovereignty of God.[9] However, the Formula also rejects an overstated theistic position that would take from the redeemed children of God the responsibility and capacity to cooperate with God that he himself has given them. The authors of the Formula wrote:

> As soon as the Holy Spirit has initiated his work of regeneration and renewal in us through the Word and the holy sacraments, it is certain that we can and must *cooperate* by the power of the Holy Spirit, even though we still do so in great weakness. Such *cooperation* does not proceed from our carnal and natural powers, but from the new powers and gifts which the Holy Spirit has begun in us in conversion [italics added].[10]

Thus the Formula of Concord guards, on the one hand, against a self-confident humanism that trumpets our freedom to will and carve out our own destiny, and, on the other hand, it cautions against an overstated theism that effectively denies the power of the Holy Spirit to communicate new life in Christ.

Both sides of this dialectic are encompassed in the charismatic renewal's call for radical dependence on the Holy Spirit. On the one hand, it recognizes that in ourselves we have no ability to live the Christian life. On the other hand, it rejoices in the power of the Holy Spirit to conform believers to the image of Christ.

CHAPTER 20

SOLA GRATIA— GRACE ALONE

The Lutheran Confessions especially want to guard Christ's honor as Savior and Lord. Salvation is all his work. Wherever people seek to "imitate Christ" in order to please God and thus achieve their own salvation, the Confessions sound the alarm: by grace alone! To speak of grace immediately draws us close to the question of a "charismatic" theology, since a *charism* is, by definition, a manifestation of grace. But to speak of grace as being "alone" has suggested to some that it comes apart from any instrument or means, and to others that it remains without consequences. The Lutheran Confessions disavow both of these possibilities.

Grace alone: not antimeans

The Lutheran Confessions emphatically teach that grace comes by means of the Word and according to the Word. Grace without the divinely appointed means of its coming robs Christ of his honor by jeopardizing the comfort he would bring to sinners. Grace without means also calls into question the authority of Scripture.

Christ communicates himself to us through what Luther calls the "external Word"—an expression which for him covered the Scriptures, particularly as preached, and the sacraments.[1] Melanchthon made a similar point when he maintained that "justification takes place only through the Word," citing Rom. 1:16 and 10:17.[2] The Formula of Concord repeats this thought in many contexts and with great vigor.[3]

Although the reformers could document their contention simply by appealing to the witness of Holy Scripture, they also made the case by suggesting that any other approach would in effect be an expression of a works-righteousness that would dishonor Christ. Melanchthon, for instance, argued:

> It is good to extol the *ministry of the Word* with every possible kind of praise in opposition to the fanatics who dream that the Holy Spirit does not come through *the Word* but because of *their own preparations*. They sit in a dark corner doing and saying nothing, but only waiting for illumination [italics added].[4]

The expression "their own preparations" is the key. The enthusiasts of Luther's day reversed the direction of the means of grace: rather than speaking of the means that God uses to communicate his grace to us, they spoke of the means they had to use to gain such grace from God.[5]

This is the framework within which charismatics speak about people being filled or baptized with the Holy Spirit. It is not something that happens apart from the promises given in Scripture, nor by our initiation. Rather, it is clearly stated in Scripture that Jesus will baptize his followers with the Holy Spirit. That word of promise, responded to in faith, becomes the means or instrument by which this grace is conveyed and received. Charismatic manifestations of the Holy Spirit likewise occur as we rely on God's Word and not because we ourselves have struck on a teaching or method for getting the Spirit into our possession.

Nevertheless, the Lutheran Confessions do not impose limitations on God as to the means he must use in order to communicate his grace to us. God sets the biblically indicated means of grace before us; he does not thereby impose limits on himself:

> It is indeed correct and true what Scripture states, that no one comes to Christ unless the Father draw him. But the Father will not do this without *means,* and he has ordained Word and sacraments as the *ordinary* [the possibility of extraordinary intervention is left open] means or instruments to accomplish this end. It is not the will of either the Father or the Son that any one should refuse to hear or should despise the preaching of his Word and should wait for the Father to draw him without Word and sacraments. The Father indeed draws by the power of the Holy Spirit, but according to his *common* [an unusual possibility is again left open] ordinance he does this through the hearing of his holy divine Word [italics added].[6]

The charismatic renewal has challenged a humanist-dominated culture with an uncompromising declaration of the sovereignty of God. Implicit in its challenge to the status quo is the understanding that God has a sovereign right to set his own agenda for the church. At the same time, however, with its strong emphasis on biblical authority, its experience in worship, including eucharistic worship, and its experiments in building Christian community, the charismatic renewal has implicitly taught people to expect encounter with God preeminently through the same means of grace emphasized by the reformers: Word, sacrament, and Christian fellowship.[7]

Grace alone: not antiworks

The Lutheran reformers took the apostle Paul's "exclusive terms" seriously. In order to do justice to such terms as "freely," "not of works," and "it is a gift," the reformers spoke of grace *alone*. Ever since, Lutherans have had to explain that this does not do away with good works.

The reformers did not mean to exclude good works, but rather any trust in good works for one's *justification*. Justification occurs alone "by grace, for Christ's sake, through faith."[8] The reformers did not reject good works as such, as their opponents frequently charged, for the reformers were ready to admit that there is a sense in which faith or grace "is at no time ever alone."[9]

The chief concerns that have been expressed by the charismatic renewal fall into that area of theology that Lutherans have traditionally called the "Third Article" or "sanctification."[10] Two points are emphasized in the Confessions: justification and sanctification are to be neither mingled nor separated. Applying this to a charismatic context, one could say: *charis* (grace) and *charism* (manifestation of grace) are to be neither mingled nor separated. Sanctification, including that aspect of it that has been related to the word *charismatic,* is the natural and expected consequence of our justification. Good works, including the manifestation of spiritual gifts, are not optional extras. They are the necessary accompaniment to justification.[11]

Grace alone: not antilaw

The Reformation's discovery of the gospel of "grace alone" brought with it obvious dangers, two of which we have discussed above. A third danger is expressed in the term *Antinomian,* which means "without law." An Antinomian is one who questions the usefulness of the "law" for a Christian; an Antinomian relegates the use of the law to the unregenerate. The Lutheran Confessions, however, from Luther's Catechisms (1529) to the Formula of Concord (1577), maintain that the law is useful also for the Christian.[12]

The usefulness of an objective standard is not limited merely to its *accusing* function. (Most "Lutheran Antinomians" would grant this use of the law also for Christians, since the Christian remains *simul justus et peccator* [righteous and sinner at the same time].) The Confessions, however, say that the usefulness of the law for a Christian also includes its *content,* insofar as this is revealed in Scripture and in nature. The exhortations of Scripture continue to instruct even the Christian as to what God's will expects. Yet this all takes place in the context of "grace alone," for a Christian's obedience is not his or her own achievement, but is by the working of the Holy Spirit.

It is for this reason that charismatics' strong emphasis on *charis* and *charism* can be so closely wedded to what the Confessions call "delight in the law of the Lord."[13] The experience of grace has been so profound that for the "new creature" the law is no longer a threat of judgment: it is a call to trust the Lord to accomplish in us the "works and fruits of the Spirit."[14] The charismatic renewal has done as much as any contemporary movement to encourage the recovery of the Lutheran Reformation's dynamic dialectic of law and gospel.[15]

CHAPTER 21

SOLA FIDES— FAITH ALONE

More than any other expression, "faith alone" pinpoints what the Reformation was all about. Its proper interpretation is dependent on all the other "alones" that are here being discussed, but the reformers saw faith as the pivotal word in their theology. Without it Christ could not be honored and could not comfort the needy sinner. The opponents of the Reformation could speak of Christ, grace, Scripture, and many other things belonging to the Christian tradition, but without faith, the reformers said, "our opponents bury Christ." [1]

> This *faith* is the true knowledge of Christ, it uses his blessings, it regenerates our hearts, it precedes our keeping of the law [italics added]. [2]

From the outset, the word *faith* has had central significance in the charismatic renewal. One of the early Lutheran writings to gain wide circulation in the renewal pointed out that faith was the common denominator in most personal testimonies:

> I have spoken and corresponded with a number of people [who have come into the New Testament experience of speaking in tongues]. They describe the results of their experience in a variety of ways: one testifies to a new joy in his Christian faith; another witnesses to a deeper or more constant awareness of the Spirit's indwelling presence; some have found a new freedom to witness to others of what Jesus means to them; another says that he has a far keener sense of the Spirit's guidance than he did before; many testify to an awakened interest, indeed a deep hunger, to study the Bible; a keener awareness of one's own sins and shortcomings is frequently mentioned. The common denominator in all of these seems to be

this: it has intensified the sense of the presence of God—the word of God has become more contemporary, believable—Christ the Lord has become more real—in a word, *faith has been strengthened*.[3]

Faith alone: not antimeans

Faith, like the grace on which it depends, does not come without means. The means that God ordinarily uses to communicate his grace to us are the same means by which we come to faith.[4]

> If a person will not hear preaching or read the Word of God, but despises the Word and the community of God, dies in this condition, and perishes in his sins, he can neither comfort himself with God's eternal election nor obtain his mercy. For Christ, in whom we are elected, offers his grace to all men *in the Word and the holy sacraments*, earnestly wills that we hear it . . . . God does *not coerce anyone to piety*, for those who always resist the Holy Spirit and oppose and constantly rebel against acknowledged truth . . . will not be converted [italics added].[5]

Such an understanding of faith honors Christ and affords peace to struggling sinners. It relieves people of the notion that they must create faith within themselves. It invites them instead to receive faith as a gift that the Spirit brings through the gospel.

Faith alone: not antidecision

In contemporary Lutheranism there is a strong bias against understanding faith as decision in a psychological sense.[6] This concern is appropriate insofar as it is directed against a mere act of the will, an independent human decision to believe God. The human will is involved, of course, but the power behind it is not human autonomy; it is rather the Holy Spirit.

> After such conversion man's reborn will is not idle in the daily exercise of repentance but cooperates in all the works that the Holy Spirit does through us.[7]

Nevertheless, even such "cooperation" does not occur "the way two horses draw a wagon together."[8] The source and origin of faith's dynamic is always found in God alone. Thus even after rebirth our response is by the gracious working of God.

This being said, it must still be maintained that decision is an important element of what is meant by "faith alone." Faith needs to be understood both theologically and psychologically. Some recent descriptions of faith utilizing the developmental terms of modern psychology have proven helpful.[9] It is possible to compare the variety of meanings given to faith in the Lutheran Confessions with the following developmental model:

WHAT OCCURS	WHAT IT AFFECTS	TYPE OF DESCRIPTION
reception (*accipere*)[10]	Spirit/spirit	theological
trust (*fiducia*)[11] }	emotion	
knowledge (*notitia*)[12]	intellect }	psychological
decision (*assentiri*)[13]	will	

The above model fits the situation of a person baptized in infancy. God's action (theological) permeates the entire subsequent development. Through the means of grace God communicates himself to the infant. The infant's passive reception of this is already saving faith.

At the infant stage of development, "decision" is not an appropriate term. An infant does not "decide" to trust its mother. Trust is created and effected as the child receives its mother's love. Likewise God's grace, communicated through Word and sacrament, creates and effects trust in the infant as it is received.[14]

Christian parents may bring a daughter to the Lord in Baptism. As she matures in this Christian environment, her trust is linked more and more explicitly with knowledge. She hears stories about Jesus. She is drawn to express herself to God in confessions of love, faithfulness, and commitment. She comes to the point where she consciously and personally decides to heed Jesus' call to discipleship, which she may remember as a milestone along her pathway. As one aspect of her growing experience in Christ, she hears about the need to be filled with the Holy Spirit (Acts 1:8; 2:4; Eph. 5:18). She decides to pray for this (Luke 11:9-13). She comes into a dramatic experience of being filled with the Spirit, accompanied by a manifestation of spiritual gifts, and this also becomes part of her Christian experience and testimony (Acts 8:14-19). Her life in Christ continues to grow and develop (Eph. 3:14-19).

What this says is simply that Lutheran theology should not overreact against "decision theology." There is a wrong sense in which this kind of language could be used, that is, if it would imply that human decision is the actual power that changes things. But that is not the kind of emphasis you encounter in the charismatic renewal. On the contrary, testimonies tilt heavily toward the side of telling what *God* has done. Decision is simply a response to what God says or does. It adds nothing to the salvation or the gifts that God gives: it only reaches out to receive them. Christ is not honored, nor is the whole person properly involved in God's dealings, when the element of personal response is downgraded or set aside.

Faith alone: not antiexperience

Scripture indicates that the experience of the gifts and fruit of the Holy Spirit serve to confirm, seal, and guarantee the reality of our life in Christ which, before our resurrection, is possessed by faith alone (Eph. 1:13-14; Mark 16:14-20; Luke 24:49; John 4:46-54; Acts 1:4-5,8; Rom. 15:18-19; 1 Cor. 1:4-9; 4:20; 2 Cor. 1:21-22; Gal. 3:5; Heb. 2:3-4; 2 Peter 1:5-11,16-19).

In this confirming sense the Lutheran Confessions make room for *sight* and *experience*.

> Since the Holy Spirit dwells in the elect who have come to faith as he dwells in his temple, and is not idle in them but urges them to obey the commandments of God, believers likewise should not be idle, still less oppose the urgings of the Spirit of God, but should exercise themselves in all Christian virtues, in all godliness, modesty, temperance, patience, and brotherly love, and should diligently seek to "confirm their call and election" so that the more they experience the power and might of the Spirit within themselves, the less they will doubt their election.[15]

The Confessions hasten to add, however, that such experience may in times of temptation grow weak and that then the promises of God are nevertheless to be trusted.[16]

Luther, in his commentary on John (14:21), spoke confidently about faith being confirmed by experience:

> Thus this is a sermon not only of words but of experience as well. To be sure, Christ begins with the Word, when he lets us hear the gospel and receive Baptism and the sacrament. But the devil comes on the heels of this; he assails and hinders us on all sides, in an attempt to check and obstruct the Word. At this point, experience must enter in and enable a Christian to say: "Hitherto I have heard that Christ is my Savior, who conquered sin and death; and I believed this. Now my experience bears this out. For I was often in the agony of death and in the bonds of the devil, but he rescued me and manifested himself. Now I see and know that he loves me and that what I believe is true."[17]

In his commentary on Zechariah (4:1-3), Luther makes the same point with reference to charismatic manifestations:

> For as I have often said, the signs and visions that God gives in addition to the Word are needed to strengthen all the more the faith of weak or saddened souls who cannot cling to the mere Word as well as to a picture or sign. For it is a great thing to believe that God is gracious and favorable to us but a difficult thing for human hearts to achieve. The frivolous fanatics, however, come rushing and roaring along and at once can praise the Spirit so confidently that they tolerate neither picture nor sign but in one moment are able to believe everything without

a sign—even the bare word. But though Joshua and Zerubbabel are great men in the eyes of God and indeed have a strong faith, conditions are still so bad that God must use visions and interpretations to nurse them along in the faith as though they were young children. Faith and the Spirit are not so easy a matter, however glibly the noisy spirits may be able to chatter about them.[18]

In reporting on the closing session of a conference of church leaders in Tanzania in 1985, which had followed five days of intense Bible study, preaching, prayer, worship, and a eucharistic service, and in which there had been noticeable manifestations of the Spirit—visions, prophecies, speaking in tongues, healings—W. Dennis Pederson wrote:

> It was obvious to the people present that the Lord had "plans" for Tanzania, and all became aware of it as we joined in praise and songs of thanksgiving for the "filling and empowering of the Spirit of the Lord."
> But in our minds the subtle thought intrudes, "Was it real? Will these days together really mean a change from traditional business-as-usual church practices? Will Holy Spirit revival come to Tanzanian churches?" Only the Lord knows for sure, but he did confirm our ministry through reports received before we left.
> When self-doubt enters and human reasoning returns to reassert its analytical control, the more objective "signs following" reaffirm a ministry like our team engaged in at the Mrango conference center. Thanks be to God, he doesn't leave our faith unconfirmed. He finds a way to say, in spite of our ordinariness, weaknesses, and failings, his affirming word, "Well done, good and faithful servants."
> There were young Catholic nuns attending the school who served us unselfishly as kitchen and dining room helpers. One especially was noticeable to me because she was the first Christian Masai tribal woman I'd seen. She looked fresh and lovely without the usual jewelry dangling from ears and nose. In broken English she told that they had seen for a long while a light "brighter than the sun" above the roof of the auditorium meeting place. Her report was confirmed by an Anglican Church Army captain who was a member of our team. He had heard a similar report while preparing to witness to a group of 150 college students the night following our conference. [These were students enrolled at the teachers' college where the conference was held, but they themselves were not participants in the conference.] He asked the whole group if the report of the light over the assembly hall at midday had been seen by others. About 30 students raised their hands, and reported the light was "brighter than day light" and remained above the building for quite a while, long enough to gather groups of friends to witness the phenomenon.
> We all concluded with agreement that our faith can accept these reports because of the scriptural promise that "signs and wonders will follow those who believe." We can't make them happen, we concurred, but at times those evidences do follow Spirit-led and Spirit-dependent ministry.[19]

Such an understanding of faith is a precious heritage that both grounds and interprets charismatic experience. "No one," said Luther, "can correctly understand God or his Word unless he has received such understanding immediately from the Holy Spirit. But no one can receive it from the Holy Spirit without experiencing, proving, and feeling it."[20] Far from undermining true faith, this kind of emphasis is "directed against a faith that is solely a concern of the mind. We learn to know God through the Holy Spirit, but the Holy Spirit uses experience as his school."[21] Such an understanding of faith honors Christ by giving to sight and experience the role assigned to it both by Scripture and the Lutheran Confessions: that place is following faith as its expected fruit and confirmation rather than preceding faith as a necessary foundation.[22]

CHAPTER 22

SOLA SCRIPTURA— SCRIPTURE ALONE

Next to "faith alone" as the pivotal truth of biblical revelation, the reformers insisted on "Scripture alone" as the proper source and norm for all Christian teaching.[1] The passage most frequently cited in the *Book of Concord* is Matt. 15:9, "In vain do they worship me, teaching as doctrines the precepts of men."[2] The position taken by Melanchthon in the *Augsburg Confession* on "matters in dispute," and his commentary on these in his *Apology of the Augsburg Confession,* make it particularly clear that Lutheranism is committed to a *sola scriptura* principle.

What are the implications of this for understanding the role of tradition, on the one hand, and the possibility of divine guidance, on the other?

Scripture alone: not antitradition

The reformers recognized that though they stood for "Scripture alone," Scripture, like faith, "is at no time ever alone."[3] Scripture must be interpreted. A false application can dishonor Christ. Thus while Scripture stands unrivaled in authority, we are concerned for its proper interpretation.

The process by which the canon of Scripture was formed is not free from tradition. The Lutheran reformers from the start recognized the three ecumenical creeds as traditions conveying an authoritative interpretation of Holy Scripture. They also honored liturgical tradition and maintained it, except at those points at which they were convinced that it dishonored Christ.[4]

The charismatic renewal has given a high place to the authority of Scripture. At the same time it has been able to appreciate and affirm good traditions that in themselves do not require what Scripture does not require, or that do not contradict the gospel. The charismatic renewal has found expression in a variety of denominational settings, and it has been notable for honoring those respective heritages and traditions. Such traditions, according to the Lutheran Confessions, can help promote tranquility, good order, discipline, and harmony.[5] We should not scorn such traditions, though we should oppose their misuse.

Scripture alone: not antiguidance

Scripture is recognized by virtually all Christians as in some sense the normative expression of divine revelation. The question raised by the charismatic renewal, however, is whether the text of Scripture itself is the only channel by which God speaks to people, or whether people can expect to experience divine guidance through believing the promises that Scripture makes in regard to such things as prayer, counsel with fellow believers, or charismatic gifts such as the word of wisdom, knowledge, prophecy, and discernment of spirits.

People involved in charismatic renewal maintain that such revelatory gifts belong to the promise of Pentecost and that the promise of Pentecost belongs to the entire era of the church, not merely to its formative years.[6] Does the standard of "Scripture alone" allow room for the experience of divine guidance?

Some important distinctions must be made. The Lutheran Confessions call Scripture the only source and norm "according to which as the only touchstone all doctrines should and must be understood and judged as good or evil, right or wrong."[7] Lutherans have traditionally distinguished between what Scripture as a whole *prescribes* and what it merely *describes*. What it prescribes as normative doctrine cannot be essentially modified or augmented, but only applied—in all times and places. However, what it describes may or may not find parallels in contemporary experience; if parallels do occur, they need to be judged by what Scripture does in fact prescribe.

For instance, both in the Old and New Testaments the Lord guides his people by means of charismatic revelations. In special situations he speaks through prophets, visions, and dreams in order to encourage, console, warn, and help them. The kind of thing we find in Scripture might in fact happen today—visions (Acts 10:19; 11:6), discernment of secret thoughts (13:9-10; 5:3-9), divine guidance of the work of missionaries (8:29; 11:12-17; 16:6-10), and direct insight into God's will and purpose (10:19). But we are always obliged to test such experiences by Scripture (Acts 17:11).

The point of this essential distinction is that Christ's atoning work *for us* is finished, and therefore the revelation about it is also finished; but that which the risen Christ accomplishes through his Spirit in the church still goes on. We cannot modify or augment that which has been finished by Christ, but we must allow his finished work to bear its promised fruit in our lives. To have visions or revelations similar to those reported in Scripture need not compromise the finished work of Christ. Indeed, Scripture itself encourages believers to expect this kind of fruit in their lives.

Essentially that is what Luther was saying in the oft-quoted but seldom understood passage taken from the *Smalcald Articles,* in which he insisted that the Spirit and the "external Word" always go together.[8] He was not trying to drive a separating wedge between revelations in Scripture and contemporary revelations. He simply insisted that all revelation be rooted not in mere subjective experience but in the external Word—an expression that Luther equated with "the Scriptures," especially as proclaimed, and with "the sacraments."[9]

Luther's concern was to preserve the honor of Christ by carefully maintaining the distinction between the finished work of Christ and that which he is still seeking to accomplish and effect in us. To fail to build on the former as foundation reduces Christ to a mere model that we strive to imitate more or less in our own strength. The finished work of Christ is thus buried and rendered useless as gospel.

Luther's insistence on the essential priority of the external Word helps set charismatic experience in the right context. Because we believe this Word, there is no reason to doubt that the Holy Spirit can by faith and prayer be stirred (2 Tim. 1:6-7) to move us to prophesy and to manifest his revelatory gifts (1 Cor. 12:7-11; 14:26-33). Scripture itself gives us this expectation, and nothing in the Lutheran Confessions contradicts that expectation, as long as the finished work of Christ for our salvation is in no way compromised.[10]

Scripture alone: not anti-Spirit

In spite of the reformers' insistence on the sole authority of Scripture as source and norm for all doctrine, they did not think of Scripture as something that could be divorced from God's sovereign Spirit, something we could take into our own hands and manipulate for our own purposes. Any attempt to wrest the authority of Scripture from the sovereign God, whose Spirit resists domestication, was abhorrent to them. Even while contending against the enthusiasts' attempt to divorce Word and Spirit, Luther rigorously insisted on the sovereignty of the Spirit—the Spirit's resistance to manipulation and domestication.[11]

How did Luther resolve the tension between Scripture as bearer of the Spirit and the Spirit as sovereign Lord distinct from Scripture? Rather than resolve the tension, he creatively maintained it in his understanding of the dynamic role of prayer and its relationship to the means of grace.[12]

CHAPTER 23

FOUR MORE *ALONES*

Most summaries of Lutheran doctrine confine themselves to the four *alones* discussed in the preceding chapters. However, the Lutheran Confessions draw from Scripture four additional *alones* that are relevant to a charismatic theology: prayer alone, the church alone, Baptism alone, and the Spirit alone.

"SOLA ORATIO"—PRAYER ALONE

In his Large Catechism Luther spent more time discussing prayer than any other subject except the Ten Commandments.[1] His treatment was calculated to stimulate the reader to fervent and joyful prayer, but not by arguing that it is necessary in order to achieve grace; rather, it is necessary because one has already been "graced."

Prayer alone: not antigrace

Having already been made God's children in Holy Baptism, we are both obligated and privileged by God the Father's command and promise to approach him in expectant prayer. Luther wrote:

> This we must know, that all our safety and protection consist in *prayer alone*. We are far too weak to cope with the devil and all his might and his forces arrayed against us, trying to trample us under foot. Therefore we must carefully select the weapons with which Christians ought to arm themselves in order to stand against the devil. . . . But by *prayer alone* we shall be a match both for them and for the devil, if we only persevere diligently and do not become slack. For whenever a good Christian prays, "Dear Father, thy will be done," God replies from on high, "Yes, dear child, it shall indeed be done in spite of the devil and all the world" [italics added].[2]

Contemporary Lutherans, who have been conditioned to be suspicious of "earnest prayer," because it supposedly breathes the spirit of a subjective pietism, have not yet learned to appreciate Luther's own pious and audacious prayer life.[3] Although he was sharply critical of the prayers of "monks and priests, who howl and growl frightfully day and night," his criticism was based on the following generalization:

> None of them has ever undertaken to pray out of obedience to God and faith in his promise, or out of consideration for his own needs. They only thought, at best, of doing a good work as a payment to God, not willing to receive anything from him, but only to give him something.[4]

For Luther, "prayer alone" was no contradiction of "grace alone," but an inevitable expression of it.

Prayer alone: not antimeans

There is a nervousness in some parts of Lutheranism that by urging the importance of prayer we will diminish appreciation for the "means of grace," the Word and sacraments. One Lutheran study commission expressed the concern this way:

> Only Baptism, the Lord's Supper, and the use of God's Word are external means. By these alone the Holy Spirit has chosen to work among us in grace. Prayer, for example, is not a means of grace but a proper response to God's grace as offered in the sacrament of Baptism.[5]

The theological concern behind such a statement is understandable: it is a concern for "grace alone." But its practical impact can lead to the worst kind of imbalance, producing passive Christians who don't expect any experience of the Holy Spirit outside the doors of the church. It does not reflect Luther's vigorous concern for prayer. It tends to make prayer an optional extra by speaking of it merely as "a *proper* response" rather than as "a *necessary* response." Luther wrote:

> To pray, as the Second Commandment teaches, is to call on God in every need. This God *requires* of us; he has not left it to our *choice*. It is our *duty* and *obligation* to pray if we want to be Christians [italics added].[6]

Again:

> And I suspect that people turn out so badly after Baptism because our concern for them has been so cold and careless; we, at their Baptism, *interceded* for them without zeal. . . . See to it, therefore, that you are present in true faith, listen to God's Word, and *earnestly* join in *prayer*. . . . For as I said, the human additions

do not matter very much, as long as Baptism itself is administered with God's
Word, true faith, and *serious prayer*. [italics added].[7]

And again: God wants us to acknowledge faith as his gift. He wants it
recognized as a proffered gift *for which we must ask him*.[8]

A theological distinction relative to the expression "means of grace" could
prove helpful at this point. The *Book of Concord* distinguishes between the
following:

- means of *communicating* God's grace = Word and sacraments[9]
- means of *receiving* God's grace = faith[10]
- means of *realizing* God's grace = prayer[11]

These three distinguishable aspects of the term "means of grace" should
neither be lumped all together nor disengaged from each other. If we lump
them together, we confuse the question of *source:* we expect too little from
God as the sole *source* of grace. If we separate them, we confuse the question
of *power:* we expect too little from God by way of the powerful consequences
of his grace. God has joined Word and sacraments, faith, and prayer together.
They cannot accomplish his purpose if we separate them.

A matter of practical application in charismatic theology at this point would
be giving prayer (Acts 1:4, 12-14) its necessary role relative to Jesus' promise
to baptize with the Holy Spirit (Acts 1:5; 2:32-33). If "Scripture alone" is
our source and norm, then Word and sacraments, faith, and prayer for the
Holy Spirit will be found in a close relationship, which, if not heeded, will
frustrate the grace of God, dishonor Christ, and rob believers of their full
inheritance (Acts 20:27; Rom. 15:19, 29). Specific prayer for the Holy Spirit
(Luke 11:9-13) and his "good things" (Matt. 7:7-11) is not optional, either
for Scripture or the Lutheran Confessions.

"SOLA ECCLESIA"—THE CHURCH ALONE

Bishop Cyprian of Carthage insisted that "outside the church there is no
salvation"; and again, "he cannot have God as a Father who has not the
church as his mother." Provided that the church is understood as the "creature
of the gospel" and not the "creature of the hierarchy,"[12] Luther would concur.[13]

The Lutheran Confessions manifest a deep appreciation for the church,
because the church also honors Christ. Christ wills and creates his church.
The church consoles and equips struggling sinners through its gospel ministry,
which includes "the mutual conversation and consolation of brethren."[14]

The church alone: not anti-Christ

A church that blurs the distinction between Christ the head and the church his body is not the church of Jesus Christ but one that has opened the door to Satan and is therefore anti-Christ. At the heart of any understanding and expression of the church is the primitive confession, "Jesus is Lord!" Historically, renewal movements have often led to division and the forming of new religious groups or denominations. The extent to which the charismatic renewal has remained within the churches is closely related to its strong emphasis on the lordship of Christ. Although many charismatics have left or been put out of their churches, many more have remained because they believed it to be the Lord's will. They have generally been supportive of the church. [15]

When the medieval church dealt with Luther and the gospel in a self-aggrandizing, absolutist fashion, being itself disobedient to the Lord and head of the church, Luther called its head "the real Antichrist." [16] On the other hand, Melanchthon wrote:

> Concerning the pope I hold that, if he would *allow the Gospel,* we, too, may concede to him that superiority over the bishops which he possesses *by human right,* making this concession for the sake of peace and general unity among the Christians who are now under him and who may be in the future [italics added]. [17]

Thus, on the one hand, we need to be extremely wary of absolutizing church structures that usurp Christ's authority as head of the church. On the other hand, we should take pains to avoid a privatizing and individualizing interpretation of "faith alone" that succeeds only in breaking up what should be the unified body of Christ, "a holy community." [18] Unity among Christians is surely one of the key priorities of the Spirit—a priority that has received strong emphasis in the charismatic renewal. Working for the unity of churches which are "creatures of the gospel," to the full extent that truth allows, has been one of the most noticeable marks of the renewal.

The church alone: not antiworld

That the church is "*in* the world but not *of* the world" does not imply that the church lives a ghettolike existence in the world, finding its end in its own existence. Rather, it is sent *into* the world, consecrated to extend the kingdom of Christ, not by using the world's sword but by using the sword of the Spirit. Accordingly, Luther wrote:

> God's kingdom comes to us in two ways: first, it comes here in time, through the Word and faith, and secondly, in eternity, it comes through the final revelation.

Now, we pray for both of these, that it may come to those who are not yet in it, and that it may come by daily growth here and in eternal life hereafter to us who have attained it. All this is simply to say: "Dear Father, we pray Thee, give us thy Word, that the Gospel may be sincerely preached *throughout the world* and that it may be received by faith and may work and live in us. So we pray that thy Kingdom may prevail among us through the Word and the power of the Holy Spirit, that the devil's kingdom may be overthrown and he may have no right or power over us, until finally the devil's kingdom shall be utterly destroyed and sin, death, and hell exterminated, and that we may live forever in perfect righteousness and blessedness" [italics added].[19]

Charismatic experience must be understood in the context of the Holy Spirit's work of equipping the church for world evangelization, thereby honoring the risen Christ, who breathed his Spirit on his apostles and said: "As the Father has sent me, even so I send you" (John 20:21-23; see also Matt. 28:16-20; Mark 16:14-20; Luke 24:44-49; Acts 1:4-5,8).

The ecumenical thrust of the charismatic renewal has been closely related to its perception that without unity the church lacks both the resources and the credibility needed for the task of world evangelization.

The church alone: not anticlergy

The Lutheran Confessions do not pit the "priesthood of all believers" and the "pastoral office" against one another. The distinction between laity and clergy is one of call and function, providing a way for the variety of gifts and callings in the body of Christ to come to expression. Those who are ordained to the pastoral office (1 Tim. 4:11-16; 2 Tim. 1:6-7; Titus 1:5-9) represent Christ, particularly in his shepherding role, and as such exercise an oversight function (1 Peter 5:2-5). A primary function of their oversight is to raise up, encourage, order, and release other ministries in the body of Christ. The Lutheran Confessions value the pastoral office not as an end in itself, but because it serves to build up the entire church when it faithfully represents Christ. Thus Melanchthon wrote:

It is necessary for the church to retain the right of calling, electing, and ordaining ministers. This right is a gift given exclusively to the church, and no human authority can take it away from the church. It is as Paul testifies to the Ephesians when he says, "When he ascended on high he gave gifts to men" (Eph. 4:8,11,12). He enumerates *pastors and teachers* among the gifts belonging exclusively to the church, and he adds that they are given for the work of ministry and for building up the body of Christ. Where the true church is, therefore, the right of electing and ordaining ministers must of necessity also be.[20]

Curiously, Melanchthon cited Ephesians 4 and specifically mentioned "pastors and teachers," but he entirely omitted discussion or even mention of "apostles, prophets, and evangelists." This has prompted one commentator to ask:

> Is the doctrine of the one church office of preaching the Word and administering the sacraments perhaps a human arrangement that overlooks the wealth of spiritual gifts? Or, was the wealth of spiritual gifts intended only for the time of the founding of the church?[21]

On the one hand, therefore, those involved in charismatic renewal can affirm the pastoral ministry as a God-given office in the church, exercising oversight particularly for the indispensable ministry of Word and sacraments. At the same time they want to leave room for the Spirit to raise up the entire variety of ministries promised in Scripture.

We must confess that historically speaking, Lutheran churches have been clergy-dominated. Far from raising up and releasing the ministry of the laity, the pastoral office has all too often simply taken over: *pastor* and *minister* have become synonymous terms, applied exclusively to the ordained clergy. In the New Testament, every believer was a "minister," that is, serving in some capacity.

One of the concerns being expressed by the charismatic renewal is that the priesthood of all believers, one of the great Reformation insights, come to practical expression, not only in one's personal relationship with God but also in one's calling and ministry in the body of Christ. This would magnify the honor of Christ as a full range of gifts and ministries are used to build up the fellowship and carry out the evangelistic commission.

The church alone: not antidenominational

The epistle to the Ephesians speaks against the notion of two separate but equal churches—one for Christian Jews and one for Christian Gentiles. Paul testified to the necessity of *one* church. Anything else would dishonor Christ and rob the church of the hope afforded in Christ (Eph. 2:11-22; 4:15-16). How does this square with a church divided into a multitude of denominations?

Melanchthon distinguished between defining the church "properly speaking," namely, "God's true people, reborn by the Holy Spirit,"[22] and "according to the outward associations of the church's marks."[23] He said, in effect, that "properly speaking," the church *is* one, though this essential unity is still "hidden under the cross."[24] He argued that unity can be exercised where there is agreement in the teaching of the gospel and in the administration of the sacraments—otherwise not.[25]

This parallels the thought of the apostle Paul, who seemed to distinguish between differences that are foundational, that is, at the very heart of the

gospel and therefore divisive (Gal. 1:6-9), and those that do not break the
unity of the Spirit but need to be worked at until a unity of the faith is attained
(Eph. 4:1-3,13). He did not indicate how much the exercise of unity is curtailed in the latter case. He simply exhorted the believers with great passion
to work at the problem in the confidence that it can be overcome.

The quest for unity is certainly one of the significant marks of organized
Christianity in the 20th century. The charismatic renewal has had a strong
ecumenical thrust from the beginning, which found expression at different
levels.

At a personal level, Christians found each other, as fellow believers, across
denominational lines. At another level, charismatic ministry in congregations
and conferences and publications often came from people of other traditions
as well as from one's own. There were few denominational barriers on the
so-called charismatic circuit. The ecumenism that occurred at these levels
was noteworthy for its spirit of love, mutual respect, and patience. It is most
readily associated with the work of the Pentecostal statesman, David J. du
Plessis. His tireless efforts to establish understanding and relationships with
leaders in mainline denominations over more than three decades was an ecumenical tour de force. The spirit and the determination with which ecumenism has been pursued throughout the renewal bears the stamp of his
personal ministry, and would be recognized by charismatics as a notable work
of the Holy Spirit.[26]

At another level, charismatic leaders have undertaken to wrestle with some
of the tough theological and pastoral questions that have historically divided
the church. Here distinctions must be made between foundational, divisive
issues and issues of lesser moment.[27] Given the strong ecumenical thrust of
the movement, and recognizing this as a genuine work of the Holy Spirit,
charismatic leaders must exercise the spiritual discernment necessary to deal
with disunity on the basis of both truth and love. They must clarify sound
biblical norms for unity, and not advocate the exercise of church unity simply
on the basis of agreement in matters of charismatic experience.

At the same time, they must press forward in a humble and untiring quest
for an ever-increasing manifestation of unity in the body of Christ. Disunity
with other believers can never be taken lightly. It, too, is an evidence of sin
and hinders the work of the Spirit. It militates against spiritual growth (cf. 1
Corinthians 1–3).

"SOLUM BAPTISMA"—BAPTISM ALONE

Closely related to the issue of whether one dare speak of the "church alone"
as the "mother that begets and bears every Christian" is the question regarding

the role of sacramental Baptism. Is "Baptism alone" the seed by which "mother church" legitimately conceives? If so, do Word and faith and charismata become optional extras?

The earliest Lutheran reformers did not speak of "Baptism alone" as explicitly as they spoke of most of the other "alones" that have been discussed above.[28] However, their sharp disagreement with the Anabaptist reformers slowly pushed their successors to formulate their teaching in such a way that one could speak meaningfully also of "Baptism alone." The *Formula of Concord* states:

> We reject and condemn the erroneous and heretical teachings of the Anabaptists . . . that the children of Christians, because they are born of Christian and believing parents, are holy and children of God even without and prior to Baptism. Therefore they do not esteem infant Baptism very highly and do not advocate it, contrary to the express words of the promise which extends *only* to those who keep the *covenant* and do not despise it (Gen. 17:4-8,19-21 [italics added]).[29]

The Scripture cited to establish the point is from the Old Testament, even though the particular issue is a New Testament one. That does not invalidate the point if its presupposition is valid, namely, that *Baptism* is God's fundamental means of establishing a *covenant* relationship with his people in the New Testament.[30] Paul did operate with this conviction in Col. 2:8-15 (also Rom. 4:9-12; Eph. 2:12; 1 Cor. 11:25; Matt. 26:28), but it is a conviction that requires qualification.

Baptism alone: not anti-Word

A passage such as John 3:5 would seem to call for a "Baptism alone" interpretation, although the verses immediately following make clear that the connection between water and the Spirit is not one that robs the Spirit of his sovereignty. And the "born anew" passage in 1 Peter 1:23-25, found as it is in a letter considered by many commentators to be at least in part a baptismal homily, lets the reader know what Luther later also emphasized:

> It is not the water that produces these effects, but the Word of God connected with the water, and our faith which relies on the Word of God connected with the water. For without the Word of God the water is merely water and no Baptism. But when connected with the Word of God it is a Baptism, that is, a gracious water of life and a washing of regeneration in the Holy Spirit.[31]

The connection between water and Spirit was for Luther never a naturalistic one, such that the effect of Baptism is achieved merely through the application of water. Rather, the effect is always dependent on the Word (God's institution). And this in turn leads to another qualification of the meaning of Baptism alone.

Baptism alone: not antifaith

With remarkable consistency the New Testament connects Baptism with faith. Only faith is able to receive and manifest the salutary effects of Baptism (for example, Mark 16:15-16; Matt. 28:18-20; John 3:5,16-18; Acts 2:37-42; 8:12; 9:10-19; 10:44-48; 16:25-34; 18:8; 19:1-7; 22:12-16; Gal. 3:23-29; Eph. 2:8-9; 5:21-27; Col. 2:8-15; 1 Peter 1:3—2:3; 3:21). In other passages faith is at least implied (Acts 8:35-38; Rom. 6:3-19; Titus 3:4-8).

The Lutheran Confessions recognize this relationship between faith and Baptism and direct it with great vigor against any notion that Baptism saves magically, that is, simply by virtue of its ritual performance. The fact that the heart of Baptism is the objective Word of promise signaled to the reformers the necessity of faith, since, as they repeated over and over again, only faith can receive such a promise.[32]

On this question Luther steered a course between two extremes. Some scholastics had said too little about faith. Baptism became a near-magical rite that guaranteed salvation. Luther, however, said:

> Without faith Baptism is of no use, although in itself it is an infinite, divine treasure. . . . We insist on faith alone as so necessary that without it nothing can be received or enjoyed. . . . Where faith is lacking, [Baptism] remains a mere unfruitful sign.[33]

The Radical Reformation, on the other hand, had said too much about faith: Baptism was not valid unless a certain standard of faith were present. Of this Luther wrote:

> My faith does not constitute Baptism but receives it. Baptism does not become invalid even if it is wrongly received or used, for it is bound not to our faith but to the Word.[34]

The promises relating to Baptism hold "Baptism alone" and "faith alone" in tension: each one expresses an aspect of the truth that honors Christ and saves sinners. Neither is complete by itself. It would be contrary to the Confessions to set a rigid standard of belief and life as a precondition for receiving Baptism; it is, after all, the beginning point of the Christian life, not an achievement along the way. On the other hand, it is contrary to the intention of the Confessions when pastors in state-church situations are required to administer Baptism to every child, even when those who bring the child and promise to raise it in the faith do not participate in the life and worship of the congregation and are ignorant of basic Christian beliefs.

Baptism alone: not antirepentance

As fundamental as Baptism is in Lutheran confessional theology, it is not reduced to a mere past historical event. It is expected to produce positive results in one's life as the Christian in faith lays continual claim to the benefits promised in Baptism. Thus we read in Luther's *Large Catechism:*

> A *Christian life* is nothing else than a *daily Baptism,* once begun and ever continued . . . . Repentance, therefore, is nothing else than a return and approach to Baptism, to resume and practice what had earlier been begun but abandoned [italics added].[35]

Baptism must be seen not only in terms of what it initiates but also in terms of what it continues to produce in the life of a Christian. The charismatic renewal recognizes this active, daily effect of Baptism by emphasizing the practical results that the Holy Spirit accomplishes in one's life and ministry.

Baptism alone: not anticharismata

A strong emphasis on justification in Baptism has sometimes led Lutheranism to a curtailed emphasis on sanctification, in terms of both the fruit of the Spirit (for example, Gal. 5:22-23) and the gifts of the Spirit (for example, 1 Cor. 12:4-11). However, the Lutheran Confessions themselves never understood justification in such a limited way. Their teaching on Baptism, linked as it was to justifying faith, clearly set forth Baptism's all-inclusive, sanctifying consequences.[36]

Later Lutheranism was tempted to understand this faith in a merely passive sense, as that which "receives" the fullness of salvation, without recognizing sufficiently how this faith then grows and develops and actively proceeds to acknowledge, to trust, and to assent to everything that the lordship of Jesus implies.[37] This faith goes on to pray that what has been objectively received in Baptism will be increasingly expressed in daily life.[38]

> In order that we may see it through and abide and persevere in it, we should *implore* God to give us his grace, of which he has assured us in *holy Baptism,* and not doubt that according to his promise he will give it to us. We have his Word, ". . . how much more will the heavenly Father give the *Holy Spirit* to those who *ask* him?" (Luke 11:11-13 [italics added]).[39]

Thus "Baptism alone" is not to be understood in a way that unbiblically limits the scope of God's gift. The working of the Holy Spirit, including his charismatic manifestations, is an expected accompaniment of Baptism.

Baptism alone: not anticonfirmation

The charismatic renewal takes no issue with the Nicene Creed that "one Baptism for the forgiveness of sins" is sufficient. Luther said that rebaptism could add nothing but the external sign of more water to the "one Baptism" whose effect and signification continues and remains constant. He said simply, "We need not again have the water poured over us."[40] Lutheran charismatics have taken the same position.[41]

However, the continuing results of Baptism are such that they confirm our Baptism. Church practice has narrowed the concept of confirmation down to a once-in-a-lifetime rite. In Scripture, however, confirmation is experienced repeatedly, as faith exercises itself in prayer and obedience.[42]

Confirming signs and wonders were experienced by Jesus at his baptism, his transfiguration, and on many other occasions. His disciples experienced them particularly at Pentecost, but also before and after.

Neither Scripture nor the Lutheran Confessions pit the one Baptism against continuing charismatic manifestations of the Holy Spirit. Rather, they confirm the abiding reality of Baptism. The issue of rebaptism has no essential connection with charismatic experience as such.[43] The focus is rather on that which continues to express and confirm what God has done in Baptism.

Baptism alone: not anti-Eucharist

"Baptism alone" is directed against the notion that Baptism is not a sacrament, or that it is optional, or that it does not communicate grace in its most fundamental and comprehensive form, as new life. It is not directed against those things that nurture or express the new life.

The expression "Baptism alone" thus does not downgrade or eliminate the Eucharist. The Lord's Supper, as a matter of fact, functions in relationship to Baptism, nurturing in its own, God-appointed way the life bestowed through Holy Baptism.

The charismatic renewal among Lutherans has given particular recognition and expression to the centrality of the Eucharist in the life of the Christian.[44] Lutheran charismatic leaders have echoed the teaching of the apostle Paul that the life of baptized persons will be expressed in lives that are both eucharistic (1 Corinthians 10–11) and charismatic (1 Corinthians 12–14) to the end of their full salvation, which is indeed to the honor and glory of God the Father, through his Son Jesus Christ, and in the power of his Holy Spirit.

"SOLUS SPIRITUS SANCTUS"—THE HOLY SPIRIT ALONE

In his explanation to the Third Article of the Creed in his *Large Catechism,* Luther wrote: "But *God's Spirit alone* is called *Holy Spirit,* that is, he who has sanctified and still sanctifies us."[45] Then he commented briefly on how the Spirit sanctifies us through "placing us in the bosom of the church" where "he preaches to us and brings us to Christ," where we "daily obtain full forgiveness of sins through the Word and through signs [sacraments]," and where he causes us to "become strong in faith and in the fruits of the Spirit" and to be "illuminated and blessed by the gifts of the Holy Spirit" until our holiness is instantly perfected and eternally preserved through "the resurrection of the body and the life everlasting." Thereupon he summarized his thought with the assertion: "No human wisdom can comprehend the Creed; it must be taught by the *Holy Spirit alone*" [italics added].[46]

Thus Luther did not shrink from speaking of the "Holy Spirit alone," even in the face of what he considered to be the aberrations of the enthusiasts. Like every other "alone" of which Luther spoke, it must not be absolutized outside of its context, but applied specifically to the falsehood he wished to negate.

The church cannot become holy, that is, the unique people of God, by dint of mere human effort, but the *Holy Spirit alone* can accomplish God's purpose in God's people. That is why many in the church today who long for the church's renewal are seeking it there, where Jesus promised we could find it—in the Holy Spirit alone (John 16:5-15).

DIALECTICAL THEOLOGY

Lutheran theology is dialectical theology. It lives in paradox and tension. It recognizes that many aspects of biblical truth come to us in the form of contraries—statements that are logically contradictory, yet each of which expresses an aspect of the truth. Dialectical theology takes hold of both sides of paradoxical truth: the high and the low found in Mary's Magnificat, the weak and the strong in Paul's theology, the law and the gospel in the prophetic and apostolic writings. It recognizes that the life of a Christian is marked both by the humiliation and suffering of the cross, and by the glory of the resurrection.

Theology of the cross

Luther scholars have given special attention to what is called Luther's *theologia crucis*—theology of the cross.[47] Appeals to the theology of the cross in relation to the charismatic renewal have often been truncated. They have simply opposed the theology of the cross to a theology of glory rather than relating the two dialectically.[48] Mary's low can only be understood in relation to the fact that God made her high; Paul's weakness cannot be separated from the fact that God made him strong; the gospel has no meaning apart from the law; and Luther's theology of the cross is bound together in dialectical tension with the glory of the resurrection.

Peter tried to break the dialectic. He wanted Jesus to avoid the cross, but Jesus rejected his objection as satanic (Mark 8:31-33). Jesus did not reject the glory that the Father had ordained for him. He only insisted that the glory could not be separated from his journey to the cross as the trusting, obedient, and suffering servant of God (Mark 8:27-31; Isa. 52:13—53:12).

Charismatic theology does not oppose a theology of the cross, but it testifies that the cross of Jesus Christ is not barren. Like the grain of wheat that falls to the earth and dies (John 12:24), it bears much fruit. Charismatic manifestations are "sign-ificant" (John 20:30-31; 14:12; Mark 16:14-20) expressions of the kingdom that springs forth from the cross (Matt. 11:2-6; Acts 1:1-8). Furthermore, they help equip God's people for taking up their crosses and following Jesus in the task of evangelizing the entire world (Luke 24:44-49; Matt. 28:16-20). They glorify and honor Christ as they help to bring God's great salvation to sinners who are crying out, "Brethren, what shall we do?" (Acts 2:32-42).

PART FOUR

TAUGHT BY THE SPIRIT
Doctrinal Concerns
in the Charismatic Renewal

When the Spirit of truth comes, he will guide you into all the truth; for he will not speak on his own authority, but whatever he hears he will speak, and he will declare to you the things that are to come. He will glorify me, for he will take what is mine and declare it to you. All that the Father has is mine; therefore I said that he will take what is mine and declare it to you.

John 16:13-15

CHAPTER 24

THE SOURCE OF FAITH

One of the marks of spiritual renewal is that faith—not mental acceptance of an idea, but true biblical faith—gets rehabilitated. When the Holy Spirit brings renewal, confidence in God displaces doubt. Where bored people have endured endless talking about what they should believe and do, suddenly there is a recounting of what God is doing. Dull repetition of doctrine and duty gives way to joyful testimony. God's presence and purpose become a daily reality in the lives of people touched by the Spirit's renewing work. The doctrines and duties take on new meaning. "It seems as though every gift and every blessing I have already experienced in the Lord is refreshed and revitalized," was the way a 71-year-old Lutheran pastor described his own renewal in the Holy Spirit.[1]

Renewal of this kind cannot be understood simply by reference to psychological, sociological, or other allegedly scientific categories. It is, at its most fundamental level, the grace of God seeking us out. It is the Holy Spirit creating true and assured faith.

Faith in Christ is not a human achievement. Indeed, it is not a human possibility at all. Only the Holy Spirit can create true faith. "By grace you have been saved through faith; and this is not your own doing, it is the gift of God" (Eph. 2:8). A long tradition of evangelical scholarship has held that in this key passage of Scripture, "gift" refers to the entire preceding clause, to "faith" as well as to "saved."[2] Salvation in its entirety, including the faith to receive it, is a gift of God.[3]

Luther began his explanation to the Third Article of the Apostles' Creed by pointing out this relationship:

I believe that I cannot by my own understanding or effort believe in Jesus Christ my Lord, or come to him. But the *Holy Spirit* has called me through the gospel, enlightened me with his gifts, and sanctified and kept me in *true faith* [italics added].[4]

Faith and justification

It is especially important to see the work of the Holy Spirit at the point where faith begins, that is, when one is justified before God and becomes a Christian. Justifying faith is central to the Christian life. "Man is justified by faith apart from works of law" (Rom. 3:28) and "Without faith it is impossible to please [God]" (Heb. 11:6). But if we understand faith as our own achievement, then we have opened the door to futility and despair: faith becomes a work that I must perform in order to win God's favor, and if my faith falters, I am condemned.

This wrong understanding of faith is no theoretical problem. It is so widespread and so devastating to Christian life that one Lutheran bishop has offered the opinion that we should quit talking and thinking about "justification by faith." Shortly after his election as a bishop of the American Lutheran Church, Lowell Erdahl wrote:

> "Justification by faith" has been the hallmark of Lutheran belief and witness. I often have preached and taught it. Yet I have come to believe that we should quit talking and thinking about justification by faith, except when necessary to explain specific passages in which it is used.
> Biblical and theological writing about justification by faith seeks to make a distinction between living by faith versus living by works. Yet when I first heard of justification by faith, I misunderstood it to mean that I was justified (that is, forgiven and saved) on account of and because of my faith. Faith for me became a good work that I had to perform in order to get God to love and save me. When my faith faltered, I was doomed. Years of parish teaching and experience convince me that I am not alone in having experienced this misunderstanding.[5]

True faith versus imitation faith

There is something that goes by the name of "faith" that is not biblical faith at all but is merely the *mental acceptance of an idea*. Of course we do use ideas and words to describe faith, but if the idea is not rooted in reality, all we have is an idea in our mind. True faith holds not only the idea of Christ, but Christ himself as a living presence.

The difference between true faith and imitation faith is not easy to put down in words because, as Regin Prenter points out in his study of Luther's concept of the Holy Spirit, virtually the same words are used to describe both true faith and imitation faith.[6] There may be, psychologically speaking, a certain joy and satisfaction that accompanies imitation faith, and we may describe it similarly to the way we describe the joy that accompanies true faith. That which makes the difference, the presence and action of the Holy Spirit, is only clear to the experience of faith.

Any relationship to Christ that is less than the true experience of his real and redeeming presence is an imitation. To experience the intellectual idea of Christ is a distinct and not-too-difficult human possibility, especially if it is a truth generally held in one's culture, but it is not the same as experiencing the real Christ. One may hold orthodox views of Christ as a matter of law or principle and for a variety of reasons. But the Holy Spirit alone creates true faith, whereby one is actually united with the living Christ as the present and redeeming Lord.[7]

The dividing line between true faith and imitation faith may not be easy to mark, but one sign of spiritual renewal is a recognition that one has been hovering very near that line in everyday experience, as the following testimony illustrates:

I grew up from childhood believing in God. Like my father before me, I learned the clear difference between right and wrong from my mother and my Sunday school teachers, who diligently taught from the Catechism each Sunday at the crowded white woodframed country church located one mile from our farm. I knew the Lord's Prayer, the Apostles' Creed, and I answered all the questions in the affirmative just before the pastor laid his hands on me when I knelt at the altar in my white robe with pink carnation on my confirmation day, while mother and relatives looked on approvingly. But in my heart there was an emptiness born of an honest recognition that I was not, and likely never would be, the Christian I was supposed to be. Well, I would try to be one anyway, for a while at least, I concluded that day.

Within a few months I gave up my struggle to live like I had been taught. It was too much for me. I found that I couldn't live the goody goody life of real believers. Yet, on at least a half-dozen occasions over my teenage and young adult years, I tried again, renewing my resolve to live like a Christian. On a couple of occasions, while at Bible camp or Luther League meetings with a friend, I raised my hand to "accept Christ as my personal Savior." But it didn't work out.

At church college I decided to live the life anyway, without the inner assurance. Students and professors alike seemed to be doing it, and perhaps that's all there was to it anyway. I believed in God, I concluded, and was baptized, what more did anyone require of me? Nothing more, it appeared, so why not enroll in theological studies too? Why not be a missionary and go all the way for God? So I prepared for the ministry, was ordained, and became a missionary candidate.

But inside me there was turmoil caused by unresolved conflict between who I should be and who I actually was as a Christian. Eventually the disparity between the ought and the actual took its toll in my behavior and in my relationships with those closest to me. I ended up resigning. I turned in my ordination papers and quit the God business.

He did not, however, quit on me. At my worst he came with grace indescribable. From a Friday to a Monday in Holy Week 1972 he moved. He gave me a great, life-astounding gift. He made me a "true believer." Faith was given to me, somehow, exactly 20 years from the day of my confirmation.

He renewed my mind, primarily. I "saw" for the first time how he was always there from my Baptism, but I had not before known him as a living presence. I never "understood" before. He does not require faith: he gives faith as a gift. He himself has done all things necessary for my salvation. He required nothing of me that he himself was not willing to work in and through me.

My evangelical friends tell me that I was "born again" that weekend in 1972. Perhaps I was, but I'd rather say that I was "born again in the Holy Spirit," because since then I have found that along with the gift of true believing faith has come the gift of the Paraclete, ever present in my consciousness.[8]

We do not want to paint an idealized picture of a renewal movement. Renewal movements, by virtue of their very popularity, have their share of the problems that go with life and growth, including the problem of imitation faith. But the Spirit is disturbing the false notion that equates mental acceptance with true faith. He is warning us that we can convert people to a belief system without converting them to Christ. The Spirit is bringing people to a fresh experience of Christ, not as mere idea, but as Lord. At the center of the charismatic renewal is not an idea but Jesus himself, the Living One, present and active among his people by the working of the Holy Spirit.

Luther's understanding of faith

Luther recognized that true faith is not something that springs up from within ourselves. It is created as a gift of God; through the working of the Holy Spirit, Christ is received as the living, redeeming Lord. He recognized that this was a radical break with the common understanding of faith:

Faith is not something dreamed, a human illusion, although this is what many people understand by the term. The reason is that, when they hear the gospel, they miss the point; in their own hearts, and out of their own resources, they conjure up an idea which they call "belief," which they treat as genuine faith. *Faith, however, is something that God effects in us* [italics added].[9]

How do people today understand and use the word *faith?* According to common usage, *faith* refers to an innate ability, that is, *something that comes from within myself:* I am the subject, the one who has faith; I place this faith of mine in God, who is the object of my faith.[10]

Luther understood faith as going beyond a strict subject-object relationship to a point of dynamic identification of subject and object. In one of his writings we virtually see this development taking place:

Faith, if it be true faith, is a sure trust and confidence of the heart, and a firm consent whereby Christ is apprehended: so that Christ is the object of faith, *Yea rather he is not the object, but, as it were, in the faith itself Christ is present* [italics added].[11]

The gift of faith is inseparable from the gift of Christ himself. Apart from the experience of Christ as the living Lord, mediated by the Holy Spirit, all talk of faith is imitation and illusion.

No one can recognize or confess Christ except by the power of the Holy Spirit. Luther stated emphatically:

> True faith cannot be manufactured by our own thoughts, for it is solely the work of God in us, without any assistance on our part. As Paul says in Romans, it is God's gift and grace, obtained by one man, Christ.[12]

CHAPTER 25

THE EFFECTS OF FAITH

Faith and life

The faith which the Holy Spirit works in a believer brings about a fundamental reorientation that is described by the biblical words *repent* and *believe:* one turns away from a self-directed life (repentance) and embraces a life that confidently trusts and obeys Christ (belief). In evangelical circles this truth has been prominently taught in regard to the initial step of faith, that is, describing how one *comes* to Christ. It needs to be extended to describe also how one *lives* with Christ (Col. 2:6-7). A Spirit-filled and Spirit-directed life is nothing other than a life that day by day turns away from reliance on self to trust Christ in everything.

Continuing repentance

The church, as God's pilgrim people on earth (1 Peter 2:11), is constantly in need of renewal. Around A.D. 140, Hermas, one of the apostolic fathers, had visions that showed the development of the church as a process of rejuvenation. He saw the church in the form of an old woman who had lost her former beauty as the bride of Christ. A voice told Hermas that through heartfelt repentance and God's renewing grace the church's former beauty could be regained.[1]

Hermas thus established a major theme in the history of the church: the church's need for continuing renewal through repentance. Spiritual awakenings, not forged by human hands, yet intimately connected to sincere repentance, are signs that the Holy Spirit is doing his renewing work.

Until the final resurrection, Christians will have to contend with the painful reality of sin. Denying it only thickens the cataracts of self-deception, and calls God a liar (1 John 1:8-10). But the awareness of sin that leads to repentance comes only through the Holy Spirit. Without him we remain blind to sin and blind to Jesus (John 9:35-41; 15:22,27).

When people are reluctant to recognize and repent of sin, it is a sign that the Holy Spirit is being resisted. Individual believers commit sins: sins against righteousness, love, and humility. Congregations come under the bondage of sin: pride, neglect, party spirit. The whole church may become corrupted by sin: presumption, faithlessness, worldliness, heresy, self-seeking. All sins need to be acknowledged, repented of, and washed away in the forgiveness that flows from the cross and resurrection of Christ. The Spirit alone creates such repentance (Ps. 51:10-12).

Where the people of God are eager to recognize and repent of sin, it is a sign that the Holy Spirit is at work and being received. In one locality in Denmark a spiritual renewal began after a pastor confessed his shortcomings to his people and asked them to pray for him. It is the devil's ploy to coax God's people away from repentance, as though repentance were an admission that one was not living in victory and the Holy Spirit's presence had been lost. On the contrary, repentance is God's confirmation that the Holy Spirit is truly present, for the Spirit alone creates true repentance. Luther suggested in the first of his *95 Theses* that the entire life of a Christian is characterized by repentance.

Is the Holy Spirit present in the church today, as it encounters a charismatic renewal in its midst? Is the Holy Spirit present in the charismatic movement, as it seeks to live out its calling in the church? One place to test these questions is at the doorway of repentance, for repentance is always a key indicator of the Holy Spirit's presence.

In general, the encounter between church and charismatic renewal has not been characterized by repentance. On one side or the other, or on both sides, repentance has been rejected or simply ignored. And then follows the evidence of the Spirit's absence: a lack of the unity and harmony that the Spirit creates.

The primary response of Lutheran churches to the charismatic renewal has been to caution, analyze, and advise. Out of 17 official documents produced by Lutheran church bodies between 1960–1979 in response to the charismatic renewal, there is but one single sentence suggesting that the renewal represents a call to repentance on the part of the church, and this is mentioned only as a theoretical possibility.[2] Lutheran officials have given their people copious theological evaluation and pastoral counsel. They have lectured both charismatics and noncharismatics on their responsibilities. But they have not seen the charismatic renewal as an occasion for calling the church to repentance.

There is a similar lack of repentance on the other side of the picture. Charismatics have generally been quick to register complaint about rejection by the church but slow to recognize their own rejection of the church and its ministry. They have too often held up their spirituality—gifts and ministries of the Spirit—as a rebuke to the church's deadness, forgetting the words of Jesus: "Blessed are the poor in spirit, for theirs is the kingdom of heaven" (Matt. 5:3). The Holy Spirit would call attention not to our spiritual riches but to our poverty and weakness, and not least to our lack of the unity for which Christ prayed (John 17:21). The Holy Spirit can accomplish more with an ounce of repentance than with a ton of self-confident gifts and ministries.

Where the Holy Spirit leads us to repentance, there follows the evidence of the Spirit's presence in the unity and harmony that he alone is able to create. At a Pan-African Spiritual Leaders' Conference in Nairobi in 1983, Koline Mbona, Anglican bishop from Zaire, spoke with compressed simplicity and candor to his fellow church leaders: "There is one sickness in all the world, and in Zaire: sin. There is one need in all the world, and in Zaire: a Savior. There is one answer in all the world, and in Zaire: the Holy Spirit. There is one *problem* in all the world, and in Zaire: *church leaders*. Brethren, we are the stumbling block of the Holy Spirit."[3] The most outstanding feature of this particular conference was the love and approbation expressed between church leaders and renewal leaders. A genuine appreciation for the church and for past workings of the Holy Spirit blended with an excitement and anticipation concerning his workings in the present renewal. This is not the ordinary experience when church leaders and renewal leaders get together. What made it possible? The kind of artless courage and honesty to which the bishop gave voice. In a word, repentance.

Confident belief

The word of Jesus was without apology. It moved his contemporary hearers to wonder, even alarm. They sensed his power and authority. The certainty with which Jesus spoke was characteristic of all his utterances.[4]

The early Christian proclamation carried the same certainty as the words of Jesus. The *kerygma* (missionary message) was a bold declaration that salvation was to be found only in the name of Jesus (Acts 4:12). His atoning death and bodily resurrection were convincingly testified to as historical events (1 Cor. 15:3-11; Luke 24:34).

The faith of primitive Christianity bears the stamp of deep, joyful certainty. Believers *have* peace with God through Jesus Christ; they *stand* in grace (Rom. 5:1-5). They *experience* forgiveness of sin as a present reality (Eph. 1:7; Col. 1:14; 1 John 2:12). Hebrews speaks of the *parrhesia*—the unshakable certainty—of a Christian's direct access to God (10:19) and urges believers to approach God in this way (4:16). The first epistle of John also speaks of the gift of *parrhesia* toward God, with special reference to the coming judgment (4:17): believers have nothing to fear in the judgment because of the certainty of God's forgiving love. Paul was *certain* that God, who began a good work in the Philippians, would bring it to completion at the day of Jesus Christ (Phil. 1:6). In 1 Thessalonians, Jesus is characterized as the one who *most certainly* saves us from the wrath to come (1:10; also 1 Thess. 5:9; Rom. 5:9; 8:30). With great certainty, Paul testified that *nothing* can separate us from the love of God (Rom. 8:38-39). Clearly, the New Testament is out of step with modern notions that exalt doubt as a desirable virtue.

As certain as the declarations of Scripture are, however, they bring no assurance apart from the working of the Holy Spirit. Neither scholarly study nor the best-intentioned biblical fundamentalism provide certitude of faith, but only the Holy Spirit. The charismatic renewal has sometimes been labeled "antiintellectual" because of the way it approaches Scripture. We examined this question to some extent in Chapter 7, and will look at it in greater detail in Chapter 36. Here we simply draw attention to the fact that the use of Scripture can never be divorced from the faith-risking life of prayer and conscious dependence on the Holy Spirit.

Also in regard to the *proclamation* of the Word, there must be a conscious dependence on the Spirit. We can be content neither with correct doctrine nor with soul-stirring preaching. There must be the evidence of the Spirit: a Spirit-filled instrument, a Spirit-anointed Word, with Spirit-given signs following. Like Paul, we cannot be satisfied with plausible words of human wisdom; there needs to be the demonstration of the Spirit and power (1 Cor. 2:4).

Where certainty of faith is absent, one must pray that the Holy Spirit will make the Word certain, for faith is meant to be certain. It was fundamental to Martin Luther's theology that faith is unconditional certainty. Thus he replied firmly to the humanist Erasmus of Rotterdam: "The Holy Spirit is no skeptic. He has written neither doubt nor mere opinion into our hearts, but rather solid assurances, which are more sure and solid than all experience and even life itself."[5]

The church today languishes under the legacy of humanism. According to the canons of humanism, certainty in spiritual matters is written off as pride, spiritual rigidity, or sheer nonsense. Humanism would agree with the German poet Goethe, that to search is more noble than to have found. Doubt is widely regarded as a virtue. Yet all the while human beings long for that sense of the unconditional that will put strength and fibre into their lives.

It is well to be on guard against triumphalism, which confuses certainty with a fleshly confidence that faith always results in victory in the arena of this world. But we must also guard against the opposite tendency: the danger of slapping that same label of triumphalism on what really is Spirit-given certainty.

In the midst of a doubt-filled generation, the Spirit of God is at work today, as in every age, leading people to certainty of faith. Wherever we make room for him, skepticism must back off. And what the Spirit makes certain to us we can share with others, knowing that through the certain testimony of witnesses the Spirit brings certainty to others.

Faith and experience

The first powerful impression of both participants and observers of the charismatic movement is the central role that personal experience plays in the renewal. The hearts of those in renewal movements, from Luther through Spener and Francke, Zinzendorf and the Wesleys, and down to the present day, are at least "strangely warmed" if not set ablaze by vivid spiritual experience. Krister Stendahl terms this "high-voltage religion":

> Opening up the full spectrum of religious experience and expression is badly needed in those churches that have suppressed the charismatic dimension. Flash-light-battery-voltage Christianity is certainly not strong enough for fighting the drug habit. And no religious tradition can renew itself without the infusion of raw and fresh primary religious experience. It could well be that the charismatic movement is given to the churches as one such infusion. We non-charismatics need not become charismatics—glossolalia is a gift, not a goal or an ideal—but we need to have charismatics among us in the church if the church is to receive and express the fullness of the Christian life. Thus *we* need *them*.[6]

The need for "raw and fresh primary religious experience" is set against the backdrop of modern secular consciousness, which either denies or suppresses religious experience. The rationalism of secular culture has made wide inroads into the church, with corrosive effects on the expression of a truly biblical faith. The charismatic renewal is a needed reminder of the church's origins: the early church not only thought and talked about God in a reasoned manner; it also experienced his presence in demonstrable ways. Its faith "did not rest in the wisdom of men but in the power of God" (1 Cor. 2:5).

Biblical faith is more than an intellectual enterprise; nor can it be reduced to a moral code. It is a living union with Jesus Christ, characterized and confirmed by the intervention of the Holy Spirit. It is a faith inseparably linked with experience.

It is a faith that needs to speak as compellingly to people in our century as it did to people in the first century. When we approach people and communities in the totality of their lives, we realize that there is more to life than reason and technique. The charismatic renewal has brought this disturbingly to the forefront of the church's thinking. It is a prophetic presence that challenges Western culture's manipulative use of reason and technique in all areas of life. Not only does the charismatic renewal challenge people to experience the reality of God in their lives, it says that apart from the real experience of God there is no such thing as biblical faith.

Faith is often contrasted with unbelief, or, in other contexts, with works. In a more fundamental way, however, the real opposite of faith is *fear:* the essence of faith is personal relationship with God, and that which blocks it is fear (1 John 2:28).[7] This can have particular application in the area of charismatic experience, as Lutheran pastor David Dorpat has pointed out:

> Many, if not the vast majority of denominational Christians, feel threatened by the Pentecostal experience. This is true even though in the New Testament this experience and the experiential manifestations of the Spirit were, apparently, a normal part of daily Christian experience.
>
> I wonder if part of the reason isn't that, as one student rather facetiously said to me, "They're afraid someone is going to take over their life."
>
> The fear that someone or something might take over one's life is not altogether bad. There are powers that would take over a person's life and use that person, not for God's purposes, but for man's or Satan's. But the Scriptures tell us to present our bodies as a living sacrifice; to present ourselves, body and soul, to God and to let him control us. Every call to discipleship is a call away from self, a call that creates a battle in the will.
>
> It's the will of man in conflict that says: "I want to control my own life. There are certain things that I have planned that I want to do, and therefore I hesitate to ask God to fill me with his Spirit, because I know that if I really do surrender to him, maybe he *will* take over and I won't be able to do the things I want to do. He may even have me speaking in tongues and I don't want to be a fool for anyone, not even Christ."
>
> The fear of losing control is a real issue with many.[8]

Nevertheless, despite fears and despite misunderstandings, millions of people around the world today are experiencing the surprise of God's nearness and power. The charismatic work of the Spirit is finding expression in their lives. The Holy Spirit is confirming the experience of faith.

CHAPTER 26

THE IMPORTANCE OF THE BIBLICAL WORLDVIEW

Faith and reason

Faith and reason are sometimes contrasted with one another, as though a person with faith must of necessity lay reason aside, and vice versa. It would be more accurate to contrast faith and unbelief, and then note how each utilizes reason. For the Holy Spirit does not tell us to abandon reason when he leads us into truth. What he does is reveal to us truth that we must include in our reasoning process.

Unbelievers do not include the truths of faith in their reasoning process. The truths of faith are nonexistent or irrelevant to their considerations. "The fool says in his heart, 'There is no God' " (Ps. 14:1). A fool may reason superbly, but his or her conclusions will be skewed because they proceed from the premise that God does not exist. A believer relates the reasoning process to the revelation of God. "We have the mind of Christ . . . among the mature we do impart wisdom, although it is not a wisdom of this age or of the rulers of this age, who are doomed to pass away" (1 Cor. 2:16,6). The truth of Christ is the beginning point or premise from which spiritual reasoning proceeds.

The disturbing challenge of the charismatic renewal

A pastor in a Lutheran congregation that had begun to experience some charismatic phenomena announced an information meeting for members who had expressed misgivings about these things. The pastor presented a brief

Bible study showing that such things as healing, speaking in tongues, and prophecy were common to the experience of the early church. Some members who had recently come into charismatic experiences shared their testimonies.

As the questioning and discussion got under way, one of the members who had been upset by these goings-on said, "Pastor, it's *supernatural,* and that's what scares us!"

It would be hard to overestimate the significance of this simple statement from a disturbed church member. In seven words she put her finger on perhaps the most disturbing aspect of the charismatic renewal: it challenges the antisupernatural worldview of Western culture.[1]

Despite certain changes that have taken place in recent years, of which we shall take note, the worldview of Western culture is still largely dominated by naturalism. It forms the principal groundwork for practical decisions in most sectors of Western culture, including the bulk of the theological community.

The secular worldview of Western culture

Naturalism, according to definition, is "the philosophical doctrine denying that anything in reality has a supernatural significance; specifically, the doctrine that scientific laws account for all phenomena, and that teleological conceptions of nature are invalid; loosely, materialism and positivism. In theology it is the denial of the miraculous and supernatural in religion, and the rejection of revelation as a means of attaining truth." Closely akin to naturalism in terms of practical outcome is *rationalism,* defined as "reliance on reason as the basis for establishment of religious truth; a view that reason and experience rather than the nonrational are the fundamental criteria in the solution of problems."[2]

The influence of naturalism and rationalism is so widespread in modern, Western culture that it scarcely requires documentation. Its effect on the church has been enormous. Rudolf Bultmann, probably the most influential Lutheran theologian of his generation,[3] wrote, "The forces and laws of nature have been discovered, and therefore we can't believe in 'spirits' . . . whether good or evil."[4] He saw with great clarity that the issue at stake was that of our *worldview.* The Bible, he said, must be "demythologized":

> Modern man acknowledges as reality only such phenomena or events as are comprehensible within the framework of the rational order of the universe. He does not acknowledge miracles because they do not fit into this lawful order. When a strange or marvelous accident occurs, he does not rest until he has found a rational cause.
>
> The contrast between the ancient world view of the Bible and the modern world view is the contrast between two ways of thinking, the mythological and the

scientific . . . the world view of the Scripture is mythological and is therefore unacceptable to modern man whose thinking has been shaped by science and is therefore no longer mythological. Modern man always makes use of technical means which are the result of science. In case of illness modern man has recourse to physicians, to medical science. In case of economic or political affairs, he makes use of the results of psychological, social, economic, and political sciences, and so on. *Nobody reckons with the direct intervention by transcendent powers* [emphasis added].[5]

Like any widely held system of presuppositions, there is some unevenness in the way that this antisupernatural worldview expresses itself throughout a pluralistic culture. There are pockets of resistance to its pervasive influence in society, and there have been evident strains since about midcentury as it has rubbed up against increasingly less passive non-Western cultures.

Church members who have never heard of Rudolf Bultmann, and who would in fact be scandalized by his "demythologizing" the miracles of Scripture, nevertheless come down to pretty much the same bottom line in their everyday life: they disregard the supernatural. Bultmann did not propagate a new worldview; he simply adapted New Testament interpretation to the dominant philosophy of our culture.

Bultmann's influence in the theological community has somewhat waned; demythologizing is not the popular fashion that it once was. But when it comes down to practical ministry, as distinct from theoretical or doctrinal discussion, most seminary training still reflects a worldview that is indifferent to the supernatural. This worldview places heavy reliance on reason and on the social and psychological sciences, while paying scant attention to such things as prayer, spiritual gifts, deliverance from demonic power, or healing. And where God's Word is still used in ministry, it is frequently a Word stripped of much of its power by the tendency to conform to the prevailing worldview.

Naturalism and rationalism still provide the essential substructure for thought and practical decisions in Western culture, and to a large extent this is also true in the church. It is simply a fact that we must reckon with if we want to be understood in today's culture.[6]

The biblical worldview

In the pages of the Bible, as biblical scholar Ben Johnson has ably shown, we encounter quite a different worldview:

That worldview holds that the universe has been created by God by an act of will, that Jesus Christ is his pre-existent Son, that the universe consists of both visible and invisible creatures, among them angels, demons, principalities, and powers. It believes that God is present in his creation in a variety of ways, among them through his holy angels, through his Spirit by which he inspires people to prophesy, that he reveals himself to people in dreams and visions, as well as through natural means (clouds, fire, etc.). It believes that he acts through signs and wonders, that he intends the perfection of the world and his people, and that he will finally come again in power to set things right. Specifically concerning his Son Jesus Christ, it believes that he was born of a virgin, taught with authority, did miracles and exorcisms, raised the dead, walked on water, and was himself raised from the dead after an atoning death.[7]

No one can set this summary of the biblical worldview alongside a definition of naturalism without seeing at once an irreconcilable conflict. To accept the presuppositions of naturalism is to deny the presuppositions of the Bible, and vice versa. Any talk of biblical authority must begin here: "The issue is the adequacy of the biblical world view."[8]

Two worldviews in conflict

Many people, and not a few theologians, have shied away from the starkness of this confrontation. Some Christians have dealt with the conflict by surrendering the question of worldview to naturalism without a struggle and reducing the sphere of biblical authority simply to "religious questions," or, in some Lutheran theological circles, to "the gospel."[9] This avoids a head-on collision with the secular worldview by abandoning most of the field of human knowledge and experience to the authority of naturalism, in exchange for the privilege of setting up a private little theological belief system on the sidelines.

Theologians have been too willing to barter away biblical presuppositions in order to win a hoped-for acceptance in academic communities that are dominated by naturalism. The result has been a trivializing of the gospel. Religious belief has been consigned to a corner marked "private opinion." Whether the opinion be biblically orthodox or wildly liberal, it has been effectively domesticated by the secular worldview: realities that shaped the life and experience of the early church—answered prayer, divine guidance, miracles, encounter with demonic powers, reproach and suffering, the Holy Spirit, healing, angelic visitations—are either dismissed outright, spiritualized, or scaled down to the level of normal human possibilities. Divine intervention is excluded from the list of expectations. Except for some notion of moral influence, this kind of "gospel" speaks with diminishing authority about or to the real world in which people live their daily lives.

One certain way to make faith irrelevant is to fence it off from the arena where people make most of their practical decisions. That is what we do when we say that the biblical worldview has relevance only as regards "religious questions" or "the gospel." We tend to reduce biblical faith to a theological word game, with a veneer of moralism.

A further problem is inherent in reducing the Bible's authority simply to "the gospel." The gospel *presupposes* the doctrine of God as an active participating agent in the world. It *presupposes* the death of his Son as an expiation for sin.[10] It *presupposes*, at its very heart, the historical truth of the resurrection. All of this flies in the face of naturalistic presuppositions.

The gospel cannot be reduced to a belief system, though unfortunately that is what it has become for many, and thereby a living faith has become a lifeless doctrine. The gospel is preeminently *history*—the record of what God has done and is doing in the world and among the people whom he has created. And therefore it is impossible to speak meaningfully about "the gospel" without becoming involved in questions of worldview.

Consider a few things recorded in Scripture. Jesus spent time teaching moral and spiritual truths. People who operate within a naturalistic framework can consign that to the pigeonhole of private opinion. But Jesus also spent time healing the sick by nonmedical means, casting demons out of people, and performing a variety of miraculous acts, such as turning water into wine, walking on water, and raising the dead. And this kind of thing was not limited to the ministry of Jesus: his disciples also healed, cast out demons, and performed miracles. Naturalism has no pigeonhole for that kind of thing. The New Testament has 7,957 verses, of which 3,874 (49%) are "contaminated" with happenings that do not fit into naturalism's worldview.[11]

What kind of a world *is* this that God has created, in which we live out our lives, in which Jesus Christ carried out his mission, and in which we are called to be his witnesses?

Are there such things as invisible spirits without bodies, who are opposed to God and serve a master called Satan, who seek to influence people and do them harm, but who can be driven away through encounter with someone of greater spiritual power and authority? Can physical sicknesses be healed through such things as prayer and the laying on of hands? Is it possible to come into possession of valid knowledge through such things as dreams, visions, and prophecies? Can spiritual authority directly alter the normal course of events in the world of nature?

Some charismatics and biblical conservatives might be tempted to brush such questions aside with a confident, "Of course I believe such things! I believe everything that's in the Bible." But think about it for a moment. How do you think you would feel if you were asked to give a report on some things that had been going on in your house, asked by people to whom you were responsible and who gave every evidence of being upset by some stories that had come to their ears? You begin by reporting that an angel appeared to you during your prayer time one morning, telling you to send some men to a nearby town to fetch a person whom you did not know, and that this person, in response to a vision as well as to your invitation, came and talked to a group of people whom you had invited for the occasion, and that while he did so the Holy Spirit fell on the whole group and they broke forth in exalted speech—prophecy and unknown tongues. That incident, transposed from Scripture (Acts 10) into everyday life, could be more than a handful for even the most avowed charismatic to handle in a culture dominated by naturalism. The best one could hope for is that he or she would be written off as an irresponsible fanatic. More likely one would be referred or committed to a mental-health facility. When two worldviews that are opposed to one another come into conflict, something has to give.

CHAPTER 27

THE SECULAR WORLDVIEW UNDER SCRUTINY

THE CENTERPIECE OF THE SECULAR WORLDVIEW: EPISTEMOLOGY

The issue we must come to grips with in regard to a worldview is that of *epistemology*. Epistemology has to do with acquiring and validating knowledge. In other words, "How do I come into possession of valid knowledge?" More simply, "How do I know what I know?"

The naturalistic mind-set of Western culture has its roots in the epistemology of Aristotle. Aristotle taught that we receive direct knowledge *only* through sense experience and reason. This epistemology was imported into the church through the prodigious theological work of Thomas Aquinas in the 13th century and has remained the reigning epistemology of Western culture to the present day.[1] Aquinas steered a careful detour around the idea that we can have direct contact with spiritual realities, and Western culture has largely followed his lead.

The parade of thinkers inside and outside the church who helped shape the modern, Western mind varied their content and field of interest, but all were astonishingly unified in their epistemology: philosophers such as Descartes, Hobbes, Hume, Kant, Hegel, Kierkegaard, Nietzsche, Husserl, and Heidegger; theologians such as Schleiermacher, Barth, Bonhoeffer, Bultmann, and Tillich—to a man they were skeptical of the possibility of any direct encounter with nonphysical (spiritual) reality such as we read about in the New Testament.[2] The impact of Aristotle and Aquinas on Western culture has been enormous.

Descartes, "the father of modern thought," said that only those ideas that could be proven true by reason could be accepted. This is naturalism in a nutshell. The philosopher L. L. Whyte, author of *The Unconscious before Freud,* observed that Descartes "made one of the great intellectual blunders of all time." Some of Descartes' brilliant mathematical insights came to him through dreams and visions, yet he narrowed down the scope of human knowing so far that he excluded his own inspiration, "and the problem he left has remained to our time."[3]

Darwin posited the theory that life evolved on the earth over millions of years by a process of "natural selection." Across the spectrum of Western culture this has become a widely believed "scientific account" of the way in which all forms of life on the earth came into being, an account that requires no reference to God. Garret Vanderkooi, at the Institute for Enzyme Research at the University of Wisconsin, observed:

A theory with such a vast scope, and which by its very prehistoric nature cannot be proved, would undoubtedly have been passed off as idle speculation, if it were not for its theological implications. The theory offers a naturalistic alternative to the creation account contained in the Bible, and this is considered to be a highly desirable thing by those who do not want to recognize the Creator. The proponents of evolution have done such an effective job of propagandizing this religious theory, in the name of empirical science, that some formerly orthodox theologians are revising their interpretation of the Bible to make room for it. From the scientific point of view, evolution may have been a plausible hypothesis in Darwin's day, but it has now become untenable, as a result of developments in molecular biology.[4]

For our purposes it is particularly helpful to observe the epistemology of naturalism in relation to Darwin's theory because it illustrates how tenaciously people cling to a worldview even in the face of contrary evidence. Thoroughgoing evolutionists have had a difficult time of it even within the scientific community. Scholars as diverse as Jacques Barzun, Gertrude Himmelfarb, and A. E. Wilder Smith noted that the progress of modern science has been brutally unkind to Darwin's thesis. Even Julian Huxley, himself an evolutionist, reckoned that the odds against a higher organism like human beings coming into being through the process that Darwin suggested are an improbability of the same order of magnitude as that of a monkey with a typewriter producing the works of Shakespeare.[5] But none of this has materially affected the sway of naturalism in the culture at large. It still commands the scene. Its presuppositions are not the result of scientific analysis. They are articles of a secular faith.

The Catholic priest Pierre Teilhard de Chardin, writing both as a paleontologist and as a religious philosopher, made a compelling and passionate case for the evolutionary hypothesis. Yet he admitted that the latest achievements of paleontology go against the basic evolutionary theory. "Life presents itself to our eyes in paradoxical form: it is like a magnificent tree whose regularly placed and fully grown branches appear to hang from an invisible and imaginary trunk."[6]

This development within the scientific community illustrates the fact that an entrenched worldview will not be readily set aside. To begin with, at least, people will force new or seemingly conflicting data into the system's mold, along with a question mark, rather than abandon the fundamental mind-set. For Teilhard, evolution was more than a cold, scientific analysis and interpretation of factual data. It was the fulfillment of a basic human need:

> It is our *need for understanding* . . . it is not a hypothesis, but a condition which all hypotheses must henceforth fulfill, the expression *for our minds* of the world's passage from the state of "cosmos" to the state of "cosmogenesis." Either you regard the world as a collection of physically linked beings, traveling by way of growth as a whole towards an organic consummation; and then, once more you are *in your heart* an evolutionist. Or else you see in the universe nothing but a system of moral and juridical relationships by which contiguous beings are associated; and then you have lost all rightful means of restraining the advance of egoistic and agnostic individualism which threatens to dissolve and sweep away the thinking zone of the earth" [italics added].[7]

What we see in a thinker so capable and honest as Teilhard is that there is more here than a scientific theory. We are encountering a philosophical *passion for understanding* as the central motive in an argument for the evolutionary hypothesis. Without it, he sees humanity facing a meaningless and threatening disorder. "An absolute beginning of things would mean the ruin of the entire edifice of our perceptual universe."[8]

Naturalism came on the scene offering a reasoned explanation for life. It is not likely to quit the stage without a struggle.

CHALLENGES TO THE SECULAR WORLDVIEW

Naturalism is still far and away the dominant worldview in Western culture. It is the way the average person thinks about reality. Yet there are sober and thoughtful people who are calling it into question. They are not simply correcting this or that aspect of naturalism's worldview: they are challenging its basic presuppositions.

Challenges from the scientific community

A rigid naturalism is being called into question by some well-credentialed scientists and philosophers. Their point of view, of course, is not primarily spiritual or religious but philosophical. What is of particular interest for our purposes is their epistemology.

Werner Heisenberg, the nuclear physicist, in his Gifford Lectures said, "The general trend in the 19th century had been toward an increasing confidence in the scientific method and in precise rational explanations . . . modern physics has turned against an over-confidence in scientific explanations; they cover only a very limited part of reality, and the other part, for instance that covered by religion, is infinite."[9]

A helpful summary of some of these developments in science was given by John Magee in his book, *Reality and Prayer:*

> Developments in atomic physics have forced scientists to abandon hope of applying mechanistic "cause and effect" explanations to the ultimate particles of matter. Atomic events seem to obey a law of "wholeness." This means that every part of the atomic event is in organic connection with the rest. We are left with the strange, though experimentally established fact, that we cannot "predict" exactly what will happen until the event is past. The last moment of the event seems to have important effects on the initial moment. Where a particle is going is as important as where it has been. All the forces in the situation seem to be operating throughout the whole system just as in a living body. In *Science and the Modern World,* Whitehead refers to this as "the brooding presence of the whole onto its various parts."
>
> Proposing this same organic interrelatedness of physical events, Max Planck, celebrated physicist and discoverer of the quantum theory, writes, "It is impossible to obtain an adequate version of the laws for which we are looking, unless the physical system is regarded *as a whole.* According to modern mechanics, each individual particle of the system, in a certain sense, exists simultaneously in every part of the space occupied by the system. This simultaneous existence applies not merely to the field of force with which it is surrounded, but also to its mass and its charge." . . . An exploration of the so-called "border-line" between living and nonliving substance makes the organismic view of the universe even more plausible. Upon close inspection those interesting crystals called "viruses" betray in an elementary form the characteristics of living bacteria. The more closely we inspect the actual organization of the so-called nonliving substances in their minutest constituents, the more they appear to obey living rather than mechanistic laws. That is, they operate as wholes, partly self-determining, giving at times the appearance of a "society" of minute organisms rather than a mechanical collection.
>
> In the light of such findings we may be well justified in assuming that even in so-called nonliving matter there is feeling and awareness, however dim or minute, and that behind the outward appearance of mechanism is a "subjectivity" which corresponds in some remote way to our consciousness. Each genuinely organic unit, an atom, say, or a molecule or crystal, will have something analogous to our feelings, powers of self-direction, selective response to the environment, and the like, though, of course, in a very minimal way. The entire physical world is simply a collection of such entities. There is no matter which is merely dead machinery. At points, for example, in plants, animals, and our bodies these

organisms are collected into larger living wholes. In such cases the smaller organism is controlled in part by laws of its own and in part by the laws of the
more inclusive organism. Whitehead points out, "Molecules differ in their intrinsic character according to the general organic plan of the situations in which
they find themselves."

   If the physical world is thus made up of living parts, a question arises. How
shall we account for the mechanistic features of our experience and for the laws
of large-scale mechanics as they appear in astronomy or geology? Why does the
world, on certain levels of scientific observation, appear to be a machine? The
most plausible answer seems to be that such laws are "statistical," that is, they
are the average performance of billions of living entities, each of which obeys
its own living law. . . . These modern developments at once set aside the old
mechanistic picture of reality. The old eighteenth-century concept of nature as a
"dull affair, soundless, scentless, colorless; merely the hurrying of material,
endlessly, meaninglessly," is repudiated, and a living nature akin to mind and
spirit is put in its place.[10]

For our purposes, the value of these observations from the scientific community is essentially negative: they do not exclude the biblical worldview.
By the same token, however, they do not exclude pantheism. What they do
is call into question the overconfident naturalism of the 18th and 19th centuries.

A theologian like Bultmann took passing note of these developments, but
seemed largely unimpressed:

   Although modern physical theories take account of chance in the chain of cause
   and effect in subatomic phenomena, our daily, living purposes and actions are
   not affected. In any case, modern science does not believe that the course of
   nature can be interrupted or, so to speak, perforated, by supernatural powers.[11]

At this point a comment of Carl Jung is apropos:

   It is a rational presupposition [of modern man] that everything has a natural and
   perceptible cause. We are convinced of this. Causality, so understood, is one of
   our most sacred dogmas. There is no legitimate place in our world for invisible,
   arbitrary and so-called supernatural forces. . . . We distinctly resent the idea of
   invisible and arbitrary forces.[12]

We flatter ourselves, Jung said, that our modern worldview is based on
"facts," whereas the worldview of ancient or primitive people is based on
crass ignorance or superstition. From his study of primitive tribes he pointed
out that the difference between worldviews is not in logic or factualness but
in basic presuppositions:

   Primitive man is no more logical or illogical than we are. His presuppositions
   are not the same as ours, and that is what distinguishes him from us. We feel we

are stating a natural sequence of events when we say, "This house was burned down because the lightning struck it." Primitive man senses an equally natural sequence when he says, "A sorcerer has used the lightning to set fire to this particular house." In explaining things in this way he is just like ourselves: He does not examine his assumptions. To him it is an unquestionable truth that disease and other ills are caused by spirits or witchcraft, just as for us it is a foregone conclusion that an illness has a natural cause. His mental activity does not differ in any fundamental way from ours.[13]

The struggle between two opposing ways of thinking is nothing new. What we see taking place in our own culture is in some ways like a replay in reverse of the struggle between the epistemology of Aristotle and that of his teacher, Plato.

Plato saw reality consisting of two realms, and he had a theory of knowledge to back it up. He recognized that we gain knowledge of the physical world through sense experience and reason, but he also believed that we have direct experience of a nonphysical realm of reality. In the *Phaedrus* he spoke of four ways that one may have meaningful contact with the nonphysical realm of reality: prophecy, healing, artistic inspiration, and love.

In the West, the thinking of Plato predominated until the 13th century, when it was largely replaced by the naturalism of Aristotle. The critical difference between these two men, for our purposes, was their epistemology: whereas Plato said that we gain knowledge through sense experience, reason, *and* direct contact with the nonphysical realm, Aristotle allowed only the first two, with reason in the driver's seat directing the operation. Plato's sophisticated understanding of the human connection with another world was so completely forgotten that, even today, Platonism carries a popular meaning of devaluing the immediate world.[14] The value of Plato's thinking for our purposes is, once again, negative: it does not limit knowledge to what we learn through sense experience and reason. It does not establish the biblical world view, but it is not hostile to the biblical category of revelation.

In this limited survey of secular thinkers, ancient and modern, we do not find agreement on worldview. But we do encounter a common thread that seriously challenges the underpinnings of naturalism: *there are objective dimensions of reality that we do not come to know about simply by means of sense experience and reason.*

Challenges from the theological community

In his book *The Misunderstanding of the Church*, Emil Brunner recognized that we cannot rightly understand the church of the New Testament unless we break out of the straitjacket of naturalism and take seriously the dynamic manifestations of the Holy Spirit:

> The mystery of the *ecclesia* as the fellowship of the Spirit is that it has an articulate living order without being legally organized. When we who are so accustomed to the juridical organization of the church ask how such a "pneumatic" order is possible, the answer must be: it *is* no longer a simple possibility, but it once *was* possible thanks to the reality of whose dynamic power we can now entertain scarcely a vague surmise—the reality of the Holy Ghost. From this point of view it would have to be said: the organization of the church and in particular its legal administration is a compensatory measure which it becomes necessary to adopt in times and places where the plenitude of the Spirit is lacking. Canon law is a substitute for the Spirit.
>
> How did the fellowship of Jesus spread? We children of an era that is rationalized through and through always think first and perhaps exclusively in such a matter of what we would call evangelization, or missionary work, in which the stress lies almost wholly on the proclamation of the gospel, and this proclamation again is understood in the sense of theological instruction. Of course, teaching and in the broader sense preaching played a decisive part in the spread of the movement. But something at least as important was just that other, that "pneumatic" factor, the non-theological, the purely dynamic. . . . People draw near to the Christian community because they are irresistibly attracted by its supernatural power. . . . There is a sort of fascination which is exercised mostly without reference to the Word, comparable rather to the attractive force of a magnet or the spread of an infectious disease. . . . The obscure beginnings of faith may be, and often are, much less dependent than we theologians are inclined to admit on the word of the preacher. Here the mighty energies of the Spirit are more important than any word, although these energies, in so far as they are those of the Holy Spirit, owe their origin to the Word of God.
>
> Present day evangelists and missionaries usually realize this fact far better than we theologians who not only undervalue the dynamic power of the Holy Ghost, but often know simply nothing of it. With them the not unreasonable fear of an excess of enthusiasm, of the para-logical, has certainly had the effect of causing the apostle's injunction, "Quench not the Spirit" (1 Thess. 5:19) to be disregarded and of confining attention to his warnings against the overvaluation of the para-logical, dynamic element.[15]

The charismatic renewal, with its renewed interest in the work of the Holy Spirit, raises at a practical level the very questions that Brunner posed in a theoretical way to an earlier generation of theologians. To what degree has the epistemology of naturalism become a rule of thumb for our practical ministry—even in circles where the miraculous events in Scripture are staunchly upheld? Has the evangelical wing of the church struck a coexistence pact with naturalism when it comes to any divine action other than conversion and faith?

Lutheran theologian Bengt Hoffman has pointed out that banishing the word *supernatural* from the theological vocabulary carries with it some episte-mological liabilities:

> We "moderns" have been tutored by scientific materialism to classify as "su-perstition" *all* claims of visionary information or dreams and poetic or prophetic inspiration. Since such phenomena are beyond measurement in the conventional sense they have been rejected as sources of "knowledge." The result is that *all* manifestations of supernatural life in Luther's [and our] thought have been ignored as time-bound superstition.
>
> Whatever drawbacks there are to the use of the adjective "supernatural," it does convey transcendental overtones without which the interpretation of faith becomes locked up in scientific materialism.
>
> In the last analysis the supernatural and the natural may indeed coincide. But for pedagogical reasons we shall have to restore the word "supernatural" to theological legitimacy. It does betoken the fact that biblical revelation is in part an invasion from the [realm of the] para-normal.[16]

Episcopalian theologian Morton Kelsey makes a similar point. "Man is not only in touch with the space-time or material world [which he perceives with his physical senses] . . . he is also in touch with a non-space-time or spiritual world [which he perceives through] images, intuitions, dreams, phan-tasies, myths, and numinous contents . . . and which is independent of the individual."[17]

In making reference to the "non-space-time" realm, Kelsey sometimes uses psychological, psychic, and biblical terminology more or less inter-changeably. Especially in his book *Encounter with God,* he develops a phil-osophical model that takes the nonphysical dimension of reality with dead seriousness, and to do this he includes research of phenomena occurring both outside and inside the Christian tradition. He demonstrates that psychic phe-nomena, some of the findings of depth psychology, as well as the biblical revelation have this in common: they point to the reality of an invisible, nonphysical dimension of reality that our Western worldview has largely writ-ten off.

At the level of practical experience, however, he recognizes that Christians must exercise discernment. Although there are similarities between, say, the psychic phenomenon of ESP and biblical prophecy, the two are not identical. Intuition or "a sixth sense" is something that many people incorporate into their worldview (even though it clashes with naturalistic presuppositions), but this does not mean that they are operating within a biblical frame of reference. Where encounter with the nonphysical dimension of reality is taken seriously, as in the charismatic renewal, people must be taught to distinguish between what is good and what is not good. For, as Kelsey points out, when we begin to take this realm seriously, we soon discover the presence of the demonic as well as the angelic.[18]

Kelsey is particularly helpful when the question arises as to whether there actually is such a thing as a "natural" and "supernatural" realm, since everything is part of God's one, unified creation: "Whether these things are ultimately one or many is a question that has no meaningful answer. One's knowledge is of experiences and not of final things. One can only speak about what happens within the realm of human experience [and the fact is that man experiences or perceives these as two distinct though not unrelated realms]."[19]

According to Kelsey, "the only large group of Christians who take the idea of a direct divine encounter seriously, aside from certain conservatives, are the Pentecostals and the charismatics, and they have come in for derision from every side."[20] Evangelicals or conservatives certainly do take seriously the idea of divine encounter in relation to salvation. They have been wary, however, of the kind of expectation of supernatural intervention that one finds in Pentecostal and charismatic groups—things such as healing, speaking in tongues, deliverance from demonic powers, and miracles.

The initial value in this kind of theological work is again negative: it does not exclude the supernatural from serious and practical consideration. However, a further question must be posed: What may it *include?* Not everything supernatural is good.

Charismatics may cheer when they see the myth of naturalism exploded. They need to exercise discernment in regard to what is offered in its place. One of the greatest challenges to Christianity in our day is a movement that offers an alternative not only to the Western worldview, but to the biblical worldview as well.

Challenges from non-Christian sources

Since the 1960s, the naturalism of the West has come in for attack from quite another direction: non-Christian religions and the realm of the occult. Such diverse interests as transcendental meditation, yoga, Eastern mysticism, Satan worship, feminine spirituality with a nurturing goddess as the cultural image of deity, Scientology, Mind Dynamics, spiritism, out-of-the-body experiences, the *Star Wars* movie sagas, reincarnation, and some kinds of health and ecological concerns have emerged as a "viable contender to secular humanism on the one hand, and the Judeo-Christian tradition on the other."[21] Before 1960 these interests had been restricted to small pockets on the fringe of Western culture. Since then they have moved into the mainstream, where they have become popularly known as the New Age movement.

Robert L. Burrows' thoughtful analysis of this multifaceted, multifocused movement stresses the question of worldview:

> Because of the variety of New Age programs, it is impossible to list criteria that would serve as a basis for recognizing the unbiblical worldview that under-girds them all. *Worldview* is, however, the *key ingredient.*
>
> The New Age Movement is not tied to any particular organization, has no overarching hierarchical structure, is diverse in both practice and belief, and although it has prominent spokesmen, has no official leadership. What unites it and links it to the traditions that preceded it is a set of common assumptions about God or ultimate reality, humanity, and the nature of the human predicament.
>
> In spite of the teeming diversity of the cosmos, ultimate reality or god is pure energy, consciousness, or life force. Humanity, like the rest of creation, is an extension of god; divine essence is humanity's true, higher, or real self. Alienation caused by sinful rebellion is not humanity's problem. Metaphysical ignorance is the root of all humanity's woes; it is dispelled by knowledge that is brought about by psycho-spiritual techniques that rid consciousness of the fragmenting effects of reason and the predefining limitations of belief. That is the path to godhood, self-realization, cosmic consciousness, enlightenment, and in our day, New Age transformation.[22]

For our purposes, the New Age movement registers another critique of naturalism, indicating how widespread the attack on the Western worldview has become. It poses, however, two dangers.

On the one hand, there is the danger of *ignorance* about the real nature of the New Age movement. Christians can get caught up in some teaching or practice of the New Age movement on the naive assumption that anything opposed to naturalism must be a Christian's ally. Or, one may attempt to "take what is good" from some New Age practice and end up getting more than was bargained for. The New Age movement is not merely a mushrooming of new ideas. It is a revival of ancient nature religions.[23] Some of its expressions are clearly laden with occult power.

Generally speaking, the charismatic renewal has been alert to this kind of danger. Accurate discernment of spirits is one of the marks of a charismatically endowed body of believers. This has been regularly emphasized in conferences and publications. In the early 1960s, David Schoch, a Pentecostal pastor in Long Beach, California, was invited to speak to a charismatic prayer group in a neighboring Lutheran congregation. "The gift of discernment should be like a watchdog," he said. "It sniffs out any teaching, any practice that comes into a church, to see whether it lines up with Scripture." Looking directly at the pastor of the congregation, he said, "I hope you're sniffing me out real good, Pastor."

On the other hand, there is the opposite danger of *overreacting* to the New Age phenomenon, a knee-jerk rejection of anything that New Age adherents support:

> New Age advocates are typically for ecology, against nuclear weapons, and for grassroots democracy. Being typically New Age, however, does not imply all those who take similar positions are aligned with the New Age Movement. Those positions can be arrived at through ideologies diametrically opposed. Marx and Jesus were both concerned with the poor. That does not make Marx a Christian, nor Jesus a Communist. A concern for ecology, similarly, does not of itself indicate either a commitment to a deified creation or the Deity of creation. *Nor are issues rendered illegitimate simply because New Age enthusiasts typically address them* [italics added].[24]

Christianity has a long tradition of adapting certain things from the surrounding environment for its own purposes. The Nicene Creed, for instance, speaks of the Son being "of one *substance*" with the Father, using a term borrowed from Greek philosophy. In adopting this creed, the church certainly was not bound to accept the whole philosophical package that was linked to Aristotle's use of the word *substance*.

Similarly, the church today may find that some concepts and terms being used in non-Christian settings can be helpful in the church, if we give them a specifically Christian application. But this needs to be done with great care, recognizing the kind of "freight" that a concept may bring along with it. An example of this would be the practice of "visualization." In New Age circles, visualization is used as a psychic or occult technique: the creative imagination is used to focus mental or occult powers.

This does not mean that Christians must avoid using the creative imagination in their prayers. The Bible is full of images and metaphors that stimulate the imagination: "A farmer went forth to sow seed . . . . a woman lost a coin, and swept the house until she found it . . . . the prophet saw a basket of summer figs." Using the creative imagination can help make our prayers more vivid.

For instance, you might meditate on a scene from the Bible, visualizing it in your mind's eye. Take the baptism of Jesus, for example: you "see" it in your imagination; you "listen" to the conversation between Jesus and John the Baptist; you "watch" the waters of baptism come over Jesus; you "see" the Holy Spirit descend on him in the form of a dove as he comes up out of the water; you "hear" the voice from heaven, "This is my beloved Son, with whom I am well pleased" (Matt. 3:17).

It would be doctrinally correct to say, "In his baptism, Jesus identified with sinful humanity, and the Father affirmed him as Son and Messiah." There is value in using our intellects to state biblical truth in a clear way. But we don't have to limit ourselves to this approach. Using the creative imagination can add to our appreciation of scriptural revelation; it often helps make the truth more vivid and personal.

Instead of simply stating a promise of Scripture, it may help to visualize the promise being fulfilled in your mind's eye. In praying for healing, it is often helpful to "see" the person healed or getting better. This can help activate faith by bringing the truth of Scripture to bear on those parts of our mind that respond more to pictures and action than to logical statements.

In other words, the fact that visualization is used in the New Age movement doesn't put it off-limits for Christians. The creative imagination is a God-given gift. But, like all gifts, it can be misused. Our use of it must be governed by Scripture.

The naturalism of Western culture is a philosophy of unbelief, clearly at odds with Scripture. We can thank God that in charismatic Christianity he has raised up a challenge to naturalism. But as certainly as God raises up a standard of truth, Satan will be on hand with his counterfeit. The supernaturalism of the New Age movement is laced with spiritual poison. We need not fear it; we need only be aware of it and on guard against it.

"He who is in you is greater than he who is in the world" (1 John 4:4).

CHAPTER 28

THE BIBLICAL WORLDVIEW AND THE PROCLAMATION OF THE GOSPEL

Some might object, "Why so much emphasis on the supernatural, on divine intervention, on spiritual experiences such as healing, visions, prophecies, casting out demons, and so on? What about the experience of salvation, the experience of personal faith? Isn't that the most important intervention of all?"

It is. Jesus once said to his disciples, who had just returned from a successful mission, rejoicing that even the demons were subject to them, "I have given you authority to trample on snakes and scorpions and to overcome all the power of the enemy; nothing will harm you. However, do not rejoice that the spirits submit to you, but rejoice that your names are written in heaven" (Luke 10:19-20 NIV).

This central experience of faith—the assurance that our names are written in heaven—can be undermined, however, if we cave in to the naturalistic worldview. Naturalism rules out the possibility of God's intervention in the world. If we unconsciously accept this, then the experience of salvation—which *is* a divine intervention—can get watered down to the level of a psychological event. We end up relating to an idea about God rather than to the Lord himself. Calling attention to other kinds of divine intervention forces us to part company with a self-contained naturalism so we can relate to the living God in a realistic, objective way.

Once a man who was crippled was brought to Jesus for healing (Mark 2:5-12). Jesus began by telling him that his sins were forgiven. When some of his critics took exception to this, Jesus said, "Which is easier, to say to the paralytic, 'Your sins are forgiven,' or to say, 'Rise, take up your pallet and walk'?" Jesus then proceeded to heal the man, to demonstrate that he had authority over sin as surely as he had authority over sickness—both of which involve divine, supernatural intervention.

Most Christians facing that question today would probably confess that it is easier to say, "Your sins are forgiven" than to say, "Rise and walk." We are used to dealing with matters of faith that allegedly take place in the invisible recesses of the human soul. That, after all, is the sphere of activity and authority that the church has marked off for itself. It is a fairly comfortable arena in which to operate, because if the words are false or meaningless it could never be proved. But any kind of linkage between the invisible realm of the soul and a command to "rise and walk," such as we observe with Jesus, would be a scary thing. When you step out into that arena, it becomes evident whether you have a gospel of mere talk or a gospel of power (1 Cor. 4:20).

Donald McGavran, a well-known figure in the evangelical community through his lectures and books on church growth, was asked about the reaction of his colleagues when he began to suggest that healing might be for today:

> I would think my colleagues at first would have shared my revulsion at the idea. As they thought about it, however, I'm sure they would grant that the evidence for it is fairly strong. . . . Partly by a theological position and partly by observation of evidence [primarily in Third World countries] I came to the conclusion that missionaries—as well as pastors and serious laymen and women—ought to regard healing much more openmindedly than they have. They must not narrowly shut themselves off in a corner and say, "That's not reputable," or, "We would endanger our reputations."
>
> That's a bit cowardly. We need to be braver than that. We need simply to face the fact that healing does occur, and that God uses healing to bring men and women to Christ.[1]

The growth of Christianity in the Third World is bringing increasing pressure against the rationalism that has been exported from European and American seminaries. Charles H. Kraft observes:

> To an African, a Christian theology that can offer no more than an impersonal Western medical approach to disease is not only culturally unacceptable but scripturally inaccurate. Africans, unlike theologians bound by a Western culture world view, *know* that illness is not usually caused by germs. And when they study the Scriptures they find abundant disconfirmation of the theological understandings of the West. Illness, by the way, is a matter of theological (not simply medical) understanding in virtually all cultures except those characterized by Western secularism.

The African expects that anyone speaking for God will automatically be concerned with healing and exorcism. If, then, the person of God attempting to communicate Christ in traditional Africa will not or cannot address the illness problem effectively, the person can expect to make little if any real impact.[2]

This is not to upstage the church's call to preach and pronounce the forgiveness of sin. It simply points out a potential danger. If we find that we are comfortable only with those experiences that happen invisibly within one's heart, faith can too easily get watered down to an idea in the mind. In a culture dominated by naturalism, the miraculous aspects of the biblical revelation remind us that God is a living, intervening God; it is not an idea about God, but God himself with whom we have to do.

Biblical faith is more than my subjective response to a doctrine or an idea about God. *Faith involves a joining of my life to the life of God in Jesus Christ, through the working of the Holy Spirit.* The present-day charismatic renewal is precisely a renewal of faith in the God who *intervenes* in our everyday life. While some theologies call for accommodating the biblical revelation to the presuppositions of naturalism, the charismatic renewal is saying that the church must abandon its efforts to tailor God to fit the presuppositions of a worldview that dismisses out of hand things that Scripture presents with the greatest seriousness. Ben Johnson points out that the weight of history is on the side of the biblical worldview:

> The experience of the church through the ages affirms the biblical worldview as the way things are, or the way they can be. For neither has the world changed nor has God's way of working with the world changed. What has changed is that secular atheism has a primary belief commitment of much of modern theology. The clear and simple issue is whether God acted in the ways described in Old and New Testaments, whether he inspired prophets to mantic utterance, whether he sent his Son into the world, whether Jesus cast out demons, healed, died for our sins, was raised for our justification, will return to judge the living and the dead. The issue is really a judgment about God, the nature of the world, and God's interaction with it. If one does not believe he acted in the ways described in the Bible, he has effectively cut himself adrift from the dynamics of the Judeo-Christian faith. And to affirm that God has indeed acted as described in the Bible and still does, in a cosmic arena which is as it is described in the Bible, is not primitivism.[3]

A label like "primitivism" has stuck to the biblical worldview simply because the assumptions of naturalism have been proclaimed as fact and accepted without question by large segments of the Christian community. Morton Kelsey describes how he once encountered this phenomenon in speaking to a group of clergymen:

> Most modern, educated Christians have been brought up and taught to believe that Jesus' concern with the realm of the angelic and demonic was determined

simply by the naive worldview of his own century and by his being caught in it. It was a contemporary illusion, and therefore we must just dismiss this aspect of his ministry. At a recent conference of clergymen, when I proposed to discuss the subject of the angelic realm, exactly this objection was raised, and then suddenly the objector said, "Yes, I see. I have simply assumed that my world view was the correct one, and that Jesus was incorrect—really, without ever critically examining one against the other."[4]

The charismatic renewal is challenging the church to proclaim to this generation a Lord who is the same yesterday and today and forever (Heb. 13:8). He is not a God of caprice who changes his world or his way of working in it to conform to our latest philosophical or theological fad. He is the God who has revealed himself in Scripture, the God who intervenes and encounters people in the real and everyday world, in ways and by means that he himself determines, and to which Scripture bears faithful and accurate testimony.

CHAPTER 29

THE EFFECTS OF THEOLOGICAL TRADITION ON RENEWAL

The charismatic renewal has focused on some aspects of the message of Scripture that have been little-known, or in any case treated as stepchildren, by large segments of the church. The rediscovery of these aspects of the biblical message has led to new theological understanding and new practice in many areas of church life.

Rediscovery of neglected truth often produces its own kind of problem: people experience the truth so strongly that they lose a sense of proportion in regard to other, and perhaps more important, aspects of the faith; they may even end up in an unbalanced position in which their approach becomes unsound and biblically false.

The charismatic renewal seeks to be a challenge and corrective in two directions: (1) to a church that has ignored important aspects of the biblical message that are decisive for its life and ministry; (2) to groups that have specialized in some of these neglected aspects of truth in an unhealthy way. In what follows we want to draw attention to certain areas of truth that have been brought into focus by the charismatic renewal, areas where the Holy Spirit would inspire sound doctrine as a balance between neglect and unhealthy overemphasis.

Aspects of Lutheran tradition that encourage renewal

Over the centuries, Lutheran state-churches have experienced a variety of renewals, revivals, and spiritual awakenings. Charismatics in the Lutheran state-churches of Europe generally view Lutheran teaching and tradition in a positive way, as a help and encouragement for renewal, though they recognize that some elements in Lutheran theological tradition have not always helped the church to live in the power of the Holy Spirit.

At the center of the Lutheran understanding of the Christian faith stands the cross—the sign of humanity's total dependence on the forgiving grace of God. Life in the Holy Spirit begins at the cross: forgiveness and cleansing by the blood of Jesus is the basic precondition for the indwelling of the Holy Spirit.

Luther deserves our lasting thanks for setting aside works-righteousness, the notion that we can earn our own salvation. He turned the eyes of all Christendom to the righteousness that God freely gives through faith in Christ. He helped reestablish the biblical foundation that must undergird the Christian life from beginning to end. In his explanation to the Third Article of the Apostles' Creed, he set before us a succinct and positive expectation for a working of the Holy Spirit that reaches out from the cross to embrace the whole of Christian life and experience:

> I believe that I cannot by my own understanding or effort believe in Jesus Christ my Lord, or come to him. But the Holy Spirit has called me through the gospel, enlightened me with his gifts, and sanctified and kept me in true faith.
> In the same way he calls, gathers, enlightens, and sanctifies the whole Christian church on earth, and keeps it united with Jesus Christ in the one true faith.
> In this Christian church day after day he fully forgives my sin and the sins of all believers. On the last day he will raise me and all the dead and give me and all believers in Christ eternal life. This is most certainly true.[1]

Here, certainly, is the Lutheran *Magna Charta* for calling believers in the Lord Jesus Christ to radical dependence on the Holy Spirit. It is a charter for the renewal of the church in every generation.

Aspects of Lutheran tradition that have not encouraged renewal

Lutheran teaching and tradition, especially when approached dogmatically rather than historically, have not always encouraged spiritual renewal. A mere glance at the history of the Lutheran church confirms this. Some elements of Lutheran tradition have been used, or misused, in a way that hinders spiritual awakening. These are painful to behold. They humble us and call us to repentance—to say with Nehemiah, "Yes, I and my father's house have sinned" (Neh. 1:6; also 9:2,16).

Luther's reaction to the enthusiasts *(Schwärmer)* of his day has had, over the centuries, a traumatic effect on Lutheranism. To this day it conjures up fears that we may get too much of the Holy Spirit.

The *sola scriptura* (Scripture alone) of the Reformation brought with it a wholesome regard for the authority of the Bible. What we have so often seen in practice, however, is that practical expectations get narrowed down to the single issue of salvation, which in popular understanding amounts to "getting my sins forgiven so I can go to heaven when I die." People are not encouraged to expect—in many cases are *discouraged* from expecting—many other things that the Word also speaks about. This became evident when the charismatic gifts first began to be experienced in Lutheran congregations in the early 1960s.[2]

Since the 17th century, scriptural interpretation has been dominated almost without interruption by an intellectual and academic approach. Interpretation anchored in life and spiritual experience has been dismally absent. The single bright exception in Lutheranism has been the much maligned Pietism.

The effect of this intellectual approach has been a highly articulated theology alongside spiritual life that is often stunted and immature. The gap between clergy and laity is one evidence of this. Misapplied emphasis on the "office" of the ordained ministry has throttled a healthy development of the priesthood of all believers, for which Luther strove. Despite lip service to the doctrine of the universal priesthood and token involvement of laity on boards and committees, the Lutheran church has not generally found a way to truly release its people into vital, Spirit-filled, Spirit-gifted ministry. We are a clergy-dominated church, with the clergy themselves often preoccupied with presiding over ecclesiastical machinery.

Another evidence is the generally low level of spirituality among baptized believers. The Lutheran church has continued to practice infant Baptism. It has not often succeeded, however, in bringing the baptized to spiritual maturity. It has not consistently taught them how to live out of the riches of their Baptism.

Lutheran theology makes much of the means of grace—the Word and the sacraments. Lofty appeals to the "means of grace," however, have often degenerated into theological sloganeering: it's a weapon that some Lutherans use to club away annoying testimonies about spiritual experience. The practical effect of such a narrow understanding of this term has been to limit our field of vision. We don't really look for the Holy Spirit to work except in immediate connection with hearing the Word and receiving the sacraments. Spiritual life becomes the servant of a narrow, intellectualist theology that disdains experience and piously limits the Holy Spirit to Word and sacrament. But what is authentic spiritual experience—divine guidance, healing, answered prayer, miracles, Spirit-led evangelism with signs and wonders following—but the outworking of the divine Word?

After one has read Luther's explanation to the Third Article of the Creed, it is painful to see among so many Lutheran Christians scant reference to the Holy Spirit or to the gifts of the Spirit.

The need for theological renewal

Many Lutheran charismatics believe that the church is flooded with pastors whose theological preparation consisted of turning in papers and passing exams. Some seminary professors are seen as practicing agnostics. The seminaries give their students little practical training in Christian living. Many graduates come into the parish ill-equipped to help people enter into lives of holiness and Spirit-empowered ministry. These pastors have learned something about historical and form criticism but devote little time to personal Bible study. They have garnered a smattering of psychological skills and jargon but frequently cannot minister God's power to the soul needs of their people. They have studied the original biblical languages, but by the admission of many, they do not know how to pray.

Charismatic Lutheran pastors see professionalism displacing spiritual formation in the preparation of the clergy; ministers view their calling as something they do rather than something they are, and so end up advocating something they themselves are not. It is a reborn scholasticism, not much changed from that which the Pietist leader Philip Jacob Spener critiqued:

> Though based on the Scriptures, it assumed the form of fixed dogmatic interpretation, rigid, exact, and demanding intellectual conformity. Emphasis was laid on pure doctrine and the sacraments, as constituting the sufficient elements of the Christian life. For that vital relationship between the believer and God which Luther had taught had been substituted very largely a faith which consisted in the acceptance of a dogmatic whole. The layman's role was largely passive; to accept the dogmas which he was assured were pure, to listen to their exposition from the pulpit, to partake of the sacraments and share in the ordinances of the church—these were the practical sum of the Christian life.[3]

Spener believed that good works should be the primary witness of Christians to those outside the faith. He denounced academic debate and intellectual argumentation as a poor method for training pastors. Far more effective for winning people to the faith, he believed, was the simple fruit of upright Christian living. He accused disputants of being interested in having people become indoctrinated Lutherans but not "genuine Christians to the core."

Many charismatic Lutheran pastors echo sentiments similar to those of Spener; they experienced their denominational seminaries primarily as "head centers," with strong emphasis on intellectual pursuits but little stress on the

development of piety and good works. Seminary life was presented and promoted in terms of academic preparation. The spiritual formation of the inner
person was either ignored or mildly ridiculed.[4]

The downplaying or ridicule of practical piety is often presented as an
expression of Luther's dictum, *simul justus et peccator*—we are at the same
moment justified and sinners. This is, to be sure, one of Luther's most pen-
etrating insights, but, to be true to Luther, it must be understood dialectically.
It does not mean that everything one does is a hopeless, indecipherable mixture
of sin and righteousness (though mixed motives and behavior are a reality),
but rather that in every moment of time, looked at from one side, I am a
sinner—"Nothing good dwells within me, that is, in my flesh" (Rom. 7:18)—
while looked at from another side I am fully justified, that is, united to Christ
by faith.

The potential of expressing either of these realities is present at every
moment of time. An alcoholic is always an alcoholic, even one that has been
dry for 13 years. As one man has put it, his sobriety does not come from a
strength within himself:

> It took me a couple of bad slips to teach me that I was still an alcoholic and
> always would be. If I wasn't drinking, it was only because I wasn't myself. I
> was in the hands of Another. And he wasn't thirsty![5]

This is quite different from dismissing or ridiculing the importance of sobriety,
or reckoning 13 years of sobriety as of little account. It is of great account,
for it represents the history of the Spirit's working.

Rethinking the way we do theology

The cleft that pastors and theologians often experience between academic
theology and the knowledge of God that they gain in personal devotions and
in the practical care of a congregation is echoed in the lives of the people. It
is a painful dichotomy that cuts through the life of many Christians who want
to be open *both* to the world of knowledge that God reveals to us through
the careful application of human reason, including the scholarly study of
Scripture, and the truth that God makes known to us through prayer, meditation, listening to the promptings of the Spirit within, and exercising the gifts
of the Holy Spirit.

The charismatic renewal has begun to explore ways of healing the split
between reason and experience. It sees that the church needs a theology that
results from a reasoned thinking through of the biblical faith. But it also sees
that this kind of theology must be done in the right context: the communal
life of the living church. The believing fellowship offers certain correctives

to the autocratic rule of reason: believing prayer, the exercise of spiritual gifts, true worship, and the testing of interpretations and proposals in the experience of the body of Christ.

Where Lutheran theology thwarts spiritual renewal, where the practice of theology has become too much a captive of the academic community, the charismatic renewal calls for the theological enterprise to forge closer links with the practicing, ministering fellowship of the church. This means more than expecting theological professors to be members of some local congregation or sending candidates into congregations for some months of practical training. It means a closer partnership between seminaries and congregations. It means a greater recognition of the gifts and ministries that the Holy Spirit distributes in a body of believers. It may call for a careful and critical look at the practical consequences of our present practice of ordination, the time-encrusted, encultured distinction between "clergy" and "laity" that is routinely deplored but seldom dealt with.

The charismatic renewal raises serious questions about the adequacy of the theological enterprise in which the church is engaged. Calling for more attention to "practical" training may provide a measure of relief, but it may also avoid part of the problem, which is a fundamental inadequacy in the way theology is "done." Pastoral candidates who have gone on a nonstop academic trip through high school, college, and theological seminary, with at best a smattering of leadership experience in the body of Christ, who then descend from the splendid isolation of theological seminaries into the hurly-burly of parish life, are often ill-equipped to give pastoral care and leadership to their people. The superficial observation is sometimes made by laity that these pastors are "too theological," by which they mean "not practical." It may be that these pastors are not theological enough: they approach theology with a crippling inability to pray, to recognize the leading of the Spirit, to deal with demonic oppression, to help people discover and use their spiritual gifts.

The living body of Christ, where the Spirit reigns in power, is the crucible in which sound theology must be formed. In this wholesome context the theologian must actively seek the spiritual support of the congregation, must expect the Spirit's guidance and wisdom, and thereby help to shape the church's thinking with useful answers and also new questions.

Doctrinal concerns in the charismatic renewal

The charismatic renewal has not addressed itself to doctrinal formulation in a comprehensive or systematic way. Rather, in keeping with its nature as a movement, it has stressed certain truths that appear to have been neglected in the church, or developed in a one-sided way.

It would be misleading to say that its experience has determined its theology; its commitment to the authority of Scripture is well-established. However, a variety of experiences and happenings have to some extent determined which doctrines charismatics have concentrated on. The doctrinal questions addressed in the next eight chapters reflect some of the most prominent issues that have arisen in the context of the charismatic renewal.

CHAPTER 30

THE NATURE OF GOD
AND THE NATURE
OF MAN

The nature of God

The charismatic renewal emphasizes the indivisible unity of the triune God. It opposes any *trichotomy* that would divide the Godhead in such a way that one of the persons is related to apart from the others.

It is true, of course, that sound doctrine makes a clear distinction between the Spirit, the Son, and the Father. Yet the Spirit's essential unity with the Father and the Son makes it impossible for us to have a proper relationship with him, or to experience him, without at the same time having Christ as Lord, and God as Father.

It is likewise impossible to have Christ without having the Spirit, who makes him really present and brings to reality his redeeming reign on earth. The charismatic renewal puts particular emphasis on the Holy Spirit, not to neglect the Son and the Father, but rather to point out the fact that it is the Spirit alone who brings people into a relationship with God, a relationship in which an awareness of each person of the Godhead goes hand in hand with a distinct emphasis on the oneness of God.

The Spirit brings an understanding of God in which both his holy *transcendence* and his loving *immanence* are emphasized. The holiness of God means that he is a consuming fire. He expresses himself in wrath against all sin and uncleanness. He stands in judgment against all who oppose him.

At the same time, in Christ his holy love extends unlimited and unconditional mercy to all who come to him in faith and repentance.

A doctrinally sound church avoids a notion of God that sees him only as the stern judge who in his majesty distributes impersonal justice. On the other hand, it eschews the caricature of a God who, in the name of love, and without regard to his holy will, treats saint and sinner completely alike.

God is not a mere fulfiller of human desires; he is not a God of permissive love who answers on man's terms to man's whim. He is the holy one, drawing us to himself and causing us to bow to his will as the sovereign Lord of all. He will not be trapped in words, but he will unfailingly keep his promises in his own way and his own time.

The Spirit alone can build a people who honor God as God, who respond to him in holy fear and loving faith.

The charismatic renewal has helped restore a balance to the doctrine of God. Dr. Johannes Hanselmann, Lutheran bishop of Bavaria, has pointed out that in the 20th century particularly, the doctrine of the Holy Spirit has been forced into the background.[1] In the early years of the century, nationalistic movements in Europe forced the church to grapple with the First Article of the Creed, the doctrine of God the Father. The work of Karl Barth and his followers focused on the Second Article, the doctrine of Christ.[2] A present-day emphasis on the Third Article, the doctrine of the Holy Spirit, does not detract from, but rather complements, attention that has been given to the other two articles.

The nature of man

Sound doctrine will avoid a one-sided or distorted view of man. The charismatic renewal has helped remind the church that man, as male and female, created in the image of God, is a whole, living being, a *unity* of body, soul, and spirit. This speaks, on the one hand, against a "spiritual" view of man that focuses narrowly on the need of his "soul" for salvation, and, on the other hand, against an unduly materialistic view that gives primary emphasis to meeting his physical or social needs.

Man stands before God as *totus homo,* a whole living being, both in his fallen state under the wrath of God and apart from Christ (Eph. 2:1-3), and as a raised and renewed person under the grace of God in Christ (Eph. 2:4-10). The Spirit shows that God's care and concern extend to the whole man.

The Spirit reaches out to embrace the total person with God's grace and power. It will affect life in its totality—the physical, emotional, social, intellectual, spiritual—all that the Spirit means to bring under the lordship of Christ. At any given time, the Spirit's work will focus on one or another aspect of life. That is the nature of his sanctifying work: it is progressive. But his long-range plan encompasses the whole of life.

During a theological consultation on the Holy Spirit sponsored by the Lutheran Council in the USA in the mid-1970s,[3] systematic theologian Warren Quanbeck made the observation that categories like *substance,* which theologians worked with when the Nicene Creed was being written, may not be as useful for communicating with people today; we may need to utilize other categories of thought and expression. Asked what category he might suggest, Quanbeck responded, "Perhaps a category like 'family' would be more useful in our day."[4]

When one experiences the reality of the Spirit as the personal God, it puts a new perspective on such fundamental concepts as sin and grace. They are understood as *relational* terms. They indicate one's position in relation to God. They are more a description of "where we stand" than of "what we are." They describe how we are relating to God, not what we are in ourselves. The idea that we have, or can have, existence apart from God is the devil's illusion. By the act of creation we are inexorably related to God—either in wrath or in love.

Man's primary problem is that he is alienated from God. He is without fear, love, or faith in relation to God. Disturbance or disharmony between different parts of his own being, between himself and others, or in a situation that he faces, are derivative problems. Only as the Spirit brings one into relationship with the redeeming presence of Christ will the healing power of God be able to effect fundamental changes in his life, his relationships, and his circumstances.

The Spirit does this in his own way, according to his own timetable, following his own priorities, working out the implications of his own understanding and wisdom. It is possible, for instance, to be right with God, to be "saved," yet still be sick in the body. However, as God's purpose of salvation overshadows the whole of one's life, the Spirit can create strong faith for healing from sickness. Paradoxically, the Spirit can also root down in the heart the conviction that the believer will be raised whole and perfect in the resurrection, whether or not he or she is healed in this life.

The old saw, "After all, I'm only human," needs a designation like *archaic* or *obsolete* in the lexicon of a Christian. When the apostle Paul said, "From now on we regard no one [who is a Christian] from a human point of view" (2 Cor. 5:16), he meant that we needed a new anthropology. The old assumptions about man were no longer valid.

The old anthropology sees man as a competent entity. His life is something that he himself can determine. If you want something of him, you must ask whether he has the will and ability and resources to do it. If you measure his life or his potential, it will be in terms of what he himself has done or is likely to do. Sociologically he may have relationships and commitments that link him to other people or institutions, but ultimately he is self-sufficient.

And then comes the gospel, with the dramatic announcement of a new humanity: "If any one is in Christ—a new creation!" (2 Cor. 5:17, literal translation). It's so radical that we can't handle it. We hang on to the familiar, old anthropology and try to use it to explain the new creation. We conceive of the new creation as a change in our human nature. We may reach for biblical terms: we are forgiven and cleansed from sin; we turn from our own ways to the ways of God; we are even filled and empowered by the Holy Spirit to live a new life. As a result, we think differently about people and life and things, and we act differently. We have new values, new goals, new commitments, new hopes and dreams. Surrounded by so much that is genuinely new, we scarcely notice that the way we think about ourselves remains fundamentally unchanged. New beliefs and attitudes and behavior there may be, but who is all this happening to? The same, old, self-sufficient individual— not a new creation at all, just an improved model of the old one.

Mere words like *commitment, discipleship,* and *lordship* do not make a new creation, not even if we back them up with exemplary action, not even if we say that it is all done by the grace of God and the power of the Holy Spirit—if we think of the grace and power as a "something" that we get into our possession to help us transform this self-sufficient old failure into a self-sufficient new success. Let us overstate the matter to bring out its radicality: the new creation does not change us one iota. We, that is our human natures, remain as we were. What changes is our bent toward self-sufficiency. Our life is joined to another, and therein lies the newness. *The new creation happens when we are joined to Christ in his death and resurrection.* The key word is *joined.* As Quanbeck suggested, we are taken into the divine family.

Of course, there is change, but it comes about because we are joined to Christ, not because we have been reconstituted as self-sufficient beings. What makes the new creation new is the fact that we can never again think of ourselves simply as ourselves. In the old anthropology there is a limited focus: life is defined in terms of the self-sufficient individual. In the new creation there is an expanded focus: life consists in two lives being united. We are new creatures not because of anything we are or have in ourselves but because our life is united to Christ's life.

The difference between the old anthropology and the new anthropology is like a scene in a great dance pavilion where people come to demonstrate their individual dancing skills. Each person dances alone. Some performances are of dazzling virtuosity; others quite mediocre; some little more than a stumbling attempt. Then, suddenly, a waltz is played and a *couple* glides out onto the floor. In this pavilion people have always thought of dancing as an individual performance. They have been intrigued by new steps and new dances, impressed by new routines. But here is something really new: "That couple—why, they dance *together*!"

This understanding is especially important when we try to understand the dynamics of the Christian life. If we stay with the old anthropology, we are in a continual debate over man's performance: what can he do, what should he do? The new anthropology gets us to asking what the *Lord* will do. For it is understood that when a couple dances, one shall lead and the other follow.

CHAPTER 31

JUSTIFICATION AND SANCTIFICATION

One of the theological issues that has been brought to the fore by the charismatic renewal is the relationship between justification and sanctification.[1] This has been a particular concern among Lutherans, because of the central role that justification plays in Lutheran theology.

Like the two natures of Christ, justification and sanctification cannot be separated, yet neither can they be mingled or confused. Christ always acted as the God-man. In him the divine and the human were inseparable. Yet we understand that his life was totally determined by divine initiative (see John 5:19; 12:49; Luke 22:42). Justification and sanctification could be thought of in a somewhat analogous way.

Both justification and sanctification describe the believer's relationship with Christ, each from a particular perspective. Justification tells us what the relationship is grounded on: the grace of God freely given in the cross of Christ. Sanctification tells us what happens in the relationship: by God's grace and power, his will is accomplished in us. Both of these are continuing, operative realities in the life of a believer. Although they cannot be separated from one another, we *understand* that justification is primary and foundational; sanctification is secondary and derivative. All that we are and all that we do as Christians is built on the foundation of being justified freely by God's grace in Christ. Only as we trust in the grace of God freely given in Christ will our lives be sanctified, that is, by the Spirit set apart, shaped, directed, and empowered to do God's will.

The spiritualists of Luther's day tended toward a dualistic understanding of life: inner versus outer, Spirit versus flesh, spirit versus letter. Karlstadt proclaimed that the external witness of Scripture is not necessary for those who have the inward testimony of the Spirit as it was promised by Christ. Müntzer said that whoever does not have the inward discernment and assurance of God's Spirit, regardless of the outer, is of the devil.

What aroused Luther's wrath, however, was not the idea of inner revelation, as such, but what he felt to be a displacement of justification by sanctification. The spiritualists saw salvation as a process by which the individual's intrinsic similarity to God is developed until "like is known by like." This led to an emphasis on inner regeneration assisted by a person's obedience and fulfillment of the law of God. Karlstadt understood Christian freedom not as being liberated from the condemnation of the law, but rather the enablement and consequent freedom to follow the law. The Spirit reveals the Scriptures as a guide and pattern for the individual's regeneration and a model for the church as a holy community. Then the Holy Spirit gives believers the power to live that Christ-like life; that is, sanctification.

Luther, on the other hand, grounded his whole understanding of sanctification in justification: he said all that may be said about man's holiness when he announced how the Holy Spirit makes the crucified and risen Christ truly present as a redeeming reality; this presence calls forth constant prayer to Christ and the constant work of love for the neighbor.[2] The Holy Spirit does not give us some kind of impersonal "power" by which we can successfully imitate Christ; he gives us Christ himself, so that "it is no longer I who live, but Christ who lives in me" (Gal. 2:20). Though Luther and the spiritualists, in one sense, looked for the same result—a life of true holiness—their understanding of the dynamic by which it would be wrought was stated differently. Karlstadt's focus was on the believer empowered by the Holy Spirit. Luther's focus was on a person's relationship with the living Christ, made effectual by the Spirit. The difference was a subtle one, and in the heat of controversy perhaps overdrawn, but the implications for pastoral care, for shepherding a person's growth in sanctification, can be important.

To focus on being empowered by the Holy Spirit may tilt one's thinking about sanctification toward the idea of the believer plus the Holy Spirit, which would be a form of works-righteousness, or synergism. A trickle-down version of this is the popular nostrum that "God helps those who help themselves." There can be a thread of validity in that, as a psychological description of sanctification. It may more or less accurately convey a person's subjective perception of a genuine experience of the Spirit. We must be on guard against measuring the validity of spiritual realities solely by the yardstick of a linguistically precise slogan. We can be talking about the same truth from varying perspectives.

Nevertheless, when theology is our task, we want to be as accurate and helpful as possible. Luther's concern to preserve the primary significance of justification can wonderfully vitalize our understanding and experience of sanctification. Sanctification that focuses on the believer in union with the dynamic, redeeming presence of Christ can help reinforce the sense of total dependence on Christ's redemption, not only in reference to the past and one's need for forgiveness, but also in reference to the present and the call to step forward into the "good works which God prepared beforehand, that we should walk in them" (Eph. 2:10). Sanctification, like justification, is altogether "by grace through faith."

It is at this point that the difference between the spiritualists of Luther's day and the present-day charismatic renewal comes most clearly into focus. Charismatics share a common concern with the spiritualists, namely, the concern for concrete, "incarnational" results. Justification should produce fruit. Of course, this was a concern of Luther as well.[3]

Where charismatics differ from the spiritualists, however, is in their understanding of how this happens. The spiritualists took issue with Luther's doctrine of justification because in their view it did not bring about either individual or corporate ethical renewal.[4] Müntzer accused Luther of preaching a "honey-sweet Christ" who called only for belief without works.[5] Charismatics, however, view the issue differently: it is not an overemphasis on justification but a deficient trust in the Holy Spirit in regard to sanctification that is the problem.

Charismatics side with Luther on the centrality of justification. Like Luther, they would hold the feet of spiritualists of every age to the fire until they deal with the basic question, What makes a person a Christian?[6] The keynote message at a Lutheran charismatic conference in California set this out with unmistakable clarity:

> Justification has to do with our citizenship in God's kingdom. How do we qualify?
> The royal edict on kingdom citizenship is this: it shall be a *free gift*. It includes a number of things. It includes sonship, forgiveness, righteousness, eternal life. And it is given freely—not a word in the Bible about earning or deserving it.
> Right here that Pretender [to the throne], the flesh, turns up and mounts his little eight-word assault, "*Let me tell you what I can do*. It's nice to receive grace, but I can add something to that. I can contribute something of my own to this business of salvation."
> This is a Pretender that God dealt with through the Reformers. They stood against this particular attempt of the Pretender to push Christ off the throne. They said, "We are not going to take part in this rebellion." In their documents they take an uncompromising stand against any pretender who would seek to add anything to Christ's work of redemption: "It is taught among us that we cannot obtain forgiveness of sin and righteousness before God by our own merits, works, or satisfactions, but that we receive forgiveness of sin and become righteous before God by grace, for Christ's sake, through faith, when we believe that Christ

suffered for us and that for his sake our sin is forgiven and righteousness and eternal life are given to us" (*The Augsburg Confession*).

This Pretender has been around a long time, and is still with us today. A few years ago a research project among Lutherans discovered that more than half of the Lutherans in the United States believe that their standing with God rests partially upon their own good works. This, in a church that takes its name from the man who raised up the standard of justification by *faith*!

When the issue is our justification, we have to quit telling God what we think we can do and listen when he tells us what he is ready to do. And what he is ready to do is justify us freely, for Christ's sake.[7]

A study conducted by Philip Gehlhar, a pastor of the Lutheran Church–Missouri Synod in the United States, indicates that Lutheran charismatics may be clearer on the issue of justification than the typical cross-section of Lutheran church members. The study indicated that charismatic Lutherans hold a sharper distinction between law and gospel, and a stronger belief in salvation by grace, than other Lutherans. The extent of the difference ranged as high as 40%.[8]

The problem comes when one stops with justification, when accepting the doctrine of justification in effect becomes the total description of Christian experience. Common sense alone tells us that describing Christianity solely in terms of *becoming* a Christian, or one's *standing* as a Christian is inadequate. There is also the business of *living* as a Christian, of *walking* as a Christian (Gal. 5:25).

But now comes the crucial transition: *How* are we to live this new life? Here the same dynamics that we encounter in justification come into play, but in a reverse order. In justification, the flesh seeks to *add* something to the work of Christ: salvation by grace *plus* good works, or experience, or right doctrine, or whatever. In sanctification, the flesh seeks to *subtract* something from the work of Christ: the holiness of Christ *minus* my weakness, or sin, or bad habits, or failures, or whatever.

It is the same basic issue viewed from two perspectives, and the answer is the same in both regards: *Christ is sufficient.* He is all-sufficient for my justification. He is all-sufficient for my sanctification.

Unlike the spiritualists of Luther's day, charismatics find no fault with Luther's doctrine of justification. But neither are they satisfied with the inadequate treatment of sanctification that developed in Lutheran orthodoxy. With Luther they insist that the dynamic of justification be extended into sanctification. The keynote address referred to above pointed out the parallel:

> Sanctification has to do with how we live our life, how we behave as citizens of God's kingdom. This gets right down to the daily business of how we treat members of our family, how we manage our finances, how we drive on the freeway, how we pray, how we help those in need.

The royal edict on kingdom living is, "Be perfect, as your heavenly Father is perfect" (Matt. 5:48).

That life which is planted in us as a free gift has a way of expressing itself. It expresses itself in obedience. Paul said that he was given his apostleship "to bring about the obedience of faith" (Rom. 1:5; 16:26).

How are we able to do this? In the gift of eternal life we receive the Holy Spirit as our enabler, giving us the power to live the life that he calls us to live. "God has done what the law, weakened by the flesh, could not do: sending his own Son in the likeness of sinful flesh and for sin, he condemned sin in the flesh, in order that the just requirement of the law might be fulfilled in us, who walk not according to the flesh [not in the tracks of the Pretender], but according to the Spirit [subjects of the Rightful King]" (Rom. 8:3-4).

Here again the Pretender mounts his little eight word assault, *"Let me tell you what I can do.* You can't expect me to be perfect, but I'll do my best." This is the Pretender that God has had to deal with down through the history of the church. The apostle Paul speaks to the people who are thinking about these things. "Since we are saved by grace, shall we sin the more that grace may abound?" (Rom. 6:1).

This old Pretender is a sly fox. He will actually make his bid for the throne disguised as an ally of the Rightful King. You will hear him say things like this: "If you stress obedience and righteousness too much it undercuts grace, and we want to live by grace." That is a phony claim. Because the God who offers free, unmerited grace is the same God who calls for unconditional obedience. It's the Pretender who tries to water down grace in justification, and obedience in sanctification.

When the issue is our sanctification, we have to quit telling God what we can or cannot do in our own strength and let him tell us what he can do; and that is to call us and empower us to live lives of righteousness and holy obedience.[9]

It is a mistaken critique to charge charismatics generally with giving the doctrine of justification short shrift.[10] The problem, rather, is a distorted perception that crops up again and again in orthodox Lutheranism: the emphasis on justification becomes so dominant that a shadow of works-righteousness is cast over the whole of sanctification.[11] The practical result is that the work of Christ gets narrowed down to forgiveness and nothing more: "If God will just forgive my sin and take me to heaven, I can expect nothing more."[12]

Charismatics take issue with such a view—not by detracting from the doctrine of justification, but by calling attention to a deficient doctrine of the Holy Spirit as it relates to sanctification. One Lutheran charismatic leader said, "There is nothing more in salvation than Jesus, but there is more in Jesus than salvation."[13]

Justification and sanctification participate in the same reality, which is Christ himself. The Holy Spirit does not bring Christ in for a short visit so he can drop off a load of forgiveness and be on his way again—leaving us with a fond memory of his visit so that we will be thankful, and act accordingly, the rest of our lives. That would put the whole enterprise of sanctification back under the law. Rather, the Holy Spirit unites our life with Christ's life, ending once and for all our self-sufficient existence—the self-sufficient life that rebels against God, or the self-sufficient life that attempts to serve God in its own strength; it is all one. And so is the life of faith all one. The faith that trusts him for forgiveness is of a piece with the faith that trusts him for holiness. We can neither add to the forgiveness nor subtract from the holiness that he gives us. What the blood is to our past, the Holy Spirit is to our future: the power of Christ that overcomes the power of sin.

Our thought life and prayer life often fail to grasp and experience this reality. The natural mind reasserts itself. We pray and plan and work as though our prayers and plans and work build the kingdom. We may give credit to God for giving us the grace and power to do it, but we nevertheless end up glorying in the doing. But if we are beholding Christ, then we realize that he has already built the kingdom. We desire only to see it manifested. If we extend the dynamic of justification into sanctification, then the essence of the Christian life is not *doing* my thing for God, but rather *discovering* what God has already done in Christ, and walking in it (Eph. 2:10).

It is from this standpoint that the practical teaching on guidance which we find in the charismatic renewal takes on added significance. How a work is initiated becomes crucially important. If we initiate it ourselves, if it is in essence a self-chosen work, then we have taken authority back into our own hands and we are operating in the flesh. But if the Spirit is able to guide us to the work that God has prepared beforehand for us to walk in, then we can step out in obedience and in faith, trusting God for the results.

CHAPTER 32

THE THEOLOGY
OF THE CROSS

The new life is hidden in Jesus, under the veil of his humanity. There it must be sought and continually refreshed. To experience the essence of forgiveness is not to feel mere psychological relief from guilt but to cling to the cross and to the blood even though all feelings and evidence at the moment be contrary. Likewise, to experience the essence of holiness is not merely to experience virtue or victory, but to cling to the risen Christ even though all immediate appearances be to the contrary—habits slow to change, prayers going unanswered, ministry bogged down and going nowhere.

Charismatics have been faulted for having a theology of glory rather than a theology of the cross. In fact, the charismatic renewal has thrown fresh light on the theology of the cross by insisting that spiritual experience must be understood in relation to the real and objective working of the Holy Spirit, and not simply in terms of certain outward acts or inner responses. As Regin Prenter wrote, "Wherever in theology the Holy Spirit is taken seriously into account, we are not dealing with the theology of glory but with the theology of the cross."[1]

The heart of a theology of the cross was stated by Luther in the explanation to Thesis 21 of the Heidelberg Disputation:

> He who does not know Christ does not know God hidden in suffering. Therefore he prefers works to suffering, glory to the cross, strength to weakness, wisdom to folly, and, in general, good to evil. There are people whom the apostle calls "enemies of the cross of Christ" [Phil. 3:18], for they hate the cross and suffering and love works and the glory of works. . . . It is impossible for a person not to be puffed up by his good works unless he has first been deflated and destroyed by suffering and evil until he knows that he is worthless and that his works are not his but God's.[2]

A theology of glory glories in what we do. The theology of the cross glories in what Christ does.

What we do is open to inspection and understanding. There is nothing mysterious about it. Think for a moment of self-sufficient religious men or women. They act with wisdom or virtue; they do well; they love and serve with distinction. A theology of glory steps in and says that such behavior figures large in God's kingdom. That is its error. The flaw in a theology of glory is that it believes flesh and blood *can* inherit the kingdom (cf. John 3:3; 1 Cor. 15:50). The theology of glory does not see how radically human presumption has been dealt with in the cross.

A theology of the cross begins and ends with Christ. What Christ has done has kingdom validity. What happens in Christ and through Christ has kingdom meaning and kingdom force. At this point someone might object, "Then why not call it a theology of *Christ?*" This is where Luther's insight comes into sharpest focus. It *is* a theology of Christ. But how do we *know* Christ, how do we *experience* Christ, how do we *serve* Christ? Always under the veil of his—and our—humanity. It is in the shadow of the cross that we meet Christ, and it is through the cross that we minister in his name. This is experience, profound experience, and one enters into it only and always by the working of the Holy Spirit.

It is a paradox. As mere human beings we are helpless and weak; worse, we are spiritually dead. We need new life from God. But we do not find it by vaulting out of our human predicament, thereby coming into blessed and unbroken communion with God, experiencing his new life as strength and power in everything we do. No, paradoxically, we experience the new life as we are led by the Spirit yet further into weakness and helplessness by being joined to Christ in his humiliation and shame on the cross, and only then being raised with him (Phil. 3:8-11).

Those who fault the charismatic renewal for spreading a theology of glory may not realize how deeply charismatic experience is rooted in weakness and helplessness. A Lutheran laywoman said, "Every time I speak in tongues it is a humiliation, a reminder of my weakness." A group of lay people in a Lutheran congregation, who had a ministry of counseling and prayer, summarized their experience this way:

A person comes to you with a problem. You sense in yourself an emptiness. You realize that you have nothing to give this person. You are helpless. In your helplessness you cry out [inwardly] to God. Like the "friend at midnight," you ask for something to give to this one in need. God imparts through you a word of wisdom—maybe a vision or picture or inward impression—which helps that person. Maybe you realize at the time what the Lord is doing, but maybe not. You may have to live with the thought that you blew it, and only find out months later that the person was actually helped. (And then, sometimes, you actually *do* blow it!)

When the next person comes, you are right back to the point of emptiness and helplessness and crying out to the Lord again.[3]

A theology of the cross despairs of every situation *apart from the Lord.* One is like the psalmist, who sees himself surrounded by enemies:

In thee, O Lord, do I seek refuge;
let me never be put to shame;
in thy righteousness deliver me!
Incline thy ear to me,
    rescue me speedily!
Be thou a rock of refuge for me,
    a strong fortress to save me!
Yea, thou art my rock and my fortress;
    for thy name's sake lead me and guide me,
take me out of the net which is hidden for me,
    for thou art my refuge.
Into thy hand I commit my spirit;
    thou hast redeemed me, O Lord, faithful God (Ps. 31:1-5).

The psalmist recognized that personally he was no match for his adversaries. It was not by his own might or power, but by the intervention of God, that he would prevail. To be in such a position is the essence of the *cross:* Jesus spoke the words of this psalm as he hung on the cross.

To be always at the mercy of strong enemies, except for the Lord, is to despair of anything I might do, and reckon only on what the Lord will do. "I am weak, but thou art mighty, hold me with thy powerful hand!" The theology of the cross results in strength out of weakness; a theology of glory results in weakness out of (presumed) strength.

Some theologians tend to link a theology of glory primarily with such things as healings, miracles, and answered prayer, and at this point many fault the charismatic renewal: its emphasis on power and victory over difficulties, they say, is evidence that the renewal does not have a theology of the cross.[4] In actual practice this criticism has some validity. The strong emphasis on answered prayer and miracles has led to a certain amount of self-centeredness in the charismatic renewal. A number of charismatic leaders have spoken out against a shallow, "bless me" mentality that one frequently encounters in the renewal.

To identify either the theology of the cross or a theology of glory simply with outward or inward circumstances, however, is to miss the point. It is a question rather of whether one's life and ministry center and rest in Jesus or in oneself.[5] If a woman prays for a member of her prayer group, and the person is healed and there is great rejoicing, that fact alone does not tell us that the woman is living by a theology of glory. If she has prayed in obedience to the Spirit, recognizes the healing as Christ's gracious intervention, and continues to look only to him, she will remain under the cross because she recognizes that it was his work, not hers. In the face of the next sickness that she encounters in her ministry of healing, she will be as helpless and beleaguered by doubt as ever, looking to Christ alone.

It may be somewhat more natural to look to Christ and cry out to him in a circumstance of deep distress. On the other hand, it may be easy, when things go well and prayers are answered, to *presume* that we ourselves have things well in hand. But this, according to Scripture, is a delusion:

> As for me, I said in my prosperity,
>   "I shall never be moved."
> By thy favor, O Lord,
>   thou hadst established me as a strong mountain;
> thou didst hide thy face,
>   I was dismayed (Ps. 30:6-7).

God has only to hide his face, and the delusion of a theology of glory is exposed. The cross is a way of life that transcends circumstances, good or bad; it is a place of total and continual dependence on Christ *in any and all circumstances.* Except for him we are lost, helpless, and utterly at the mercy of our enemies—not only in regard to our own salvation, but in regard to our daily life and ministry.

The cross is the sign *par excellence* of our Christian life, for it shows our utter helplessness, the imminent triumph of our foes *except for the intervention of God.* If a "victory" takes us away from the cross, it is only because the eyes of the flesh have taken over and we do not see the true shape of our existence, which is still ringed about with enemies, still needing to cry out to the Lord.

In some ways it might actually be easier, from a human point of view, to live a theology of the cross in times of adversity, because our sense experience corresponds to or reinforces our state of dependence on the Lord. When outward circumstances seem to be going well, our sense experience can more easily deceive us as to our real condition, which is still one of total dependence on Christ, still at the mercy of enemies, except for him.

You never outgrow the weakness. In the scheme of this world, success breeds confidence, and confidence produces more success. It's an upward journey. But in the kingdom, the cross remains at the center. God may have manifested wisdom, healing, and miracles through you for 30 years, but today you find yourself back at square one again, weak and helpless, clinging to

Christ with empty hands. Luther's last written words were, "We are beggars; this is true."[6]

A gentle warning is in order at this point. There can be a subtle concession to the flesh in the theology of the cross if the personal or subjective dynamics are overstressed—the weakness, helplessness, suffering, and inner conflict (1 Cor. 13:3). Luther's own presentation runs the danger of being misunderstood as a subtle form of *imitatio* piety: inner conflict and suffering become the way that the flesh chooses to imitate Christ and obtain the favor of God. A true theology of the cross accepts adversity when God gives it as his appointed means and place of revelation, but it does not pander to the flesh's desire to make a TV documentary out of all its little struggles. Bob Mumford put it well: "When you go through a storm, it's important not to spend the rest of your life talking about it."[7] Such ego-gratifying talk can undergird a theology of glory.

Compared to the reality of Christ, our struggles are little. The cross itself was "little" to Christ, compared to that which it brought forth. Consider Jesus, "who for the joy that was set before him endured the cross, despising the shame, and is seated at the right hand of the throne of God" (Heb. 12:2; also Rom. 8:18).

From the cross flows the whole life and kingdom rule of Christ, and that—not our subjective struggles—should chiefly occupy our attention.

The problem of Antinomianism

The justified sinner who is forgiven and declared righteous for Christ's sake receives a new life. The redeeming presence of Christ, with his "alien righteousness," indwells the believer, through the working of the Holy Spirit. Living in union with Christ, he or she is brought into a new life of holiness. Christ, who lives within by the Spirit, day by day conforms the believer to his own image (2 Cor. 3:12-18).

Apart from this faith relationship with the indwelling Christ, we have no righteousness, no new life, no strength, no hope. We do not receive "righteousness" or "new life" as something that we then control and operate. We receive Christ by faith, and he *is* our wisdom, righteousness, sanctification, and redemption (1 Cor. 1:30).

The object of the Christian life, very simply, is the rule of Christ, which means the denial of self-rule—or, as the apostle Paul put it, to live by the Spirit rather than the flesh (Gal. 5:25).

While Luther sought to preserve the biblical understanding of justification, in his treatise *On the Councils and the Church* he spoke out strongly against those who separate justification from sanctification:

> That is what my antinomians, too, are doing today, who are preaching beautifully (as I cannot but think) with real sincerity about Christ's grace, about the

forgiveness of sin and whatever else can be said about the doctrine of redemption. But they flee as if it were the very devil the consequence that they should tell the people about the third article, of sanctification, that is, of the new life in Christ.

They think one should not frighten or trouble the people, but rather always preach comfortingly about grace and forgiveness of sins in Christ, and under no circumstances use these or similar words, "Listen! You want to be a Christian and at the same time remain an adulterer, a whoremonger, a drunken swine, arrogant, covetous, a usurer, envious, vindictive, malicious, etc.!"

Instead they say, "Listen! Though you are an adulterer, a whoremonger, a miser, or other kind of sinner, if you but believe, you are saved, and you need not fear the law. Christ has fulfilled it all!"

Tell me, my dear man, is that not granting the premise [Easter] and denying the conclusion [Pentecost]? It is, indeed . . . taking away Christ and bringing him to nought at the same time he is most beautifully proclaimed! And it is saying yes and no to the same thing. For there is no Christ that died for sinners who do not, after forgiveness of sins, desist from sins and lead a new life. . . . They may be fine Easter preachers, but they are very poor Pentecost preachers, for they do not preach about the sanctification of the Holy Spirit but solely about the redemption of Jesus Christ, although Christ . . . did not earn only grace for us, but also the gift of the Holy Spirit, so that we might have not only forgiveness of, but also cessation of, sin.

Now he who does not abstain from sin, but persists in his evil life, must have a different Christ, that of the Antinomians; the real Christ is not there, even if all the angels would cry, "Christ! Christ!" He must be damned with this, his new Christ. . . . But our Antinomians fail to see that they are preaching Christ without and against the Holy Spirit because they propose to let the people continue in their old ways and still pronounce them saved. And yet logic, too, implies that a Christian should either have the Holy Spirit and lead a new life, or know that he has no Christ.[8]

This statement of Luther met with a chorus of assent when it was quoted at a session of an International Lutheran Charismatic Leaders' Meeting in Finland in the summer of 1981.[9] There was a general perception that this depicted a situation present in the churches today, and any presentation of the work of the Holy Spirit must speak in a responsible way to this issue.

An emphasis on the lordship of Christ, with a clear call to obedience, has been a hallmark of the charismatic renewal. It is not understood within the renewal, however, as jettisoning justification for sanctification, but rather as a question of emphasis and balance, as one young charismatic Lutheran pastor stated in a pastoral letter to his congregation:

An imbalance has come into Lutheran theology. The imbalance is in the understanding of grace. A doctrine that sees little room for human response to divine initiative must settle for a grace that can forgive but cannot enable. God comes off looking like a coach whose team keeps losing. But that's all right—he's a forgiving coach. He talks little about discipline, about giving it all you've got, about the possibility of having a winning season. He doesn't lay anything heavy on his players. His training standards are low. His redeeming quality as a coach is that he's nice. When his players consistently lose he isn't hard on them.

Contrast this with the New Testament concept of grace. Grace according to St. Paul is the power that enables us to live the way God wants us to live. God doesn't change his absolute standards—but he supplies the power by which those standards can be met. New Testament grace goes beyond forgiveness into enablement. God is interested in doing much more than merely forgiving his people— he wants to change them. He wants to enable them to reach their destiny in Christ. Grace is what makes that possible.[10]

The Spirit teaches the church that justification promises more than a mere forensic act accomplished in heaven. It also promises a real beginning of renewal of our relation to God here on earth, whereby through faith we come to share Christ's own life and righteousness. Nor is justification related merely to the past, a once-for-all event. The righteousness of Christ is continuously imputed to the believer. It is the ever-present, ever-effectual ground of our right standing with God. It is the ground of our every action. We can take steps of obedience only because by faith we know that our whole life— including this act of obedience that the Holy Spirit now sets before us—is ordained by God and accepted by God.

A Christian's whole life and ministry is rooted in justification by grace through faith alone; and sanctification is a day-by-day manifestation of that reality by the working of the Holy Spirit. A doctrinally sound church is taught by the Spirit to see both justification and sanctification as gifts of God to be received by faith.

CHAPTER 33

THE KINGDOM
AND THE CHURCH

The kingdom of God

Charismatic experience results in a new awareness of the kingdom of God as a living, present reality. In its most primary sense, Christian experience is a foretaste of the kingdom. Signs and wonders are an integral part of the coming of the kingdom (Matt. 11:2-15; 6:10; John 14:12-14; Acts 1:6-8; 1 Cor. 2:4-5; 4:20; Gal. 3:3-5; 1 Thess. 1:5; Heb. 6:4-6; Mark 16:14-20).[1] They are not limited to the apostolic age. They are for us today also.

The significance of kingdom as a biblical category is well established, but its practical significance is an area still calling for theological spade work. The concepts "church" and "kingdom" are frequently used more or less synonymously, even though the New Testament has no tendency in this direction.[2] Is the common understanding of "gospel" identical with what the New Testament means by "gospel of the kingdom"? Bob Mumford hinted at a practical aspect of such questions with his description of the spread of the gospel in the New Testament: "What they preached was the kingdom; what they got was the church."[3] If you preach the church, you are likely to get a yawn or a squabble.

Charismatics have tended to use "kingdom" language in a fairly general sense, to contrast with "world" or simply with the status quo. For example, they will describe parish renewal as a movement "from democracy to kingdom." This may be a helpful way of communicating some important and fundamental changes in the way a congregation functions, but theologically it is not precise. More work needs to be done to draw out the meaning of the kingdom concept and its practical implications for ministry.

At the same time, the Spirit points us to the glorious and perfect fulfillment of the kingdom at the second coming of Christ (Rom. 8:18-25). The kingdom will never be fully realized until the last day, at the resurrection of the body and the renewal of the whole creation.

The church

In the final report of the Geneva Conference on questions concerning charismatic renewal (March 8-13, 1980), these things were named as elements of a renewed and unified church:

- New openness toward the healing power and the lordship of Jesus;
- Renewal of spiritual life of the church in its local congregations;
- Spontaneity, openness, freedom, and joy in praise and worship;
- New interest in the Bible as God's living Word;
- Deeper experience of the reality, holiness, and transcendence of God;
- Deeper interest and new openness in regard to the essential doctrines of the Trinity, the divinity of Christ, his death and resurrection, confirmed in experience;
- Renewal of the service of healing for the sick;
- Lay leadership;
- New incentive for evangelization, missions, and witness in the power of the Spirit.[4]

These are all marks of the church in the New Testament. The dynamic of the church, as it confronts us from the perspective of the New Testament, is challenging, even disconcerting. It presents itself to us as a sort of spiritual measuring stick. Because God remains true to himself, the goal of renewing contemporary Christianity will be nothing short of this: its participation in the spiritual reality from which the New Testament church draws its life. But what does that mean?

It is not without some hesitation that one reflects on the New Testament church. First of all, however, we should be aware of three possible dangers:

1. *The danger of idealization.* From Matthew's gospel to the Revelation of John, the church of Jesus Christ is admonished, warned, and criticized. Specific misdeeds and sins within the church are named. It is obvious to every reader of the New Testament that the congregations of that time were not perfect congregations. We should not idealize them.

2. *The danger of harmonization.* Biblical research has brought to light a great variety of approaches to congregational life and theology. The church at Jerusalem differed from the church at Corinth, and both of these were in many respects unlike the congregations addressed in the Pastoral Epistles. Some biblical scholarship may overemphasize these differences to the point

that any sense of unity nearly disappears, yet one thing is clear: *the* pattern for a New Testament church has never existed. Variety can add great richness to the church. It would impoverish the church to set forth one expression of primitive Christian church life as normative for all expressions.

3. The danger of ecclesiological fundamentalism. The danger inherent in every form of fundamentalism lies in the failure to take historical distance seriously. It seeks to recapture the truth in the same form in which it was cast by the biblical texts. Ecclesiological fundamentalists leap over 2000 years of church history in an attempt to refashion the church today after "the model of the primitive church." In effect, they discount the work of the Holy Spirit during the whole history of the church.

The Spirit is concerned to point out to us not simply the form or forms of the church that we see in the New Testament but also the *essence* of the church. Certainly what God did at the beginning has a unique place in our understanding of the church, and it is often the task of a renewal movement to remind the church of its origins, as the prophets reminded Israel of the exodus and Sinai. The origins of the church, as recorded in Scripture, provide valuable insight into God's purpose and plan for the church. Most especially, they remind us of God's faithfulness and provision, and call forth a response of faith. But God wants to lead the church not simply back to its beginnings but forward to its fulfillment. In this there can and should be a thoughtful appreciation for the ways in which the Holy Spirit has enriched the church through the centuries, yet an openness to what he wants to do today.

Metaphors for the church in the New Testament take various forms. Some terms relate particularly to Christ: "body of Christ" or "bride"; some to the Spirit: "temple of the Holy Spirit"; some to the Father: "people of God," "household of God," and "church of God." A biblical understanding of the church will be clearly trinitarian.

It is no accident, however, that the ancient creeds mention the church in the Third Article, in direct connection with the Holy Spirit. This reflects the church's awareness that only by the working of the Holy Spirit can the church live under the lordship of Christ to the glory of God the Father.

The charismatic renewal has given expression to this in highly practical ways. Making room in liturgical services for free charismatic expression— prophecy, tongues, testimony, prayer for the sick with the laying on of hands— is one example of this. Another is the attention given to divine guidance in and for a congregation. One of the workshops at the Fifteenth International Lutheran Conference on the Holy Spirit in Minneapolis, Minnesota, in 1986, for instance, carried this title and description:

> *Discerning God's Will in the Church Council.* Pastors and layleaders: How do you feel the morning after a Church Council meeting? All too often Church

Councils can get bogged down in just the "machinery" of church life. We need to give top priority to *discovering and responding to God's will,* if we are to lead a congregation into real spiritual renewal. This workshop will focus on practical helps for structuring the prayer, relationships, meetings, and work of the Church Council in ways that will make "Thy Will Be Done" a dynamic reality in the congregation.

This kind of practical dependence on the Holy Spirit does not deny, but rather illustrates, the fact that everything that the Spirit does in and through the church is based on the saving act of Jesus Christ. The Holy Spirit can only reveal what God has already actually and without qualification done in Jesus Christ; he can only develop what is already given in Jesus Christ. The Spirit stands in the service of Christ and the eschatological reality brought through him and present in him.

The New Testament often describes the relationship between Jesus Christ and his church in terms of contrast: shepherd/flock, bridegroom/bride, master/disciples, lord/servants. Other statements describe the relationship in terms of organic unity: vine-branches, head-body.

Both of these emphases are important. On the one hand, the church must see itself as over against Christ, responsible to him, submitted to his lordship. The frequent reference to the lordship of Christ in the charismatic renewal answers to this reality. On the other hand, the church must see itself as one with Christ: it has no life of its own apart from the life that Jesus Christ himself possesses. The church possesses nothing that does not belong to the substance of Jesus Christ, who came in the flesh, was crucified, and rose from the dead. The very being of the church consists in being in Christ, but this becomes reality only as the church lives in absolute dependence on the Holy Spirit.

Just as God expects nothing from individual believers other than that which they are already in Christ, so he expects nothing from the church as a whole other than what it already is in Christ. In Jesus Christ the life of the kingdom has already begun. Individual believers are drawn into this reality by the Holy Spirit through faith and Baptism. The Holy Spirit labors so that Jesus Christ may be fully formed in the church (Gal. 4:19).

It is all too easy to borrow an ideal for the church from some element in the surrounding culture: in times past, the Roman province, the feudal fief, or the town meeting; in our time, the successful corporation, the accepting fellowship, the counseling clinic, or the service agency. Any ideal for the church is irrelevant unless it clearly has its roots in the new life in Jesus

Christ. On the other hand, whatever is given by God in Jesus Christ *ought* to come to visible manifestation in the church, even if such manifestations have been absent for centuries.

CHAPTER 34

BAPTISM

A vivid experience of the Holy Spirit can be like a new beginning of the Christian life. When Luther described his own famous "tower experience," he said that he felt as if his soul were born anew.[1] The natural result of such an experience is the impulse toward commitment, a desire to make a radical break with the past and live for God in a new way.

What is at work here is the reality of one's Baptism: one's death and resurrection with Christ is taking place at the level of more conscious experience. The Holy Spirit is bringing the reality of one's Baptism into focus, whether one was baptized as an infant or later. An experience of the Holy Spirit is not a call to be rebaptized but to live in the reality of one's Baptism.

The Spirit leads us to think soundly. He grafts believers into the body of Christ in Baptism (1 Cor. 12:13). He does not repeat this work every time a believer has a vivid experience of the Spirit's life and power (Rom. 11:29). The church correctly interpreted the sense of Scripture when it confessed at Nicaea, "I believe in *one* Baptism for the remission of sins."

A man who was planning to join a charismatic Lutheran church in the United States told the pastor that he had been baptized four times, and wondered whether this presented any problem. He had been baptized as an infant in the Roman Catholic Church, baptized as a teenager in a nondenominational church, baptized in the armed services after a conversion experience, and baptized in an ecumenical prayer group after experiencing the baptism with the Holy Spirit. The pastor did not make a big issue of it. "The way I see it," he said, "you had one Baptism and three baths."

Behind that seemingly offhand response, however, lay some intense prayer and study as to the purpose and effect of Baptism. What began as an inquiry into the early church's practice of Baptism led to the realization that the overriding reality is simply the fact that *God acts in Baptism*.[2] Once that is established, a sound practice of Baptism can follow.

Infant Baptism

With our emphasis on faith in connection with Baptism and receiving the gift of the Holy Spirit, the question of infant Baptism naturally arises. Should infant Baptism be practiced? Does God grant the Holy Spirit in infant Baptism?

As is well known, the question of adult or infant Baptism is not explicitly dealt with in Scripture. The baptisms described in the New Testament were primarily baptisms of believing adults, though there is a possibility that sometimes children may also have been included (Acts 11:14; 16:33). The same thing is true today where the church is in a first-generation missionary situation: the most frequent form of Baptism is adult Baptism, even in churches that practice infant Baptism. One does not normally baptize children of non-Christian parents. The basic framework for New Testament teaching on Baptism, therefore, is the practice of adult Baptism in a predominantly pagan culture. However, if infant Baptism has been practiced from earliest times, and even by the apostles, the church must have had good reasons to do so.[3]

Infant Baptism and new life

There seem to be two basic reasons for infant Baptism. First, God has sovereignly made Baptism an integral part of Christian initiation. The Spirit is active in Baptism. In and by the Spirit, forgiveness of sin and new life are united to Baptism (cf. Acts 2:38; 22:16; Eph. 5:26; 1 Cor. 6:11; Gal. 3:27; Col. 2:11-14; Titus 3:5; 1 Peter 3:21). Through the new birth in Baptism a person enters the kingdom of God (John 3:3, 5).

Second, even small children have the need and the right to enter the kingdom of God. Jesus' words speak of the necessity for children to be born into the kingdom: "Let the children come to me, and do not hinder them, for to such belongs the kingdom of heaven" (Matt. 19:14). Jesus did *not* say that the children automatically belong to the kingdom, that they are born into the kingdom by natural birth. He said that the kingdom belongs to such; that is, the kingdom is meant for children. They are brought into the kingdom by being brought to Jesus. If Scripture points to nothing other than Baptism as the objective point of entry into the kingdom, then it seems unnatural to withhold it from children who are being raised in a Christian home. The argument that children cannot respond in faith does not rest on a secure biblical foundation.[4] Children have been baptized in the Christian community from the earliest times. "History," as one writer has said, "is a friend of infant baptism."[5]

Even if children do not have a conscious, articulate faith such as adults have, this is not a hindrance to their being accepted into the kingdom, that is, being saved. Where he does not encounter resistance, the Holy Spirit is well able to kindle faith and unite a person to Christ, whether adult or child. Not the innocence of the children but their helplessness and dependence on God for their salvation makes them fit for the kingdom. In their dependency they receive the kingdom when they are brought to Jesus and received by him.

As they grow up, their unconscious dependence on Jesus grows into a conscious dependence. Like physical life, spiritual life must grow and mature. What begins in Baptism must come to open, conscious expression.

Baptism regularly includes prayers for the Holy Spirit and his gifts, and that needs to be taken seriously.[6] A Lutheran congregation in North Carolina allows for prayer in tongues at the baptism of infants, and finds that many of these children begin speaking in tongues at a very early age.[7]

Of course, people can deliberately leave God or fall away from him after Baptism. They must be brought back to repentance and faith. They do not need to be rebaptized, for God's promises at their Baptism are still valid. Through faith they can reenter the kingdom and receive the gifts of the kingdom once again. In this sense, there is certainly a place for preaching *conversion* to baptized Christians.

Infant Baptism and the gift of the Holy Spirit

Do children receive the gift of the Holy Spirit when they are baptized? As we have seen, the primary focus in Acts is on the conscious experience and manifest demonstration of the Spirit in a believer's life. Scripture does speak of even very small children manifesting the Spirit (Luke 1:15,41; cf. Ps. 8:2; 22:9-10). While this does happen from time to time in charismatic circles, it is not yet the common experience in connection with infant Baptism.

Receiving the Spirit in the New Testament was normally a *conscious* and indeed a *manifest* experience. Accordingly, just as a little girl baptized in infancy should be encouraged to take the conscious step of faith whereby she personally appropriates and confesses her calling as a child of God, so should she be encouraged to pray that Jesus would confirm her calling by filling her with the Holy Spirit so that she can be an effective witness.

This, in effect, has been the historic focus of the Lutheran practice of confirmation—in liturgy, if not in fact:

> The Father in Heaven, for Jesus' sake, renew and increase in thee the gift of the Holy Ghost, to thy strengthening in faith, to thy growth in grace, to thy patience in suffering, and to the blessed hope of everlasting life.[8]

Our life in Christ is dependent on the Holy Spirit from beginning to end, and his working is appropriate at every stage of our life and walk.

CHAPTER 35

GOD'S FATHERLY
PROVISION

Closely connected with the charismatic renewal's emphasis on the present reign of God is a revitalized faith in such things as his guidance and direction, his healing power, and his fatherly willingness to provide for our material needs. Blessing is not only "spiritual." God touches and blesses every aspect of our lives. At root the Spirit is renewing the classical faith in the providence of God.

Guidance

A Lutheran lay leader in Germany said that the most important aspect of charismatic renewal for him was the experience of divine guidance. He was a man with wide-ranging family, church, and business responsibilities. He had experienced a marked conversion through the ministry of the Marburger Kreis, the German expression of the Oxford Group Movement, so he was no stranger to daily Bible reading and prayer, meaningful fellowship, and active participation in the life of the church. Yet, in common with many Christians, he had not seriously reckoned with the possibility of actually knowing the will of God in regard to the basic life decisions that one must make. This became a reality after his experience of being filled with the Spirit. It did not make decisions easier—if anything, they became more difficult. But the way of approaching them was different: discerning the will of God became the first consideration rather than a prayer tacked on at the end of the process.[1]

This kind of testimony has been widely repeated throughout the charismatic renewal. One of the fundamental convictions of the movement is that God still speaks to people today as he did in Bible times.[2] Such gifts as prophecy, a word of wisdom, and a word of knowledge often come to practical application at the point of guidance.

In the charismatic renewal, teaching on divine guidance is usually rich in anecdotes, based on paradigms or analogies drawn from Scripture. Witness predominates over exhortation. Whereas other aspects of charismatic renewal, such as baptism with the Holy Spirit or spiritual gifts, are often the subject for careful argument and persuasion, with guidance it is more likely to be a lively report of what happened last week.

Two principles are almost universally stressed: the authority of Scripture and the need for confirmation. Both speak to the need of testing guidance against objective standards. Aside from this, however, teaching on guidance is generally unsystematized. The sovereign freedom of the Spirit has probably been experienced here more than in any other area of charismatic life and ministry. The Spirit does not always work according to neatly predictable rules. He will catch us by surprise, confront us with the unexpected, and only afterward will we see how appropriate and wise were his dealings with us. To be led by the Spirit means that we remain open and flexible, so that he can do in us all that his wisdom determines is necessary and good.

Providential care

In this area, and especially in regard to healing, there is considerable theological diversity across the spectrum of the charismatic renewal. Lutheran charismatics have not generally drawn up a rigid doctrine about healing that sooner or later comes into conflict with reality. While Lutherans, along with charismatics generally, have had a strong emphasis on healing, they have recognized that there is mystery here that we must learn to live with. Even the most committed and faith-filled Christian may be caught in the grip of sickness. Until Christ comes again, death comes to us all, and oftentimes through sickness.

A positive attitude toward prayer and a conviction that God will provide for us does not commit a person to a "theology of success," though this charge is often leveled at charismatics. To become successful in the eyes of the world is not the same as receiving God's promise that he will supply us with the things necessary for life (Matt. 6:19-33). God measures his blessings according to a kingdom standard that we may not always understand. He causes us to abound and to be abased (Phil. 4:12). He may shower us with unexpected abundance; then he may bring us into lean times. You don't have to talk with many charismatics before you discover how real this is. God does not provide for everyone in the same way or at the same time. Faith in his provision is one side of the matter, but divine sovereignty is the other. Lack of faith is not the only reason that people may not be healed or experience material blessing.

To recognize the ambiguities that we encounter in regard to divine providence, however, is not the same as being resigned to them. It is at this point that the charismatic renewal challenges the church. When our teaching about divine providence leads to resignation or indifference, something is wrong. The problem in the church today is not that people believe too much about God's providential care, but that they believe too little or too seldom. While many church members acknowledge that God *can* heal or intervene with special blessings, they do not generally expect it to happen in their case. At the level of practical experience, God's fatherly care is little more than a theological phrase. It does not shape our day-to-day expectations.

The Lord wants that to change. Human logic may tote up a list of unanswered prayers and conclude that belief in divine providence is simplistic. The Holy Spirit, however, is the master of paradox. In one situation he can speak his quiet word of comfort when we sit in darkness with unanswered questions; then at another time he can quicken in us the faith that God will indeed intervene. The Lutheran church has generally emphasized the side of darkness and ambiguity. Overzealous charismatics have emphasized the side of God's intervention. Both sides of the paradox are true, but only the Holy Spirit can lead us to apply the right truth at the right time.

Faith

One could almost reduce the charismatic renewal to this: *it is a revitalization of faith*. God's love and power is even more overwhelming than we thought or taught. There is a passive side to faith that quietly takes God at his Word. In a sense, this kind of faith is a foundation on which all else is built. But there is also an active side to faith that is greatly encouraged by concrete answers to prayer. Jesus does rebuke "little faith" and encourages "great faith."

The charismatic renewal's teaching on faith must be seen as parallel to its theme of dependence on the Holy Spirit. As we have seen in earlier chapters, faith is not a human achievement. It is a precious gift of God given to us through the Holy Spirit. Great faith, therefore, comes through a humble willingness to be totally dependent on what God gives. It is not the product of a legalistic pressure on a person to "have faith." It comes rather from trust and openness to the Spirit, as we feed on God's promises.

Spoken confession

The Spirit today is stressing the importance not only of believing, but of giving voice to what one believes. Luther advised people in his day to recite

the Creed aloud, for God and for the powers of darkness. His letter to pastor
Severin Schulze in Belgern in 1545 applied this truth in a practical situation:

> Venerable Sir and Pastor!
>
> The tax collector in Torgau and the counselor in Belgern have written and
> asked, on behalf of Mrs. John Korner, that I give some good advice and comfort
> in order that her husband might be helped. I know of no worldly help to give.
> If the physicians are at a loss to find a remedy you may be sure that it is not a
> case of ordinary melancholy. It must be rather an affliction that comes from the
> devil, and this must be counteracted by the power of Christ and with the prayer
> of faith.
>
> This is what we do and what we have been accustomed to do, for a cabinetmaker
> here was similarly afflicted with madness and we cured him by prayer in Christ's
> name.
>
> Accordingly you should proceed as follows: go to him with the deacon and
> two or three good men, confident that you as Pastor of the place are clothed with
> the authority of the ministerial office. Lay your hands on him and say:
>
> "Peace be with you dear brother, from God the Father and from our Lord Jesus
> Christ."
>
> Thereupon repeat the creed and the Lord's Prayer over him in a clear voice,
> and close with these words:
>
> "O God, almighty Father who hast told us through thy Son, 'Verily, verily I
> say unto you, whatsoever ye shall ask the Father in my name, he will give it to
> you,' who hast commanded and encouraged us to pray in his name, 'Ask and ye
> shall receive,' and in like manner said, 'Call on me in the day of trouble and I
> will deliver thee and thou shalt glorify me,' we unworthy sinners, relying on these
> words and commands, pray for thy mercy with such faith as we can muster.
> Graciously deign to free this man from all evil and put to naught the work that
> Satan has done to him, to the honor of thy name and the strengthening of the
> faith of believers, through the same Jesus Christ thy Son our Lord, who liveth
> and reigneth with thee, world without end. Amen."
>
> Then when you depart lay your hands on the man again and say: "These signs
> shall follow them that believe: they shall lay their hands on the sick and they
> shall recover." Do this three times, once on each of three successive days. Mean-
> while let prayers be said from the chancel of the church publicly until God hears
> them . . . other counsel than this we have not.[3]

Charismatics know from experience the usefulness of this practice. Yet the
Spirit also works discernment. One cannot make magic out of spoken confession. In other words, one cannot simply confess what he or she wants to
happen, assuming that God will bring it to pass as long as it is taken from
Scripture. Romans 10:9 says that "if you confess with your lips that Jesus is
Lord and believe in your heart that God raised him from the dead, you will
be saved." This broad-ranging promise cannot be indiscriminately applied to
anything one may choose to confess out loud. The word of faith must be
quickened or energized by the Spirit. Otherwise we are dealing not with faith
but with presumption.

The experiential side of the Christian life

Whatever else people may know about the charismatic renewal, they know that it has brought the experiential side of the Christian faith to the fore again. Luther's sharp criticism against dead orthodoxy sounds like an echo of present-day conversations in the charismatic renewal.[4] If God is a real God and Jesus is a real Lord, he will not leave people unaffected in their emotions, thinking, and will—they will *experience* the reality of their encounter with him.

Lutheran Pietism echoed the same kind of concerns about neoscholasticism that one might hear today from charismatic Lutheran pastors: a stress on faith as an intellectual body of doctrine, a mechanical view of the sacraments and worship (*ex opere operato*), and suspicion of anything resembling a different or special kind of piety.[5] From this perspective, the Pietist leaders Spener and Francke help expose the poverty of much current Lutheran theological practice; they highlight the need to return to an authentic Reformation view of faith that historian Williston Walker called, "that vital relationship between the believer and God which Luther had taught [and for which] had been substituted very largely a faith which consisted in the acceptance of a dogmatic whole."[6]

The experiential dimension of the faith, however, must also be looked at from another perspective: the Spirit does not renew the faith of some of God's people in order to exalt them above other Christians. During a meeting of Anglican, Lutheran, and Roman Catholic renewal leaders in England in 1985, this word of prophecy came during one of the worship sessions: "I am not calling you to tell the church that it is wrong, but to show the world that I am alive."[7]

If anything, a renewal of faith is a renewal of servanthood. The Spirit wants to break down false barriers between charismatics and noncharismatics. It is certainly proper, indeed necessary, to make distinctions between Christians in terms of their function or calling in the body of Christ. Sometimes Scripture also makes distinctions between Christians in terms of the quality of their Christian life or commitment (for example, 1 Cor. 15:10; Phil. 2:21-22), but this is a dangerous game and generally to be avoided (2 Cor. 10:12). Historically, it has had a poor track record.

The Cathari, whose greatest activity was in southern France and northern Italy during the 12th century, laid particular emphasis on faith tested by suffering and life in the power of the Holy Spirit. The term "Cathari" comes from the Greek *catharci,* "the pure." One of their number, Alacaicus, wrote enthusiastically, "The Cathari are holy people. For the sake of Christ they suffer great persecution, while the Catholics enjoy richly all the pleasures of the world."[8] Within their ranks the Cathari differentiated between the "per-fect" and the merely "believing." The latter were lacking in fundamental spiritual experience. Acceptance in the body of the "perfect" was gained through the "consolamentum," the impartation of the Paraclete, that is, the gift of the Holy Spirit. Their rigorous ethic went hand in hand with a per-fectionistic understanding of the church. The Spirit-filled Cathari were prac-titioners of charismata. Their emphasis on experience gave vitality to their movement, but their lack of concern for biblical teaching made them highly susceptible to syncretism in many forms. Their strength became a weakness because they used it as a basis for making unwise distinctions among Chris-tians. Charismatics would well be warned by such an example.

A case in point would be the loose way that charismatics sometimes throw around terms like "Spirit-filled" as a designation for charismatics. People who have been filled with the Spirit will surely need to be encouraged to be filled again, or filled continually (Eph. 5:18). In that sense, charismatics will be as much in need of "filling" as some noncharismatics. Some noncharis-matics may be powerfully filled with the Spirit, even though they have not shared some of the distinctive experiences associated with the charismatic renewal.

All Christians have the Holy Spirit (Rom. 8:9; 1 Cor. 12:13). When personal experience is preached in a manner that exalts one group of Christians over another rather than exalting Christ, Luther's battle with the enthusiasts of his day becomes relevant once again, with his emphasis on the "external Word" (Scripture), Baptism, and Eucharist. Experience can serve to strengthen and confirm faith; it should not be a source of division among the faithful.

CHAPTER 36

TRUTH AND AUTHORITY

Pentecost was a demonstration of the lordship of Christ (Acts 2:36). It transformed the ministry of the disciples: they were supernaturally empowered to be witnesses of the truth concerning Jesus.

On the day of Pentecost Peter boldly proclaimed the truth of the resurrection in the teeth of those who had rejected Jesus as Messiah. But truth was not only what was proclaimed. The outpouring of the Spirit was truth as *event,* truth confirmed by wind and fire and tongues, truth embodied in a band of disciples who had been weak and fearful but who now were bold in the Spirit. It was truth that reverberated with authority, calling people to repent and turn to him who is the Truth.

The issue of truth and authority is at the heart of the charismatic renewal. It calls us to live under the lordship of Christ, to bring every thought captive to him who is the Truth, who has all authority in heaven and on earth.

This is not a simple human possibility, a matter merely of subscribing to the right doctrines. The ministry of the gospel, the apostle Paul reminds us, is given "by the working of [God's] power" (Eph. 3:7). Only the dynamic of the Holy Spirit can establish truth and authority in the church.

Doing the truth

An aspect of the charismatic renewal that deserves more attention than it has received is its concern for truth. Discussion of the movement often centers around the question of experience, but that is simply part of a much larger question, the question of truth. When the Holy Spirit leads, he leads into truth (John 16:13). Charismatic experience is important only because it is an aspect of truth into which the Spirit wants to lead the church.

The Spirit teaches us to consider truth in a new way. Truth cannot be adequately expressed merely in terms of scholarly opinions, theological perspectives, or even true doctrine. These things can exist quite apart from spiritual life. Truth is related to life. It is the reality of the kingdom of God, revealed in Jesus Christ, and experienced wherever the Holy Spirit makes the lordship of Christ a reality in the lives of believers.

Truth is like the promised land: it is given to God's covenant people. It is given through the Word of promise in order that we shall walk into it under the guidance of the Holy Spirit. Truth is not something we merely think about. It is something we *do*—in times of worship, in spiritual warfare, in service and suffering. As we live the truth in our ministry, experiencing its grace and its burdens, we learn what it means that "every place that the sole of your foot will tread on I have given to you, as I promised to Moses" (Josh. 1:3).

Scripture and experience

Truth related to experience and truth related to Scripture have sometimes been set in opposition to one another. This was Luther's concern in his battle with the enthusiasts. In the charismatic renewal, however, it has generally been the case that experience is measured by the standard of Scripture. Charismatics, both Lutheran and non-Lutheran, underscore Luther's insistence that the Word is primary and that experience must be weighed against that standard. This is not a substitute for the Spirit, but a recognition that this is the way that the Spirit works.

In the charismatic renewal, the Holy Spirit has created a profound respect for the written Scripture as the Spirit-inspired, eternally true, and powerful Word of God for people today. It involves more than an academic interest: the Spirit creates an *expectancy of encounter* with the triune God through personal reading and study of the Bible.

Without the Holy Spirit, the study of Scripture would be another weary effort of the flesh. Scripture would be dead letter, not life-giving truth. The focus of expectation must be not simply on the Bible, but on the Holy Spirit and his use of Scripture to accomplish God's will with us.

The Spirit creates a church that desires to be guided into the full truth of Scripture, into fresh insights and new understanding. He shows the church where it needs to be reformed, corrected, and renewed in order to be faithful and obedient to the never-changing Word. He shows where the church must stand fast in the truth without compromise. A Spirit-led church is a teachable church, willing to subject all areas of its life and doctrine to the scrutiny of Scripture, under the guidance of the Holy Spirit.

When the Spirit brings renewal, the Bible comes alive as God's personal letter to us in our present, concrete existence. The Holy Spirit inspires believers to become a Bible-believing, Bible-studying, Bible-formed, Bible-living people.

The authority of the Bible

One of the characteristics of renewal movements, according to Lutheran theologian Lloyd Svendsbye, is a renewed interest in Scripture and a heightened sense of the authority of Scripture.

This was clearly the case, for example, in Pietism. Spener and Francke advocated widespread use of the Scriptures in the life of both ministers and laity. They taught the depravity of humanity and the need for regeneration and sanctification through the biblical message. Spener emphasized that lay people should read the Bible extensively, that they should study entire books consecutively, and that they should gather for house meetings ("pious gatherings") to discuss the Scriptures in "an apostolic kind of church meeting."[1]

When Francke began his theological professorship at Halle, he banished the study of philosophy and replaced it with biblical exegesis, exchanged polemics for active Christian service, and replaced scholastic commentaries with his own Bible lectures, thus reforming theological education.[2] In general he followed Luther's distaste for philosophy and moved at every hand to establish the preeminence of Scripture for Christian life and ministry, propounding 2 Tim. 3:16: "All scripture is inspired by God and is profitable for teaching, for reproof, for correction, and for training in righteousness."

Within the charismatic movement the authority of Scripture has been assumed from the outset. At a charismatic conference in 1975 Lutheran pastor Larry Christenson made this remark:

> One of the issues that has given real strength to the charismatic renewal is the fact that it has accepted the basic ground rules [of scriptural authority] without debate. I can't recall ever participating in a charismatic teaching session or prayer group where there was a basic argument about any of the cardinal doctrines of the Christian faith, such as justification by faith, the virgin birth, the atonement, the divinity of Christ, the validity of the moral law. All of these things are accepted without question. Critics sometimes fault charismatics for not spending enough time on the basics, apparently failing to recognize how thoroughly they are believed and accepted; therefore, it isn't necessary to spend a lot of time on them.[3]

The Conference of Bishops of the United Evangelical Lutheran Church in Germany issued a document on the charismatic renewal in 1976 in which they said, "We note with gratitude that these [charismatic] communities, as arms of the Lutheran church, take their stand on Holy Scripture."[4]

During the so-called discipleship controversy within the charismatic renewal in the United States in the mid-1970s, Bob Mumford and those associated with him were charged with teaching that "the church is no longer
subject to a 2000-year-old written *logos,* but may rely on the current *rema.*"
Mumford's response to this charge asserted the preeminence of Scripture:

> I feel it almost ludicrous to have to make statements concerning my attitude
> toward the Bible as God's Word, after twenty years of teaching and preaching
> the Scriptures. Without making complicated or theological statements, let me say
> emphatically that *I believe that the Scriptures, as given to us in the Holy Bible,
> are the final rule of faith and practice.* I believe in the verbal and plenary in-
> spiration of the Scriptures without reservation. Every other form of the Lord's
> communication to his people by the Holy Spirit, that is, dreams, visions, prophecy,
> leadings, personal counsel, or the shepherd's oversight, is subject to, and to be
> judged by, God's written Word.[5]

Roman Catholic participants in the charismatic renewal, from a slightly
different perspective, likewise hold to a high view of scriptural authority:

> Strong and increasing pressures on God's people are trying to choke out the Word
> of God. Within the church these pressures are manifested in a subtle but powerful
> spirit of criticism, skepticism, and uncertainty. Once these seeds of doubt are
> sown, the protection that the certainty and clarity of God's Word was intended
> to provide for his people is removed, and it is easy to be seduced into many
> different things. The Catholic church teaches that once you have formed your
> conscience on the objective word of God and the teaching of the church, then
> your conscience is in a position to tell you the right thing to do. But today many
> people are saying, "I'm going to read everything, experience everything, and
> see what I feel is right to me." This is an incredible attack on the Word of God
> and on the authority of God.[6]

Danish renewal leader Ole Skjerbaek Madsen's statement on biblical authority illustrates the high regard for Scripture that one typically finds among
Lutheran charismatics:

> If the church wants to be the church, and to know God, it must continue steadfastly
> in the apostles' teaching. With the Confessions of our church, we declare that
> the Word of God, as it is found in the prophetic and apostolic writings—the whole
> Bible—is the authority in the church. A church that does not honor the whole
> Bible as God's Word and authority in the church, by the same token does not
> know Christ Jesus as Lord—he who is the Word of God.[7]

Critics who contend that charismatics "set experience above Scripture" are
hard put to come up with the evidence. John MacArthur once wrote a magazine
article in which he said that Larry Christenson "had often indicated that the

Christian faith is based on experience and that theology is only an explanation of that experience." Christenson replied in a letter:

> Nothing could be further from the truth. I do not know where you are drawing your instances from in alleging that I have "often indicated" this position. I am quite sure that I have NEVER done so, for it is absolutely contrary to my personal conviction. I accept the Bible as the inspired Word of God and as the only infallible rule of faith and life. In 20 years of pastoring a Lutheran congregation this has been my consistent teaching, and the basis of my pastoral practice. If a parishioner were to come to me and claim some experience that stood in clear contradiction to the Scriptures, I would insist that the Scriptures define, explain, interpret, and take precedence over the experience, not the reverse.
>
> I *have* said that Scripture itself is the (inspired!) record of what the men of God who wrote the Scripture *experienced*. In other words, they did not arrive at their writings by mere speculation or imagining, as is true of many humanly wrought philosophies. The Christian faith is the *empirical* faith, par excellence (cf. 2 Peter 1:16-19; 1 John 1:1-4). Men encountered the living God in outward events, and inwardly, as they were given to understand the meaning that God wanted them to see in those events. The Bible, seen as a whole, is the "raw data" of our theology . . . something like all the empirical findings of the chemist are the raw data out of which he formulates a theory.
>
> Theology is the attempt to understand, and to some degree systematize and to communicate the truth that is inherent in that raw data of revelation. When I teach an adult membership class about the doctrine of the Trinity, I do not go to some person's "experience" of this. I show how that doctrine, though not specifically so named in Scripture, is nevertheless implicit in the (unimpeachable) data of Scripture. If some person were to report some kind of "experience" that corroborated this teaching, I would view it as just that, corroboration.
>
> Of course, in one sense the Bible does not need any corroboration; it is a faithful testimony whether received or not. Yet it is the nature of our evangelistic enterprise to bear personal witness that what the Bible says has also proven true in one's own experience. It is in this sense that I recognize and appreciate "experience," namely as that which bears witness to the truth revealed in Scripture. Whether this is a testimony to forgiven sin, answered prayer, healing, or growth in understanding . . . is a secondary matter. The primary thing is that it accord with Scripture, not be in contradiction to Scripture.[8]

Through the experience of the Spirit the Bible ceases to be merely a formal authority. It becomes a practical authority for everyday Christian believing and living. The gap of 2000 years is bridged. The Spirit makes the words of the prophets and apostles relevant for people today.

Bertil Gärtner, bishop of the Gothenburg diocese in Sweden, challenged his audience with this thought in a workshop at a European charismatic conference in 1986: "There will never be renewal if the Bible is not at the center. It must be the book above all others that we study. It must be our authority." He went on to say, however, that if we accept the Bible as our authority, we will walk contrary to many theologians and leaders in the church today. He quoted a Harvard theologian who described the Bible as "a great but archaic monument in Western culture."[9]

Charismatics would respond that although the languages of the Bible are those of different human cultures and the biblical revelation took place in distant history, the Bible remains in every generation the Spirit's primary instrument for conveying God's wisdom and will to those who will receive it. The Bible brings us the account of God's saving acts and the Spirit's authentic interpretation of those acts. This is not a demonstrable fact, but a statement of faith. Only the Holy Spirit can establish the authority of Scripture in the believer.

The place accorded to tradition

In the Roman Catholic and Orthodox churches, the authority of sacred tradition is placed alongside the authority of Scripture, and charismatics from these churches generally hold to this understanding.[10] Some Protestant charismatics are bemused by this emphasis on tradition, considering it a vestige of the past that Catholic charismatics will slough off as Scripture gains a stronger foothold among them. Among other Protestant charismatics, however, there seems to be an increased appreciation of the place and value of tradition.

The influential group of teachers associated with *New Wine* magazine in the United States all came from conservative Protestant backgrounds. Nevertheless, their teaching reflected a cautious appreciation of some aspects of Catholic tradition, especially in the area of ecclesiology. This apparently came about primarily as a result of practical experience, rather than through academic study.[11] A more unusual example is seen in the newly formed Evangelical Orthodox Church in the United States. Most of the leaders in this group were formally associated with Campus Crusade for Christ, a conservative evangelical movement. They express a keen appreciation for Orthodox theology and spirituality and have undertaken an intensive study of Orthodox tradition with the zeal of converts.[12]

In less formal ways, of course, tradition is operative among any group of Christians. Anglicans have their *Thirty-Nine Articles;* the Reformed, their *Westminster* and *Heidelberg Catechisms,* Lutherans, their *Book of Concord;* Baptists, Methodists, Congregationalists, Pentecostals, and independents of every stripe, not to mention local congregations and fellowships, have their distinctive traditions in theology, worship, and practice that can, on occasion, carry the weight of considerable authority.

One of the characteristics of the charismatic movement has been a heightened appreciation of the corporate aspect of the Christian faith, and this has resulted in a practical, if not a formal, emphasis on the place and value of tradition. The movement has tended to play down the Protestant myth of an authoritative Scripture that hangs suspended between heaven and earth, unaffected by human interpretation and tradition. At a large gathering of charismatic leaders in Kansas City, Missouri, in 1975, one of the speakers made this observation:

> What we teach is based first of all on our understanding of Scripture, and we don't make that an absolute; it is *our understanding* of Scripture. Secondly, what we teach is based on what we believe the Holy Spirit has said subjectively to us. We don't have chapter and verse for everything we are doing. I used to live in a situation where if I couldn't find a verse of Scripture for it I wouldn't do it. I thank God for deliverance from that kind of bondage.[13]

A similar note was struck in another of the talks given at this same conference:

> How many of the divisions in Christendom have come about because we have canonized our own understanding of Scripture at a particular point in time? Some groups contend, "We don't listen to men. We just follow the Word. We believe the Bible." Let's face it. When we say, "I am following the Bible," what we really are saying is, "I am following what I understand the Bible to be saying in this situation, at this particular point in my spiritual development." Any time we canonize something that is as limited as that we have moved in the direction of stupidity instead of wisdom. It's not the written Bible that is going to protect us from error. It's the written Bible *as it is lived and experienced and understood among a body of brethren who are [led by the Spirit], committed to one another, and can mutually correct one another.*
>
> Let's admit it. As Protestants, that's a hard word for us to swallow. For years we've been looking down our nose at the Catholic understanding that it isn't only the Scripture, but the teaching office that interprets the Scripture. While we may not agree with the way in which that idea has been worked out in the Roman Catholic communion, we ought to be honest enough to admit that the principle is essentially correct. There must be a check and balance in the interpretation of Scripture. The whole sad story of Protestant division has been written as people have walked off in opposite directions with their Bibles clutched firmly in hand![14]

What good is an inspired Scripture in the hands of men and women operating independently of the Holy Spirit? It is worse than worthless, for it can be used to further human ends in the name of God. As the Scripture itself is the work of the Spirit, so also must be our understanding and interpretation of it. One of the ways that he instructs us is through the wisdom and understanding that he has already given to the church in times past.

CHAPTER 37

CONFIRMING THE WORD

Without the leading and the empowering of the Holy Spirit, any "truth" that we proclaim will be without authority, however orthodox it may be. Truth without authority—spiritual authority—will be without effect in spiritual matters. "For the kingdom of God does not consist in talk but in power" (1 Cor. 4:20).

Spiritual authority does not depend on acceptance by the secular system. A secular system may accept or resist spiritual authority, but it cannot control it. Nor does spiritual authority derive from an ecclesiastical system. It may provide the framework in which spiritual authority is exercised, but without the dynamic of the Spirit there will be no functioning of real authority. Spiritual authority is an authentication given by the Spirit when he leads us into truth. It is God's confirmation of the Word of God.

Spiritual authority "bears God into the midst of life"

This understanding of spiritual authority has a long and honorable tradition in the church. Ignatius, the martyr-bishop of Antioch (ca. A.D. 115), was the forerunner of an "Asia Minor theology," and he is numbered among those theologians who, along with the gospel of John, gave the Eastern church its unique character. He is described as a "charismatic" bishop.[1] He is generally recognized as the first "monarchical bishop," yet he did not see his authority deriving from an ecclesiastical office. He usually began his letters with the words, "Ignatius, the God-bearer" (*theophoros*). He based his spiritual authority on the knowledge that God and Christ lived in him. The expressions "indwelling" (*enoikesis*) and "union" (*henosis*) with Christ make clear the nature of his own spiritual experience and pneumatology.

For Ignatius, as in the New Testament, experience of Jesus Christ and of the Holy Spirit were clearly and inseparably linked. In his letter to the Ephesians, Ignatius noted his intention, in a later communication, to discuss in detail the necessity of union with Christ, and added, "especially if the Lord reveal to me that you all severally join in the coming meeting in grace from his name, in one faith." [2] In what we might consider a prosaic affair—convening a meeting of church leaders—he deferred to the guidance of the Holy Spirit.

Ignatius sealed his testimony with his blood. Like Stephen, he saw heaven opened (Acts 7:55). [3] Before his martyrdom, Ignatius wrote to the church at Rome: "Let me be given to the wild beasts, for by their means I can attain to God. I am God's wheat, and I am being ground by the teeth of beasts, so that the pure bread of Christ may be made of me." [4] Ignatius did not speak as a hero, brave unto death. Rather, Christ, the one who is present in his church and who brings the dead to life, spoke in him. Therein lay Ignatius' authority.

In charismatic leadership conferences one frequently hears charismatic authority defined as "the authority of influence rather than of office." It is interesting that one so strongly associated with ecclesiastical office as Ignatius should speak so "charismatically" on the question of authority. To some extent it reflects the observation of Lutheran theologian Hans von Campenhausen that in the second century ecclesiastical authority and charismatic authority still had a good working relationship. [5]

Confirmation of truth through signs and wonders

The Father confirmed the truth and authority of Jesus' ministry by the signs that followed, and Jesus promised the same kind of confirmation to his disciples: "Truly, truly, I say to you, he who believes in me will also do the works that I do; and greater works than these will he do, because I go to the Father" (John 14:12).

The charismatic renewal has been sounding this theme in most of the established churches of Western culture. But the note is being heard even more clearly from some of the independent churches and parachurch movements in the Third World, almost all of which are charismatic, though many have had little or no connection with the charismatic movement as such. These churches are concerned about truth, but by that they do not mean simply a more carefully worded statement of church doctrine. Behind their phenomenal growth is the biblical understanding of truth as something that must not only be taught but also *done* in the power of the Spirit. They are churches that expect the proclamation of truth to be accompanied by signs and wonders. [6]

What they are saying to some of the established churches is something like this: "If you talk about salvation and sing about God's marvelous deeds but do not pray for the sick, do not deal with demonic bondage, leave no room for God's miraculous intervention and confirmation, your 'truth' is too theoretical. If you declare that the Holy Spirit brings us to faith, but do not demonstrate his presence in your ministry, your 'truth' is deficient."

In 1960, representatives from American, German, and Scandinavian missions met together with African synods to discuss the formation of one united Lutheran church in southern Africa. Many voices were raised against coming together into one united church. Just before the vote was taken, a loud thunderclap was heard. The people were stunned because it was the dry season and there were no clouds in the sky. The Africans spontaneously cried: "The Lord has spoken!" The vote to form the united church was unanimous.[7]

This kind of experience is not easily accepted in churches in which ecclesiastical machinery is expected to operate in a predictable way. Some charismatic groups would have trouble with it as well. The uncomfortable fact for us to ponder, however, is that it is not particularly foreign to Scripture.

Demonstration of truth in life

As a spiritual awakening initiated by the Holy Spirit, the charismatic renewal is called to help the church not only articulate truth, but demonstrate it. As a movement, it is spreading and having effect worldwide—in deeply traditional churches, in congregations, in groups, in the lives of individual Christians. In the setting of Lutheran state churches the movement is often referred to simply as "spiritual congregational renewal." That says several things: renewal is genuinely taking place; the Holy Spirit is the one behind it; it comes to a focus in the congregation. It also says that truth is more than simply a correct statement of doctrine: it is a reality that must be continually renewed in the life of God's people.

If the charismatic renewal is to be an advocate of the truth, it must itself be as open to the judgment of Scripture as it calls the church to be. Is the fruit of the Spirit (Gal. 5:22-23) evident in the lives of charismatic leaders? Does the ministry taking place in the context of the renewal measure up to biblical standards? This kind of evaluation, of course, is somewhat subjective. But charismatics should welcome it. They should invite church leadership and membership to test the renewal on the basis of biblical criteria. Charismatic leaders should also encourage participants in the movement to place their beliefs and practices under the scrutiny of the Scriptures.

At the same time, charismatics challenge church leaders, and all segments of the church, to examine their positions and practices in the light of the Word of God. Testing is vital in order to avoid deception, on the one hand, or rejection of truth, on the other. The institutional church needs to examine itself as diligently as it scrutinizes renewal movements. Frequently the rise of renewal groups is an evidence of the institution's failure to hear and adjust to the purposes of the Spirit.

Charismatics have not always given sufficient attention to the manner in which they challenge the church. The renewal cannot force its message on the church. It can only declare it and live it in the power of the Spirit, openly inviting the church to test the message against the Word, leaving the results to God. The truth and authority radiating from revivals depends on their willingness to have no official power and influence, to serve the cause of truth from a position of weakness.

Charismatics often experience a loss of prestige as a gateway into new freedom and new authority in their ministries. A fresh experience of the Spirit may put them at odds with institutional goals and leadership and bring them to that old doorway into the kingdom: death to self, resurrection with Christ, fellowship in his sufferings, and freedom to proclaim and do the truth, which is the ground of true authority.

Unashamed commitment to biblical truth will inevitably bring church leaders into conflict with standards of truth and behavior that prevail in secular society and in secularized segments of the church, a reality that church leaders are not always eager to embrace. It is interesting that a significant number of Anglican and Roman Catholic bishops have sought and received the gift of tongues in connection with the charismatic renewal, whereas Lutheran bishops who speak in tongues are virtually unheard of. This is a small thing in itself, yet what might it be telling us? Charismatics are sometimes accused of making too much of tongues, but here is a phenomenon that raises an opposite kind of question: Is *not* speaking in tongues a price that Lutheran officials are implicitly expected to pay in order to maintain their credibility in Lutheran circles? During an open forum at the Thirteenth International Lutheran Conference on the Holy Spirit in 1984, psychiatrist Lee Griffin offered the opinion that Lutheran tradition, with its heavy accent on controlled intellectual content, makes it particularly threatening for Lutheran leaders to become identified with more spontaneous kinds of spirituality.

One of the characters in Hemingway's novel *For Whom the Bell Tolls* says, "To me, now, the most important thing is that we be not disturbed. To me, now, my duty is to those who are with me and to myself."

His comrade responds, "Thyself. Yes, Thyself now since a long time. Thyself and thy horses. Until thou hadst horses thou wert with us. Now thou are another capitalist more."[8]

Leaders who are bound by the settled conformity of colleagues and tradition may have too much to lose—too much status, too much acceptance, too much influence, too much approval, too much prestige. The presence of a widespread renewal movement challenges church leaders to weigh their commitment to institution and tradition and human opinions against their commitment to biblical truth and authority.

Charismatics are not what Luther called *Schwärmer*—spiritual enthusiasts who reject biblical authority, institution and organization, order and tradition.[9] But their experience helps them recognize a neglected biblical perspective: truth is something we enter into as we are led by the Spirit. Only as we *do* the truth can we come to *know* the truth (John 7:16-17).

Not one way among many

The charismatic renewal does not represent simply one way among several possible ways of building or renewing the life of individuals and congregations. Its central emphasis is not something that could just as well be replaced by another renewal emphasis. Rather, it focuses on the truth by which the church and every other movement in the church must live, which is *total reliance on the Holy Spirit*. This is not an optional way, but is the only way in which the Lord continually refreshes and renews his church.

As in other areas, so in questions of truth, charismatics call for a radical dependence on the Holy Spirit. This is not a stance or a blessing for the few. It is a challenge to the whole church to be led by the Spirit into the truth.

What effect this approach to truth will have on one's standing in the established church or in the secular community is hard to tell. For some, surely, it will mean a loss of prestige or position. For some, persecution. Others will find an eager response to their words and ministry. All of that is, in a sense, incidental. It is the province of the Spirit. Our part is to do the truth. The Lord tells us plainly how that will happen: "When the Spirit of truth comes, he will guide you into all the truth" (John 16:13).

PART FIVE

LED BY THE SPIRIT
Practical Concerns
in the Charismatic Renewal

So then, brethren, we are debtors, not to the flesh, to live according to the flesh—for if you live according to the flesh you will die, but if by the Spirit you put to death the deeds of the body you will live. For all who are led by the Spirit of God are sons of God.

Romans 8:12-14

CHAPTER 38

THE POWER OF THE INDWELLING CHRIST

In many mainline Protestant and Catholic churches, highly personal expressions of the faith are muted or absent altogether.[1] Charismatics talk freely about Jesus' presence and activity in their daily lives. Part of this difference may be cultural. A renewal movement creates a substructure in which it is more acceptable to share personal religious experience.

It would be an oversimplification, however, to see in it nothing more than that. A readiness to talk about Jesus points to a widely shared reality in the charismatic renewal: a heightened awareness of Jesus' presence, not only in regard to salvation, but in one's daily life. Jesus pictured our inner life as a well that receives from him a spring of living water that never runs dry (John 4:14). He said that when people come to him and drink, the Holy Spirit flows out of them like a river (John 7:37-39). Charismatics see Scriptures like these as both the source and confirmation of a relationship with Christ that is all-consuming.

UNION WITH CHRIST

Our relationship with Christ is not a matter of cooperation between two independent partners, not even if we allow the Lord the greater share of the credit and take the smaller part for ourselves. It is not a matter of asking him to help us, as though we were essentially self-sufficient creatures but could turn in a more creditable performance if we had a little help. It is rather that we have no existence, no life, no possibilities except as the Spirit joins Christ's life to our life.

Just as Christ does not live and cannot be accurately understood in terms of his divine nature alone, nor in terms of his human nature alone, but only

227

in terms of the two natures existing in a supernatural union, so we can live and understand our own existence as Christians only as a supernatural union of our life and Christ's life. For this kind of life the word *cooperation* is too clumsy, too weighed down with connotations of independent existence. The Reformation term *communicatio* ("communication") is more helpful: Christ communicates his life to us, and we respond in faith to this impartation of life.

Our response is critical, of course, because God will not do anything in us against our own will, without the "yes" of faith. But this is something quite different from striving in our own strength to grow spiritually—clenching our teeth, screwing up our willpower, targeting our resolve—and then calling for an assist from "grace" when we come up short. The way of growth is, rather, along the lines of faith, recognizing the mighty presence of the Holy Spirit, yielding to him as he communicates Christ's life to us, surrendering to him and allowing him to direct and control us in such a way that Christ's life can be released.

Why is this life foreign to so many? Why is spiritual immaturity the rule, and dynamic growth the exception, in large segments of the church today? Maybe it is because we simply have not in faith welcomed the Holy Spirit into our lives. We have not prayed expectantly, with Luther and with the church through the centuries, "Come, Holy Spirit." For it is the powerful working of the Spirit that creates, sustains, and makes fruitful our life in Christ.

THE INFILLING OF THE HOLY SPIRIT

How one grows as a Christian has been a more widespread emphasis in the charismatic renewal than how one becomes a Christian in the first place. Especially in the first two decades of the movement, charismatic conferences and publications gave more attention to teaching than to evangelism. The teaching was experience-oriented: it sought the practical application of spiritual truth in people's lives. Central to this quest has been teaching on the infilling of the Holy Spirit as the dynamic that makes true growth possible.

A new dimension of growth and Spirit-anointed ministry can open up when one prays to receive the infilling of the Holy Spirit. When the Lord fills or immerses us in the Holy Spirit, he often effects immediate and even surprising changes in our life and behavior. It is as though at the outset he wants to imprint on our consciousness the reality of the Spirit's presence and power, perhaps with a view to sustaining us in times of struggle that lie ahead.

An experience of being filled with the Spirit can be tremendously important in releasing the dynamic of Christ's life. It can help bring balance to a Christian faith that has become overly intellectualized.

The theology of infilling

As we have suggested earlier, the manner in which one experiences the infilling of the Spirit can vary considerably, *but it is necessary.* Perhaps the greatest single theological contribution of Pentecostalism has been its insistence that effective ministry requires the infilling of the Holy Spirit. Theologians in mainline churches have tended to dismiss the so-called "second blessing" theology of the Holiness and Pentecostal movements, which holds to a distinct work of the Holy Spirit subsequent to salvation. What they cannot dismiss, however, is the essential truth that is imbedded there. The idea of a distinction between the work of the Holy Spirit by which we receive new life and a work by which we are empowered for ministry was not introduced by Pentecostalism. A "charismatic work of the Spirit" can be traced from the pages of the New Testament, through the church fathers, into every century of the church's history.[2]

Pentecostal theology has had an undeniable influence on the charismatic renewal, especially in the early years of the movement. Charismatic theologians, however, have also sought to bridge the gap between the Pentecostal way of describing the Spirit's work and the traditional Protestant and Catholic ways of doing it.[3] The task is twofold: on the one hand, to affirm the essential truth of a charismatic work of the Spirit: on the other hand, to bring an added historical perspective to the way that truth is presented theologically. Lutherans, for instance, will bring to the inquiry their particular understanding of the Reformation and Pietism, Catholics and Anglicans their understanding of confirmation, Methodists their emphasis on sanctification.[4]

This work is going on at the present time, and theologically things are in flux, but what comes out will be more than a restatement of old positions. With the experience of the charismatic renewal, the Holy Spirit has thrust us beyond the point of simply theorizing. Around the world and across the whole spectrum of the body of Christ, people are experiencing the reality of being filled with the Spirit. It may take some time for theologians to catch up with explanations, but the reality is already here.

The need for infilling

What the charismatic renewal sees missing in the life of the church is the *appropriation* of the power to lead a new life. It is not enough to include the Holy Spirit and his gifts in our theology: he must come to expression in our lives. In a broad sense, justification must be followed by sanctification.

It is in regard to the broad question of sanctification—the exercise of spiritual gifts being but a part of this—that Lutheran charismatics have placed their understanding of the infilling of the Spirit. As part of a larger discussion

of Baptism, Larry Christenson presented two basic ways in which the infilling
of the Spirit may be experienced:

> In any relationship there will be times of quiet growth and moments of more
> dramatic breakthrough. The balance between two modes of development will vary
> from individual to individual. Also, the times in which one lives will to some
> extent affect the interplay of the "growth" and "breakthrough" motifs. In war-
> time, for instance, large numbers of young military people move into sober,
> responsible adulthood by means of crisis; in quieter times many would tend to
> mature somewhat more gradually.
>
> We live in a time of great upheaval. Behind the scenes of social and political
> unrest, spiritual warfare is raging, and its tempo is mounting. In such times, more
> people will have breakthrough-type experiences than in times of spiritual tran-
> quility.
>
> How else are we to explain the fact that suddenly a charismatic "movement"
> surfaced in the church, and in less than a decade, with no central organization,
> circled the globe, and moved into every major denomination? It is not that Chris-
> tians today are more holy and zealous, nor more gullible and unbalanced, than
> in former generations. It is that we live in a time of spiritual crisis. The widespread
> experience of the baptism with the Holy Spirit is a barometer of the hour in which
> we live.
>
> For a time, to begin with, a breakthrough experience may separate a person
> from his or her roots. That person is all caught up in the exploration of a new
> dimension of life. One thinks of young people who fall in love, and all but lose
> contact with the world around them.
>
> But if a breakthrough experience is to contribute something of value to life, it
> must establish itself in relation to the basic foundations of the life from which it
> sprang. The young lovers, as Dietrich Bonhoeffer has said, begin by seeing only
> themselves in the world. In marriage, they must go on to see themselves as a
> link in the chain of generations, which God causes to come and to pass away to
> his glory, and which he calls into his kingdom.
>
> Those who have experienced the blessing of a baptism or renewal in the Holy
> Spirit will find that blessing deepened and enhanced as they come to see it as a
> means of continuing and multiplying that life into which one has been initiated
> by water and the Word.[5]

Without the Holy Spirit, the most precious truths can become a snare.
Renewal movements from the Radical Reformation to the present time have
warned that the Lutheran emphasis on unconditional forgiveness can lead to
a gospel of "cheap grace." The antidote to this is not a vigorous restatement
of our theology but the working of the Holy Spirit. He alone can make costly
redemption and costly discipleship realities in our lives. As regards our theology, one of the most important things we Lutherans can do is remain open
to prophetic critique. The best-formulated theological motifs can be perverted.
Lutherans justly prize the theological insights of Luther, but too easily they
can become an occasion for pride and contention. Without the willingness to
see our desperate need for renewal, such motifs as "law and gospel" and

"simultaneously sinner and saint" can degenerate into sloganeering defenses of the status quo and become excuses for resisting the Spirit.

We do not hold title to the spiritual treasures that we recognize and appreciate in our own tradition. They belong to the treasure store of the Spirit. At most, we hold them in trust for the body of Christ. But even then, they remain only a remembrance, a description of what the Lord once did—until the Spirit fills us and makes them live again. The charismatic renewal, with its emphasis on being filled with the Spirit, is not the enemy of our traditions: it points to the only way that traditions remain alive.[6]

CHAPTER 39

HOLINESS

It was the day of a national election, and a men's morning Bible study group was holding its regular weekly meeting. They were reading Matt. 28:18, "All authority in heaven and earth has been given to me."

One of the men commented, "Won't it be great to know that, finally, the right man is in charge?"

It was an understandable slip, putting this little election-day thought on the authority of Christ into the future tense. It's the way we often talk about the lordship of Christ: something that happens somewhere out there in the future, or somewhere up there at a higher stage of the Christian life that we may aspire to, though we fall short of it in experience.

The Holy Spirit glorifies Christ by revealing who he is. He does this not only with words, but also by example (2 Cor. 3:2). He reveals Christ as Lord by actually establishing his lordship in the lives of believers.

The lordship of Christ: foundational truth, not afterthought

The Holy Spirit is very present-tense about Christ's lordship. The Spirit does not come with a bare-bones gospel of salvation: Repent, have your sins forgiven, go to heaven when you die. That truncates and caricatures the gospel, which is a gospel of the *kingdom*. The Holy Spirit comes with the good news that he has "delivered us from the dominion of darkness and transferred us to the kingdom of his beloved Son" (Col. 1:13). It is a unified action: as surely as he *delivers* us, just as certainly he *transfers* us. The Holy Spirit gathers the redeemed people of God under the lordship of Christ—not some-time in the future, not at some higher stage of the Christian life, but here and now, present tense, active.

232

The Holy Spirit is letting it be known that a gospel without lordship is no gospel. "Cheap grace" is not grace at all; it is a perversion of grace. The Spirit does not come with the good news of salvation, then tack on the lordship of Christ. The lordship of Jesus Christ *is* the good news. As certainly as we are saved *from* sin, we are saved *into* the kingdom where all authority has been given to him. On that fundamental truth Scripture is unmistakably clear.

Obedience: a work of the Holy Spirit

But the Spirit does not leave it there—or, more properly, he does not leave *us* there. That would consign us, at best, to a valiant striving in our own strength to demonstrate our gratitude for the gift of salvation, a kind of works-righteousness on the installment plan: "Saved Now, Pay Later!" The end of that is either a burdensome life under law and obligation, or the opposite danger of throwing off law and restraint in the name of liberty. Human flesh can do no better or other. It cannot live under the lordship of Christ—not with the best of will and good intention, not with the most orthodox belief nor most heartfelt gratitude. Human flesh cannot live in obedience to this King.

The Lord calls us to radical dependence on the ongoing work of the Holy Spirit within and among us. The Spirit alone can produce obedience to the lordship of Christ.

The charismatic renewal has laid particular stress on the issue of Christ's lordship. The Holy Spirit comes to make that lordship real. Through the Holy Spirit Jesus takes authority. He works his will in us in new ways. Spirit-inspired obedience glorifies Christ, for it testifies to his lordship. Before the Spirit is released, we can plunk ourselves down in the driver's seat. When Jesus immerses us in his Spirit, he once again asserts his lordship. A sign that one has truly received the outpoured Spirit is that the authority of Christ becomes more operative in one's everyday life (Acts 5:32).

Obedience: a theme deeply rooted in Christian tradition

The theme of obedience is applied to the monastic tradition, often in a negative sense. Protestants are prone to dismiss monasticism as a legalistic system. Yet if one goes back to the root, one often discovers a distinct emphasis on divine initiative; obedience is willed and wrought by the Holy Spirit.

Though having its roots in the East, monasticism took on a decidedly Western form through Benedict of Nursia, founder of the monastery at Monte Cassino. Until the 12th century, the Rule of St. Benedict held sway in the Western church.

In a vision Benedict had seen the whole world before his eyes, as if purged and purified in a single sunbeam.[1] He saw the fallen world in divine light, as the new earth to be created by the God who makes all things new (Rev. 21:5). For the world illumined by the light of God, no effort is too great, no prayer in vain, and no time wasted by honest toil. The rigid, tightly organized Benedictine Order was a church-renewal movement for the sake of the world, which Benedict had seen restored—transfigured—in heavenly light.

True enough, spiritual disciplines can degenerate into a legalistic system. But the other side must be held in perspective also: many of the men and women who founded renewal movements and religious orders, calling people to lives of obedience, were acting in response to a revelation of the Holy Spirit.

Obedience is the fundamental mark of a Spirit-filled believer. Scripture uses the plainest imagery to bring home this truth. The apostle Paul introduced himself to the Christians in Rome quite matter-of-factly as "Jesus Christ's slave" (Rom. 1:1, Living Bible). He thanked God for their life in Christ, in turn characterizing them as "slaves of righteousness" and "slaves of God" (6:18,22). He both introduced and concluded his letter by stating that the God-given goal of his ministry was "to bring about the obedience of faith among all nations" (1:5; 16:26).

It is not enough merely to hold this as a doctrine. It must be a reality that the Holy Spirit works out in our lives. Day by day we live out of the scriptural expectation that the Holy Spirit is applying the Lord's will in our lives, working in us a glad obedience.

He does this in many ways. Willingly and patiently he teaches us to recognize and respond to his ways. Even when our flesh rises up in rebellion, the deeper reality of his indwelling presence teaches us to obey and to rejoice in obedience—because "the right man really is in charge."

The call to holiness

To become *holy* is God's urgent call to his people. Today as always, God calls his people to be holy because God himself is a holy God (1 Peter 1:15-16; Rom. 1:7; 1 Cor. 1:2; Eph. 1:4). Christ died in order to sanctify the church, which is his bride and body, so that he might present the church to himself and to God as "holy and without blemish" (Eph. 5:25-27). In the Lord's Prayer, Jesus taught his disciples to pray that the holy name of God would occupy first place in their prayers. Jesus prayed, "Holy Father, keep them in thy name . . . that they may be one, even as we are one" (John 17:11,21). The life of God's people and the credibility of their witness to the world depends on holiness.

To be holy means quite simply that it becomes visible in our lives that we—as individuals and as the church—belong to God, that we are indeed the body of Christ. It means to be transformed into the image of Christ, because the best description of holiness is the character of Christ. To be holy is to bring forth the fruit of repentance, to forgive as Christ forgives, to love as Christ loves, to be compassionate as he is compassionate, to be righteous as he is righteous, to be honest, selfless, and pure as he is honest, selfless, and pure.

The call to be holy is a command. Yet beneath the command lies the promise: God gives what he demands. It is this perception, perhaps more than anything else, that has been a bulwark against legalism in the charismatic renewal. The emphasis is not on a self-produced but a Spirit-wrought holiness: "And we all, with unveiled face, beholding the glory of the Lord, are being changed into his likeness from one degree of glory to another; for this comes from the Lord who is the Spirit" (2 Cor. 3:18). God's Holy Spirit transforms us into the image of Christ. He alone can do it.

The ways of the Spirit

Though they sometimes surprise us, the ways of the Spirit are not arbitrary or whimsical. He is a God of order. It can be helpful to recognize in a general way how he works, so long as we do not seek to turn this knowledge into abstract principles and begin to govern our life by them. The Spirit may direct us to apply particular biblical principles. That is something quite different from using principles as a pious basis for acting independently of the Spirit. That would thrust aside the sovereignty of the Spirit and bring us back under the bondage of the law.

Scripture and *prayer* are two of the principal tools that the Spirit uses to shape our lives. He uses them in known and dependable ways.

Through the words of Scripture the Holy Spirit teaches us basic truths and principles of the holy life. When spiritually renewed people begin to talk about biblical standards of holiness, the cry of "Legalism!" is not far behind. But this may be a superficial judgment. One must come closer and discern the root of this quest for holiness. It *may* be a wooden, Spirit-less application of Scripture to a present situation, an attempt of the human will to live a holy life. But possibly it is something quite different, and truly given by the Spirit: a humble recognition that we really are fallen creatures. No part of us has escaped the ravages of the fall, including our faculties of moral judgment. It is not only our will that is defective; our understanding of what constitutes true holiness is flawed. The presumption that we know perfectly well what constitutes holiness is as much an evidence of our fallenness as is greed or sexual perversion. Biblical standards of holiness are the gift of a gracious

God to those who have been called to live holy lives and recognize that they don't even know where to begin.

Christian growth begins with the humble recognition that we are strangers to the ways of God. We must be instructed in the ways of holiness. Through the words of Scripture the Spirit must show us that which we cannot know by natural reason alone, namely, the kind of life that is pleasing to God.

In the school of prayer the Holy Spirit makes the truth of Scripture real and personal to us. He enlightens our understanding. He guides us to its proper application. It is no accident that spiritual renewal and prayer are inevitably linked together.

Through both Scripture and prayer the Holy Spirit reveals to us *our own heart*. This is critical to the life of holiness. Often one struggles with the same faults and weaknesses, commits the same sins again and again. The way out of this is not to pull oneself together by one's own efforts. At best that may produce a temporary result, and then one is overtaken again.

The way out is to turn to the Lord in prayer and ask for the Holy Spirit to reveal the nature of the difficulty. Perhaps its hidden roots lie buried in our unconscious and must be revealed through the operation of a spiritual gift. It may be festering away in a forgotten memory about a situation in which we sinned and did not receive forgiveness or were hurt and did not forgive. A major part of our "old nature" is made up of memories in which forgiveness did not take place. As long as these remain buried in our hearts, they can exercise control over us, and we are quite helpless to prevent it. Jesus spoke with great concern about what we carry in our hearts. In writing about the holy life, many of the church fathers stressed the importance of the self-knowledge given us by the Holy Spirit. When the Spirit reveals an area that needs to be dealt with, we may also trust him to quicken the faith by which we can forgive and receive forgiveness.

It takes time to come to a place of inner silence in our prayer life so that we can truly begin to listen. The young Luther was deeply influenced by the words of the mystic Johann Tauler: "God must be born in us in a spiritual and contemplative manner." [2] By nature, without the leading of the Spirit, we do not permit God to speak out his mind: we do not hear and thus cannot obey. Luther picked up the sense of such pre-Reformation awakenings when he depicted the true church not as a system of doctrines, the way scholasticism would have it, but as something grounded in the *experience of God.* [3] One does not simply think about God, one must hear and hearken to his voice. Luther was fond of Tauler's words: "If God would speak, you must be still."

It takes patience and endurance to come to the place where prayer really does become a two-way conversation. But without a prayer life that includes real listening, no deep and lasting growth can take place. A decade before

Transcendental Meditation became one of the cult expressions of the counterculture in the West, the charismatic movement had been quietly cultivating the practice of Christian meditation as one aspect of its concern for renewal.

What happens in the heart must be worked out in terms of practical faith and obedience. One cannot simply "wait for something to happen." Often we do not experience that the Holy Spirit has dealt with an area of our heart until it is tested in practice. We must step out in the freedom Christ has given us, yielding ourselves in obedience, living the life of holiness and obedience that is ours in him.

Two dangers

While clearly rooted in Scripture, Luther's teaching on justification was also an expression of his own experience of justification. It stressed the new attitude of the pardoned sinner before God. Luther himself sometimes included in his explanation of justification not only the legal sense of absolution (forensic justification) but also the sense of sanctification (sanative justification). "God, in Christ, conquers and heals the nature of man as that of a sinner, hostile to God."[4] Christ's substitutionary, atoning death is the basis for a new relationship with God (Rom. 4:25). God himself works the wonder: out of his enemy, he makes a friend (Rom. 5:10).

In applying this to daily life, two ditches must be avoided. On one side is the soft shoulder of passivity: "If the Holy Spirit alone can make me holy, then I have no responsibility." On the other side is the gully of willpower and self-determination: "I must accomplish my own sanctification."

A person driving into the first ditch careens headlong toward moral breakup and a spiritual standstill. In the second ditch we may plow on a ways, striving with our own power to steer a holy course, but then we stall out. Despite the best of intentions, the life of holiness gets mired down. So we thumb through the New Testament and determine, perhaps, that traveling this highway is, after all, an impossible ideal. Or we begin to compare ourselves with others along the wayside and happily conclude that we're just as good or better than our neighbor, and this is the beginning of spiritual pride. On both sides the problem is the same: *we do not reckon realistically with the persistent purpose and dependable power of the Holy Spirit to bring us to holiness.*

Philippians 2:13-14 is a critical passage for a right understanding of Christian growth. "Work out your own salvation with fear and trembling; for God is at work in you, both to will and to work for his good pleasure." Here Paul uses the term *salvation* to cover the whole process of redemption, which Christ works out in us through the Holy Spirit. The Holy Spirit creates in us the will to be holy, and he gives us the power to live a sanctified life. Paul knew from experience that this is no life of passivity. It is work, effort, striving (1 Cor. 9:25; Col. 1:29; Phil. 1:27; 2 Tim. 4:7). Yet it is crucial, in the very moment of striving, to depend on the Holy Spirit, who is giving both the will and the power to live a holy life (1 Cor. 15:10).[5]

CHAPTER 40

TRAINING
IN DISCIPLESHIP

Pastoral care

Jesus commissioned his apostles to make *disciples,* not merely believers in an intellectual sense, students in an academic sense, or converts in a statistical sense. People do not necessarily grow in discipleship by making a decision for Christ, accepting a doctrine, attending a class, or participating in a seminar. While these and other things may be appropriate steps along the way and may help people become more knowledgeable, they do not necessarily make people more faithful.

Disciples are made not simply by teaching but by training. Maturity comes not only by obtaining information *from* the Word of God, but by having spiritual formation *in* the Word of God. Spiritual formation involves more than preaching and teaching: it requires pastoral care that helps people to live in the Word of God. In the charismatic renewal the idea of teaching is being broadened to include practical training in discipleship, in which believers are encouraged and supported in Christian growth not only by teaching in an academic sense, but by the personal association and example of a spiritual mentor.

"Feed my sheep" is still Christ's commission to the shepherds of his church, and it requires many more shepherds than are presently available. The task of effectively applying the Word to individual lives is too large for the ordained clergy alone. One of the concerns that the charismatic renewal has addressed is the need to equip shepherds, lay as well as clergy, to nurture Christ's flock.

The small group

The initial rapid spread of the charismatic movement came primarily through prayer groups and house meetings that were spontaneous and largely unstructured. As the movement developed, the small group continued to play a decisive role as the place of pastoral care and directed spiritual growth. Small-group experience from other movements, especially the church-growth movement, was freely adapted by charismatics. People who made some initial steps of faith and experienced a measure of spiritual renewal were encouraged to commit themselves to meet with others on a regular basis for prayer and directed spiritual growth. Between renewal of the individual and renewal of an entire congregation rose up the renewing, nurturing, evangelizing ministry of the small group.

The precise format of small groups varies greatly throughout the renewal, but certain elements tend to predominate:

- biblical teaching that is simple and practical;
- prayer, intercession, and the practice of spiritual gifts;
- stress on committed, loving relationships;
- personal ministry, primarily through prayer, in which the Word is applied to people's practical needs.

Through intercession and training, small groups can serve as cells of spiritual renewal, sending fresh impulses of life into congregations. They help extend the shepherding ministry among the laity. They become a training ground for leadership in the congregation, "schools of discipleship" that both directly and indirectly affect the spiritual life of the entire congregation.[1]

Giving

A mark of the Spirit-led believer and Spirit-led church is a giving attitude, reflective of God's nature. It is a basic principle of life; it is a practice that the Holy Spirit leads us into. It begins with the conviction that everything belongs to the Lord and is at his disposal. It touches every area of life—time, abilities, gifts, money, property. It is the invitation of a gracious God to share in and give expression to his life. It is grace, not law or legalism.

Lutheran churches in Europe have traditionally been supported by a government- or church-taxing system. In other countries they are generally supported by free-will contributions of the members. In the latter case, even critics of charismatic renewal admit that giving patterns among charismatics are above average. Charismatic Lutheran pastors consistently report that the renewal results in less need to talk about stewardship, yet increased giving.

Generous giving is certainly not unique to the charismatic renewal. The fact that it often occurs more or less spontaneously, however, indicates that it is linked to an understanding of faith that moves quickly toward practical expression. The event that sparked the charismatic renewal was John and Joan Baker, members of an Episcopalian congregation in Van Nuys, California, coming into the experience of baptism with the Holy Spirit in 1959. One of the first things they did—that which caught the attention of their rector, Francis MacGuire—was that they began to tithe. After he had heard their testimony, he called the Episcopal priest in the neighboring parish, Dennis Bennett, and asked him what he thought about it all. Bennett is reported to have said, "If they're tithing, it can't be all bad."

Generous givers frequently testify that scriptural promises of blessing in connection with tithing, such as Mal. 3:10, prove true in their own experience, though this is not a primary issue. The motive for giving is not to receive reward. Generosity is its own reward. It is a way of life. "It is more blessed to give than to receive" (Acts 20:35).

The central truth of stewardship is that God is the source of material possessions. This fits well with the dynamic understanding of faith that is threaded through the charismatic renewal, the expectation that God intervenes in everyday life. The believer places faith not in possessions but in God, trusting God for all one's needs (Phil. 4:19). The focus of expectation is on God's fatherly care, not on one's visible income or resources. We are able to give generously because we are children of a generous Father.

It is not a question of our giving something to God and his kingdom either out of duty or gratitude. If that is the motivation, we are back under the law; giving quickly becomes either a burden or a source of pride. Rather, as in every other area of life, we depend on the working of the Holy Spirit: we can give generously because the giving, serving, sacrificing presence of Christ is alive within us by the Holy Spirit.

This understanding is essential. If stewardship becomes an inflexible obligation, it loses its spiritual dynamic. The Spirit must remain in control, which also means that there will be some understandable variety in stewardship practices. The giving patterns in countries where there is a folk church, well supported by taxation, may differ from what happens in countries where church support is voluntary. In the former case, spiritually renewed believers may direct more of their giving to voluntary associations such as mission societies or evangelistic works, while in the latter, one's primary giving may be through the local congregation. In a family where not everyone is Christian, the income may have to be considered differently than if everyone were Christian. What is essential is that the way we handle material possessions comes fully under the lordship of Christ.

The temptation to a materialistic outlook, finding our essential comfort and security in material things rather than in the Lord, is always close at hand. It is no accident that covetousness and greed appear prominently in various catalogs of sins in the New Testament (Rom. 1:29; Eph. 5:5; Col. 3:5; 1 Tim. 6:10). The emphasis on stewardship that has been prominent in the charismatic renewal has not been used primarily as a money-raising technique. That could become a matter simply of transfering a materialistic outlook from the personal to the congregational level. Rather, it is a recognition that stewardship represents a *need for the believer.* Cheerful and generous giving is the Lord's antidote to the love of money. Personal stewardship would be a necessary emphasis even if a congregation had a huge endowment and needed no offerings to carry on its ministry.

Generous givers say that they cannot outgive God. One man, who had the true spiritual gift of liberality (Rom. 12:8), put it this way: "I shovel it out the front door, and God shovels it in the back door, and he's got a bigger shovel than I do." Another person noted that he had never heard anyone say that he had given up tithing; there is no "ex-tithers club." Those who have taken this step of faith share with enthusiasm the blessings of giving. A newly converted couple told how they had increased their giving each Sunday for a period of weeks and discovered that they did not miss the money that was given. They discovered the joy of giving.

Charismatic churches challenge believers in all areas of activity, including the church's financial needs. This does not mean, however, that they continually dun the people for money. The direction of the challenge is more toward God than toward the people, a matter of prayer more than of promotion. There may actually be very little said about money in the open gatherings or services of the congregation. The emphasis is on the working of the Spirit, trusting God for the church's finances. In one charismatic Lutheran congregation the "stewardship program" one year consisted solely in a group of men who gathered every Tuesday morning at 6:00 A.M. to pray for the financial needs of the congregation. The congregation's income increased dramatically.

In 1973, after years of financial struggle, North Heights Lutheran Church in St. Paul, Minnesota, decided to shift from the traditional "promotional" approach in stewardship to trusting God and his Word in regard to finances. Individually and as families, the members sought to step out in faith in order to implement what they sensed to be God's will. They looked to God as their source of income. Groups of spiritually renewed members met weekly to pray for the finances that would enable the congregation to carry out the ministry God had entrusted to it. In the ensuing years the church's income rose from 30% to 50% annually, from $78,000 to $1,500,000 in one decade.

During a discussion of poverty that took place at an ecumenical meeting of charismatic leaders in the United States, Joseph Garlington, a black pastor serving an inner-city church in Pittsburgh, made this statement: "The first thing we need to do is ask whether poverty is an economic or a spiritual problem. I believe it is a spiritual problem." He went on to say that when people in his congregation started tithing, many of them moved off the public-assistance rolls.

Many Pentecostal churches, with exemplary standards of stewardship, can trace their origins to storefront missions that served the most impoverished segment of society. "From the beginning," said Pentecostal patriarch David du Plessis, "we taught our people to tithe."

If we focus our expectations only on observable human resources, we will always look to the rich as the givers, the poor as the receivers. Although there is a certain logic, and also biblical support, for this approach, it may be less than the whole answer. In a Third World church, when tithing was taught, people began to prosper. They moved from subsistence-level living to financial freedom. The government was so impressed that they asked church leaders their key to economic prosperity.

In Ethiopia, both in terms of percentage of income and in overall amount, poorer Christians outgive their more prosperous neighbors. These and other illustrations suggest that we need to look beyond our traditional approach to stewardship. Tithing or sacrificial giving can be practiced with great blessing by believers without particular regard to income.

Generosity that flows from the heart does not come naturally to us. The believer must ask the Holy Spirit to bestow and release the gift of generous giving. When it happens, it is God's work and God's glory.

A lifelong process

Christian discipleship is a lifelong process in which the Holy Spirit conforms us to the image of Christ so that our lives reflect his glory. It will not be completed in this life (Phil. 1:6). Yet Christ clearly expects that when our lives are joined to him we will be "fruitful" (John 15:5; Phil. 1:11). When the Holy Spirit has control of us, he produces observable results. For he works according to the Father's will, and that will is for us to become holy and to bear fruit. It is not an option, it is a demand. But it is a demand that God himself makes possible through the indwelling of Christ by the Holy Spirit.

CHAPTER 41

MANIFESTING SPIRITUAL GIFTS

The early church manifested an astonishing abundance of spiritual gifts. It proclaimed the gospel not only in truth but with power. God underscored the spoken message with the signs that followed (Mark 16:20; Acts 4:30; 1 Cor. 1:4-8; Heb. 2:3b-4).

Many aspects of the Christian faith are assumed to have present-day relevance. This has not been true, however, in regard to all of the spiritual gifts. Any serious talk of manifesting spiritual gifts must therefore begin by considering what the Bible says about their use.

The apostle Paul introduced the concept of *charism* (spiritual gift) into the vocabulary of the New Testament. The term is related to the word *charis* (grace), and should therefore be understood as an outworking of God's grace, a gift freely given. It may refer to the gift of salvation (Rom. 6:23; Rom. 5:15-17). It may also refer to other gifts granted by God, the content of the gift being determined by the context (Rom. 1:11; 11:29; 1 Cor. 7:7).

In the charismatic renewal, *charism* has been used primarily in the technical, specialized sense that one finds in Romans 12, 1 Corinthians 12, Hebrews, and in the Pastoral Epistles (see especially 1 Peter 4:10), where it means specific gifts granted by the Spirit to individual members of the congregation. Charisms are spiritual endowments that the Holy Spirit gives to believers in order to equip them for powerful and effective service.

Unity and diversity of gifts

By comparing the various lists of charisms in the New Testament, it becomes evident that they embrace great diversity. There are references to events and to persons, to spontaneous acts of supernatural power and to permanent, unspectacular ministries, to directly inspired speech and to premeditated instruction, to the breaking in of the transcendent God, and to patient and humble service.

Distinctions between charismatic and natural gifts are not always clear-cut. There may be a connection between natural talent and charismatic ministry, though this is not necessarily so. Sometimes the Spirit grants gifts that seem contrary to a person's natural endowment. He reserves the right to do the unexpected (see 1 Cor. 1:26-31).

The characteristic thought of Paul, which all ages find difficult to grasp, was the enormous freedom and diversity of the Spirit's gifts on the one hand (2 Cor. 3:17; 1 Cor. 12:14-26), and on the other hand, the common foundation and common goal of the gifts. The diversity of gifts is grounded in a strong unity. Scripture clarifies this distinction in two particular ways.

First, the varieties of gifts, service, and working have their origin in the one, triune God (1 Cor. 12:4-6). In 1 Cor. 12:4-6, three terms are linked together: "Now there are varieties of gifts (*charismata*), but the same Spirit, and there are varieties of service (*diakoniai*), but the same Lord, and there are varieties of working (*energemata*), but it is the same God who inspires them all in every one." The charisms are given by the Spirit, but at the same time they express the servant nature of Christ and the fatherly provision of God. The doctrine of the charisms is a part of the New Testament doctrine of the Spirit, but it is set in a trinitarian context.

Second, the church is the body of Christ in a real sense (1 Cor. 12:12). Different members with differing gifts all belong to the one body. The place and function of each member is determined by the gift that one exercises (1 Cor. 12:14-16; Rom. 12:4-8).

The gifts are a manifestation of Christ's life. They should come to expression in every aspect of a congregation's life and ministry (1 Cor. 11:23-30; 14:26; Eph. 5:18-20; Acts 2:42-47). There should be a profound, Spirit-directed interplay of the various gifts in the ministry of a congregation. No member should lack all gifts, and no member has all gifts.

In seeking to explain or encourage the use of spiritual gifts, charismatics sometimes take an overly individualistic approach. They underscore such texts as, "You can *all* prophesy . . ." and "I want you *all* to speak in tongues" (1 Cor. 14:31,5; italics added). This can come across to noncharismatics as pressure or manipulation.

Certainly there is a time and place for individuals to be confronted with their own need to be empowered by the Holy Spirit, and this may include the manifestation of specific gifts. But the full panoply of spiritual gifts needs particularly to be urged in relation to the congregation. The congregation is a microcosm of the body of Christ. Our goal for the congregation should be nothing less than the full spectrum of spiritual gifts in full and effective operation. If that goal is declared in power, we can trust the Holy Spirit himself to address specific members in regard to specific gifts.

Receiving and evaluating spiritual gifts

Charisms can and should be sought: "Earnestly desire the higher gifts. . . . Make love your aim, and earnestly desire the spiritual gifts, especially that you may prophesy" (1 Cor. 12:31; 14:1).

The gifts of the Spirit are sought primarily through prayer (1 Cor. 14:13). They may be given by intercession and laying on of hands by leaders in the church (Acts 13:3; 14:23; Rom. 1:11; 1 Tim. 4:14; 2 Tim. 1:6).

The criterion for evaluating spiritual gifts is threefold:

First, spiritual gifts manifest the primitive confession of the church, "Jesus is Lord" (1 Cor. 12:3). They also express the unity of the one body, one Spirit, one hope, one faith, one Baptism, and one God and Father (Eph. 4:4-6).

Second, they build up the church (1 Cor. 12:7; Eph. 4:11-12). All charisms should contribute in some way toward this goal.

Third, they are governed by love (1 Corinthians 13; Rom. 12:9; Eph. 4:15-16). Those who manifest gifts without love are counted as nothing (1 Cor. 13:1-3).

The dispensational question

Does the Holy Spirit distribute spiritual gifts today, or was that a special consideration given only at the beginning, to "get the church established"? This is a familiar argument, which usually goes by the name of dispensationalism. The idea is that history is divided up into different epochs or dispensations. God's purpose, and therefore his action, varies according to the dispensation; for example, God dealt differently with people before the Flood than he did after the Flood, differently before the giving of the law at Sinai than afterward.

According to some dispensationalists, the early church lived in a different dispensation than the church today. When the New Testament was completed, God inaugurated a new dispensation in which the gifts of the Spirit were no longer necessary. Today we have the Scripture. All we have to do is proclaim the Word and invite people to accept it "by faith."

While this theology is primarily taught among certain groups in the Anabaptist tradition, it has also found its way into some circles of Lutherans.[1] Hints of it can be found in both Luther and Calvin, though it is not a developed or consistent position.[2]

The implication in dispensationalism is that signs and wonders were a necessary scaffolding for establishing the authority of the Word in the early church. Once the Word was enshrined in an authoritative Scripture, these primitive means could be dispensed with. According to this understanding, spiritual gifts belong to the infant stage of faith; the church today walks in faith along a higher plane. This is flattering to our spiritual ego, and it offers a superficial explanation for the widespread absence of gifts and miracles in the church today. But it compromises the foundation of the church, which from the beginning was the Lord Jesus Christ, received by faith alone. It is a mistake to interpret signs and wonders as the ground of faith—either in the early church or today.[3]

In comparing the situation of the early church with the situation today, it misconstrues the issue to set faith and signs in opposition to one another. The Spirit-inspired declaration of the gospel in the early church was in Word and in deed. Those addressed by this audible-visible gospel responded to it in faith, or rejected it in unbelief. In regard to faith, the situation of the early church was no different from ours: it came as a gift through the working of the Holy Spirit.

The dispensationalist explanation separates what God has joined together: the Word and signs that follow are two sides of the same coin. The issue, rather, is this: Has the Holy Spirit, in our day, chosen to work in a different way than he did in the early church? In the early church proclamation and signs were joined together. Now, we are told, signs are not necessary because we have an authoritative Scripture. Neither Scripture itself, nor history, nor common experience bear out such a contention.

Today, as at the beginning, the Holy Spirit desires to manifest the sovereign power of Christ's victory over sin and death in an incarnational way through specific and varied gifts given to members of Christ's body. Spiritual gifts flow from Christ himself, who is *the* gift to the church. The fullness of the kingdom is hidden in Christ. Through the Holy Spirit we have access to the rich store of Christ's gifts. In a sense, spiritual gifts represent a continuation of Christ's incarnational ministry. Through them the Holy Spirit ministers Christ's love in a demonstrative way.

The twofold expression of spiritual gifts

All spiritual gifts are an exercise of the power and authority of Christ. Within the body of Christ, however, the gifts interrelate in a particular way.

Some gifts involve the exercise of a Spirit-given ministry or office. Here the "gift" is a Spirit-anointed person who manifests a particular office of

Christ within the body of believers: apostle, prophet, evangelist, shepherd, and teacher (Eph. 4:11; 1 Cor. 12:28).

Other gifts involve the exercise of a Spirit-given ability or power. Here the gifts are specific demonstrations of the Spirit, manifested through believers, enabling them to minister to other members or to nonbelievers with resources beyond their own natural abilities (1 Cor. 12:4-11; Rom. 12:6-8; Heb. 2:4; 1 Peter 4:10).

It is important that these two types of gifts be recognized and properly related in the daily life of a body of believers. An office gift could be compared to a captain or a coach: it encourages, develops, enables, and orders the functioning of the charismatic gifts. The primary task of the office gifts is to equip the saints. Office gifts manifest Christ's headship in the body. They inspire faith in a way that encourages and releases the charismatic gifts. They help brothers and sisters recognize and use their gifts for the good of all. They see that the charisms are exercised in an orderly and biblically consistent manner for the equipping of the saints for the work of ministry, for the building up of the body of Christ'' (Eph. 4:12, New King James Version).

To speak of order, however, without active encouragement of spiritual gifts is more or less pointless: there will be nothing to order. Scripture tells us that we should ''earnestly desire the spiritual gifts'' (1 Cor. 14:1), and for a very good reason. Without desire, there will be no quickening of faith and expectation.

A simple question was once put to a group of people gathered for a seminar on spiritual renewal at Luther Northwestern Theological Seminary in St. Paul, Minnesota: ''In your experience, has the Lutheran church encouraged people to earnestly desire the spiritual gifts?'' It was met with a shaking of heads. Generally speaking, mainline churches have not taught people to seek the full scriptural range of spiritual gifts.

In discussions about spiritual gifts you often run into the contention, ''Oh, I am open to any spiritual gift that the Lord wants to give me.'' The scriptural word, however, is much stronger than ''being open'': The Greek word *zaylow* (1 Cor. 12:31; 14:1) means to ''strive,'' ''desire,'' ''exert oneself earnestly.'' ''Being open'' is essentially a passive attitude. It does not yield the same practical result as ''striving after.''

Jack Eichhorst, president of the Lutheran Bible Institute in Seattle, Washington, once shared with Larry Christenson his concern that the school provide a hospitable climate for charismatic spirituality. The proof that the climate was not merely tolerant, but truly hospitable, he agreed, would be that some students come to the school not having experienced some spiritual gifts, and leave having experienced them. ''Charismatic spirituality'' includes encouraging people to earnestly desire the spiritual gifts.

It is a responsibility of those who lead God's people to encourage an active faith and expectancy for all of the spiritual gifts. Scripture leaves no doubt that spiritual gifts are to be recognized, sought after, and used. God does not only *commission* disciples, that is, give them a task or calling; he also *empowers* them with spiritual gifts so that they can carry out that calling.

Where gifts are absent from the life of the church, the primary responsibility must rest with the leaders. They must, first of all, *proclaim* the availability and desirability of spiritual gifts, as did the apostles. Faith is kindled by the Word. Then they must provide a climate that actively welcomes the gifts, gives them a place to grow and develop, and disciplines and orders them in the Lord's service. A truly Spirit-filled church helps its people enter into the Spirit-filled life, informs them about spiritual gifts, helps them to discover their gifts, encourages them to seek gifts, aids them in releasing their gifts, instructs them in the proper use of gifts, and provides the setting for corporate use of gifts.

Spiritual gifts in the early history of the church

The exercise of spiritual gifts, as described by Paul in Romans 12 and 1 Corinthians 12, into the second and third centuries, is well-documented. Justin Martyr (beheaded in Rome in 165) examined the charismata in his discussion with the educated Jew, Tryphon. In his *Dialog with Tryphon* (ca. 160), Justin wrote: "Among us one can see men and women who have received gifts from the Spirit of God."[4]

Irenaeus (bishop of Lyon after 177), the most significant theologian of the second century, also spoke of spiritual gifts. In his *Denunciation and Refutation of the False Gnosis,* which won him renown as an opponent of heresies, we find the following: "Yet we hear in the church of many brothers who have prophetic gifts, who speak through the Holy Spirit in tongues, who bring to light the hidden things of men, for their salvation, and explain the mysteries of God."[5]

Origen (died 253/54 at age 70, as a result of torture during the Decian persecution), the greatest scholar of ancient Christendom, referred expressly to the gifts of the Spirit in a letter to his opponent Celsus: "Christians cast out demons, accomplish many healings and, according to God's will, see into the future."[6]

The ancient church bore witness not only to the exercise of spiritual gifts, but also, in accord with St. Paul, to the fact that use and misuse of such gifts are often quite close to one another. The institutional church came to suspect Spirit-gifted laity as sectarian troublemakers. Fear of pseudoprophets increased with the passage of time. The charismata were mentioned less and less—in some places ignored altogether.

Montanism arose during the second century in reaction to this trend. One might call Montanism the Pentecostal movement of early church history. In A.D. 156–157, Montanus and two women, Prisca and Maximilla, appeared as prophets in Phrygia (Asia Minor). They strove against the increasing worldliness of the church. Maximilla declared: "The Lord has sent me. Whether I want to or not, I must proclaim his will."[7]

It seems that the form of prophecy in Montanism was almost more of a problem than the content. The Montanists were accused of speaking in a trancelike state, which was considered a sign of a false prophet. They often spoke in the first person, for example: "I am the Paraclete . . . I am the word and the Spirit and the Power." Their opponents apparently chose to take such expressions in a literal sense, contending that Montanus claimed to be the incarnation of the Holy Spirit.

The historical questions in relation to Montanism are difficult to answer because the only references to Montanism that we have, aside from brief comments by Tertullian, occur in writings by its opponents. Montanus expected the imminent return of the Lord, and the outpouring of spiritual gifts in his movement was seen as inaugurating the final stage of history in which the Holy Spirit would be operative in a special way. This claim, and the ecstatic form of the prophecy, seem to be the only fair arguments against Montanism that can be historically substantiated. There was no major doctrinal error. The main burden of Montanus and his followers was ethical, and it was their ethical rigor that attracted men like Tertullian.

If the Montanist controversy did not immediately lead to a common skepticism towards all prophecy in the church, this was nevertheless the ultimate outcome. In modern volumes of church history, Montanism is respectfully dubbed "a reform movement within the church."[8] The unhappy result of the movement, however, was that in later periods charismata were met with an exaggerated skepticism; lay people with extraordinary spiritual gifts were routinely judged to be heretics or sectarians.[9] The judgment of Kilian McDonnell, that "the church never really recovered its balance after it rejected Montanism" is possibly overdrawn as such, but it is a fairly accurate assessment of how the church came to regard the charismata.[10]

In the theologies of the Greek and Latin Fathers, teaching concerning the gifts of the Spirit was widely debated, yet in practice skepticism held sway.[11] Charismatic piety was revived in cenobitism, the style of monastic living originated by Pachomius around A.D. 320.[12] In the hermit monks influenced by Antonius the Great, there was also a rebirth of charismatic piety, reflected, for example, in the sayings of the desert fathers. Their spiritual life had its source in the contrite heart, the fruit of which was humility. Through the ascetic life the hermit fought desire and temptation; fasting and silence were central to their way of life. Out of the silence the charismata grew, especially the word of knowledge, wisdom, and prophecy. Gifts of healing and power over evil spirits were also known among the desert fathers.[13]

In Book Eight of the so-called *Apostolic Constitutions,* a collection concerning liturgical and jurisprudential matters that originated in either Syria or Constantinople around 380, there is an extensive discussion of early Christian charismata. God bestows spiritual gifts *so that unbelievers of good will might more easily come to belief.*[14] Also stressed is the following: "There is no one who believes in God through Christ, who should not also receive spiritual gifts."[15]

There are different sorts of charismata: some "express themselves in miracles"; others simply constitute the substance of belief, such as the gift that one honors no false gods but worships "God, the Father, through Christ." Whoever is kept clear of heresy should be seen as having received a spiritual gift.

As highly valued as the more exceptional gifts were, the church's negative experiences gave rise to the strong admonition: "Whoever can perform signs and wonders ought neither judge nor cast suspicion on those believers who have not been granted such gifts."[16] In principle, the ancient church clung to the recognition of the charismata, even though, with the passage of time, the practical reality diminished. Reinhold Seeberg is essentially correct when, with a view toward this reality, he says, "The church set aside the dwindling charismata and blocked the Spirit with the word of the New Testament gospel."[17]

Spiritual gifts: their use in the church today

The Holy Spirit is no different today than he was in the days of the early church. He still has this unimaginable store of spiritual gifts for building up the body of Christ and bringing its witness to the world. The "priesthood of believers" (1 Peter 2:9-10) becomes functional as people begin to discover and use their spiritual gifts.

The charismatic renewal is sounding this word of hope and faith in the church today: "Spiritual gifts—*all* of them—are part of God's provision for the church. Let us use them!" The *us* is important, for the exhortation is addressed to the renewal as much as to the church. The charismatic renewal is not in a position to lecture the church on its neglect of spiritual gifts, though we have done this time and time again, and need to ask forgiveness. The renewal itself has scarcely begun truly to make room for receiving and developing spiritual gifts. We have seen in Scripture far more than we have experienced, and it is this—the promise of Scripture—that we hold up in the midst of the church: "Come, as brothers and sisters of the Lord who went about doing good, healing all who were oppressed, let us together seek the gifts promised in his Word. Let us spread his gospel in demonstration of the Spirit and of power."

Even though imperfectly understood and used, spiritual gifts are a practical part of the gospel ministry (1 Cor. 13:9). They help build the congregation and the individual believer; they glorify Jesus; they put the love of God into action.

Discernment

The congregation needs to test spiritual gifts for authenticity. Precisely because spiritual experience is so important, life in the Holy Spirit must be subject to the closest scrutiny. The history of the early church reminds us how important is the ministry of "discernment of spirits" (1 Cor. 12:10; 1 John 4:1-3). What spirit is at work in a given situation—God's Holy Spirit, the human spirit, a demonic power, or a mixture of influences? Special watchfulness must be exercised in regard to the use of spiritual gifts, for instance, where prophecies are directed to specific individuals.

Theological perspective is indispensable. Otherwise the work of God can be damaged by spiritual Lone Rangers, pride, wrong understanding, unteachableness, and sectarian isolation. These dangers, however, dare not lead to such an overcritical stance that every spiritual outbreak gets squashed before it gets started. We must live with a measure of risk if we want to experience life in the Holy Spirit.

We must allow room for some learning to take place, which includes the possibility of failures and mistakes. A sailboat under full sail can capsize. The important thing is to learn something from that experience so that we can, without fear, bring the boat into full sail again.

An examination of three gifts

While the charismatic renewal has called for the church to be open to the full range of spiritual gifts, some gifts have been more prominently associated with the movement than others. It would go beyond our purpose to discuss in detail all the different charisms, but it is worth taking further note, in the following three chapters, of three gifts that are particularly associated with the movement and which play an important role in charismatic spirituality: *prophecy, speaking in tongues,* and *healing.* They are also controversial in the church at large, and a clarification of their meaning and practice can be helpful.

CHAPTER 42

THE GIFT OF PROPHECY

The basic meaning of the word *prophecy* is the proclamation of a divinely inspired message. It denotes a special charism in the New Testament church (1 Cor. 12:10; 13:2; 14:22). It was a widespread phenomenon in the early church until about A.D. 300.

Christians who speak prophetically in public proclaim God's Word by the inspiration of the Spirit. Peculiar to prophetic speech as distinct from ordinary speech is the element of revelation, *apokalypsis* (1 Cor. 14:26,30). What is revealed is not necessarily the future; more often, prophecy deals with the present situation, especially deeper and hidden truths about the situation of individuals and the church (1 Cor. 14:24-25). Prophecy leads to a keen awareness of God's presence. Prophecy may evoke confession of sin and acknowledgment of the presence of God.

A congregational prophet is not in a state of ecstasy. There is no irresistible constraint to deliver the message. He or she may begin or stop speaking at will (1 Cor. 14:29-33). A true prophet can speak prophetically, however, only if a message has been received from God.

The function and purpose of the gift of prophecy is to bring the Word and will of God to bear on a particular situation. This may take place through the convicting and judging of sin, and through pointing to God's promises (Revelation 2–3). Prophecy is primarily directed toward the church.

Although prophecy is a charism by which the Spirit conveys his message in a spontaneous, unpremeditated way through believers to believers, prophets speak within the framework of the apostolic tradition contained in the New Testament. Prophets may play a role in the development of doctrine, but they cannot go beyond or against the message delivered to the church by the apostles. Scripture is the norm for testing all prophecy. The words of prophets are tested in the light of the final revelation in Christ (1 Cor. 12:3; Matt. 7:15-20; 1 Thess. 5:20-21; 1 John 4:1-2). This can be done by believers with gifts of prophecy (1 Cor. 14:29) or the ability to distinguish between spirits (1 Cor. 12:10). Basically, all Christians are encouraged to test messages on the basis of the revealed Word of God (Acts 17:11; 1 Thess. 5:20-21).

Prophecy is a particularly valuable gift for edifying or building up the church. It should be sought by Christians (1 Cor. 12:31; 14:1). It can bring the truths of Scripture to bear in particular situations with great force.

Prophecy in the New Testament sense is utterance given by direct inspiration of the Holy Spirit, through which God's true will is proclaimed. There is, to be sure, a theological criterion applicable to prophetic utterance (its content must agree with the confession of faith, cf. Rom. 12:6), and it must be confirmed in a responsible way, yet the utterance is not simply a theological conclusion.

The practice of the gift of prophecy in churches today can be considered in the light of a series of basic questions:

What is prophecy?

The Hebrew idea of a prophet (*nabi*) carried with it the understanding that the prophet spoke words that had been divinely revealed, as a messenger of God, and the declarer of God's will.[1] Prophecy may include an element of prediction, but not necessarily so. The central meaning of the word *prophesy*, both in Hebrew and Greek, is to speak forth, to proclaim on behalf of someone else.

This basic meaning of the word *prophet* sheds light on the function of New Testament prophecy. The word describes someone who makes something known or public, especially one who speaks for God, who proclaims God's will. Prophecy involves something other than a faith-awakening missionary proclamation, something other than didactic instruction, something other than mere information concerning some future occurrence (even though prophetic speech *can* touch future events).

God's prophets receive direct inspiration to speak a divinely given message. The message can come in a variety of ways: word by word, as a picture or inner impression, through dream or vision, or through application of a particular Scripture.[2]

Prophecy, as distinguished from the gift of teaching or counseling, is not arrived at by a direct process of study or reasoning. It has a certain quality of spontaneity. It has more the immediate sense of being received than of being arrived at by logical process. Prophecy is different from the prophet's own general wisdom, biblical insight, or recognition of needs among those that are being addressed. A prophecy does not start in the prophet's brain, but in God himself. When God sees the need for prophetic revelation and finds someone who is ready and able to speak for him, then he will impress his message on the prophet by the Holy Spirit. Therefore, though it may exercise his or her thought and concern even over a considerable period of time, the message that the prophet brings is essentially unpremeditated.

The biblical meaning of prophecy is not identified with every inspired utterance. There can be testimonies, teaching, and preaching that are certainly inspired by God. The difference between these and what the Bible means by prophecy is not the content of the message but the way in which the message is given. In the case of teaching, the message depends partly on a person's knowledge, training, and insight, whereas prophecy has its origin in God alone. Prophecy does not depend on a man or woman's natural talents or intellectual powers, though these may influence to some degree the way in which he or she conveys the message.

What is the biblical role of prophecy?

In the Old Testament, God revealed his message through his prophets, a term widely used in Scripture. Besides those usually named as prophets, the term was applied to people like Abraham, Aaron, Miriam, and Moses.

Above all, God has revealed himself through his Son (Hebrews 1; John 1:18), who is *the* prophet. Although Jesus outwardly bore certain similarities to the scribes, he lacked the prerequisites for rabbinical service in the usual sense. As far as we know, Jesus had neither studied theology nor been ordained a scribe. In any case, he was not viewed as a professional theologian, but rather as a charismatic figure (Mark 1:22), and the unanimous opinion was: "He is a prophet." This was continually expressed among the people (Mark 6:15; Matt. 21:11-46; Luke 7:16; John 4:19; 6:14; 7:40-52; 9:17) and even among the Pharisees, if with a touch of skepticism (Mark 8:11; Luke 7:39). The religious leaders demanded a sign from Jesus precisely because he was viewed as a prophet; the sign was a means by which he could legitimize the claim. According to Luke 24:19, Jesus' disciples also saw him as a prophet. Jesus was finally arrested and accused as a false prophet.[3] Jesus himself did not reject the opinion that he was a prophet. Although his own (divine) commissioning was not described in detail, he did see himself in the ranks of the prophets (Luke 13:33; Matt. 23:31-39; also Mark 6:4; Luke 4:24; John 4:44).

As the true bearer of all spiritual gifts, Jesus continues his prophetic ministry as exalted Lord through his body, the church. The Pentecost message proclaimed that the age had now come when prophecy should be frequent among God's people (Acts 2:17; cf. Joel 2:28). The importance of the prophetic office in the ancient church is indisputable. It is immediately evident in the regional expansion of the church: in Palestine (Matt. 7:22; 10:41); in Caesarea (Acts 21:9); in Antioch, with its prominent Gentile congregation (Acts 13:1); and especially in Jerusalem (Acts 11:27-30; 21:10; 15:32). The presence of prophets in Thessalonica (1 Thess. 5:20), in Ephesus (Acts 19:6), and in Rome (Rom. 12:6) may be assumed as well. The significance of prophecy in the early church is further evidenced by the fact that specific individuals are named as prophets.

The high regard for prophecy in the church at Corinth is well known. Paul reckoned the ministry of the prophet among the charismata given to the body of Christ (Rom. 12:6; 1 Cor. 12:10,28). He urged the Corinthians to seek this gift earnestly (1 Cor. 14:1,39). Prophetic speech was esteemed as the gift of the Holy Spirit, more valuable, for instance, than speaking in tongues, unless the tongue is interpreted.[4] The importance of this spiritual gift was underscored when Paul stated that God had "appointed" the prophetic office (1 Cor. 12:28). It is noteworthy that he used this same verb to indicate that the ministry of reconciliation was established by God's will (2 Cor. 5:19). Paul himself possessed the gift of prophecy and employed it in his letters (Rom. 11:25-27; 1 Cor. 15:51-58). Ephesians stresses the fundamental significance of the postresurrection prophetic ministry for the entire church (Eph. 2:20; 3:5; 4:11).

New Testament prophecy often operates in the direction of spiritual or pastoral care: "He who prophesies speaks to men for their upbuilding and encouragement and consolation" (1 Cor. 14:3). The extent to which one, through prophetic utterance, may come face to face with God is made abundantly clear from 1 Cor. 14:24-25: "But if all prophesy, and an unbeliever or outsider enters, he is convicted by all, he is called to account by all, the secrets of his heart are disclosed; and so, falling on his face, he will worship God and declare that God is really among you."

And finally, the book of Revelation, taken as a whole, is an outstanding testimony to the place of prophecy among the early Christians. The seven letters to the churches in Asia Minor are presented as direct, prophetically received words from the risen Lord. The ministry of prophets receives prominent mention throughout the book (11:18; 16:6; 18:20-24; 22:9). The reader is urgently warned against undervaluing the claims of this prophetic writing (22:6-7,18-19).

What role does prophecy play in the history of the church?

It would be incorrect to state that the church has known no prophecy at all in the post-New Testament era. There is evidence of prophetic activity over the centuries. For example, the Swedish seer Birgitta (d. 1373), as a result of particular revelations, was active in the political life of her homeland and was prophetically involved in the ending of the "Babylonian Captivity" of the papacy (1309–1377). In a vision she was given the task of founding an order. The Birgittine Order was the most significant institution of its type in Scandinavia. Birgitta's piety was in the tradition of the great mystics, such as Meister Eckhart (d. 1327), Johan Tauler (d. 1361), Heinrich Suso (d. 1366), and Johannes von Ruysbroeck (d. 1381).

In a vision, the glorified Christ told Birgitta of the suffering that the sorry condition of the church was causing him. She heard Christ saying to her, "Even the Christians are lifting me onto the cross through their love of sin; they slay me through their impatience. They can bear no words concerning me."[5] In her visionary meetings with Christ, it became clear to her that the church's history is essentially nothing more than the continuation of his passion.[6] Birgitta exerted great effort to call the church, which was sliding away from its Lord, to repentance. Through the order she founded, she strove to arouse a great penitential movement, one fruit of which would be that the church would again practice the New Testament spiritual gifts.

Birgitta stands in a long tradition of renewal movements in which the prophetic gift was evident. Lutheran Pietism, for instance, experienced a renewal of prophetic gifts. There is no evidence that Spener or Francke spoke in tongues.[7] However, they did believe and practice the kind of prophetic manifestations common among charismatics, such as "visions, dreams, raptures, miracles, and special revelations." On the basis of Scripture they also rejected the arguments of Anabaptist and Calvinist dispensationalism, suggesting that spiritual gifts ended with the apostles.[8]

Yet, taken as a whole, prophetic utterance is a slender thread in the tapestry of church history. Bruce Yokum is correct when he writes, "It is clear that since the third century prophecy has been neither continuously manifest in the church nor common to the whole church at any one time."[9]

In the charismatic renewal the gift of prophecy has come to the fore perhaps more widely than at any time since the second century. The church is being challenged by a vigorous movement that maintains that all spiritual gifts, and preeminently prophecy, are an expression of Jesus himself, manifesting himself through members of his body.

How is prophecy understood today?

As it is used in the church today, the word *prophetic* often means simply a penchant for social criticism. The sense of a spontaneous utterance inspired by the Holy Spirit is foreign to our whole way of thinking and responding.

Most Christians have no sense of lack because of the absence of prophecy in the church. The church has learned to trust in theological and scientific wisdom, in churchly and worldly methodologies, rather than to expect that God will speak prophetically to us today. Prophecy has not found a place in everyday church life, but the Spirit is working toward the day when the church will again expect and take to heart his prophetic Word.

Most thoughtful participants in the charismatic renewal recognize that prophetic revelation in the renewal has often been elementary. At charismatic conferences, for instance, most of the prophecies are rather generalized words of encouragement and exhortation. This is not to say that they have not been genuine or important (perhaps we need more encouragement than we realize), but it probably also illustrates the fact that "we prophesy in part . . . according to the measure of faith" (1 Cor. 13:9 KJV; Rom 12:6 KJV). We have been schooled in the ways of reason, but not in the more spontaneous modes of revelation. We should expect to grow and develop in the exercise of spiritual gifts. It is worth the time and effort, for it will make the church more responsive to the leading of the Spirit.

God never meant for his church to be guided only by the natural and spiritual wisdom that we have accumulated. On occasion, he wants to break through with prophetic revelation. When the prophetic Word is again spoken and received, the church will have taken one more believing step toward biblical normalcy.

How does present-day prophecy relate to biblical authority?

Jesus confirmed the Old Testament as the true Word of God. By word and deed he declared the will and plan of God when he was on earth, always consistent with the written revelation (see, for example, Matt. 8:17; John 10:35b; Luke 24:27). He entrusted his mission to the apostles and equipped them by the Holy Spirit to remember and correctly interpret all that he had taught and done (John 14:26; 16:14). He wrapped their apostolic witness in the mantle of his own authority (see, for example, Matt. 10:40-41; Acts 15:7; 1 Cor. 14:37). Thus the written Scriptures of both the Old and the New Testament rest on the authority of Jesus Christ. Our confidence that the written Scriptures are the Word of God is rooted in our trust in Christ himself.

Christ himself submitted all that he said and did to the test of Scripture. We can point to no better model. All present-day prophecy must be submitted to and tested by the Bible. The Bible is God's authoritative Word. He will never inspire a prophecy that contradicts his own Word.

Prophecies are not meant to bring fundamentally new doctrinal material to the church. Rather, a prophetic message applies or expands on biblical truth, emblazoning certain passages or truths on the hearts of individuals, groups, congregations, or even the church as a whole.

It is possible, of course, that God could expand on scriptural truth through prophetic revelation—give providential direction on issues not directly dealt with in Scripture. For instance, if space travel were to become a reality, we might encounter things for which there would be no immediate scriptural paradigm. Scripture itself does not prescribe precise limits for prophetic revelation. This lies within the sovereignty of God. In the meantime, we can receive with thanksgiving the gift of prophetic revelation, faithfully submitting it to the authority of Scripture.

Do we need prophecy today?

Prophecy brings home with added force the fact that God really does speak to us. It highlights his nearness and concern. Prophecy can increase our trust in the living and caring God, in his willingness to guide us even in the most ordinary situations. We need this in a secularized culture, in which God, if he is considered at all, is kept at a distance and has no real influence on everyday life and decisions. The gift of prophecy can help restore a lively trust in the Lord who guides in his steadfast love the people whom he has redeemed (cf. Exod. 15:13), helping us to walk in faith step by step.

Prophecy serves especially to upbuild, encourage, and console the people of God (1 Cor. 14:3). A good illustration of that is the seven prophetic letters to the churches in Asia Minor (Revelation 2–3). Some of these churches were drifting away from their devotion to the Lord; some were falling victim to dangerous heresies; some were headed into hard times. They needed a clear Word that would rebuild their relationship with the Lord and prepare them for what lay ahead. It is easy for us to drift off center in our Christian calling, to be taken up with peripheral things and lose sight of that which concerns the Lord. Through the prophetic gift our real needs can be addressed, and God can edify, encourage, and console his people.

Prophecy makes the Word of God more personally effective because it pinpoints the Word that God has for a particular person or situation. We live in a culture that is virtually oblivious to the biblical concept of sin and guilt, and in some regards leans toward an almost hedonistic understanding of Christianity. In America, according to one poll, 74% of the people considered themselves Christian, yet fewer than half of these believed that they were sinners; they saw Christianity only as a way to have a fuller, more abundant life. It is the ministry of the Spirit to convict of sin and create faith in Christ, and he knows what an individual needs to hear in order to see his or her sin and the need for salvation. The gift of prophecy can make our evangelistic outreach more effective by pinpointing the Word that the Spirit wants to bring in a given situation (2 Sam. 12:7; 1 Cor. 14:25; Acts 8:30-35).

In the New Testament, prophecies normally dealt with the current time and situation, showing hidden things that needed to be uncovered, applying biblical truths to a present need. On occasion, however, prophecy can throw light on future events, in order to prepare people for what is to come. A group of Armenians emigrated to the United States in the early years of this century because the prophecy of an 11-year-old boy accurately warned them of an impending persecution.[10] Both in Acts and Revelation there are numerous examples of prophecies that predict future events. These enable the church to prepare for what lies ahead. A Word from the risen Lord, who through suffering has defeated death—what a preparation for those headed into a time of persecution! The church that is prophetic today will be stronger tomorrow.

In the Old Testament, God's prophets attacked social unrighteousness and the oppression of the poor. Even though this was in the context of theocratic Israel, it has relevance for today. Lutheran doctrine speaks about the "first use of the law," *usus politicus,* that is, the application of God's law in civil, social, and political affairs. God's desire for social righteousness and his concern for those who suffer has not changed. Prophetic messages, directed first of all to the church, can help Christians see God's agenda for righteousness and justice in society at large.

Anyone who has listened to debate in the public marketplace knows that the theme of social justice evokes a clash of wildly divergent opinions. There is disagreement not only as to how to achieve justice in society but also as to what constitutes justice. As Christians we can do better than simply pick up our social agenda from the editorial page of the local newspaper. Through the prophetic gift we can discern God's priorities and plans and therefore serve him more effectively in the social arena.

Prophets in the Old Testament also attacked false spiritual security, superficial worship, and empty religious traditions. Christians can fall victim to the same ills. A Lutheran congregation that hadn't moved forward spiritually in more than 25 years and was quite content with its religious routine, suddenly found itself with a new pastor who preached faith, surrender, and commitment to Christ as though it really ought to matter. After about a year had gone by, a small group began to agitate for his removal. They arranged a congregational meeting to force his resignation. At the meeting they rehearsed a litany of grievances with considerable acrimony and at some length. Finally someone called for the question. The chairman asked if there was any further discussion. A teenage girl who had sat silently throughout the meeting stood up and quietly said, "Let him who is without sin cast the first stone." The meeting was thunderstruck. Someone said, "I move that we table this matter indefinitely." It was tabled without even the agitators raising a dissenting voice. A prophetic Word can jar people out of complacency because it is pointed and direct, alerting them to the fact that God himself is concerned about them and dealing with them.

The nature of the prophetic gift answers to its function in the church. The church is the body of Christ (Rom. 12:5; 1 Cor. 12:27). Christ is the head (Eph. 1:22-23). Prophets are a communication link between the head and the members: they transmit the mind and will of the head to the members. As the members in a physical body pay heed to the impulses that come from the nerve center of the brain, so members in the body of Christ need to listen to what their spiritual head wants to say to them through his prophets. In this way the prophetic gift becomes a strategic part of Christ's ministry for bringing the church on earth to maturity.

Does God want a prophetic church?

The whole of Scripture testifies to the fact that prophecy is a key element in God's dealings with his people. The strong evangelistic outreach of the early church was closely linked to the ministry of prophets (see for example, Acts 13:1,3). This was a logical consequence of the Old Testament promises that in the age to come there would be an outpouring of the Spirit on all believers.

God himself has appointed some to prophetic ministry in the church (1 Cor. 12:28; Eph. 4:11). The order in which the gifts and ministries are listed is worth noting. Prophets are consistently listed as number two, right after apostles (see also Eph. 2:20; 3:5). The prophetic ministry has particular significance for the well-being and upbuilding of the church. There is no suggestion in Scripture that God intends this ministry to be superseded or dispensed with prior to the second coming of Christ. He wants prophets in the church today, and that is a call to obedience: we should seek in every way to encourage a responsible exercise of the prophetic gift.

God is looking for more than a passive, theoretical acceptance of spiritual gifts in the church. A passive acquiescence to "whatever gifts he wants to give me" can be the cover for an unbudging resistance to any actual mani-festation of spiritual gifts.

The early church seems to have had a deeper dependence on receiving prophetic direction from the Lord than does the church today. When they faced important choices, they sought the Lord's guidance through prophets. When a congregation today has important choices to make—setting right priorities, recognizing the gifts and ministries of the different members, com-ing up with a strategy for evangelism or a building program—we might well take a cue from the early church (see Acts 13 and 15). So also with individuals and groups that seek guidance from the Lord: we should ask those whom God has gifted prophetically to help us discern the Lord's will.

Spiritual gifts, and preeminently prophecy, must be actively encouraged among us. In public worship, prayer meetings, and private gatherings we need to cultivate an expectant faith in the God who speaks through his proph-ets. We need to create an atmosphere in which the prophetic gift can be freely expressed, grow, and mature. Then the Lord can more perfectly edify, en-courage, and comfort his church. Then the church can minister not simply in the power of human understanding, but in the power of divine knowledge and wisdom.

How does the prophetic ministry function?

Prophecy has nothing to do with uncontrollable ecstasy. The prophet who receives a message from God is not compelled to speak it out immediately (1 Cor. 14:32). In a worship service, prophecy should be offered in an orderly way, at a time provided for it.

Not everyone will prophesy, even though prophecy seems to be one of the more widely distributed spiritual gifts. Some believers may never receive a prophecy; others, only a few times in their lives. Some may prophesy rather freely, but the prophecies remain quite general or superficial, or of a mixed spirit; leaders in the congregation may need to impose some restraints. But others prophesy regularly under a clear anointing of the Spirit; the gift is manifested with increasing maturity and authority. The congregation comes to see that they have among them one with the "office" of a prophet.

A prophet is under a holy call from God to convey the revealed message. The form in which this is done may vary. Since the message is God-given, in the Old Testament it was often introduced with the phrase, "Thus says the Lord." In the New Testament we see the phrase, "Thus says the Holy Spirit" (Acts 21:11). At other times, however, a prophecy is given with no distinctive introduction (Acts 13:2). The form "Thus says the Lord" could be so un-familiar in some Lutheran churches that it would actually hinder the acceptance of the prophetic word. A lower-keyed introduction, such as, "I sense that the Lord wants to tell us . . ." might be a more helpful way of preparing people to receive a prophetic word. Prophets should seek to be sensitive not only to the content of the message but also to the most appropriate way to convey it, for that, too, is part of the wisdom of God.

The church today needs obedient prophets who faithfully speak the word given to them by God. The counterpart to this is a people who listen to that word with reverence, discernment, and with a predisposition to obey the Lord.

CHAPTER 43

THE GIFT OF TONGUES

The gift most prominently associated with charismatic renewal in the popular mind is speaking in tongues. It has played a major role in the spread both of the Pentecostal and the charismatic movements.[1] In our century it has become more widely experienced than at any time since the days of the early church. By any reckoning it has been the most controversial of the gifts.

Those who have experienced speaking in tongues testify to the blessings that the gift has brought into their lives, especially their personal prayer lives.[2] Critics say that it occasions spiritual pride, causes division among Christians, or at least is overemphasized in charismatic circles. It raises questions that call for serious and balanced consideration.

What is the basic meaning of the term?

The gift of tongues is sometimes called *glossolalia,* a transliteration of the Greek terms *glossais* (tongues) and *lalein* (to speak). The basic meaning of the word *tongue* in classical Greek, as in other languages, is the physical organ in the mouth. It is also used analogically in Greek: it can mean an antiquated or obsolete expression that needs explanation, or a language or dialect. In English, also, the word can be used analogically to mean language or a manner of speaking, as in "one's mother tongue" or "a silver-tongued orator." In the New Testament, however, *glossolalia* is a technical term that refers to a special kind of religious or spiritual speaking.[3]

Speaking in tongues is speech inspired by the Spirit (Acts 2:4); it is one of the gifts of the Holy Spirit (1 Cor. 12:10). It is not understood by the speaker, and usually not by anybody else (1 Cor. 14:2; Acts 2:6). It is not framed by the speaker in the way of a learned language. It is a spontaneous

266   LED BY THE SPIRIT

linguistic expression; the speaker does not consciously determine what he or she is going to say. It does not proceed from the conscious reasoning process (1 Cor. 14:14). It is pararational speech prompted by the Spirit.

This does not mean that speaking in tongues is necessarily ecstatic in an emotional sense or that it is uncontrolled.[4] The gift itself has no particular emotional aspect: there can be as little or as much emotion as with any other speaking, depending on the emotional state of the person who is speaking. It is subject to the speaker's conscious control; he or she can start or stop it at will, speak louder or softer, slower or faster, and so forth, even though the actual procession of words or sounds is not consciously determined.

What is the purpose of the gift?

It is mentioned in three places in the New Testament: Acts, 1 Corinthians, and the ending of the gospel of Mark. In Mark and Acts it serves primarily as a *sign* that one is a believer (Mark 16:17), or that one has been filled with the Spirit (Acts 2:4; 10:46; 19:6). In 1 Corinthians it is described as a form of *private prayer* or *personal edification* (14:2,4,16,28). When used with the sister gift of interpretation, it can be a communication to the church (1 Cor. 14:5,13,27).

Like the other charisms, the purpose of speaking in tongues is to edify or build up the church. Unlike other gifts, however, it most commonly does this indirectly: it builds up the individual believer, who then is able to contribute more effectively to building up the church (see 1 Cor. 14:18-19, where the private edification of tongues is related to public edification through prophecy). The gift of tongues is uniquely suited to private devotions, and this has been its primary application in the charismatic renewal. Many charismatics, who have seldom if ever spoken publicly in tongues, do so regularly in their private prayer times, and testify to its value.

The common occurrence of "singing in the Spirit" in charismatic worship takes place when everybody begins singing in tongues, each one using his or her own "tongue" and improvised melody. Sometimes it blends into a rich harmony. The practice is not attested to in Scripture, though one finds something like it in the history of Christian worship in the practice known as "jubilation."[5] It is not a single voice speaking out to be heard by the congregation, which would call for interpretation. It is a chorus of praise directed toward God, and therefore no interpretation is required. Although it may not benefit the minds of those present, it can still build up their spirits in the same way that speaking in tongues does in private. Moreover, the corporate dimension can help prepare the congregation for the exercise of other spiritual gifts in the worship service.

Speaking in tongues, because of its unusualness, can serve in a special way to alert us to the reality of God.[6] A Lutheran pastor's wife described it as "a daily reminder of the Spirit's presence." On occasion it may serve as a sign to skeptics or unbelievers (Acts 2:4; 1 Cor. 14:22). A person in Denmark described his encounter with tongues in this way:

> When I first went to a charismatic meeting, I heard the singing in tongues, and I knew that the Lord was in the midst of these people, but I was not one among them. This led me into a year of wrestling with the problem of sin and unholiness in my life until I finally confessed my sins to a brother and asked other Christians to pray with me for the Spirit.[7]

Tongues may also serve as a sign to other Christians that the gift of the Spirit has been received (Acts 10:45-46; 19:6). In Acts it is the most consistently mentioned sign that accompanies the reception of the gift of the Spirit. However, other signs are also mentioned in connection with receiving the Spirit—prophecy (Acts 19:6), extolling God (Acts 10:46), and miracles (Acts 9:18).

There is no indication that there are two different kinds of tongues: one a sign of receiving the Spirit, the other a spiritual gift. The same term is used throughout the New Testament without significant variation. It is a case, rather, of the same basic gift being used by the Spirit in different ways, to accomplish different purposes.

The occurrence of speaking in tongues on the Day of Pentecost was particularly unusual because it was understood by those who stood by and listened (Acts 2:6,8). This was not typical in the New Testament church, though the fact that the gift was apparently understood to be genuine language would seem to allow for the possibility (1 Cor. 14:2, 10-11).[8] Occurrences of *xenoglossia* (speaking by the Spirit in a known foreign language which the speaker has never learned) have been reported in present times. Risto Santala, a missionary in Israel, analyzed a tape of glossolalia utterances that a research team of the American Lutheran Church had obtained during a visit to Trinity Lutheran Church in San Pedro, California, and determined that it was a clearly spoken mixture of Hebrew and Aramaic, a hymn of praise cast in Old Testament bridal imagery.[9] There are no theological or other reasons for excluding the possibility of such an occurrence today.

What is the value of speaking in tongues?

For many people, speaking in tongues is an unparalleled experience of God's presence. The comprehensive study of charismatic renewal made by the Lutheran church in the German Democratic Republic characterized speaking in tongues as "a praying in the Holy Spirit remarkable for its clarity and simplicity, bypassing critical intellectual reflection, a standing in the presence of Christ that comes ever and again as a surprise, each time it is experienced. Speaking in tongues ushers the worshiper into the presence of God." [10]

Speaking in tongues may be one of the ways that the Spirit is dealing with an overweening dictatorship of rational processes in Western culture. It is not against reason, but its utterances are not determined by reason. In explaining his experience to some skeptical colleagues, Dennis Bennett said, "Speaking in tongues is not a feat of the intelligence, but it's the most intelligent thing I've ever done." There can be wisdom in recognizing not only the benefits of reason, but also its limits. *Time* magazine, reporting on the spread of charismatic gifts into mainline churches, noted the observation of a Lutheran charismatic pastor that "the gifts are God's answer to the hyperintellectualism of our age and the cold impersonality of formal worship." [11] It is not a question of downgrading the intellect, but of recognizing its limits, and restoring a measure of balance. In the life of faith, a restrictive rule of reason can close us off from those workings of the Spirit that come along other lines, and without which faith can degenerate into an intellectual belief system.

A teacher of a high-school Bible class came into the experience of speaking in tongues, and several months later one of his students remarked, "You know, he's *changed;* he believes it more now than he used to." This is not the kind of change that one learns out of a book. It springs from deep personal experience of the Holy Spirit's work in one's life. The teacher did not make extravagant claims in regard to his own experience. "I realize," he said, "that many people have come into blessings similar to mine without speaking in tongues. But this is the way that God chose to lead me into a deeper walk with him, and I thank him for it."

When many people witness to an experience that has deepened and strengthened their Christian faith, we would serve the church poorly to whisk it aside without a hearing, slapping on it a label of "fad" or "emotionalism." Especially so, since we are not dealing simply with a new church "program" or "approach" or "technique," but with a manifestation of the Holy Spirit that is clearly spoken about in the Bible. [12]

The testimonies of people who speak in tongues often illustrate what the Bible says about the gift, even though the person may not consciously plan it that way:

- "It is a form of prayer." One who speaks in a tongue speaks not to men but to God (1 Cor. 14:2).
- "We don't understand what we are saying, but we know that we are communing with God." He utters mysteries in the Spirit (14:2).
- "Sometimes, however, we do get a sense of what we are praying about. It may be a rather general sense that the prayer is a confession or a

petition or an intercession, but then it may also be a very specific sense of exactly what is being prayed." He who speaks in a tongue should pray for the power to interpret (14:13).

- "One of the most beautiful aspects of the gift is *singing* in tongues, where words and melody flow spontaneously together. It helps overcome our stiffness and formality—a new dimension of freedom in praise and worship." I will sing with the spirit (14:15).
- "We are spiritually strengthened and built up through the use of this gift." He who speaks in a tongue edifies himself (14:4).
- "It is praise and worship. That is what we sense most often." You are praising God with your spirit . . . you may be giving thanks well enough (14:16-17 NIV).
- "Occasionally we use the gift in a public meeting—a prayer group, church service, or charismatic conference—with interpretation following." If any speak in a tongue, let there be only two or at most three, and each in turn; and let one interpret (14:27).
- "Most often, however, we use it in private devotions. Far and away, this is the greatest blessing of speaking in tongues. It enriches the personal prayer life." He speaks to himself and to God (14:28).
- "Sometimes we don't know how to pray, or what to pray for. Then we can pray in tongues, trusting the Spirit to give the prayer that is needed in that situation." We do not know how to pray as we ought, but the Spirit himself intercedes for us with sighs too deep for words (Rom. 8:26).[13]
- "We had been pretty vague on the Holy Spirit. We 'believed' but it was more a theological than a personal conviction. The experience of speaking in tongues has helped make the Holy Spirit a fresh and personal reality in our lives." They were all filled with the Holy Spirit and began to speak in other tongues. . . . The Holy Spirit came on them; and they spoke with tongues (Acts 2:4; 19:6).

Practically speaking, how should the church handle the question of tongues?

Speaking in tongues can be overemphasized or abused. The apostle Paul addressed that kind of a situation in the church at Corinth, and what he wrote is part of Holy Scripture. Nothing that he wrote can support an argument *against* tongues, only against its abuse. Once this basic truth is grasped, our consideration of tongues can be cast in the positive framework that Paul himself reflected when he said, "I thank God that I speak in tongues more than you all" (1 Cor. 14:18). The cure for abuse is not disuse, but proper use.[14]

Churches have generally handled or responded to speaking in tongues in one of three ways. We will look briefly at each of these ways, then suggest a fourth way that we believe is more suitable both to the teaching of Scripture and in the context of the Lutheran church.

One common response to tongues has been simply to banish or disallow it. Sometimes this is backed up with a theological rationale such as dispensationalism:—"tongues were intended only for the apostolic age." We have dealt with the question of dispensationalism earlier: there is nothing in Scripture that allows us to limit certain spiritual gifts to the apostolic age. Scripture does not draw that kind of distinction between any of the gifts—assigning some to the apostolic age, while others continue. To be consistent, dispensationalism would have to consign *all* of the charismata to the apostolic age, including the charism of eternal life (Rom. 6:23), something that not even the most thoroughgoing dispensationalist has ever suggested. Dispensationalism is not a scriptural way of addressing the question, but is an attempt by Bible-believing Christians to reconcile the miracles of Scripture with the absence or decline of miracles in the church, and/or the rationalism of Western culture.[15]

Churches may disallow tongues with less elaborate theological rationale. In the early days of the charismatic movement, Episcopalian bishop James Pike branded speaking in tongues "heresy in embryo," and banned its public use in the parishes of his diocese.[16] Churches, or influential individuals, can effectively discourage speaking in tongues on other grounds, or in less formal ways, as well: for instance, tongue speaking will be explained in terms of psychological aberration or emotional instability;[17] the occurrence of tongue speaking in non-Christian settings will be cited to cast a shadow of suspicion on the practice as such;[18] tongues will be charged with causing controversy and division; it will be dismissed as contrary to a church's tradition.[19]

No argument or oblique tactic that seeks to banish speaking in tongues from the church can take its stand on Scripture. "Do not forbid speaking in tongues" (1 Cor. 14:39) stands like a sentinel, guarding the place of even this so-called least of the gifts. This includes its occasional use in public. While the gift of tongues is used primarily in one's private devotions, the fact that the Spirit gives the companion gift of interpretation indicates that tongues can also play a role in public worship. To allow it in private but prohibit it in public is a mediating position that does not rest on solid scriptural ground.[20] Paul's discussion of the question, and his final admonition to "forbid not," deals primarily with how the use of the gift is to be ordered in public worship.

Some biblical scholars argue that these words of Paul are directed to a particular congregation in a long ago time, and are not necessarily authoritative for the church today.[21] According to this view, Paul's words are "descriptive, not prescriptive." Without addressing the larger question of scriptural authority which this raises (we have dealt with that in earlier chapters), one might ask quite pragmatically: Who is better able to offer good counsel on speaking in tongues than the apostle Paul? We are not looking here at a situation or question unique to the first century. When we consider how spiritual gifts should contribute to orderly and edifying worship, we have to deal with essentially the same kind of questions that the congregation in Corinth dealt with. There is more of the universal than the particular in Paul's advice.

Even if 1 Corinthians were not considered binding on the church in this regard, the apostle Paul's credentials for offering sound counsel on speaking in tongues would still put any present-day theologian in the shade. Paul spoke in tongues himself. He knew what the gift was all about from personal experience. He had firsthand experience and a Spirit-given understanding of a whole range of spiritual gifts that most theologians have only read about.[22] He was not angered, nor was he intimidated, by speaking in tongues; he was not hostile to the gift, nor did he overvalue it. He probably saw more abuses of speaking in tongues than any modern bishop. He dealt with the abuses without defensiveness, in a pastoral way that works well today, if one takes the time and trouble to put it into practice.

Whom could we turn to in the church today who could counsel us on speaking in tongues with the measure of understanding, wisdom, and balance that the apostle Paul brought to this question?[23]

A second response to tongues has been to tolerate it; to allow its presence in the church, but to discourage its "promotion." If this were understood as a counsel of balance, spoken into a situation badly out of balance, it would be consistent with Scripture. In practice, however, church officials have said this in situations where speaking in tongues has barely made an appearance, where the mere presence of the gift, not its abuse, had raised questions. To forestall potential problems, without openly repudiating scriptural authority, they tell those who have the gift that they may use it, but they should not promote it in any way. The other side of that coin is that one should not seek the gift.[24] This approach sees tongues essentially as a problem to be contained, an infection that hopefully can be kept from spreading.

Scripture takes a decidedly different approach: "Earnestly desire the spiritual gifts" (1 Cor. 14:1). Paul openly promoted spiritual gifts, including tongues: "I want you all to speak in tongues" (14:5). His concern was not that too many people might speak in tongues, but that tongue speakers might neglect to seek and value other gifts as well: "Even more, I want you to prophesy" (1 Cor. 14:1).

On the surface, the counsel against promoting tongues appears benign, even pastoral. But what does this counsel actually say? "Speaking in tongues is unimportant. If you have it, it may be good for you, just keep it to yourself. If you don't have it, don't bother."

To begin with, this faults God: he has given the church a gift that is insignificant, causes problems, and which we could just as well do without. Our attitude toward spiritual gifts touches on our attitude toward God himself. If we demean a gift, do we not denigrate the one who gives it? In providing for the church, God does not do foolish or inconsequential things. Here we must guard against the tendency of the flesh to judge and control even the things of God. Paul's warning not to despise prophesying (1 Thess. 5:20) could be applied to any of the spiritual gifts, including tongues.

From another point of view, the counsel that allows speaking in tongues but discourages its promotion is simply unnatural. On the one hand, it seeks to affirm the gift as a good thing for those who have it, but, on the other hand, to discourage sharing this good thing with others. In what other area of church life would we take such a line? Here is a congregation with a successful stewardship program—they came out of a building program completely debt-free. Here is a Lutheran congregation with a remarkable evangelism outreach in its community—they have more adult baptisms than infant baptisms. Or, here is a person who studies the book of Ephesians in her personal devotions and comes to some tremendous insights. We would hardly say, "These things are all fine, just don't promote them. The Spirit may have given you something good in stewardship or evangelism or Bible study, but don't share it with others." A bishop who gave such advice would be rightly accused of speaking out of both sides of his mouth. It's in the nature of human relationships, not to mention Christian fellowship, to share your good experience with others. If speaking in tongues is a good gift of God that comes back into the church after a long period of disuse, some healthy promotion of the gift is both inevitable and desirable.

A third response to tongues is one which, in a sense, underlies the other two: the position of classical Pentecostalism that speaking in tongues is "the initial physical evidence of baptism with the Holy Spirit." Mainline churches generally, and evangelical Protestants in particular, have opposed this theological formulation. Attempts to banish or merely tolerate tongues can be traced in part to a reaction against the doctrine of "initial evidence." The implication of this Pentecostal teaching, of course, is obvious: if you haven't spoken in tongues, you haven't been baptized with the Holy Spirit.

Lutheran charismatics have generally steered clear of this Pentecostal position.[25] They recognize that tongues was a widespread experience in the early church and that many people are experiencing it today in connection with being filled with the Spirit, though it may be less widespread among Pentecostals and charismatics than has been supposed.[26] Lutheran charismatics would recognize it as *an* evidence of being filled with the Spirit, but stop short of calling it *the* evidence.[27]

While Lutheran charismatics do not agree with the Pentecostal doctrine of initial evidence, they probably would agree with Stephen Clark, a leader in the Roman Catholic charismatic renewal, that a person must be fundamentally open to tongues in order to be filled with the Spirit.[28] This would not put tongues in a special category, however. The same thing could be said about any of the gifts. In other words, we must be surrendered to the lordship of Christ in order to be filled with the Spirit. If we take a position against tongues, or any other gift that the Lord may want to give us, we have usurped the lordship.

How then should we handle tongues—if the gift should not be disallowed, nor merely tolerated, and if it should not be touted as *the* evidence of being baptized with the Spirit? A practical outline takes shape if we look at the positive alternative imbedded in each of the three positions that we have described:

- Speaking in tongues should be recognized and permitted in the church. It is a gift of the Holy Spirit.[29] The first major Lutheran treatment of speaking in tongues to come out of the charismatic renewal set the context for a sane valuation of the gift: "God does all things well. What he has appointed for his Church has behind it wise purpose and meaning, for the mere reason that *he* is the one who has appointed it. His wisdom, though often beyond the clumsy reach of human reason, is perfect. Our task is neither to defend nor downgrade a gift of the Holy Spirit, but rather to *discover* the purpose and meaning that God had in mind when he appointed the gift for his church" (1 Cor. 12:28).[30]
- The gift of tongues should not only be permitted in the church, it should be welcomed and encouraged, along with the other gifts of the Spirit. Hand in hand with encouragement must go sound teaching on the proper use of the gift. Scripture holds these two elements continually in balance.
- Speaking in tongues should be kept in an appropriate theological context. It goes beyond the clear implication of Scripture to tie the Holy Spirit exclusively to this one gift, as the initial evidence of his coming. This in no way detracts from the unique blessing that tongues is meant to bring in the life of the believer.

What this comes down to is not so much a doctrine as an attitude that leads to *wise pastoral care*. The American Lutheran Church published a series of essays on the charismatic renewal that included the following set of pastoral guidelines. They were formulated by a charismatic pastor in regard to the renewal as a whole, but with particular reference to speaking in tongues as a focal point of the movement.

PASTORAL GUIDELINES

1. Become informed

Seek to obtain an accurate and balanced view of what is happening in the charismatic movement. Discuss the matter with other pastors or laity who have first-hand experience.

2. Offer guidance, direction, authority

People who have had charismatic experiences need to realize their need for spiritual authority. An experience may awaken a person to new potential in the Christian life, but it may not mature one. Maturity comes through patient discipleship, which includes submission to those whom God sets over us. The lawless, independent spirit hinders the work of God. The pastor must be ready to accept the responsibility of guiding members who have had charismatic experiences.

A Lutheran charismatic one day approached his pastor and said, "You can't get off the hook on this charismatic thing. You are my spiritual authority." A week later the pastor met the man and said laconically, "I accept." It was the beginning of a warm pastoral relationship.

When a congregation has a fair number of charismatics, a prayer group could be started within the congregation itself. This should be set under the leadership of a responsible person who would keep in regular touch with the pastor and leaders of the congregation. The pastor may want to assume leadership of the group. If the prayer group is publicly announced and open to all who wish to attend, there need be no divisiveness. Indeed, its ministry of prayer and intercession can become a great blessing to the entire congregation.

When a congregation has only a few charismatics or when no one wishes to assume leadership of a prayer group, it may be that those interested could attend an ecumenical prayer group in the community with the knowledge and blessing of the pastor. They would, of course, be expected to maintain their loyalty and service to the congregation.

3. Accept

People who have had charismatic experiences need to feel that they and their experience are accepted by their pastor. Rejection or mere tolerance closes the door to effective pastoral ministry.[31] In 1969, the American bishops of the Roman Catholic Church issued a statement on the charismatic movement which evidenced a warm and wholesome pastoral attitude:

It must be admitted that theologically the movement has legitimate reasons for existence. It has a strong biblical basis. It would be difficult to inhibit the working of the Spirit which manifested itself so abundantly in the early church. The participants in the Catholic Pentecostal Movement claim that they receive certain charismatic gifts. Admittedly, there have been abuses, but the cure is not the denial of their existence but their proper use. We still need further research on the matter of charismatic gifts. Certainly, the recent Vatican Council presumes that the Spirit is active continuously in the Church.

Perhaps our most prudent way to judge the validity of the claims of the Pentecostal Movement is to observe the effects on those who participate in the prayer meetings. There are many indications that this participation leads to a better understanding of the role the Christian plays in the world. Many have experienced progress in their spiritual life. We are attributing this to the reading of the Scriptures and a deeper understanding of their faith.

4. Evaluate

To accept a person and that person's experience does not mean that the pastor must accept the person's own theological description of that experience. Lutheran charismatics have sometimes described their experience in terms which are foreign to our heritage, for example, the categories of classical Pentecostalism. With patience, this kind of problem can actually become the occasion for a deepened apprehension of spiritual truth both for pastor and people. The very name by which it has come to be known, that is, the charismatic movement, suggests that its uniqueness is primarily historical, not theological. It is a phenomenon in the life of the church which began at a certain point in time. To accept the charismatic movement, therefore, does not mean that one accepts some set of strange doctrines. Rather, one accepts a particular work of the Holy Spirit which is taking place in our time, seeking to understand it and relate to it in a positive way. With patience and care, it can be understood and experienced within the framework of our Lutheran heritage and tradition.

5. Establish order

In the manifestation of the charismatic gifts in the congregation, two extremes should be avoided: (1) undue emphasis on any one gift; (2) suppression of any one gift. No gift of the Holy Spirit is without its special value, or God would not have set it in the church. When manifested in an orderly way, according to scriptural guidelines, each gift can bring its distinctive blessing to the body of Christ. The pastor must offer guidance and direction so that order and balance are maintained. In the early years of the charismatic renewal, Lutheran theologian George Aus offered this advice in regard to the gift of speaking in tongues:

A. To those who have experienced the gift: (1) Be sure that the purpose for which you use it is positive, that is, for edification—whether private or corporate. (2) Let the Spirit sift your motives in the public use of the gift. (3) One of the risks in this gift is that it can become divisive. Be in prayer that if it becomes divisive it be not due to you or to your use of the gift, for example, when it is used to exalt self in the display of spiritual excellence. (4) Beware of spiritual pride.
B. To those who have not experienced the gift: (1) If the exercise of the gift by others edifies you, thank God. (2) Do not be disturbed by the fact that it has not been given to you. This fact does not mean that something is wrong with you or that you are an inferior or carnal Christian. (3) Your function in the edification of the congregation may call for other gifts. What kind of a body would it be if everyone were a foot?

6. Counsel patience

Where differences or disagreements crop up in a congregation, precipitous action should be avoided. Both sides should be counseled to prayer and patience with the expectation that the Holy Spirit will bring unity. This will not necessarily mean uniformity, but more likely, a deepened respect for one another and for the God-given variety of our experiences. Both those involved in the charismatic movement and those not involved need to learn to appreciate the gifts that the others have. And both need teaching in order to understand more fully how the charismatic movement can serve in helping to build up the life of the church.

7. Take a positive, pastoral attitude

Essentially the charismatic movement is people; some of those involved are our people. There is no need for them to be lost to the Lutheran church. As we relate to them in a positive, pastoral way, the majority of them will respond with gratitude. The statement of the Catholic bishops, mentioned above, concluded with these words:

> It is the conclusion of the committee on Doctrine that the movement should at this point not be inhibited but allowed to develop. . . . Bishops must keep in mind their responsibility to oversee and guide this movement in the Church. . . . In practice we recommend that Bishops involve prudent priests to be associated with this movement. Such involvement and guidance would be welcomed by Catholic Pentecostals.

The same would be true for Lutheran charismatics. For, deep down, sheep know that they need a shepherd![32]

In light both of the biblical testimony and of practical experience, speaking in tongues should be regarded as a valuable spiritual gift to be sought and practiced in the church. It can contribute to spiritual renewal in one's personal devotional life, and open up new levels of prayer and praise both for the individual believer and for the congregation.

CHAPTER 44

GIFTS OF HEALINGS

When charismatics talk about miracles, their most common illustration is likely to be healing. When they talk about proclaiming the gospel with "signs following," the sign that is uppermost in their mind is almost certain to be healing. To some extent this is a reflection of their experience, but more importantly it reflects the proportions of Scripture. In the New Testament, healings outnumber all other miracles combined.

Although speaking in tongues, interpretation, and prophecy have had only limited expression outside the Pentecostal and charismatic movements, the ministry of healing has been more widely accepted. Among Lutherans, while healing through prayer had never been a major emphasis,[1] it did find expression in the ministry of Luther himself,[2] and, closer to our own time, in the influential ministry of Christoph Blumhardt in Germany;[3] other influences in Lutheranism, such as Norwegian pietism, were likewise hospitable to the healing message.[4] In the Anglican communion there was a contemporary renewal of the healing ministry several decades before the charismatic movement arrived on the scene. In 1932, Episcopalian clergyman John Gaynor Banks began to publish the magazine *Sharing* to encourage the ministry of healing in the historic churches. This led in 1948 to his founding the Order of St. Luke, which included members from all the mainline Protestant churches, both clergy and laity, with significant participation also by members of the medical community.

The charismatic renewal has drawn on these sources and added its voice to a rising chorus of prayer for God to "stretch forth his hand and heal" (Acts 4:30). Physical or psychological healing, whether as an instantaneous event or a gradual process, is recognized as God's personal and direct intervention to bring a person from sickness to health, as an expression of his will and power to alleviate suffering and make people whole.

A biblical perspective on healing

In circles that do not feel comfortable with talk of miracles, serious discussion of biblical healing is sometimes deflected by citing medical science as God's gift of healing for today. A favorite sermon illustration is the story of the doctor who puts a cast on a boy's broken leg and tells him, "God heals your leg. We just hold it in place for him." Of course it is true that all healing comes from God. When a broken leg mends, it is because God has built into the leg the power to mend. When antibiotics fight infection in our bodies, it is because medical science has discovered certain things about the created order and put them to use. But the Bible, in speaking about healing, usually has reference to an intervention of God that brings about healing by other than natural or medical means.

In situations where people become narrowly preoccupied with the miraculous, it may be necessary to broaden their vision by calling attention to the blessing of God through medical healing. But this is not usually the case. In Western culture we have gone to the opposite extreme: we have narrowed healing down to medical science alone. We need the biblical perspective to restore balance.

Actually, by focusing on the intervention of God, the Bible immeasurably broadens our perspective on healing. Healings were an integral part of the ministry of Jesus. His motive for healing was love and mercy toward human beings who were suffering—suffering not only the immediate pain of physical sickness, but the oppression of Satan (Luke 13:16). When Jesus healed the sick, he illustrated the essence of his entire mission, which was to make well what had become sick; his healings established the reign of God in territory that had been usurped by the devil. Biblical healing is a miraculous intervention, an incursion of the kingdom of God into the kingdom of Satan, a foretaste of the age to come in which an all-embracing healing will extend even to the whole creation (Rom. 8:21).

When Peter preached to the household of Cornelius (Acts 10:34-43), he set miracles of healing, deliverance from demonic power, and the proclamation of forgiveness in one unified context: wherever sickness has entered the creation, Jesus does his healing work.

The root sickness is our broken relationship with God (Isa. 53:4-6; Mic. 6:13). The atonement brings the deep healing of forgiveness, reconciliation, and deliverance (Hos. 6:1; Mal. 4:2; 1 Peter 2:24). He heals our faithless backsliding (Jer. 3:22). He conquers the ultimate sickness, death (1 Cor. 15:26).

His healing extends to our relationships with other people. The individualistic view of human life that we have inherited from Greek philosophy and the Renaissance has hidden the extent of our sickness. The Bible does not see us as well apart from wholesome relationships in family, community, and society (Isa. 3:4-7; Rev. 22:2). The ability to live together as God intends us to do—to love one another, forgive one another, pray even for enemies—is impossible until the Holy Spirit brings the healing presence of Christ into our lives.

Jesus heals a sick and fallen world. Poverty, famine, and calamity are evidences of a sick and fallen creation. His feeding of the hungry and his stilling of the storm are signs that he comes to heal the whole creation.

The Bible's perspective on healing goes far beyond the meaning that we normally attach to the word; like salvation, healing takes in all of life. This perspective can open the way to a Spirit-empowered ministry of healing, but it poses a particular danger: the very breadth of the vision can tempt us to neglect the Bible's more frequent and specific meaning, which is healing people's physical and emotional sicknesses. It could invite the same kind of unfortunate results that took place in overseas missionary work when mainline churches began speaking about *mission* rather than *missions*. The mission of a church embraces everything that it does, not just establishing world missions. This is true enough, but along with this shift in perspective came a tragic neglect of missionary work in mainline churches.[5]

The intellectual culture of the West has a certain fascination with abstractions. Abstractions can come to be treated as an ersatz reality. The danger of an enlarged perspective on healing is that we could satisfy ourselves with a new definition of healing while our ministry remained unchanged. Everything we do can be understood in some sense as "healing," so we content ourselves that we really are a healing church, even though actual healings, in the traditional sense, are not part of the picture.

The biblical perspective should be the basis for an altogether different result: not a complacent neglect of physical and emotional healing, but increased confidence that this, too, can be part of our experience. In essence, as we have seen, physical healing is of one piece with such things as forgiveness or the final conquest of death. Therefore we should lay hands on the sick and pray for them to be healed with the same certainty that we proclaim the forgiveness of sins or preach the resurrection. This is what Jesus did when he healed a paralytic man:

> "Which is easier, to say to the paralytic, 'Your sins are forgiven,' or to say, 'Rise, take up your pallet and walk'? But that you may know that the Son of man has authority on earth to forgive sins"—he said to the paralytic—"I say to you, rise, take up your pallet and go home." And he rose and immediately took up the pallet and went out before them all; so that they were all amazed and glorified God, saying, "We never saw anything like this!" (Mark 2:9-12)

Lutheran pastor William Vaswig has reported widely how his son was healed of incurable schizophrenia through prayer.[6] The well-documented healing was not only a blessing to the young man and his family, but became an arresting testimony of faith. Actual physical and emotional healings are signs that tell a skeptical world that our gospel really is a gospel of total healing, not just a stream of nice-sounding words.

Establishing a ministry of healing in the local congregation

Healing presents a secularized age with a different set of dynamics than some of the other spiritual gifts, such as speaking in tongues or discernment of spirits. A church where people speak in tongues or cast out demons may be dismissed as fanatic, quaint, or irrelevant. The general response to a church that heals is likely to be more positive, for it touches people at a point of great need. Theoretically, spiritual healing is as foreign to the Western world-view as any other spiritual gift. But in the face of the pervasive and painful reality of sickness, theory tends to become more pliable. In many otherwise traditional congregations, introducing a ministry of healing is likely to meet with a favorable response.[7]

One thing, more than any other, keeps pastors and leaders from introducing a ministry of healing into their congregations: *fear of failure*. This is often camouflaged by theological objections to charismatic healing, but the real issue is a fear that nothing will happen. At this point, ironically, it is not charismatics, but their critics, who place experience above the Word: from the church's nonexperience of healing they proceed to build a theology that dismisses spiritual healing as a present-day reality. If a theologian were to lay hands on half a dozen sick people and see them dramatically healed before his or her eyes, theological objections would melt away.

Charismatics, however, do not rest their case for healing on their successful experience. John Wimber, whose ministry includes a strong accent on healing, said, "We fail more often than we succeed."[8] In 1962, Oral Roberts said that he estimated as few as 10% of the people he prayed for were healed.[9] Those kind of statistics in themselves would not hold out much encouragement for beginning a healing ministry. *The motivation for entering into a healing ministry is not experience, but the promises in the Word.* Charismatics are not seeking to rally the church around the banner of their own experience; even when they testify to some miracles of healing, they know that they have only scratched the surface of what is promised in Scripture. A. O. Aasen, a pioneer Lutheran pastor in Canada and the United States, who quietly practiced a ministry of healing for more than 60 years, and was himself dramatically healed of cancer at the age of 80, said to a young seminary student who had an interest in healing: "Don't be discouraged if things don't happen overnight. We are surrounded by a world of unbelief—some of it is in the church—and even Jesus could do no mighty works in Nazareth, because of their unbelief. But it's in the Word. If it wasn't in the Word, we'd have no business talking about it. Because it is in the Word, we have no business neglecting it." [10] Charismatics are saying to the church, "Come, let us together seek the Lord. Let us take him at his Word. Let a ministry of healing be restored to God's people."

A ministry of healing depends on the dynamic working of the Holy Spirit. Agnes Sanford, whose Schools of Pastoral Care for many years helped pastors in the English-speaking world to bring a ministry of healing into their congregations, once said, "We must continually remain alert to the danger of a ministry of healing becoming an empty form. The saddest thing I see is pastors who recite prayers for healing without the power of the Holy Spirit; no actual healings take place." [11]

On the other hand, a healthy ministry of healing must include sensitive pastoral care to help people deal with unanswered prayers. A simplistic approach, that explains every failure as a lack of faith on the part of the sick person, has wrought untold and unnecessary grief to people living under a burden of sickness; it is true neither to Scripture nor to experience of any depth. The issue is more complex. There is much we have yet to learn about healing. But that should not detain us from making a start. When the central focus of our prayers is on Christ the Healer, and not simply on healing as such, we can enter with confidence into a ministry of healing. He will work healing among us. And, by the Holy Spirit, he will remain with us in times when prayers go unanswered.

Scripture suggests a variety of ways in which a ministry of healing may come to expression.

Healings take place as members simply pray for one another. "These signs will accompany *those who believe:* . . . they will lay their hands on the sick, and they will recover" (Mark 16:17-18). If prayer really is our access to the healing power of God, what is more natural than that believers should pray for one another—not only in their private intercessions, or only in cases of desperate extremity, but personally and directly—in our everyday encounters with sickness?

The pastor of a small Lutheran congregation in northern Minnesota felt led to begin having a Sunday evening praise and prayer service. A small group gathered for singing, a brief Bible teaching, free prayers, and a time of informal sharing in which people could ask for prayer and also report answers to prayer. In a quiet and unspectacular way it encouraged the growth of a natural use of prayer in the congregation. One evening a longtime member said, "I feel almost a little foolish telling this, but why shouldn't I? I had a bad case of hiccups this week. I tried every trick and home remedy you can name—bending over and touching my toes while holding my breath, putting my head in a paper sack and sucking in. None of them worked. Finally I went to the doctor about it. He gave me some medicine, but that didn't help either. The hiccups kept on for three days, and it was really wearing me down. Then a couple of our members here came over, laid hands on me, and prayed. That did it. The hiccups stopped. God did the job." A healing ministry begins with the simple conviction that God really does answer prayer. Any believer can on occasion be part of the congregation's ministry of healing.

Healings may come through the exercise of charismatic gifts. Scripture uses a double plural in reference to charismatic healing: "gifts of healings" (1 Cor. 12:9, New American Standard Bible). This suggests some variety. Some people have a general gift to pray for the sick. Others seem to have a gift to pray for certain kinds of illnesses. Sometimes healing comes after long periods of intercession, sometimes at a single word of command. Sometimes people are healed through their own prayers, sometimes through the prayers of others. One thing is certain: there is no one formula for spiritual healing. Healing is a sovereign intervention of the Holy Spirit. He himself will frustrate any attempt to reduce the ministry of healing to a method.

Healing may be linked to the exercise of other charismatic gifts. For instance, a word of knowledge given by the Spirit may show people how to pray more accurately and effectively in regard to a particular sickness. Robert Whitaker, a Presbyterian minister, told how their adopted son was healed after an elderly couple received a word of knowledge that his epileptic seizures were related to a trauma the boy had experienced before he was adopted.[12]

Healing, especially emotional healing, can come through private confession and absolution.[13] Scripture links together confession and healing: "Confess your sins to one another, and pray for one another, that you may be healed" (James 5:16). Both Scripture and medical science alert us to the close link that can exist between guilt and sickness. Private confession appears to be especially necessary and helpful in dealing with certain categories of sin and guilt: bad relationships with parents, sexual misconduct, and traffic in the occult.[14]

Evangelistic preaching should ideally be linked with a strong ministry of healing. It was this way in the ministry of Jesus, and it was carried on by his disciples. The apostles prayed, "Grant to thy servants to speak thy word with all boldness, while thou stretchest out thy hand to heal, and signs and wonders are performed through the name of thy holy servant Jesus" (Acts

4:29-30). In his book, *The Case for Spiritual Healing,* Don Gross draws out the implication of our modern tendency to separate faith from miracle:

> It has frequently been observed that in earlier centuries people accepted Christ because of his miracles while now people accept his miracles because they believe in him. This could happen only in a decaying Christian culture. It does not happen in the youthful vigor of faith. Now we go forth and preach everywhere without signs to attend our message, hoping that our listeners will not be offended by the signs that confirmed the preaching of our forebears.[15]

The linking together of faith and miracle is not something peculiar to the mind-set or culture of the first century. It is a demonstration of the Spirit that is effective in every age and culture. In 1979, James Roberson, pastor of Our Savior's Lutheran Church in Albany, New York, was a guest speaker in a small congregation in Japan. His proclamation of the gospel included the scriptural promise, "These signs will accompany those who believe: . . . they will lay their hands on the sick, and they will recover (Mark 16:17-18). The service was not particularly inspiring, as pastor Roberson remembered it. "As a matter of fact," he said, "it was dead. Nothing I said seemed to connect with the people. I could hardly wait for the benediction so we could go back to our hotel."

At the end of the service a man in the front row stood up and came forward to grasp Pastor Roberson's hand—and suddenly the whole congregation began to praise God. Not knowing the language, Pastor Roberson didn't understand at first what was happening. Later his translator told him that the man who came forward was well-known in the congregation, and for years had been crippled on his right side from a paralytic stroke.

In the Bible, healing is frequently associated with the ministry of spiritual leaders: in the Old Testament Moses and the prophets healed (Num. 12:13; 1 Kings 17:21-22; 2 Kings 5:10-14); in the New Testament the apostles and other leaders carried on Jesus' healing ministry (John 14:12; Acts 3:7; 6:8; 8:7; 9:34; 19:11; 28:8-9). The elders of a congregation are given special responsibility and authority to pray for the sick. "Is any among you sick? Let him call for the elders of the church, and let them pray over him, anointing him with oil in the name of the Lord; and the prayer of faith will save the sick man, and the Lord will raise him up; and if he has committed sins, he will be forgiven . . . . the prayer of a righteous man has great power in its effects" (James 5:14-16).

It is important to note that while healing may be linked to the faith of the sick person, this is not necessarily the case.[16] Here healing is attributed to the faith of the elders. There are times when it is appropriate to challenge the sick person to have faith for healing, other times when it is not. In cases of

severe depression, for instance, a sick person is often too weary and discouraged to exercise faith. The Holy Spirit must guide us in the way that we
minister healing in individual cases.

Inner healing

An aspect of healing that has gained particular prominence in the charismatic renewal goes by the name of "inner healing." The concept seems to
have originated with Agnes Sanford, who called it "healing of the memories."
The idea is that Jesus can heal the psychological, emotional, and spiritual
wounds that fester in the memory. She focused on two basic factors that must
be taken into account in this kind of healing, which she illustrated in her
Schools of Pastoral Care with a verse from a familiar hymn:

> There is a balm in Gilead to *make the wounded whole;*
> There is a balm in Gilead to heal a *sin sick soul.*

The concept of healing the memories can bring fresh meaning and reality
to a foundational truth of Scripture: it can be a helpful restatement of the
doctrine of forgiveness. Its particular value lies in the emphasis that it places
on the actual appropriation of forgiveness, and healing from the effects of
sin, through the ministry of prayer. Care needs to be exercised that the emphasis on healing does not bypass the reality of guilt and the need for repentance.

Healing the memories can deal not only with the wrongs that we have done,
but also with the wrongs that have been done against us. One reason for the
phenomenal response to the ministry of inner healing is the fact that the need
is so widespread. Our common life structures—family, church, school, community—can deal harsh blows to the individual, especially the young and
defenseless. Who pauses even to note, much less deal with, the wounds
inflicted by rejection, neglect, fear, unkindness, ill-begotten humor and teas-
ing, shame, and failure? Many unhealed hurts lie buried or undealt with in
our memories. It is true that anyone who is in Christ is a new creation; the
old has passed away, and the new has come (2 Cor. 5:17). But for many there
is a gap, sometimes a gigantic gap, between the promises of redemption and
the actual experience of it. Healing of memories, again, emphasizes appropriation: Jesus came to heal the brokenhearted, and through prayer for inner
healing that can become an experienced reality.

Healing and atonement

It is debatable just how closely we can link healing to the atonement, and
therefore to the Lord's Supper. Jesus' own ministry of healing was seen as a

286 LED BY THE SPIRIT

fulfillment of the prophecy of Isaiah that "he took our infirmities and bore our diseases" (Matt. 8:17; Isa. 53:5); in its context this is one of the clearest Old Testament references to the atonement. In a comprehensive sense, therefore, we can say that on the cross Jesus dealt with the full effects of sin, including sickness (1 Peter 2:24). This can be appropriated in regard to an immediate need: a person may receive faith for healing in connection with receiving the Lord's Supper, and many testify to this. What better way to encourage faith than to remember Christ (1 Cor. 11:23-25)?

This does not mean, however, that the Holy Spirit will invariably bring healing in the Lord's Supper. We cannot draw a straight line here between forgiveness and healing: "as certainly as he took my sins, just as certainly will he heal this sickness." The Lord's Supper is not only a remembrance of Jesus, but also an anticipation of his return (1 Cor. 11:26). It is a misunderstanding of the biblical evidence to affirm that because of Christ's atonement perfect healing can be received in this life in the same way as forgiveness of sins. Forgiveness takes away the guilt of sin; it does not necessarily remove all the effects of sin. A drunken driver may careen his truck into a bridge abutment, sheer off his leg, and barely escape with his life. He may later repent and be forgiven, but he will go through the rest of life with one leg. Results of sin may remain until "the creation itself will be set free from its bondage to decay and obtain the glorious liberty of the children of God. . . . We ourselves, who have the first fruits of the Spirit, groan inwardly as we wait for adoption as sons, the redemption of our bodies. For in this hope we were saved" (Rom. 8:21,23).

Perfect healing is never a reality in this life, where sin and the results of sin have permeated the whole cosmos. However, healing is a foretaste of the coming world, a sign of the kingdom. Although the "mystery of evil" will not be fully solved in this world, and suffering will persist until the end, Christians may glory in the fact that on the cross Christ has conquered sin, death, and the devil and therefore also broken the power of sickness. In reference to the Lord's Supper, the church fathers set healing in the broadest possible context, calling it the "medicine of immortality."[17] In a special way the Lord's Supper points us to the ultimate healing of the resurrection.

CHAPTER 45

THE CHURCH:
WORKSHOP OF THE SPIRIT

At a charismatic conference on church renewal, one of the speakers began his address by stating, "I want you to know that I have discovered the New Testament pattern for the church—37 different times!" He wanted at the beginning to disabuse people of the idea that church renewal is a matter of finding and following a biblical formula. Renewal of congregational life is a renewal of the life of Christ in and with his body. It stems from a fresh release of the Holy Spirit among the people of God. It is not simply a set of principles that we discover and put into practice; it is first of all something that we receive.

When charismatics hold seminars on church renewal, they do not propound elaborate or esoteric visions of an ideal church. They focus on some practical ways that the lordship of Christ and the power of the Holy Spirit can become greater realities in present-day church life.

Charismatics generally use the word *church* in an uncomplicated, pragmatic sense: they mean simply the institutional church as it is presently known.

Jesus, the source and model for the church's ministry

Jesus himself was, in all the fullness of his ministry, the model and source of what the church would become:

- Jesus was *apostle,* the one truly commissioned and sent by God (Heb. 3:1; Mark 9:37; Acts 3:20,26; John 3:17; 5:36-38; 6:29,57; 11:42; 17:25).
- Jesus was the *prophet* "like unto Moses" (Deut. 18:15; Matt. 11:2-5).
- Jesus was *evangelist,* who proclaimed the promised good news (Isa. 61:1; Luke 4:43; 8:1; 20:1).

LED BY THE SPIRIT

- Jesus was *teacher,* who spoke the words of God (John 17:8). It is, however, important to note the difference between Jesus and the Jewish
scribes. Unlike the pupils of a rabbi, Jesus' disciples never became rabbis
themselves (Matt. 23:8). Jesus was a unique teacher and wanted to remain
such.
- Jesus was *healer,* who bore our diseases (Matt. 8:17; 1 Peter 2:24).
- Jesus was *shepherd,* who cared for his own (Heb. 13:20; John 10; 1 Peter
2:25; Matt. 26:31).
- Jesus was *deacon,* who came not to be served but to serve (Luke 22:27;
Mark 10:45; Rom. 15:8; John 13:1-5).
- Jesus is *high priest,* who always lives to make intercession for us (Heb.
7:25).

The church as a continuation of the incarnation is a frequently echoed idea
in the charismatic renewal: Jesus' supernatural ministry is carried on through
the church.

The church as the body of Christ

In the theology of the New Testament, the concept of the church as the
body of Christ is most fully represented by Paul, though Pauline churches
were not the only variety of New Testament church. Perhaps the Pauline
churches even differed among themselves, depending on individual circumstances. Other models are also present in the New Testament: the "spiritual
church" of John, insofar as we can infer it from available texts; the Jerusalem
congregation, led by a council of elders, a form taken over from the synagogue;
and congregations with the structures described in the Pastoral Epistles, which
may evidence a development within the New Testament itself. However, "Paul
is the first and, within the New Testament, the only one who has developed
a genuine, explicit, and hence for us, comprehensible, doctrine of church."[1]

This doctrine confronts us, though with certain differences, in Romans, 1
Corinthians, Ephesians, and Colossians. It is the doctrine of the "body of
Christ," to which every believer belongs, and in which every believer is
blessed with spiritual gifts and ministry. According to this view, every believer
is meant to function as a charismatic (1 Cor. 12:7,11).

The relationship between the spiritually gifted members and Christ, as head,
is critical to the understanding of this image of the church, as Edmund Schlink
has pointed out:

> Through the rich variety of spiritual gifts Christ in his fullness comes to present
> day manifestation—in the congregation first of all, then through the congregation
> to the world. The variety of spiritual gifts can appear in different congregations
> at different times and in differing forms. But the variety is always in essence a

manifestation of the one gift, Jesus Christ. As head of the body, he is the source and bearer of all spiritual gifts. They function at his behest. They manifest the power of his name, each gift bearing its appropriate witness.

Fellowship among the spiritually gifted people exists because of their common possession of the one gift, Jesus Christ. Christ himself is the one who really "has" the spiritual gifts. He is the one apostle, the one teacher, the one evangelist, the one shepherd, the one deacon of the new covenant. He is the head of his body, the leader of his church. He makes known divine power, and is the author of all powers, signs, and wonders in Christendom. It is in thus sharing together the one gift, Jesus Christ, that the church becomes "the fellowship of spiritual gifts."[2]

The understanding of the congregation as the body of Christ had particular application to worship. Worship was not only a celebration *for* the congregation, but was also in large measure a celebration *by* the congregation, each member actively participating. Paul taught that when the body comes together for worship, every member should have something to contribute (1 Cor. 14:26). Of course this admonition assumed that spiritual gifts were widely distributed in the body.

As early as the post-apostolic era, the practical implications of this teaching began to be lost. Especially in the area of worship, the idea of a spiritually gifted fellowship was replaced with a model in which the gifts of the Spirit were centralized in one person, or at most a few persons.

In the second century, the monarchical episcopate arose, which elevated the idea of "office" and further removed the gifts from the people. The Lutheran Reformation developed a modified interpretation of "office," consciously oriented toward belief in justification.[3] The office was understood as a service appointed by God to kindle faith by proclaiming the Word and administering the sacraments. This provided a more functional understanding of the pastoral office. The officeholder is first of all a Christian among Christians. The biblical idea of rule and oversight, however, was also maintained: the office stands over against the congregation with divine authority.

The "priesthood of all believers" was a central teaching of the Reformation, but its scope was limited to the area of personal access to God: one did not need to go through a priest to obtain forgiveness. The wider implication of the teaching—that every believer participates in the gifts and calling of priesthood—was not developed. The traditional distinction between clergy and laity was maintained. The early church's understanding of a fellowship of spiritually gifted and ministering people was not fully recovered. The Lutheran church, as a whole, remained a church dominated by clergy.

The doctrine of the priesthood of all believers still awaits practical realization. If we agree with Paul that the church is a fellowship of spiritually

290 LED BY THE SPIRIT

gifted people, then we must take practical steps—not least in the church's worship life—for these gifts to come into service.

If a person has, for example, the gift of prophecy, how do we make room in our worship services for this gift to be manifested? Paul said that in a time of worship two or three may speak in tongues, with interpretation following. What might the Spirit wish to do with that gift today? We do not suggest that worship should be given over to prophesying and speaking in tongues. Even in outspokenly charismatic worship services, these particular gifts are not given undue weight. But because these gifts are not commonly manifested in our churches, they help bring the basic issue into focus: How ready are we to let the Spirit bring a fully gifted body into operation? By giving attention to spiritual gifts, the charismatic renewal has brought this question to the fore.

The church as a ministering fellowship

The Spirit is working to recover the early church's practice of allowing many Spirit-gifted ministries to function in the congregation. This is not something that can be consigned simply to the infancy of the church. It belongs to the nature of the church; Edmund Schlink is again helpful:

> Paul taught the variety of spiritual gifts so fundamentally that his statements can in no way be limited to the congregations in Corinth or Rome or even to the Pauline congregations of the church's formative period. Rather, according to Paul's declarations, the rich variety of the Spirit's gifts belongs to the essence of the church in all places and at all times. The church, as the Body of Christ, is an organism having many gifts and many ministries. Paul formulated his teaching so generally and so basically that it cannot be relegated to one historical period. On the contrary, these statements must be included in the doctrines of church and office, even if they are not reflected in most of the other New Testament Scriptures.[4]

This emphasis is finding practical expression in the charismatic renewal against the background of differing ecclesiastical traditions. It has not yet brought significant change in traditional points of view regarding the official or ordained ministry. The Lutheran doctrine of office, the Roman Catholic doctrine of consecrated priesthood, Presbyterian polity—these views remain essentially unchanged. What is changing in many places is the role of the laity.

In charismatic churches and groups, Spirit-gifted laity are increasingly ministering with evident and acknowledged spiritual authority. They function in leadership; they give spiritual care; they preach and teach; they speak prophetically; they pronounce blessing. In many areas they minister alongside trained theologians and ordained clergy. In 1985, Fred Hall, a charismatic

Lutheran layman from the United States, was invited to give a series of Bible studies at an annual conference of pastors and deacons in Tanzania. At the end of the conference Lutheran bishop Erasto Kweka said, "It has been unusual to have a layman teach the Bible to pastors, but we see how the Holy Spirit has used him, and we are thankful."

Increased lay participation in ministry has been vigorously championed in charismatically renewed Lutheran congregations. In worship services they are moving beyond traditional support roles, such as ushering and baby-sitting, into leading worship, teaching, preaching, and public prayer. Some Lutheran congregations find it useful to have lay members wear a robe or an alb when they minister before the congregation in public services. It helps break down the artificial distinction between clergy and laity, and at the same time conveys the sense of special calling that is symbolized by distinctive dress.

In other areas of church life, outside the worship service, laity are doing more of the ministry that people have traditionally expected from the clergy: visitation of the sick, spiritual counseling, basic doctrinal instruction. That which is distinctive in the charismatic renewal is not simply that laity are urged and recruited to become more active, but that there is a more conscious recognition of the sovereignty of the Holy Spirit to call and anoint people for ministry.

This is not something that happens suddenly. It is a deepening conviction that must imbue both those who minister and those who receive ministry: they must see that the essential factor in *all* ministry, whether by clergy or laity, is the working of the Holy Spirit. The problem of a clergy-dominated church is not something that has been one-sidedly imposed on the laity by the clergy. Dwarfed expectations on the part of the laity in regard to their own ministry is at least half of the problem.

On the one hand, many lay members have a self-imposed spiritual inferiority complex. They entertain no realistic expectation that they could receive gifts and anointing to minister in the power of the Holy Spirit. An insurance executive who belonged to a charismatic Lutheran congregation was asked by his pastor to become part of a group of men who conducted a special prayer service in the congregation each month. The men were stationed in teams at the altar of the church, and people desiring personal ministry would come to them for prayer. A variety of spiritual gifts would be manifested— prophecy, word of wisdom, word of knowledge, healing. At first the man declined. He had experienced the power of this ministry firsthand, when he himself received it from his fellow members, but he couldn't imagine something "as far out as prophecy coming through *me*." When the pastor persisted, he agreed to "stand up there and pray silently while the other men do the ministry." It was not long, however, before he began to receive prophetic revelation himself. He became a permanent member of the prayer-ministry team. The first barrier to be overcome is within the lay ministers themselves.

On the other hand, many lay people are not prepared to accept the ministry of other laity as fully authentic. They have a professionalized view of the ministry: a pastor is educated, trained, official; ministry by a nonordained person is a well-intentioned effort by a spiritual amateur. The surest way to overcome this mind-set is for a person to actually experience Spirit-empowered ministry at the hands of a fellow lay member. One of the pastor's important tasks is to present and commend the ministry of those whom the Spirit has gifted, so that other members will be encouraged to avail themselves of a ministry that the Holy Spirit has raised up.

The increased attention that the charismatic renewal has given to spiritual gifts is helping make the doctrine of the priesthood of all believers more than a theological phrase. This is an appropriate way for the formal structure of the church to be augmented, or even corrected, by a substructure. We may never arrive at the place where there are a specific number of gifts and offices, bearing the same name, in every congregation. But when the grand total of Spirit-anointed ministries in the congregation and in the church as a whole increases, then the church will manifest more and more of the fullness of Christ. The body of Christ will be strengthened, to the glory of God.

The church as community

One of the unique features of the charismatic renewal has been the formation of a worldwide network of parachurch ecumenical communities. They have grown up principally in metropolitan areas and provide a corporate expression for charismatic renewal. They often begin as a prayer fellowship and grow to include such features as extended households, regular meetings, disciplined teaching, pastoral care, private schools, and community-service projects. Some Lutherans belong to these communities, but the majority of members are Roman Catholic.

According to Kilian McDonnell, the recognition of church as community is a distinctive emphasis that the charismatic renewal contributes to the renewal of the whole person and of congregations. True Christian community embraces both Jesus' intimate concern for the welfare of the individual members of his body, and his desire for each member to lose his or her life in fruitful service for the kingdom. McDonnell claims that the churches have "only sporadically grasped the importance of community in the charismatic renewal. Unless the role of community is grasped one has failed to understand what the renewal is saying. It seems to me that the primary consequence of the resurrection and of Pentecost is not the exercise of gifts but community formation."[5]

Among Lutherans, the experience of community has most commonly been an extension of congregational life. A Lutheran congregation moving strongly in charismatic renewal often has many things in common with ecumenical charismatic communities.

Lutheran charismatics generally understand community in the practical sense that a layman in one charismatic Lutheran congregation described it: "submission to the lordship of Christ, and a high level of personal commitment of the members to one another." A church in renewal will gather together frequently for worship, preaching, teaching, sacraments, prayer, fellowship, and service. The distinctive experience of communty, however, requires smaller groupings within the congregation. The importance of cell groups for healthy body life is being increasingly recognized. This is where the members' personal commitment to one another can be most readily expressed. They provide pastoral care, personal nurture, and also evangelistic outreach. Both the larger gatherings of the congregation and cell groups are necessary ingredients for building Christian community. Both of these elements were present in the earliest days of the church, in Jerusalem (Acts 2:46-47; 5:42).

CHAPTER 46

THE CHURCH: INSTITUTION AND FREE MOVEMENTS

When charismatics talk about the church, they often fall into "us/them" patterns of speech. Traditional church members do the same thing in talking about charismatics. Speakers at church conventions can usually garner a quick guilt reaction by calling attention to this phenomenon, but the habit persists. Properly understood, us/them talk may not be all that bad. It expresses something that is essential to an understanding of church renewal, namely, how free movements relate to the institutional church.

TWO STRUCTURES WITHIN THE CHURCH: INSTITUTION AND MOVEMENT

Throughout the history of the church there have been two structures in which Christians have gathered together: *institution* and *movement*. In our day, "institution" is represented by denominational structures, from national and regional offices down to local congregations. "Movement" is represented by groups that operate outside normal parish structures, such as evangelistic organizations, mission societies, religious orders, charismatic communities, Bible-study fellowships, and prayer groups.

Both structures necessary

In April 1984, a study of these two kinds of structure was presented to the Commission for a New Lutheran Church as part of its consideration in designing a merger of three Lutheran bodies in the United States.[1] The study demonstrates that these two structures have been part of the Christian church from the beginning, and concludes that they are both necessary for the healthy functioning of the body of Christ:[2]

> The Christian congregations that were established in the New Testament era were structurally patterned on the model of the Jewish synagogue. This structure embraced the community of the faithful in any given place. The defining characteristic of this structure is that it included the full age-sex spectrum of the entire community.
>
> Paul's missionary band was patterned on the model of the Jewish evangelists who "traversed land and sea to make a single proselyte." This structure was organized by persons who committed themselves to a complementary mission endeavor. The defining characteristic of this structure is that it did not include the entire community but was selective.
>
> Thus, on the one hand, the structure we call the New Testament church is a prototype of all subsequent Christian fellowships where old and young, male and female are gathered together as normal biological families in aggregate. On the other hand, Paul's missionary band can be considered a prototype of all subsequent missionary endeavors organized out of committed, experienced workers who affiliated themselves (as members of a second additional structure).
>
> Neither of these two structures was "let down from heaven"; they were "borrowed patterns." The New Testament shows us how to borrow effective patterns; it frees [us] from the need to follow precise forms . . . and allows [us] to choose comparable indigenous structures . . . structures which will correspond faithfully to the function of the patterns. We are directed to dynamic equivalence, not formal replication.[3]

The historical development of institutional authority

From the outset, the institutional aspect of the church was faced with the problem of maintaining order and orthodoxy in the face of a variety of influences and movements. This is one of the main tasks of the institutional aspect of the church, and it almost invariably sets it in tension with all movements, whether good or bad. While institution and movement serve complementary functions, they are not usually complimentary toward one another.

In A.D. 96, Bishop Clement of Rome wrote his letter to the Corinthians. His shrill admonition was directed against elements threatening the unity and order of the congregation: "Submit yourselves to the priests, accept chastisement unto repentance, bend the knee of your hearts."[4] Disharmony in the Corinthian church was evident even in St. Paul's time, when the charismatics were unwilling to maintain order. Thus the command: "Learn obedience!"

The Roman church had its roots in the church at Jerusalem, with its strong emphasis on the church's institutional elements. Even in early Christendom, the Roman church had taken on the task of defense against heresy. When Irenaeus spoke of "the greatest and oldest church, a church known to all men, which was founded and established at Rome by the most renowned Apostles Peter and Paul," he wished to establish its claim to institutional leadership.[5]

The major threat to the young church, aside from the Marcionite heresy, was posed by gnosticism. Gnostic heresy refused to take the incarnation seriously; neither did it take in earnest the attendant problem of sin. The stumbling block for the gnostic was Jesus' shameful death on the cross. The foundation of Christian faith, as expressed in John 1:14, "the Word became flesh," was inconceivable. The Holy Spirit was understood by many gnostics as a sort of heavenly light ray which is imprisoned in the bodies and supracosmic souls of mortals.

Gnosis ("knowledge") had its practical side. Gnostics claimed to know the escape route from the labyrinth of existence. They knew how their souls could reattain the realm of light. Because of their knowledge they felt themselves superior to mere believing church Christians.

Here was a movement that perverted the gospel and threatened to corrupt the church. How did the church deal with this kind of challenge? The development of firm, hierarchical authority was greatly accelerated. Rigid order was raised up as a bastion against the assault of gnosticism.

The so-called *Didache* ("The Teaching of the Twelve Apostles") is thought by many scholars to have originated in Syria in the first half of the second century.[6] It was not rediscovered until 1873. It puts us in touch with earlier practice in the church, when the charismatic dimension was still generally accepted, and when the responsibility of the institutional structure to provide discipline and order was also recognized.

Like St. Paul, the *Didache* referred to the gift of prophecy. True prophets would speak in the Spirit and differentiate themselves from false prophets primarily by their life-style. The life of real prophets would resemble the Lord's.[7] Their words would include concrete instructions for the congregation.

The *Didache* permitted prophets to "give thanks as much as they desire" in the course of a liturgical service of the Eucharist. While the prophets were speaking in the Spirit, their words became liturgical language. Their utterances were worship and praise for the gift of the Eucharist.[8] Their prayers were the wellspring of liturgy in the early church. On the other hand, according to the *Didache*, false prophets gave themselves away in that their instructions were not bound up with continuous praise of God. Pseudoprophets sought honor for themselves and made a business of their prophetic abilities. The *Didache* warns emphatically: "Whoever speaks in the Spirit saying, 'Give me money' or some such thing should have no hearing . . . but whoever enjoins giving for those who suffer want should be judged by no one."[9]

This healthy interplay gave way to increasing distance between institutional and charismatic authority. Generally speaking, by about A.D. 150 a monarchical episcopate had developed out of the ranks of the clergy. One official in a given congregation bore sole, final authority as leader. The institutional aspect of the early Catholic church was clearly moving into ascendancy over free charismatic influences. The early Catholic church did practice the gift of spiritual discernment, as apocryphal gospels (special favorites with the gnostics) were rejected and the New Testament Scriptures were given canonical status and became the basis of a binding Rule of Faith.[10]

The negative side of this development was that the sphere of ministry for spiritually gifted laity was greatly reduced. In the battle against heresy, spiritual gifts freely operating among the laity became suspect. As time passed, it became ever more difficult to distinguish their proper use from their misuse.

During the Middle Ages, institutional authority greatly expanded its sway in the church. The church stood under the standard of the papacy's universal rule. The pope enjoyed highest respect as possessor of supreme authority. Considered to be the successor of St. Peter, he established infallible, unalterable rules of faith.[11] Because of the might of his hierarchical office, to him was attributed the "charism of power." The book of canon law was regarded as divine law. At the new universities, Scholasticism was flourishing. According to the scholastics, the fundamental spiritual gifts were science, law, art, and the priesthood.[12] The gift of understanding, it was taught, was expressed in theology and science; in law and hierarchy the administrative gifts; the prophetic gifts could be seen in those artists whose work was dedicated to the church. Charisms were eclipsed by canon law.

The development of charismatic authority

In spite of hierarchy and rigid legal structure the Middle Ages were rich in spiritual awakenings. Several religious orders became fountainheads of spiritual activity.

> The monastic tradition . . . developed a second structure. This new widely proliferating structure undoubtedly had no connection at all with the missionary band in which Paul was involved . . . it more substantially drew from the Roman military structure than from any other single source. [It] carried forward a disciplined structure . . . which allowed [members of the parish church] to make . . . an additional specific commitment.
>
> Meanwhile, in its institutional aspect, the congregational pattern of the early church became pervasively replaced by a geographical pattern adapted from the Roman government. This new pattern, the Christian parish church, still preserved the basic constituency of the early church, namely, the combination of young and old, male and female.
>
> There were, then, by the fourth century two very different kinds of structures in the church—the *diocese* and the *monastery*—both of them significant in the transmission and expansion of Christianity.

> The diocese and the monastery are each patterns borrowed from the cultural context of their time, just as earlier Christians adapted the patterns of the Jewish synagogue and missionary band. It is important . . . to note that while these two structures are formally different—and historically unrelated to the two in New Testament times—they are nevertheless functionally the same.[13]

It is not possible here to discuss in detail the rich charismatic traditions to be found in the history of monasticism, but out of the many examples in various times and places, four individuals, two men and two women, can be cited whose spiritual activity bore fruits of revival and brought blessing to the universal church: Benedict of Nursia (d. 550), Hildegard of Bingen (d. 1179), Francis of Assisi (d. 1226), and Birgitta of Sweden (d. 1373). Their movements, although at first resisted by ecclesiastical officials, were finally accepted and helped strengthen the tradition of charismatic authority in the church.

Other spiritual movements such as the Cathari, Waldenses, Joachimites, and Hussites, however, did not find a home within the established church, to the detriment both of the church and the movements. The Roman church became more worldly. Spiritual awakenings were increasingly perceived as threats to the established order. Birgitta of Sweden had painfully sensed this as the real suffering of Christ. The history of the church in the Middle Ages proves that the church as the body of Christ suffers when office and charismata stand irreconcilably opposed to one another.

The Reformation experience

Though the Reformation itself began as a movement within the church, the Protestant reformers made no provision in their churches for anything akin to free movements.

> The Protestant Reformation started out by attempting to do without any kind of structure [comparable to the religious orders of the Catholic church]. Luther and the Protestant reformers attempted to renew the life of the church through congregational structure. The renewal was attempted at the general level of church life. Even though Luther was an Augustinian and had found faith in that order, neither he nor any other Protestant reformers adopted any [of these] patterns. Lutheranism produced a diocesan structure which to a considerable extent represented the readoption of the Roman diocesan tradition . . . but did not in a comparable sense readopt the [structure of movements], the Catholic orders, that had been so prominent in the Roman tradition.
>
> Dr. Trygve Skarsten, professor of church history at Trinity Theological Seminary in Columbus, Ohio, perceives the lack of Protestant [movement] structures as a far-reaching weakness in the resulting tradition: "Protestantism, and to be more specific Lutheranism, resembled an unwieldy torso with its arms and legs

severed and with little possibility of movement and mission. Not until new structures were devised could the Lutheran churches reach out effectively at home and
abroad. An attempt to devise new [movement] structures occurred in the early
eighteenth century . . . [but] foundered. It was not until the evangelical awakening
of the early nineteenth century had unleashed the pent-up spiritual energy of
Christendom on both sides of the Atlantic that the new structure known as the
'voluntary society' came into its own." From this time on, these societies have
contributed in a most phenomenal way to Lutheranism and Protestantism.

History has demonstrated time and again that the church does not renew or
reach out effectively unless the structures [of institution and movement] are working in harmony. This is evident in the history of Lutheranism, Protestantism, and
Catholicism.[14]

Both structures contribute to the life and health of the church

Institutional structure provides for stability and permanence. Movements
provide for spontaneity and change.

The place of the church's institutional structures is generally understood.
The role of movements is less clearly understood and accepted. Especially in
their early stages, movements are often resisted by the institution. What is
needed, as the above report points out, is a new perception of the interde-
pendence of these two basic structures within the church:

Both movements and movement organizations can be, and usually are, seen
as protest or criticism of the society or institution in relation to which they exist.
While this dimension may be intrinsic to movements and movement organizations,
it may not be the primary focus. In many instances, the primary focus is a positive
one—joyful growth, a free sharing of gifts, a compassionate caring for people in
need.

But if it is assumed that the institutional church is the only legitimate form in
which the church exists, it is highly unlikely that movement structures will be
seen in a positive light. Rather, movement organizations will almost always be
perceived in negative and hostile terms as illegitimate, competitive, and destructive. This puts the institutional church in a defensive and recalcitrant posture. In
this posture the institutional church is apt to reject the reform and renewal brought
to bear by movement organizations and is likely instead to intensify the situation
needing reform and renewal. When this happens, movement organizations tend
to be cut off from the institutional church, are apt to become suspicious of it and
may become sectarian. In this kind of polarization, change tends to be an ag-
gravating—even if needed—process.

But if it is assumed that the church truly exists in both institutional and movement structures, movement organizations may be perceived in an altogether different perspective: as complementary, constructive, "glad responses . . . to the
Spirit of God." It is from this perspective that movement organizations in general
seek to be understood. This does not necessarily diminish the critique or challenge
a movement organization brings to bear on the institutional church—it may even

enhance its challenge in the sense that the challenge is now perceived to be born out of a caring spirit rather than a negative reaction. This perspective views movement organizations and institutional structures in such a way that mutual correction and growth are encouraged. It does not, however, naively accept everything any one church movement or institution promotes.[15]

This is a framework of understanding within which the charismatic movement makes its appeal to the church. The charismatic movement has been called into life to meet a special need: to remind the church that God calls it to radical dependence on the Holy Spirit in every area of its faith and life. The church cannot lift its voice in worship nor its hands in service except by the initiative and power of the Holy Spirit. This is no new teaching, but a fundamental of the faith that needs to be recovered in thought and experienced in life.

INSTITUTION AND MOVEMENT: HOW THEY RELATE

Renewal movements need the institutional church, and the institution needs the inspiration and new life offered by movements. Frequently, however, the two are in conflict with each other. Every individual and institution needs continuous renewal in order to remain vigorous. Renewal movements can be vital correctives. However, most renewal efforts are rejected or at best tolerated by the establishment. At the same time, many renewal groups take a judgmental position in relation to the institution. They desire radical, immediate change. But seldom does correction come rapidly. Change is usually a slow process. Both institution and movement need to give serious thought to how they relate to one another.

Institution faces movement

It is proper for the church to test the charismatic movement to evaluate whether it is from God, man, or Satan. Indeed all church teachings and practices should be reexamined on a continuing basis to guard against creeping error.

The primary test is the biblical one: is it true to the whole and heart of Scripture?

Charismatics believe that this renewal is truly biblical, that it represents an initiative of the Holy Spirit to bring neglected aspects of the biblical faith back into the active life of the church. It is not an innovation, but a renewal of basic elements of the Christian faith as attested to in Scripture.

Lutheran charismatics not only call attention to neglected truth, they also strongly reaffirm the foundations of the faith. They are trinitarian both in emphasis and practice. The authority of the Bible as God's Word is strongly stressed, yet not as legalistic biblicism. The distinction between law and gospel is maintained. Appropriation and assurance of salvation in its full sense is emphasized and experienced. Christian living based on the Scriptures is strongly underscored, that is, sanctification by grace through faith. The call to Christian witness, service, and mission is sounded clearly and frequently.

Every society has its ideal and norm, with the ideal always higher than the norm. Several options are available to deal with this perfomance gap. One remedy is to scold society for its low performance level, then apply the law more strictly. Eventually this approach produces negative and rebellious reaction. Another method is to lower the ideal in order to bring it more in line with the norm. Instead of narrowing the gap, lowering the ideal results in lowering the norm, because the two follow parallel lines. A third option is to defend the norm and neglect the ideal, thus in effect resisting and restricting change. This tends to be the approach of the establishment. A fourth approach is to focus on the ideal and thus raise the norm. The approach of the charismatic movement is to stress the biblical model and trust the Holy Spirit to raise performance.

Every society has individuals who are deviants from the norm. Deviants on the high side are often ostracized from the mainstream of society and sometimes even persecuted. The next generation may honor them as prophets ahead of their time and may erect monuments in their memory. On the other hand, deviants on the low side are frequently placed under discipline, unless they become too numerous and powerful, in which case they drag down the whole society. In time this may generate a counterrevolution from the idealists or the law-and-order segment of society. Deviants on the low side are often made folk heroes in the next generations; one thinks of characters like Jesse James and Billy the Kid in the folklore of Western America. Deviation on the low side appears to be more acceptable to society in general than that on the high side.

As a social order, the church responds in similar fashion. Renewal movements have been rejected consistently throughout biblical and church history, not just by society but principally by the ecclesiastical hierarchy, which sees no need for renewal and does not recognize renewal when it comes.

Three basic choices face institutional church leaders in relation to the charismatic movement: *reject* it, *ignore* it, or *recognize* it.

The church may choose to *reject* the renewal in a deliberate manner for doctrinal, political, pastoral, psychological, or sociological reasons. This may be done with or without a hearing. Church officials may define the charismatic renewal as being in biblical or theological error. Or they may decide that the renewal threatens the church's harmony and peace. Or they may declare that the movement has been found wanting on the basis of some bad examples and unfortunate experiences. They may declare that the leadership and participants are psychological misfits. Or they may describe the movement sociologically as foreign to the church's traditional pattern of behavior, and thus unacceptable.

In the 1960s, most mainline Protestant churches tended to reject the charismatic renewal in one way or another.[16] When charismatics talk about persecution and suffering, most often it is in reference to the institutional church. If this persecution had happened to a handful of malcontents, it could be dismissed, but such suffering is widespread among charismatics who have remained loyal to their churches. It tells us something about the way church authorities have related to the movement.

By the early 1970s it became apparent that the movement was not going to go away, and since then the response has commonly been to *ignore* it. The practical effect of this is that the renewal is rejected.

Church officials may, however, choose a third option, which is to *recognize* the renewal, so that it can positively influence the life of the church. Both church officials and charismatics must see clearly what this option entails. It does not mean that the church adopt or take over the renewal in an official or semiofficial way.

Lutheran charismatics, especially among the clergy, have sometimes so yearned to be accepted by the church that they have not seen this clearly. They unconsciously model their idea of acceptance after official programs or institutions of the church. This kind of acceptance, however, could be disastrous. One of the fundamental dangers faced by any renewal movement is that of being domesticated by the establishment. A thoroughly domesticated renewal can easily lose its prophetic edge, and therefore its calling, and end up becoming just another piece of burdensome ecclesiastical machinery. This does not call for an adversary relationship between a renewal movement and the church. A healthy tension is necessary, but this can be in a spirit of love and communication.

Recognizing the charismatic renewal is something different from adopting or endorsing it. It is more subtle. It is less official, yet at the same time more effective. Recognition may not involve an official statement by the church, but it may occur when an official states his or her agreement with a charismatic. Recognition may not mean an ecclesiastical office for charismatics, but may be an occasion when charismatics present a position that is seriously heard and considered. Recognition has to do with the way that church officials and charismatic leaders speak about each other and relate to each other. It is more a matter of tone than of official policy. It is a concrete and consistent demonstration of regard that can be expressed in a variety of ways. For instance, a theological seminary or a church convention may invite a charismatic to be the speaker for an annual lecture series. A bishop may risk his popularity by taking a stand against those in a congregation who want to reject a pastor simply on the ground of the pastor's being charismatic. A church commission may seek counsel from charismatic congregations that have demonstrated effective ministry in a particular area. A church official may bring greetings, or celebrate the Eucharist, at a charismatic convention.[17]

These kind of actions do not involve official endorsement of a movement. What they do is recognize the presence of a renewal movement in the church and encourage its healthy expression. More importantly, they say convincingly that people involved in the renewal are fellow members, whose calling and gifts are appreciated in the church.

In giving this kind of recognition to the charismatic renewal, the church does not and should not lay aside its responsibility to continue to evaluate and, where necessary, to correct the renewal. Theologians, officials, pastors, and parishioners need to examine the renewal in the light of Scripture. Church leaders owe it to their constituency to make such an evaluation. If the charismatic renewal is truly from God, it will stand up under scrutiny.

Movement faces institution

The charismatic movement is faced with major options also: *isolation, institutionalization,* or *witness.*

Large numbers of charismatics have felt frustrated with or rejected by their church. Some have chosen to leave their congregation or denomination and join more active churches. In the absence of a lively alternative church, some have established home meetings as a substitute. The net result is that valuable members have become lost or isolated.

Lutheran charismatic leaders have generally counseled charismatics to have prayerful patience with the church and not to reject it. They have challenged charismatics to love the church, to pray for it, and to serve it, just as Jesus does (Eph. 5:25-27). Leaving the institutional church is always a last resort.

A renewal movement may become institutionalized either by becoming a parachurch organization within the denomination or by leaving its historical setting and forming a new denomination. Church history records numerous examples of renewal movements moving in these directions. Many have organized themselves as a mission society, a Bible society, an evangelistic association, a Bible-school movement, spiritual-life federation, or religious order. These spiritual life structures within the larger church run the danger of being relegated to the periphery of church life, exerting only a limited influence on the larger church. After an initial surge and peak the renewal's influence gradually wanes. When the renewal becomes a new denomination, formed around newly discovered experience and teaching, the life span of the movement may be greater, but its influence is restricted to its own membership, and it runs increased risk of falling victim to imbalance.

A third alternative is that the renewal becomes a witness in and to the church. On the one hand, this means being a bold, prophetic voice, recalling the church to its high calling. On the other hand, it means being a servant—repenting of sin, allowing the Holy Spirit to do his cleansing and painful work first of all in the renewal, giving and serving in humble and unnoticed ways, laying down its own life for the sake of the church, interceding for the people of God as Moses interceded for Israel (Exod. 32:7-14,30-32), praying with persistence for the church's renewal.

Being a witness means seeking out ways to express love and regard for the church. Charismatic leaders need to model this in their relationships with church officials. Again, it is not a matter of setting up official structures, but of finding natural ways to recognize and honor brothers and sisters who have been called to positions of authority in the institutional church. A church leader may be invited to speak or conduct a workshop at a charismatic conference.[18] A bishop who takes an unpopular stand in the church may receive a telephone call or a letter from a charismatic leader, supporting and encouraging him.[19] Charismatic leaders and church officials may meet informally from time to time to discuss questions or problems of common interest, to pray with one another, or simply to socialize. How many Lutheran charismatic leaders have ever taken their bishop and his wife out to dinner—not to criticize or agitate, but just to spend some time together?

Generally speaking, relationships between institutional and movement leaders function most effectively if they are kept informal and unofficial. Leaders of free movements need to guard against the temptation to use these relationships to gain acceptance or status. Church officials are understandably wary of being co-opted by a particular group or movement in the church. They may have genuine sympathy for some of the objectives of a renewal movement, but be reluctant to voice it if renewal leaders are addicted to name-dropping or are likely to quote them out of context.

When relationships of mutual trust and regard are built between institutional and movement leaders, each respecting the integrity of the other, the us/them dichotomy can be lived out under an overarching *we*. The church in both its expressions—institution and movement—will be a more credible witness to the lordship of Jesus Christ over all things in the church.

THE BURDEN OF THE CHARISMATIC RENEWAL FOR THE CHURCH

The institutional church is in serious need of renewal. The Lutheran church in many parts of the world is experiencing a measureable decrease in membership, as well as a perceived decline in influence and effectiveness. Its evangelistic zeal has been waning and its missionary force declining. Church attendance and program participation involve only a small fraction of the total baptized membership. Responsible polls indicate that many Lutherans lack assurance of personal salvation or proper understanding of justification by faith.[20] That alone constitutes a crying need for renewal in the Lutheran church.

Scripture gives prophetic images of renewal that come to the whole people of God: Ezekiel's vision of the valley of dry bones (Ezekiel 37), Joel's prophecy of an end-time outpouring of the Spirit (Joel 2).

The shape of a renewed church may be quite different from its present form, yet the essentials of our life in Christ will be abundantly evident. The Holy Spirit will be recognizably present in the church's life and ministry. There will be a strong biblical orientation in preaching, teaching, and daily life. The gifts of the Spirit will be in operation in the public life of the church and the private life of church members. Jesus will be acknowledged as head of the church and his will sought for all things. The rule of God will be established in the belief system, structural order, worship, and ministry of the church. The church will be increasingly ecumenical. The growing unity of the body of Christ will be demonstrated to the world as a positive witness to the gospel. The church in renewal will seek to fulfill the great commission. It will be both an example and an advocate of justice and righteousness.

One of the unique and encouraging features of the charismatic movement as a whole has been its determined insistence to remain within the church. By and large it is a movement *within* rather than *outside* of the institutional church. Richard Hutcheson, a Presbyterian church official, points this out:

Unlike many previous spirit-centered movements, the charismatic movement is not essentially anti-institutional, but is rather making a conscious and generally successful effort to remain within the existing churches. A remarkably high percentage of individual charismatics and charismatic groups are making a determined effort to support, remain loyal to, and work within the existing structures of their own congregations. They are often the most loyal, most enthusiastic, and most active workers and supporters. A great many non-charismatic ministers would be startled to learn how many of those they regard as pillars of the establishment speak in tongues in their private and small group devotions.[21]

Present-day charismatics are not more holy than participants in earlier renewal movements. They have certainly done their share of complaining about the institutional church. They have not always borne rejection and criticism with grace. And yet it is true, as Hutcheson points out, that the movement has so far tended to remain within the church more than many previous movements. This must be seen as a special grace of God, both for the church and for the charismatic movement. The Spirit is holding both institution and renewal in his embrace, softening fleshly dogmatism, quieting the voices of strident intransigence, giving our generation the chance to grasp and experience more deeply the true nature of the church.

The church has its *institutional* side, which embraces all believers, providing structure and stability; and it has its *movement* side, which the Spirit calls into being to meet special needs. Can these two, in our day, so submit to the Spirit's authority that the church will recover what has been lost—a mutual regard that bequeaths to the people of God both the strength of institution and the innovation of movements?

CHAPTER 47

THE CHURCH:
AN ORDERED BODY

Charismatics have addressed themselves to questions of order in regard to the two primary areas in which the renewal has functioned: the movement itself, and the local congregation. It has had little or nothing to say about larger church structures, though its experience both within the movement and in local fellowships is not without implications for the church at large.

ORDER IN THE CHARISMATIC MOVEMENT

To speak about "order" in the same breath with "charismatic movement" may seem to fulfill the classic definition of humor: the juxtaposition of the incongruous. Certainly the renewal has nothing comparable to the defined structure and established procedures of a denomination. If one looks at the worldwide phenomenon of the movement in terms of structure, then one must say that innovation and variety are the rule; uniformity, the exception. In this sense there is no standard or well-defined "order" in the charismatic movement. Yet a crucial component of order *is* exercised in and by the renewal, and that is *authority*.

Benedictine scholar Kilian McDonnell once asked David du Plessis, widely recognized as classical Pentecostalism's ambassador to the historic denominations, to speak to a group of bishops, and commented, "We want someone who can speak from a position of *authority*."

Du Plessis, who held no office, represented no organization, demurred: "I have no authority."

"Indeed you do," countered McDonnell. "It carries no title, is subject to no election, has no jurisdictional boundaries, is recorded in no minutes; it is nonofficial, nonlegal, nonbinding. But it is *authority!*"

It is characteristic of renewal movements that they give rise to another stream of authority in the church, alongside that of the official institution. As McDonnell rightly observed, it is a different kind of authority: not the authority of office, but the authority of influence. Yet its effect in the church can be considerable, and may in particular matters even go beyond that of official institutional authority. Where charismatic authority is recognized and received, it can significantly shape individual lives and the life of the church as a whole.

The charismatic renewal has raised up a considerable cadre of leaders who, in varying degrees, make up part of this second stream of authority in the church. Many renewal movements have come to a focus in the person of a single charismatic leader who, at the least, symbolized the movement. Names like Francis of Assisi, Martin Luther, John Wesley, Hans Nielsen Hauge, Nicolai Grundtvig, Carl Olof Rosenius, and William Booth spring immediately to mind. No such single figure has arisen in the charismatic renewal. Because the movement is so widespread—on every continent, in every denomination—the leadership is also widespread. What one sees is not a single leader who leads or represents the movement, but rather a network of relationships among many leaders.

Order is related to goal or purpose. A single family, a business enterprise, a church, or an entire nation establishes an order that it believes will help it accomplish certain goals. The goal of the charismatic renewal is neither to take over nor to replace the institutional church. Individual charismatics may have positions in the structure of their denomination (charismatic parish pastors would be the prime example), but the purpose of the charismatic renewal, as a movement within the church, is to *speak* to the church, be a *presence* in the church, *encourage* the church, *serve* the church, *bear witness* to the church.

The kind of order that will accomplish that goal in all the different nations and cultures of the world, and in every denomination throughout the entire body of Christ, calls for incredible diversity and a great deal of grass-roots initiative. The order that has grown up in the charismatic renewal is appropriate to its purpose: not a centralized or highly coordinated organization but a relatively loose and fluid set of relationships among charismatic leaders. These relationships form a communication link that encompasses the globe and reaches into virtually every denomination in Christendom. Charismatic leaders know each other, correspond with each other, meet together in a variety of situations and configurations, consult with one another, and undertake common projects that serve or give expression to the renewal. All of this with a very minimum of structure and organization.

Charismatic leaders have not sought to organize much of anything beyond the level of denominational renewal committees and ad hoc committees that convene meetings or initiate special projects. The order that they give to the charismatic renewal is a sense of solidarity in the common purpose of calling the church to a renewed dependence on the Holy Spirit. This solidarity is expressed in their relationships with one another.

More significant than anything that charismatic leaders do or organize is just the way that they move about in the body of Christ with evident love and regard for one another, recognizing, honoring, and drawing on one another's ministries. While there have been some noticeable and unhappy breaks in relationships between some charismatic leaders, on the whole these relationships have served to give an order to the movement that is commensurate with its purpose.

When Philip Potter, general secretary of the World Council of Churches, asked David du Plessis whether the charismatic movement was the "real ecumenical movement today," du Plessis is reported to have said, "My dear Philip, we are so far ahead of you we can't even see if you're still coming."[1] In an open seminar at the World Council of Churches Assembly in Nairobi in 1975, Kilian McDonnell, himself a professional ecumenist for the Vatican, said that "the most significant thing happening ecumenically today is in the charismatic renewal."[2] It is a different kind of ecumenism, unofficial and relatively unprogrammed. Yet, through an infrastructure of relationships among its leaders, the charismatic movement is sending strong impulses for reconciliation, unity, and renewal throughout the body of Christ.

ORDER IN CONGREGATIONAL LIFE

The second area in which the charismatic movement has addressed itself to the question of order is in regard to congregational or parish renewal. The reason for this is that the place where the renewal has had the greatest freedom to reshape structure is at the level of the local church. A charismatic Lutheran pastor who has the support of the lay leadership can exercise considerable freedom in bringing changes to a local congregation. This is the level at which the charismatic renewal has had its greatest impact in the Lutheran church, especially in the United States. At regional and national levels the overall influence of the renewal has had some effect on the church as a whole, but, generally speaking, regional and national church leadership has not included charismatics.

Concern for congregational order in the charismatic renewal has been an extension of its emphasis on the lordship of Christ. If Christ is truly Lord of the church, then its structure and operation cannot be a matter of indifference or mere preference, but should be reflective of his will in the matter.

Scripture, the point of departure

In this, as in most other matters, charismatics have taken Scripture as their point of departure. Lutheran charismatics have generally steered a middle course between claims of having discovered *the* scriptural pattern for a "New Testament church" and the liberal notion that Scripture has nothing whatever to say on the subject.[3] What this has boiled down to in practice is a readiness to evaluate some present-day practices in the light of scriptural patterns and precedents.

On the one hand, as we have noted earlier, it seems clear that the New Testament does not present a single, universally normative structure for a Christian congregation. On the other hand, Scripture is certainly not silent in regard to questions of order, structure, and authority in the church. What the Holy Spirit led the church to do in its formative years in regard to order ought not be turned over to antiquarians with never a sideward glance. It is part of the apostolic witness, part of canonical Scripture. We cannot assume *a priori* that the Spirit will not apply the same or similiar wisdom to our situations.

It is true that "situations change," but parroting that slogan should not be our point of departure in establishing the order of a congregation. For it is also true that the Spirit is able to apply the same basic truth in a great variety of situations. The Spirit may indeed set aside some patterns from the past and utilize present-day practices in ordering the life of a congregation, but he is not bound to do so, nor are we free to do so if he wills something else. We must at the very least take into account the possibility that the Spirit may find some of his own precedents in the church more to his liking than the latest fad from the political or management marketplace.

Alternative concepts for ordering congregational life

If one were to look for a touchstone of the charismatic movement's teaching on congregational order it would probably be focused in words like *elder* or *church council*. This stems first of all from the study of Scripture. The role of elders figures prominently in governing structures both in the Old and New Testaments. The other side of this is the fact that charismatics have recognized some of the weaknesses inherent in a congregation that structures itself after the model of a democratic assembly. The transition from one to the other is essentially a matter of concept; it does not necessarily, or at once, involve external changes in structure, for instance, in the constitution or legal basis of a congregation.

A change in concept is sometimes described as a transition from democracy to kingdom. In explaining this transition to a group of pastors, Herbert Mirly, pastor of Resurrection Lutheran Church in Charlotte, North Carolina, said,

"We did not need to change the constitution of our congregation as this transition got under way. It was a matter of how we understood and used the existing structure. For instance, we used to come to a congregational meeting with the idea that *we* must 'make certain decisions.' When we began to see the congregation as an expression of 'kingdom,' we approached the whole thing differently. *God* makes decisions. Our business is to discern as accurately as we can what he has decided and then proceed to obey him. The so-called 'voters meeting' became a prayer meeting or a 'discernment session.' We still discuss the issues, but the attitude and approach is altogether different: instead of choosing up sides and seeing who can muster 51% of the vote, we are all standing on the same side of the line participating in the process of listening to the Lord and seeking his will in the matter."[4]

A related concept for understanding congregational order has been that of family. The model of family tends to produce in a congregation an ordered set of relationships rather than simply a procedure for handling issues. The church council answers to the role of parents; the congregation, to the role of children. At first glance this seems to lead to a more centralized, authoritarian structure, but the opposite is more usually the case. Loving and sensitive parents probably listen more sympathetically to their children than an elected official does to his or her constituency. They listen because they love and seek the best for their children, not because the children have the leverage of a vote in the next election. A typical church constitution might permit a church council to do certain things with a majority or two-thirds approval of the congregation. Charismatic congregations that have developed the family concept, on the other hand, might well decide to wait if as few as 10% of the members feel uneasy about a particular action; in a family, maintaining unity is normally more important than pushing through a particular decision.

A charismatic Lutheran congregation that had experimented with a family model of church government for about 10 years included the following statement in its annual report:

> What we see emerging in our midst is a particular understanding of church order and leadership that is significantly different from that which many people have grown up with and have come to take for granted. It has several inter-related features.
>
> *1. Leadership is a particular calling.* The old idea was to give almost everyone who was willing to serve a turn on the church council. If we saw those whom we would like to see develop further, we would grab them for the council. "That way we will get them involved," so we thought. The council was looked on as a place to develop leaders.
>
> What we have come to see is that leadership is a particular gift and calling in the Body of Christ. While there will inevitably be some real development in any person who serves on the council, the council is essentially a ministry for those

who have already demonstrated the gift and calling for leadership. Our concern in nominating people for the council is not to "get them involved," or to "give them a chance to grow," but rather *to discern the ones whom the Lord has given the calling of leadership in the congregation.*

We must set aside the worldly notion that leadership is a place of higher status, while those not in leadership occupy a lower status. The call of a council member is in essence no different than the calling of a Sunday School teacher, a pastor, a custodian, an usher, or a nursery attendant. The calling of each and every one is to *serve.* Leadership is simply a necessary function in the Body of Christ to which some members are called, because God has gifted and equipped them for serving in this particular way.

When we understand leadership in this way, then it becomes evident that not everyone is called to serve on the council. Just as not everyone has a calling to teach, or play the organ, or manage finances, or do marriage counseling. Some members will never be called to serve on the council. Not because they are less important or respected in the congregation, but simply because that is not their calling under God.

Indeed, it has been our experience that the very nature of congregational life is such that a relatively small number of people have the calling to serve on the church council. Council members rotate off the council at least every three years, but after a year's "sabbatical" have frequently been called back into active service. What we have had in effect is a small pool of leaders from which we each year select a council. New members may be drawn into this "pool of leadership" as their gifts and calling for leadership become evident.

If one looked at this practice from a human point of view, it could be dubbed a clique. "The same old people back on the council again." But what is it from *God's* point of view? Does God call people to the important ministry of leadership for three years, and then set them aside so as to "give somebody else a chance"? This is a human way of reckoning, which attaches some special status to the ministry of leadership. We repeat: no member of the Body of Christ is more honored or significant than any other. Each simply has a different function. Those who have had the calling to serve on the church council, in a congregation our size, consist of a pool of probably no more than twenty people. With the simple passage of time, some people will be added to this pool, while others will move away, be called to another ministry, become less active, or be promoted to the heavenly councils!

We do not see the evolving of a small cadre of leaders in our congregation as a sign that we are in a rut, or having the same old people run everything. Rather, we believe this is the result of a definite leading of the Spirit. It has resulted from his work among us, to strengthen and build up the Body of Christ.

2. From political assembly to family. As we enter into a deeper apprehension of the church order and leadership which the Spirit is working among us, we have to unlearn some of our traditional ways of thinking about church order. As Americans we have experienced great blessings from the political system of representative democracy. But the foundational concept of democracy is alien to the church. Under democracy, the leaders are ultimately responsible to the people who elect them. In the church, leaders are ultimately responsible to God.

A political system is a poor model for church order. Far better is the model of a *family,* "the household of God" (1 Tim. 3:15). The nature of a Christian congregation is much more akin to a family than to a democratic government. According to the family model, the leaders of the congregation fulfill the role of parents. They are responsible for the leadership and direction of the family.

Parents' ultimate accountability for their family is to God. They are *responsive* to their children, but they are *responsible* to God. Likewise, the leaders of a congregation must be responsive to each and every member. Leaders are expected to have wisdom, and one of the qualities of the "wisdom that is from above" is that it is easily entreated" (James 3:17), which means that a church council member is someone you can feel free to come and talk to, someone with whom you can share your problems and concerns. God may use something that you share to help formulate a decision or direction taken by the council.

While leaders must be responsive to the people, they cannot ask simply, "What does the congregation want?" If they take that line, they would be like parents who make decisions simply on the basis of "What the children want." Those called by God to leadership responsibility will have to press on to ask, "What does *God* want?" Leaders who end up being simply an echo of the people have abandoned their God-appointed calling to *lead*.

The family is an appropriate model for the church because it embraces people at all different levels of (spiritual) development: tiny babes (a 40 year old man can be a babe in Christ), children, young men and women, mothers, and fathers. It is the calling of the spiritual parents to give leadership to the family. They are the ones that God has equipped for the task. Blessed is the congregation where such "parents" have been raised up by God, have entered into their calling, and have been gratefully received by the people.

Where the responsibility and authority of leadership rests in a council of spiritual elders, the congregation is spared on the one hand the mistakes and immaturities of purely democractic decisions. (Even in the secular sphere, especially given the enormously increased power of the mass media, we are beginning to see how subject the decisions of the people are to whim and passing fad.) On the other hand, the fact that leadership rests in a *council,* and not in a single individual, protects the congregation from the dangers of a spiritual dictator. Council members serve as a healthy check and balance on each other. Indeed, as we look at the leadership God has given us, the diversity of gifts, talents, and personalities he has put in the same "pool" is truly amazing.

3. Esteem them highly. Those who are called to the ministry of leadership bear a heavy responsibility. They need your prayers, your support, your counsel and conversation, your heartfelt cooperation. They are not in a position of leadership because they are perfect but simply because the call of God is on their life for this particular service. By God's grace their service will bless and upbuild the congregation.[5]

THE GOAL OF GOOD ORDER

Order is not an end in itself, but a means for achieving a right balance between freedom and unity. When the church is well ordered, individual members will experience freedom, yet the body as a whole will be able to live and act in unity. It is not something achieved at a single stroke. Bodies

314 LED BY THE SPIRIT

of believers grow into it as they allow themselves to be led by the Spirit. If the charismatic renewal has a contribution to make in this area, it will not be a successful formula for ordering congregational life, but a demonstrated willingness to hear and follow the leading of the Spirit.

CHAPTER 48

THE CHURCH: A WORSHIPING COMMUNITY

During his life on earth, Jesus had spoken of a time when people would worship the Father in Spirit and truth (John 4:23). When the disciples on Pentecost were filled with the Holy Spirit, the first thing they did was break forth into exalted praise and worship of God.[1] The 3000 who came to faith that day entered into a community that centered its life in worship and prayer (Acts 2:42,46-47). In equipping the church for mission, the Holy Spirit brings people into a new dimension of worship.

A pastor in a Lutheran congregation that had been deeply affected by the charismatic renewal routinely asked people in his adult membership class, "Why do you want to be a member here?" The most common response was, "Because of the love that I have felt in the worship." When a study of the charismatic renewal was made in the German Democratic Republic, one of its chief marks was seen to be the central place given to praise and adoration in renewal gatherings. For many people, charismatic renewal has brought a heightened sense of God's presence in worship, and this has led to a greater degree of personal involvement. Spectators at worship have been converted into participants.

Even to outside observers, an accent on worship has been one of the most noticeable characteristics of the charismatic renewal. News items on charismatic conferences typically carry a picture of a crowd of people with hands upraised in worship. This is an interesting phenomenon: even secular editors, who may see nothing more than an interesting departure from staid decorum, nevertheless recognize that worship is somehow central to this movement.

But it is more than a matter of upraised hands. That is just one of the ways that the Spirit may choose to help people respond to a sovereign God. Perhaps our response to God has been so controlled and intellectual that we need to do something like raise our hands to enhance the sense of abandonment. But we would miss the point if we became preoccupied simply with outward gestures. The Spirit wants to lead us in exactly the opposite direction: away from reliance on our own efforts or forms of worship into a dependence on him to orchestrate our meeting with the Lord. At the heart of charismatic worship is a radical willingness to obey the Lord, which is as much a challenge to the charismatic renewal as it is to the church at large.

David Preus, speaking as presiding bishop of the American Lutheran Church, once complained that in many of the Lutheran churches he visited, the worship was just plain dull. The same kind of complaint can be heard in regard to some charismatic prayer groups, after they have been going for a while. To begin with, people often find charismatic worship a refreshing experience. Some of this can be due simply to novelty: new songs, new expressions, new style—a welcome break from liturgical routine. But if it does not get beyond mere novelty, the work of the Spirit is wasted. When the newness wears off, charismatics can find themselves back in essentially the same place that Bishop Preus described. The liturgical procedures have been shuffled around, but the same old problem is there again: dull worship.

Worship in Spirit and in truth is simply not a human possibility. Only the Holy Spirit can bring it about. It cannot be reduced to set forms, though it may find expression in a structured service. It cannot be equated with any particular mood or feeling or style. It is what happens when the Holy Spirit fills us, making our bodies his temple (1 Cor. 6:19), and prompts us to respond to God our Father, and Jesus our Lord and Savior. The Spirit may lead us to express this in a variety of ways, but the worship never becomes our possession, in an absolute sense. It is God's work. The essence of charismatic worship is not found in particular forms, but in the awareness that every occasion of worship calls for a fresh dependence on the Holy Spirit.

Through the ministry of the Holy Spirit, the Lord himself is present in worship. Divine worship is a festival of his presence. It is a foretaste of heaven, where life centers around the worship of God.

The charismatic renewal has had two principal gathering points: the local prayer group or home fellowship that meets on a regular basis, and regional or national charismatic conferences that people attend once or twice a year. In these settings, the worship elements that have been most prominently emphasized in the renewal are praise, ministry of the Word, and prayer.

PRAISE

One of the popular choruses of the charismatic renewal is from Psalm 92:

It is a good thing to give thanks unto the Lord.
It is a good thing to give thanks unto the Lord
And to sing praises unto thy name,
O Most High (v. 1 KJV).

An upsurge of praise has been one of the marks of the renewal. Praise as an intellectual concept or a liturgical expression may have been familiar, but for many people, spontaneous and heartfelt expressions of praise have come as a new and refreshing experience. It is worth noting that one of the distinctives of the charismatic renewal, speaking in tongues, is chiefly a vehicle for praise (see Acts 2:4; 10:46; 1 Cor. 14:16). The fact that one writer could turn out a spate of books on the single topic of praise that would sell several million copies suggests that there is a considerable gap between formal belief in praise and its practice in people's everyday lives.[2]

Praise engages the whole person

Praise cannot be reduced to a formula, yet, as Lutheran pastor Paul Anderson has pointed out, Scripture portrays praise in more vigorous terms than we would normally use to describe a Sunday morning Lutheran church service:

The Hebrew word *halal,* from which the word *hallelujah* comes, means "to make a noise." Praise enlists the vocal cords. We did not learn silent meditation from the Hebrews; they were an expressive bunch. The Hebrew word *zamar* [praise] includes the playing of musical instruments, and the verb for thanking includes the motion of holding out the hands. Clearly, praise is meant to engage the voice and body. Those who only worship God in silence miss the joy of exuberance. They would do well to read Psalm 47 and obey the commands: "Clap your hands, all peoples! Shout to God with loud songs of joy! God has gone up with a shout, the Lord with the sound of a trumpet. Sing praises to God, sing praises! Sing praises to our King, sing praises." Those whose devotional life includes only quiet meditation may have precious moments with the Lord, but the *hallelujah* is missing.[3]

Praise honors God for who he is. When the Holy Spirit reveals God to us, praise is the appropriate response. In essence, praise expresses our love to God. One of the things that continues to attract people to the charismatic renewal is an affecting and unashamed love for God that expresses itself in praise.

Spontaneity and tradition

The charismatic renewal has sometimes tended to equate unstructured spontaneity with the Spirit. Its most common form of worship has been the "prayer and praise service" with spirited singing, free prayer, exercise of spiritual gifts, and biblical teaching—all of this with a bare minimum of structure. This has helped open up the worship experience to greater participation by the people, and it has produced a significant new body of worship songs. But it has also had the tendency to separate the renewal from the church's heritage of formal worship.

In some places, such as Resurrection Lutheran Church in Charlotte, North Carolina, there has been a conscious effort to blend together charismatic worship and liturgical worship. This does not happen spontaneously. It requires thought, planning, and a sustained effort by both leaders and people to enter more deeply and fully into the reality of worship, but it has produced the renewal's finest contribution to the worship life of the church. Through the Spirit, liturgical worship, which may have become lifeless, can be filled with joy, love, warmth, and a sense of God's presence.

This may require a decisive step by the leaders of a congregation to open up the liturgical order and allow for charismatic expression—free prayer, prophecy, tongues and interpretation, and testimony. Lutheran liturgies can be readily adapted to this kind of free expression without losing their traditional character. Early Christian liturgies made room for free expressions following the reading of Scripture and during the distribution of Holy Communion.[4] In larger congregations, or in services that draw people from a wider circle than the local parish, new charismatic liturgies and worship styles may also be introduced.

Luther once expressed the desire for services that would be oriented toward ministering to people's personal needs, but said that he didn't have the people for it.[5] Today the people are there, in growing numbers: the Spirit is distributing the gifts by which we can minister to one another's needs. When we encounter the living God in worship, we often find that he himself turns our attention to some of the practical needs of those around us and opens up the service to a time of personal ministry.

Neither liturgical form nor nonliturgical expression will in itself produce vibrant worship. Liturgy is an outline for worship. It can help release the corporate and individual adoration of God in an orderly, yet free expression. But the Holy Spirit is the initiator and inspirer of true worship. When he directs our worship, questions of spontaneity and structure are caught up into the greater awareness that we are encountering the living God, and that he is in control.

MINISTRY OF THE WORD

Wherever the Holy Spirit is welcomed and honored, the proclaimed Word can be experienced. What God says, God does. We should expect the Word to be at work in many ways and at many levels during worship.

Through the enacted Word, the sacraments, God draws near for fellowship. The charismatic renewal has not made any significant contribution to sacramental theology, but the realism of its worship has helped intensify the sense of encounter that is inherent in the sacraments.

In Baptism God initiates us into a covenant relationship with himself. We become part of the body of Christ. The death and resurrection experience of Baptism can become a reality not only for the person being baptized, but also for those remembering their own Baptism during the liturgy. During the general confession and absolution, people can be set free from bondages just as certainly as through a pointed ministry of deliverance. Jesus, truly present in the Eucharist, is the same Lord who forgave sin and healed the sick. When we celebrate his precious presence in the eucharistic meal, we are proclaiming and living in the reality of his death until he comes again; we appropriate the benefits of his death for ourselves and for others; and we manifest our unity in him (1 Cor. 11:26-32; 10:16-17). Burdens of sin, sickness, and alienation can be lifted at the Lord's table.

Through the proclaimed Word, both the judgments and the promises of God come into the midst of a worshiping people—not merely as ideas, but as realities. The charismatic renewal represents a reaction against preaching and teaching that contents itself simply to articulate doctrine. "Your problem," said David du Plessis in addressing a group of Protestant clergymen, "is that you have made doctrine terminal." The end product of the Word is not a body of teaching, but the demonstration of the Spirit in changed lives and situations.

The most widespread ministry in the charismatic renewal has been that of teaching, but it has been action-oriented teaching, short on explaining and long on doing. This partly explains the hostility that has sometimes been directed against the movement. The opposition that a renewal movement encounters stems more often from what is done than from what is taught. Ern Baxter, a popular charismatic Bible teacher, made the observation that we are not hated for our ideas, but for putting our ideas into practice.[6]

When the Holy Spirit stands at the center of the teaching, the "doing" is what God accomplishes. This is obvious when the Word is confirmed by miraculous signs and wonders. But it is equally true, though less obviously so, in manifestations of love and holiness: it is his gracious doing, not ours.

PRAYER

Is it really necessary to make a case for prayer? Of course prayer belongs to the life of the church!

But what is the actual shape of the church's prayer life? Here we must consider not only the setting of people gathered for worship, but the whole life of God's people. Worship as event is part of a larger tapestry: worship is a way of life, and prayer is one of its principal expressions.

The charismatic movement came on the scene calling for a renewal of spiritual gifts in the ministry of the church. This occurred in a particular setting. The principal locus of the movement in its early stages, the instrument through which it was spread, was the prayer group. Many people who had grown up in churches in which prayer found little expression outside of formal liturgies began to meet in homes and hotels and church basements to pray. People's involvement in the renewal could be fairly accurately gauged by their participation in a prayer group. The emphasis on *charismata* occurred in the larger context of a renewed emphasis on prayer. For those within the renewal, such charismatic distinctives as being filled with the Holy Spirit and experiencing spiritual gifts had the character of a personal response to the Word of God, kindled by prayer.

Renewal movements always bring with them an element of rebuke. The charismatic renewal is a rebuke to a church whose prayer life has drifted into formalism or disuse. How often do long hours of discussing and planning church business end with the half-guilty reminder that we should ask God's blessing on our efforts? Activities, discussions, seminars, teaching—how efficient are they? What is the end result of efforts that rely merely on human intelligence and methods? Do they achieve God's purpose? Have we not abandoned the greatest privilege and the most revolutionary power available to us as Christians? The Holy Spirit does not flow through mere methods and institutions. He needs people who pray.

Through the ministry of the Holy Spirit we experience the power of God in our prayers. Through prayer, offered in the name of Jesus, the Spirit causes the intercession of Jesus in heaven (Heb. 7:25) to become effective on earth (Rom. 8:26-27). Prayer in the power of the Spirit is God's powerful instrument for bringing his kingdom to reality among us.

The New Testament shows us that Jesus was much given to prayer (Mark 6:46; 14:23; 14:32-39; Matt. 14:23). He is the model of a person who lived out of conversation with God. Prayer was a central factor in key events of his life: his baptism and transfiguration (Luke 3:21; 9:28-29), the choosing of the Twelve, and being recognized as Christ (Luke 6:12-13; 9:18). Jesus withdrew himself from the crush of those seeking healing in order to pray (Mark 1:35; Luke 5:16). Jesus frequently prayed in solitude, on a mountainside, for instance (Mark 6:46; Matt. 14:23; Luke 6:12). In each case, Jesus was a person bound to the Father through prayer. In Gethsemane he showed by example the foundation on which all true prayer is built: subordinating one's own will to that of the heavenly Father.

Just as Jesus is himself the pray-er preeminent, so he is also the master teacher of prayer. The disciples asked Jesus for instruction in prayer (Luke 11:1); they observed that his ministry and prayer were closely linked together. He directed those who pray to go to a secret place (Matt. 6:6). On the other hand, he made a special promise to those who pray together (Matt. 18:19). He encouraged prayers of faith (Mark 11:24). He consistently affirmed that such prayers will always be heard (Matt. 7:7-11; Luke 11:9-13). Above all, he gave to his disciples the name of God that is particularly appropriate to prayer: *Father.*

The Acts of the Apostles shows clearly that prayer held great significance for the early Christians (1:14; 2:42; 6:4; 6:6; 12:5; 12:12; 13:3; 20:36; 21:5; see also the statements concerning pray-ers in 9:11; 10:9; 16:25). The working of the Holy Spirit is experienced through prayer and, conversely, always leads one back to prayer (Acts 2:1-4; 4:24-31). In the Epistles, as well, one sees that prayer was a decisive component of congregational life. The admonitions to unceasing prayer confirm this (Rom. 12:12; Col. 4:2; 1 Thess. 5:17; Eph. 6:18; Jude 20; 1 Peter 4:7; Phil. 4:6). At meetings of early Christians it is clear that everyone, men and women alike, had the opportunity to speak aloud in prayer (1 Cor. 11:4-16).

Prayer played an essential role in the expansion of Christian faith (Acts 4:29; 2 Cor. 1:11; Col. 4:3; 2 Thess. 3:1). The apostle Paul made clear how dependent he was on the prayers of the church (Rom. 15:30-32; 2 Cor. 1:11; Phil. 1:19; 1 Thess. 5:25). On the other hand, the apostle prayed constantly for his churches (2 Cor. 13:7; Eph. 1:16-23; Phil. 1:9; Col. 1:3,9; 2 Thess. 1:11). Intercession extended beyond the bounds of the Christian community, with special concern for secular rulers (1 Tim. 2:2-4).

Given all of the above, it is striking that nowhere is mention made of any prayer technique. Questions about prayer concern content: prayer depends on its object. Most decisive is the fact that *all* prayer proceeds from faith. We cannot pray aright by virtue of any inherent power. The ability to pray must be given, just as the ability to believe. This is clear, above all, from Romans 8:26-27. Some exegetes find a reference here to prayer in tongues, which is altogether possible.[7] The point which the apostle makes is that only the Holy Spirit can bring forth in us prayer that is pleasing to God. Thus we remain, at all times, dependent on the Spirit of God in our seasons of prayer.

Jesus told his disciples that they could not do anything apart from him (John 15:5). This is a difficult word. Something in us must die if we are to say, "I can't do *anything* apart from Jesus." No, not even pray. Like the disciples, we need to come to the master Teacher, and say, "Lord, teach us to pray."

Jesus responded to the disciples' request with the words of the Lord's Prayer, which in the context was more than a formal prayer. It was like a curriculum of his own intimate conversations with the Father. He wanted to share this with his disciples. His high priestly prayer underscores this same theme of intimate communion with the Father: ". . . even as thou, Father, art in me, and I in thee, that they also may be in us" (John 17:21). After Christ's ascension, the disciples joined together in prayer and waited for the coming of the Spirit. On Pentecost the Lord ushered them into a new dimension of fellowship with God. Immediately this found expression in exalted prayer, and nowhere was their relationship with God more evident in the time that followed than in the dynamism that animated their prayers.

What practical steps does God set before us?

• *Humility.* We must humble ourselves before God and confess our complacent contentment with lives so meager in prayer. We enter into the riches of prayer first of all by recognizing our poverty.

• *Commitment.* God's presence must become the center of our lives; daily we must seek his face. In personal audience we must ascribe glory to him, the holy and almighty God. This means a significant commitment of *time.*

Luther's scribe and companion, Veit Dietrich, said of him, "No day passes that he does not give three hours to prayer, and those the fittest for study."[8] Luther wrote to his coworker Philip Melanchthon:

> Whatever aspect matters may assume, we can achieve all through prayer. This alone is the almighty queen of human destiny. Therewith we can accomplish everything, and thus maintain what already exists, amend what is defective, patiently put up with what is inevitable, overcome what is evil, and preserve all that is good.[9]

For Luther, prayer was no mere matter of the intellect or of memorized sentences. It was the heart in conversation with God. We see what is before our eyes, but God looks on the heart. The more naturally and truly the heart opens up to God in prayer, the more certainly and freely the time of prayer will have its effect in one's daily life.

Of course, regular study of the Bible will comprise a part of this time. This is necessary for one to learn to distinguish between the voice of God and other voices, including one's own thoughts.

The Holy Spirit stands by, the teacher who helps us recognize the thoughts and guidance of God and apply them to our lives. "Watch and pray that you may not enter into temptation" (Mark 14:38).

Closely linked with prayer is the ministry of spiritual counsel and direction, which can take place in a natural way within the intimate and accepting atmosphere of a prayer group. This points to another important step in the renewal of prayer.

• *Praying together.* Nothing so undermines fellowship as scheming and contention, and nothing so works against this as a fellowship of prayer in which together we come into the presence of God.

Fellowship in prayer calls us out of isolation and loneliness. It calls us to listen to one another and bring one another's needs before God. It can foster a childlike trust that the Father will influence and change things now happening in one another's lives.

To begin with, prayer groups are often surprised by specific answers to prayer, even though Scripture is full of such promises.

Fear and timidity about praying for one another ebbs away where people are bound together in the love of God. Simply and directly, they can lay their common concerns before God. The Holy Spirit is their Paraclete, their Counselor before the throne. He directs their thoughts, helping them recognize the Lord's will in specific circumstances. When they pray in the name of Jesus, they know that their prayers are heard and will be answered (see John 14:13-14; 1 John 5:14-15).

Prayer for the sick with the laying on of hands carries with it a particular promise of Jesus (Mark 16:18).

• *Representative prayer.* In worship services the pastor or leader may bring the concerns of the entire congregation before God. The pastor must depend on the Holy Spirit's guidance in preparing this kind of prayer. This may come as members of the congregation bring word of particular needs in some area of their common life. The members stand behind the pastor in prayer. They silently identify with what is spoken, which is an indispensable part of the prayer. They understand that the pastor gives voice to their own prayers. While one voice speaks, many hearts are joined together in prayer.[10]

• *Special prayer burdens.* The Holy Spirit may entrust some people with prayer responsibilities for particular needs of the time. Some members of the congregation may sense an urging to form a prayer fellowship that will meet together regularly to seek the Lord's face, or a handful of people will receive a burden to intercede for the sick.

What a divine mystery, that God, who knows all things and has all power, nevertheless waits for our prayers! What changes have been wrought in community, church, and nation through persistent and prevailing prayer!

The above actions are not meant to present a comprehensive program for prayer renewal, but on the contrary are simply illustrative of the immense variety of practical steps that the Holy Spirit may prompt us to inaugurate.

Prayer and power

The emphasis of the charismatic renewal on power—on signs and wonders—is not born of human bravado but of the humbling recognition that in ourselves we have nothing to give to desperate people. We have come into a dead end and need to repent. Jesus taught us to begin prayer by recognizing the holiness of God. In the biblical context, God's holiness refers not only to his purity but also to his power to deliver and save. Only the heavenly Father is holy. There is no holy father on earth. Martin Luther's hymn verse is the testimony of the charismatic renewal:

> Did we in our own strength confide,
> Our striving would be losing.

Through the Spirit God makes the impossible possible, and for this we should pray with expectation. Out of many churches and denominations God is summoning a company of pray-ers who fully expect him to bring renewal through the Holy Spirit.

The priority of prayer

In a renewed church, prayer has an essential priority: prayers of thanksgiving, praise, and worship; urgent intercession; assured claiming of divine promises; and ever-fresh prayers of repentance. Prayer rests on the simple conviction that all good things in the church are worked by God. "Apart from me you can do nothing" (John 15:5). At its heart, prayer is a confession of faith, an agreement with the Word and will of the mighty triune God, Father, Son, and Holy Spirit.

When we say that the Holy Spirit makes us a worshiping people, it is another way of saying that he leads us into the *experience* of God. Worship is the experience of God. In worship, the Holy Spirit causes us to experience the presence of God in praise, the grace of God in Word and sacrament, and the power of God through prayer. For people who experience this kind of reality, worship becomes a way of life.

Jesus said, "Where two or three are gathered in my name, there am I in the midst of them" (Matt. 18:20). Paul said that together we are the temple of the Holy Spirit (1 Cor. 3:16). In a distinctive—perhaps we could say in an *intensified*—way the Lord is present when Christians come together for common worship and celebration of the Lord's Supper. In the gathered community of believers we should expect to experience the manifest presence of God.

As the church learns to pray and praise in the Holy Spirit's power, it will experience an increasing measure of new life and vitality. God seeks a praying church.

Prayer groups and personal ministry

Spiritual renewal of congregations often begins in small prayer and Bible study groups that meet in private homes. Here people experience the presence of Jesus in an intense way, learn to live from the Word of God, and experience the Holy Spirit and his gifts.

Retreats, conferences, and visits to renewal centers and communities serve a similar function: they help people respond to the reality of God in a new way.

Spiritual counseling also plays a leading role in renewal. Here people experience, some for the first time, the reality of repentance, forgiveness, and absolution. Frequently this is the setting for a ministry of deliverance from bondages, through prayer and blessing, command, and the word of power.

Prayer in tongues can be a special help in the ministry of counseling. As a counselor exercises this gift, usually in silent petition, the Lord will often give a vision or revelation that pinpoints a need in the person's life.

In the Pietistic renewal, Spener and Francke urged people to come together to discuss the Scriptures, pray for each other, and sing. In these informal settings, ministry was dependent on lay people who led in the exposition of Scripture and in the prayer ministry.

Home fellowships, prayer meetings, and cell groups are commonplace in the charismatic renewal. This is the setting in which lay leadership is most often identified and developed. The leadership and ministry of the laity is the lifeblood of these meetings.[11]

The experience in small groups becomes a foundation for the Holy Spirit to work in the entire congregation, so that the healing power of the gospel streams forth from a healing fellowship.

Small groups that meet under the leading of the Holy Spirit are often dynamic and unconventional. Their form will vary and change. One thing, however, remains constant: worship and adoration occupy the foreground.

MINISTRY BY THE BODY, IN THE SPIRIT

Although the charismatic renewal has emphasized the need for anointed leadership in worship, it recognizes at the same time that it is the Holy Spirit, not the pastor or worship leader, who gives life to the worship. It is the Spirit who makes us aware of Jesus and causes us to experience his presence.

The ministry of the Spirit is not limited to the ordained clergy. The Holy Spirit longs to work through a many-membered body. Paul said that the agenda of worship should allow for anyone to bring a hymn, a lesson, a revelation, a tongue, or an interpretation (1 Cor. 14:26). Where we do not restrict the Spirit, he will inspire gifts and ministry in the whole body of believers. Our worship will rise to the Father as a symphony, manifesting the presence of Jesus and releasing his abundant blessing (Matt. 18:19).

CHAPTER 49

THE CHURCH: A MISSIONARY COMMUNITY

THE HOLY SPIRIT EMPOWERS A WITNESSING CHURCH

Jesus declared the power and extent of the church's evangelistic task when he told his disciples, "You shall receive power when the Holy Spirit has come upon you; and you shall be my witnesses in Jerusalem and in all Judea and Samaria and to the end of the earth" (Acts 1:8).

Evangelism is telling "the good news about Jesus" (Acts 8:35). It is the primary purpose of the church (Mark 16:15) and the privilege of every believer (Acts 8:4). It is the purpose for which the Spirit's power is given.

Much has hampered Christian witness in the past. Some suffer from a minority complex, saying, "We are so few; what can we do?" In practice, church leaders have often failed to recognize the laity as the primary witnesses who are to spread the gospel to the ends of the earth. Throughout the church there has been a widespread neglect of the Holy Spirit, and a corresponding dependence on human techniques for spreading the gospel.

Some churches have become program- or activity-centered, always eager to launch new projects. It has been said, "If God would remove his Spirit from the church, 95% of the work would continue as if nothing had happened." Even admitting the hyperbole, it is a statement worth pondering. For according to the command of Jesus, only as we receive the power of the Spirit can we be effective witnesses and useful instruments for him.

The Holy Spirit does not make us witnesses automatically. We may have clear teaching about the Holy Spirit in our theology. We may have come to

328 LED BY THE SPIRIT

faith in Christ through the working of the Spirit. Yet the Lord says that we need to be empowered by the Holy Spirit if we are to become his witnesses.

The early church consisted of a small group of people who not only believed in Christ for their own salvation, but who received the charismatic anointing of the Holy Spirit to become powerful witnesses. A fundamental perception of the charismatic movement, which it holds in common with earlier renewal movements, is that what the Spirit has done in the past he can do again, and that nothing less is adequate to the church's evangelistic task.[1]

Every member a witness

In general, the Lutheran church has been more interested in being evangelical than evangelistic. "Evangelism in the Lutheran church is a tragic joke," wrote Noel Boese, the pastor responsible for directing evangelism emphasis in the Michigan Synod of the Lutheran Church in America.[2] Orthodox theology has not necessarily led to active evangelism; this emphasis has come more through revival movements. We need to ask ourselves why it is that in Lutheran churches it is typical for people to become Christians without becoming active witnesses or missionaries.

The Spirit is urging on the church the realization that Jesus' statement, "You shall be my witnesses," was an all-inclusive designation. In Christ's body every member is important and needed. Not every Christian may be called to be an evangelist, yet all Christians are called to be witnesses. A teenager called to be a witness in court is not required to know the legal process of the court case or to know the full content of the law, but only to tell what he or she has seen or heard. The Spirit is opening the ears of many to heed the call to become witnesses and to ask for the empowering of the Spirit.

Evangelism may take place spontaneously or in a planned way. Charismatics have laid special stress on spontaneous witnessing. North Heights Lutheran Church in St. Paul, Minnesota, has been one of the fastest-growing Lutheran churches in the world. It has no organized evangelism program. Growth comes as people are filled with the Spirit and become witnesses at home, work, and school in spontaneous ways.

Many opportunities to be a witness arise in the normal course of everyday life when there is no opportunity for a planned approach or response. The Holy Spirit works changes in our lives that become like walking sermons to other people. They evoke curiosity and interest, and often the question, "What is it that you've got?"

Evangelism can also involve thorough training, in which people receive knowledge, tools, and help from other people. Evangelicals have been in the forefront of this kind of evangelism. In some places, such as Norway, charismatics have taken the lead in utilizing evangelistic programs such as the popular "Evangelism Explosion." Wherever and however evangelism takes place, the power of the Spirit is indispensable.

A charismatic approach to evangelism has certain emphases that may differ in degree and basis and method from some traditional approaches to evangelism. One charismatic Lutheran pastor pinpointed *hearing from God* as the first key to what he termed "radical evangelism." The second key was obeying God.[3] Evangelism in charismatic circles tends toward more conscious dependence on the Holy Spirit, greater emphasis on participation of all members, emphasis both on proclamation and on miraculous signs following, and witness both by individuals and through the life of a body of believers.

A primary fruit of congregational renewal, through the working of the Holy Spirit, is that witnesses are produced. By the power of the Holy Spirit they are able to share with others what they themselves have experienced—the Lord who saves them, grants them new birth, equips them with his Spirit, and opens to them the secret of his joy. The missionary power of the Holy Spirit works through individual witnesses.

The Spirit also works through the Spirit-filled congregations in assembly. Walther Kallestad, pastor of a fast-growing Lutheran church in Phoenix, Arizona, says that their primary tool for evangelism is Sunday morning worship. There is no more convincing evidence of the reality of God than a truly Spirit-filled assembly of believers. In such assemblies God is not a theory or teaching. He is a flaming reality. And he enkindles in his people a love and service that reaches out to those in need—those in sickness, sorrow, bondage, and despair.

THE HOLY SPIRIT SENDS FORTH A MISSIONARY CHURCH

The church is called into mission, that is, extension of its life and ministry outward. The Spirit-renewed church not only does mission work, it *is* missionary. Its very being and nature is missionary.

The focus of the church's mission is given in the great commission: to make disciples of all nations. The church that neglects missionary responsibility is spiritually stunted or misdirected.

The Spirit's outpouring is meant to empower people for witness, beginning with one's immediate sphere of influence and extending without limit to the whole world (Acts 1:8). Every Spirit-anointed Christian is a witness. Without Spirit filling, witness can become legalistic duty. The outpouring of the Spirit shifts mission from law to gospel.

A heightening of missionary zeal is characteristic of renewal movements. This was not immediately apparent in the charismatic renewal. In the first years of the movement, priority was given to personal spiritual renewal. By the mid-1980s, however, the theme of world evangelization had clearly gained the high ground. The strongest witness of the charismatic movement, the standard by which history will judge it, will be its contribution to the spread of the gospel into all the world.

The missionary challenge before the church today

Experts estimate that the world's population at the time of Jesus was around 170 million people. Today a population explosion has swelled the earth's population by 2700%, to more than four billion people, and that number is expected to top six billion by the year 2000.

Jesus spoke of discipling the *nations*. Today the Spirit can direct missionaries into more than 200 nations. Besides these existing political units, missionary research has catalogued 19,000 "people groups" that possess common territory, language, and culture.

Today an unprecedented number of people have not yet been evangelized. Christian churches list a combined membership of a little more than one-and-a-half billion people. Another estimated one and three-quarter billion people have at least heard the Christian gospel. But more than one-fourth of the earth's population—one billion, three hundred million people—have never even heard that a man called Jesus lived on earth, died on a cross, rose from the dead, and sent forth disciples with the message of salvation.[4] More than 70% of the earth's 5700 languages still have no part of the Holy Scriptures translated into their own language. And hundreds of millions are illiterate and cannot read the Scriptures that are available in their mother tongues. The magnitude of the missionary task facing us staggers our imagination, to say nothing of our faith.

Christians, even including nominal believers, are a minority in the world today, and becoming more so. The Holy Spirit is calling them to do battle in the face of mounting opposition. More Christians live under governments hostile to the Christian faith than live in free societies that permit them to work and worship unhindered. More Christians have been martyred since 1900 than in the first three centuries of the Christian era. A militant, anti-Christian Islam numbers 750 million in the world today and is growing. Ancient religions, such as Hinduism, Buddhism, and Shinto, which in the past have lost members to Christianity, have adopted aggressive mission methods to regain members and new adherents to their faiths. Eastern religions are sending missionaries to the Western world in growing numbers. In Western culture, systems of unbelief—humanism, secularism, scientific materialism, hedonism, naturalism, rationalism, idealism—have led millions to deny the truth of Christianity, or in any case to live as practicing atheists. A frightful array of addictions hold millions in physical, emotional, and spiritual bondage. The Holy Spirit is sending us into a world of unprecedented challenges.

Direction and power for mission: the Holy Spirit

God's mission for the church requires the guidance of the Holy Spirit at every stage. Derek Prince, a well-known and widely traveled Bible teacher in the charismatic renewal, has said that the history of the church can be characterized as an almost continuous attempt by church leaders to find some system so safe that we would not have to rely on the Holy Spirit:

> We have ignored and slighted the Spirit of God almost systematically, for centuries. Someone has said, "In recent centuries, the greatest sin of the church has been snubbing the Holy Spirit." We have made our own rules, we have made our own programs, we have drawn up our own lists of objectives, and we have not in any way consulted the Holy Spirit.
>
> In my own experience, in the various areas of the church where I have moved, time and time again I have been present at meetings in which men sought to make plans and strategies for the work of God, but very little real attempt was made to seek the counsel and direction of the Holy Spirit.
>
> The Scripture asks, "Who has given counsel to the Spirit of God?" (see Isa. 40:13), and the answer is that no one gives counsel to the Spirit of God. *He* is the Counselor. And we have not sought his counsel.
>
> When we do not give the Holy Spirit priority in our planning and in our activities, we cannot possibly achieve the real purposes of God. The word of God is always the same, "Not by might, nor by power, but by my Spirit, says the Lord of hosts" (Zech. 4:6).[5]

Mission history knows failures. Without the power and gifts of the Holy Spirit, God's church is helpless to reach the nations (Luke 24:49). The great commission presents the task of a world-embracing mission; but motivation, guidance, and power for the task awaits Pentecost.

Pragmatic observations of mission work, of "success" and "failure," played a large part in initiating the experimental course entitled "Signs, Wonders, and Church Growth" at Fuller Seminary in Pasadena, California, in the early 1980s, according to the in-depth report of *Christian Life* magazine:

> The seminary catalog described the course as focusing "on understanding the effects of supernatural signs and wonders on the growth of the church. It is approached from Biblical, theological, historical and contemporary perspectives. Special attention is given to the ministry of healing. Field experience is an important dimension of the course."

Early Christians shared their faith in Jesus Christ with the confidence that God also would confirm their witness "by signs, wonders and various miracles and by gifts of the Holy Spirit" (Heb. 2:4).

After a long period of decline, a renewal of these signs and wonders is appearing in both Protestant and Catholic church circles.

For the most part, this emergence of spiritual life has stemmed from the grassroots, not from ecclesiastical or theological sources. Groups of believers—sometimes led by a single courageous pastor, sometimes not—have provided the launching pad from which the Holy Spirit has moved.

The renaissance first began in the 20th century. But not until the early 1950s did it surface in the historic Protestant denominations; in the early 1960s in the Roman Catholic Church.

Now, for the first time, it is being given serious consideration by theologians and scholars. According to Peter Wagner [one of the professors who team-taught the experimental course at Fuller], it came out of the reaction of Third World students to the various courses on church growth developed by Fuller's famous professor, Dr. Donald A. McGavran, recognized worldwide as the dean of the theory of church growth.

These Third World students said, "We appreciate the great help Fuller's courses have been to us. But something else is happening in our countries that Western theologians and missiologists are ignoring. The result is enormous church growth of a first century type."

McGavran, who has repeatedly visited Asia and Africa, reported it true: in many cases native evangelists prayed for the sick, they were healed and an astonishing number of conversions resulted.

Other professors contributed similar reports of signs and wonders resulting in massive church growth in other parts of the Third World they had visited. Later, when the faculty of the School of World Mission huddled to consider the phenomena, they came up with the recommendation that an experimental course on the subject of signs, wonders and church growth be offered.

For Dean Gilliand, professor of Contextualization of Theology at Fuller Seminary, the experimental course came as no surprise. He explained that Dr. Peter Wagner had become convinced that if something appears in the Scriptures, then Christians today ought to be seeing it. Wagner maintained that the churches who were manifesting the signs and wonders were the growing churches.

"What we saw as a faculty, in the beginning," Gilliand said, "was that we should offer this as a course because we ought to be open to the Holy Spirit. If there is something that the Spirit should be teaching the churches today, we here at the School of World Mission don't want to resist."

Gilliand felt that Wagner basically was supporting the fact that God is doing something in certain churches today, and that those churches are growing.[6]

This linking together of world mission and supernatural signs challenges the charismatic renewal as much as it does the institutional churches. While the renewal has had an emphasis on spiritual gifts, a burden for world mission was largely absent during the first two decades of the movement. Its energies were taken up with establishing an experiential and theological base for charismatic phenomena in a deeply secularized Western culture. Now, it would appear, there is a fresh initiative of the Spirit to bring these two things together: to let the gospel spread according to the New Testament pattern, "with signs following." Interestingly, this latest initiative of the Spirit surfaced outside the charismatic renewal, as such, and outside the historic churches in Western culture, as though the Spirit were underscoring our poverty and his sovereignty.

CHAPTER 50

THE CHURCH:
A SERVANT

Jesus came into the world to serve (Mark 10:45). Every believer is called to serve. Christians serve each other; they also serve those who are not yet believers.

Serving underlies all Christian life and activity. This is a profound truth, but one easily corrupted by legalistic posturing. A recital of human needs, calculated to induce a guilt reaction, does not produce a servant church. Serving is a gift of the Holy Spirit. Jesus' serving is incarnated in those who live near him in his church, responsive to his lordship, built up by his forgiveness, by his Word, and by his body and blood. Serving comes by the working of the Spirit, not humanistic imperatives.

Serving is a gift as truly as are the signs of prophecy, tongues, healings, visions, and revelation. The more spectacular gifts are not higher or more valuable than the humbler gifts of helping and serving. Both are *gifts,* which means that they are not produced by human talent or in response to legalistic demands, but are the result of the Holy Spirit's gracious visitation and empowering.

A charismatic Lutheran pastor in Scandinavia reported:

> We have seen more or less dead Christians and congregations come alive in serving as an answer to their prayers for the Holy Spirit.
>
> Rich people say: "My money isn't mine. It is God's. I am only a steward." They are happy to give to the poor people, to evangelistic and missionary work. They not only share their money, but their homes and tables too.
>
> But not only rich Christians share—also people in ordinary circumstances. The Holy Spirit lays other people's needs on their hearts. They help each other in a practical way, take care of each other when anyone is sick. They look after each

other's children and dogs. They comfort each other when they feel sorrow, and so on.

When their pastor or fellow Christian is persecuted, they gather in prayer and let the one who is under attack by mass media or the children of this world know that he or she has their and God's love.

We have seen Christians who have served an unfortunate neighbor, hit by mental disease, by taking them 50 or more miles to visit their home church when there was an intercession service. Others have given their time to known and unknown prisoners, alcoholics, and drug addicts.

Eyes have been opened to see others. Feet have become willing to go to others. Hands have been lifted to serve others.

Why do people do this? Why do they bother about each other in this unselfish way? The answer is: the Holy Spirit has worked it in them. He has given them new hearts. He has given them the gift of serving—not as something they must do to qualify as "good Christians," but as the living presence and power of Christ in the heart.[1]

Jesus, the servant

Jesus is the very picture of a servant. He characterized himself as such: "But I am among you as one who serves" (Luke 22:27). The word that he used for "serves" has the primary meaning of a person who serves at table (Mark 1:13,31; 15:41). At issue is a life given to meet the needs of others.

Everything Jesus said and did demonstrated an attitude of service. His life in its totality was service. Paul expressed this comprehensively in his hymn to Christ in Philippians: "though he was in the form of God, [he] did not count equality with God a thing to be grasped, but emptied himself, taking the form of a servant, being born in the likeness of men. And being found in human form he humbled himself and became obedient unto death, even death on a cross" (Phil. 2:6-8).

The cross was the final and ultimate expression of service, as Jesus himself described it: "The Son of man came not to be served but to serve, and to give his life as a ransom for many" (Mark 10:45).

Through word and example Jesus set before his followers the model of service. He declared service to be the basis for interpersonal relationships, especially within the church (Mark 10:43-45; Matt. 20:26-28; Luke 22:26). A servant does not make his or her way in the fellowship by means of power and force of law, but rather by serving the needs of others (Luke 22:24-26). This attitude of servanthood was continually emphasized in early Christian preaching.

The servant church

The church early recognized that service lies at the heart of the Christian life and mission. This came to practical expression in the wide-ranging use of the word *deacon* (one who serves) as a designation for every form of ministry, from apostle to those who wait on tables (see Acts 6:1-4). Paul understood and taught that spiritual gifts, which are given to every believer (1 Cor. 12:7), are instruments of service. It is a theological insight of far-reaching significance. It describes the basic attitude that motivates the use of spiritual gifts.

The servant mentality runs contrary to human nature. When the flesh reasserts control, the desire to dominate others crops up in every area of the church's life—in relationships between individual believers, in groups of Christians, within the local church, and beyond. Pastors try to lord it over their congregations, congregations over their pastors, men over women, women over men. Sometimes spiritual gifts are misused as instruments of domination. Missionary work can be twisted into a means of manipulating people. Especially dangerous have been attempts by the church to exercise power in the world and over society, instead of simply serving.

In the Reformation period, Müntzer attempted to apply the spiritual dynamic of the Reformation to the conversion and purification of the total society. When this proved unsuccessful, the spirit of domination was reoriented toward the church as a holy community withdrawn from the world; in the holy community true and living faith, as opposed to the dead scribal faith of Wittenberg (Luther) and Rome, was to be exemplified in the regenerate, Spirit-filled believers.[2]

Against such mixing of law and gospel the Holy Spirit works incessantly. In all ages he has worked to conform us to the image of Jesus Christ, the servant. Through Baptism and faith we have a share in Christ's life and his serving love. Wherever we have become servants of one another, the Holy Spirit has wrought a miracle indeed. The more we become servants, the more God is able to entrust to our care.

The needs facing us are beyond counting, and the willing servants so few. Where does the servant church begin? How can the church determine its servant role? It cannot serve everyone everywhere; it must be selective. The Spirit-led church looks to the Holy Spirit for guidance. The question then is this: Where does the Holy Spirit want us to serve? Through revelation and confirmation by the Spirit the church must be guided into those places where he calls it to serve.

The gifts of the Spirit are valuable spiritual tools both in discerning the Lord's will for the servant church and in carrying it out. Spirit-led service is not simply a human or humanitarian ministry. It is a divine work, accomplished through human instruments in spiritual power.

Suffering

A servant church will inevitably be a suffering church; the two cannot be separated.

Suffering has not been a prominent theme in the charismatic renewal. Serious critics from within the movement cite this as one of the renewal's major weaknesses. Teaching on spiritual power and faith has not been balanced with a biblical perspective on suffering. This is ironic, inasmuch as some of the greatest suffering of Christians in our day has been among those who share a charismatic spirituality and perspective—in China and some Third World countries. Their experience, however, did not begin to receive major attention in the charismatic renewal until the late 1970s. In the beginning, the formative influences of the movement came more from the United States and Western Europe.

Suffering is not something alien to the life of Christians. God chooses it for us. It is one of the ways that we share the life of Christ. It is not a call to heroism but to humble dependence on the Spirit, who enables us to walk in the suffering that belongs to our calling.

Suffering needs to be distinguished from punishment. God does punish his children, and the one punished suffers pain (Heb. 12:5, 11). This is not identical, however, with the suffering that we encounter because of our witness for Christ. Punishment and suffering can produce similar results: purifying of motives, cleansing of attitudes, strengthening of character, and change in behavior. They serve, however, somewhat different purposes. Punishment comes because of disobedience and has to do with the crucifixion of the flesh. Suffering for Christ's sake is not linked to disobedience, but with being his witnesses; it has to do with overcoming evil with good.

Paradoxically, suffering is twin to hope. The believer's hope emerges in the midst of suffering—hope not only for the age to come, but also for this life. Suffering helps prepare us to share in the reign of Christ (Rom. 5:2-5, 17).

Jesus, the suffering servant

The Gospels provide us with a picture of Jesus as one who suffers. "The Son of Man must suffer many things" (Mark 8:31) could serve as a superscript over his whole life.

Jesus prepared his disciples for the path of suffering (Matt. 5:10-12). This was especially true of those whom he sent out. Joachim Jeremias wrote, "Suffering for the sake of Christ is inseparable from service as his messenger. All primary sources are in agreement that Jesus emphasized this continually."[3]

Jesus sent his messengers out as sheep among wolves (Matt. 10:16; Luke 10:3).

The suffering church

The Acts of the Apostles portrays the path of the first Christians as a path of suffering. It describes the injunctions against their preaching (4:17-18; 5:40), physical punishment (5:40; 16:23), the imprisonment of the apostles (4:3; 5:18; 16:23-24), the martyrdom of believers (7:57-60; 12:2). The rest of the New Testament also reports sufferings that believers had to endure for the sake of Christ (Heb. 10:32-34). The book of Revelation prepares Christians for even greater suffering, as the day of Christ draws near (Revelation 13). According to the New Testament, being a Christian and suffering go hand in hand.

The history of the church records times of great persecutions for Christians. This continues in our own time: countless believers have offered up their lives for Christ in the 20th century. Many followers of Jesus today suffer persecution under various political and social regimes. At the conclusion of an all-Africa charismatic leaders' conference in 1983, participants from one of the countries said their farewells with tears: "We may not see you again in this life," their spokesman said. "Some of our brethren have already been imprisoned. We do not know what will happen to us in the days ahead. Pray for us. Our trust is in the Lord."

Our prayers especially need to include those who will be honored to give up their lives for the glory of Christ. According to New Testament prophecy, believers will come into times of unparalleled suffering as the end approaches.

Suffering may come in a variety of ways. One may be laughed at or mocked. Good friends may be lost or an unbelieving family alienated. One's job security or professional advancement may be threatened because of one's active Christian witness. In some places, an open witness for Christ will put one's life at risk. Whoever walks the pathway of discipleship will experience suffering.

The more Christians are filled with the Holy Spirit, the more powerfully they bear witness, the more heartily they live the Christian life, the more consistently they follow Jesus, the more suffering will come their way. A movement that urges people to be filled with the Spirit cannot avoid the consequences: it must help prepare them for suffering.

This does not mean training people in survival techniques. It means extending the central theme of the charismatic renewal into this area of life also: we enter times of suffering, like everything else in the Christian life, totally dependent on the Holy Spirit. We do not shrink from suffering. We recognize it as an integral aspect of Christian experience. In the power of the Spirit we resist the temptation to avoid or ease the suffering by accommodating ourselves to the world. We trust the Spirit to maintain our fellowship with the serving, suffering Christ.

CHAPTER 51

THE CHURCH: A BATTLE-READY COMMUNITY

God calls his church into *spiritual warfare*. Like it or not, we are involved in a "war of the worlds" (Eph. 6:12; Matt. 10:34; 1 John 3:8). Spiritual awakening and renewal means that we will be engaged in heightened spiritual conflict. Over every day of a believer's life stands the banner: "Fight the good fight of the faith" (1 Tim. 6:12).

This presupposes the kind of worldview that has emerged in the charismatic renewal, which reckons realistically with an invisible, nonphysical, spiritual dimension of reality, and with the conflict that rages there. The church appropriates and applies Christ's victory over Satan, even as we await and hasten the day of final triumph. The gifts of the Spirit are necessary weapons in this spiritual conflict (2 Cor. 10:4).

We have considered the church as a gathering of believers, growing in the knowledge and experience of Christ. We need to see it also as Christ's instrument for establishing his reign over human lives and institutions.

The lordship of Jesus needs to be established first of all in the lives of believers and the life of the church, with Scripture as the standard of kingdom life. First priority for every decision must be the will of God. Jesus is head over the church in all things (Eph. 1:22-23). This involves not only bringing people into the obedience of faith (Rom. 1:5; 16:26), but also doing battle with demonic forces. Casting out demons, or deliverance, is a necessary ministry if Christ's rule is to become reality.

Beyond this, the church needs to engage in spiritual warfare against demonic forces that control various sectors of society. The foundation for this ministry is intercessory prayer. In bringing the witness of Christ to society at large, we particularly need to be reminded that we are not contending against flesh and blood (Eph. 6:12). We are engaged in a life-and-death struggle with supernatural evil powers that control much of this world. Many well-intentioned attempts to speak or act prophetically in society fail because they have not first dealt with the powers of darkness through intercessory prayer in the power of the Holy Spirit.

The rule of Christ includes what he wills and works not only in the church, but in society at large. In facing issues of justice and morality, society is encountering Christ the Lord, even though it does not yet recognize him as such. When the Holy Spirit involves Christians in these issues, he brings into the battle the power of prayer, discernment, and dependence on him. Much of this may be a secret work, never mentioned in the public arena. But we dare not forget or neglect it. By God's grace we participate in the struggles of society with more responsibility and power than meets the eye.

The biblical perspective

The Lord deploys the church for spiritual warfare against principalities, powers, spiritual rulers, and massive numbers of evil forces (Eph. 6:12). The church is empowered and equipped for battle with weapons supplied by the Spirit (Eph. 6:10-17; 2 Cor. 10:3-6). The gifts of the Spirit (1 Cor. 12:4-11) are spiritual tools for doing spiritual work and fighting spiritual battles.

The world was created to be a part of God's kingdom under his sovereign rule. Man and woman were to be God's delegated authority to govern the world. In their fall into sin the devil stole that rule.

Jesus came to earth to defeat the devil and to bring the world under his own reign and then at the close of the age under the Father's sovereignty (1 Cor. 15:24-28). Jesus is God in human flesh. He conquered the devil and his kingdom through his own cross and resurrection (John 12:31-33; Col. 2:15; Heb. 2:14-15; 1 John 3:8). Jesus is now seated at the right hand of the Father, from where he reigns over all things (Eph. 1:20-23; Heb. 2:5-9; Ps. 110:1-6).

The redeemed company of believers are transferred from Satan's kingdom to Christ's kingdom (Col. 1:13-14). They share the reign with Christ (Eph. 2:6; Rom. 5:17), though the form of his rule in this age is not evident to the eyes of the world; it is hidden under the veil of weakness, suffering, and servanthood.

Jesus, the deliverer

Jesus proclaimed the advent of God's coming kingdom. One of the ways that he demonstrated the kingdom was by casting out demons. Deliverance played a noticeably large role in his ministry. People marveled at his *authority*. They recognized what was taking place: a change of rulership.

Was Jesus simply a child of his age in this regard, a prisoner of superstition? Jesus recognized that some things were the product of a particular time or culture, for example, some of the traditions of the scribes and Pharisees. But he never dealt with demonic oppression as a wrong teaching or superstition that one must simply set aside. In his battle with demons, he was dealing with something other than merely cultural heritage. Wherever God's power broke forth in Jesus, satanic forces mounted opposition. Wherever the Holy Spirit involved himself in Jesus' ministry, unholy spirits were stirred into action. Whenever God's triumph is near, Satan fears for his own survival. "In opposition to the divine authority manifest in Jesus' ministry, all darkness draws itself together into one demonic kingdom under Satan. In other words, evil is not only recognized as an all-encompassing, super-human power, but it is also a power that comes into action."[1]

Especially in Mark's gospel, Jesus' casting out of demons is portrayed as a combat (see, for example, Mark 1:23-38). Jesus understood these battles as the seizing of plunder after binding the strong man, that is, Satan (Mark 3:27; Luke 11:21-23). "Every time Jesus drives out an evil spirit it is an anticipation of the hour when Satan will be visibly stripped of his power. Victories over his functionaries are an anticipation of the eschaton."[2]

Jesus commissioned his disciples to cast out demons

Jesus empowered his disciples to cast out demons in his name. He sent them out to proclaim the kingdom of God and gave them authority over the forces of evil (Mark 3:14-15). Authority over spirits is a recurring theme in Jesus' words of commissioning, and indeed becomes a mark of these words (Mark 6:7; Matt. 10:8; Luke 10:19-20; cf. Mark 6:13; Matt. 7:22; Luke 10:17).

Clearly this is part and parcel of Jesus' commissioning of his disciples: when God establishes his authority, the authority of Satan is revoked. Thus Jesus' battle against powers of darkness was central to his own ministry and to the ministry that he gave his disciples. There is no room for any "demythologizing" without adulterating everything we know about Jesus' commission.

The early church believed and confessed that through his death and resurrection, Jesus had conquered all evil powers, ultimately subordinate to Satan, which are hostile to God. He "disarmed" them, as it were (Heb. 2:14; Col. 2:15; Eph. 1:20-23). In faith, Christians have already overcome Satan (1 John 2:13b-14). Yet they are called to battle, and to spiritual watchfulness (1 Peter 5:8-9). The names of the devil are a clue to his treachery. He is called the "evil one" (Eph. 6:16; 1 John 5:18-19), the "enemy" (Luke 10:19; Matt. 13:25), the "ruler of this world" (John 12:31; 14:30); the "dragon" (Rev. 12; 13; 16:13; 20:2), or the "serpent" (Rev. 12:9; 20:2). But there is no doubt as to his ultimate destruction (Matt. 25:41; Rev. 20:10).

The book of Acts, especially, reckons with the demonic oppression of people. In various ways, it attests to freedom from such oppression through the ministry of the church (5:16; 8:6-8; 16:16-18; 19:12). How the battle against him is to be fought in its particulars is expressed metaphorically in Eph. 6:11-17, where believers are instructed to "put on the whole armor of God." All overcoming of evil spirits is ultimately linked to the authority of Jesus (Acts 16:18).

The modern attitude toward demons and deliverance

Charismatic experience makes a person more aware both of the good God and of the evil forces around and among us. Western culture has made an abstraction of evil: it is merely the absence of good, or it is embodied in human attitudes and institutions such as humanism, racism, capitalism, communism, and so on. The Bible, as we have seen, speaks about the devil in terms similar to those used to speak about God: he is a person with will, purpose, and supernatural power. The Bible does not ignore the evil that takes root in human attitudes and institutions, but it does not see that as the end of the inquiry. What power is at work behind these manifestations of evil? And how do we deal with it? For charismatics, the biblical view is more adequate than the secular view of Western culture, and accords more with actual experience. Intercessory prayer and deliverance from demonic power become a necessary part of the Christian arsenal in the battle with evil.

Luther retained prayers for deliverance in the baptismal liturgy, and added an even stronger intercession for the baptismal candidate. What began at Baptism would continue throughout one's life: conflict with the devil was seen as a basic condition of the Christian life.

The charismatic renewal has brought this issue to the fore. Where the message receives a hearing, the opposite problem sometimes surfaces and must also be dealt with: people begin to see demons behind every bush and as the cause of every problem. Not all problems are immediately demon-related. George MacAusland, a wise spiritual counselor, said, "If you could kill the devil, you'd still have me to deal with!" In other words, the old nature must still be reckoned with. Some of those with considerable experience in a ministry of deliverance have a good rule of thumb: "If everything else fails—counseling, confession, admonition, discipline—begin to look for demonic factors."

It was jokingly said that when penicillin was first discovered, doctors routinely gave it to every patient. If patients didn't improve in five days, they tried to find out what was wrong with them. That is an illustration that cuts both ways: the church has widely administered the wisdom of psychology and sociology to the hurts of its people, and some charismatics have routinely cast the devil out of anyone who came up with something less than a victory testimony. To take the reality of demons seriously is simply to ask the church—the whole church—to be as accurate as possible in the way that it diagnoses and deals with evil. If demonic activity is the problem, or a significant part of the problem, then that must be dealt with. If the problem is bad habits, ingrained attitudes, sin, neglected relationships—then those are the things that must be dealt with in the wisdom and power of the Spirit.

A Danish pastor told how his pastoral care of one particular individual had to take several factors into account:

> Claus came to me after he had left a psychiatric hospital. Both he and his mother felt that he had received no help there. He said that he could not speak with doctors about his real problems.
>
> About three years earlier he had entered an occult healing order through what he described as a "mild satanist initiation." He was given a "small helper," an accompanying spirit. Gradually he began to be assailed by thoughts of murder and suicide, and some months later ended up in the psychiatric hospital.
>
> I proclaimed the gospel to him, and made a special point of the victory of Christ over the devil on the cross. Claus found his way back into the faith of the church.
>
> The first time I just prayed a general blessing on him, and the Spirit of God gave him tears. I shared this word with him: "Jesus is crying tears of joy because you have turned to him."
>
> In subsequent meetings we dealt with the demonic aspect of his problem. I spoke to the evil spirit and commanded it to leave, in Jesus' name. This broke the occult bondage, with strong physical and psychological reactions.
>
> Over the course of half a year Claus began behaving normally within the fellowship of the congregation. Later he received the gift of tongues, and that was another step forward. He remained under my pastoral care for some time. He experienced some reverses when he became too deeply immersed in books on exorcism, which apparently can be misused in an occult way.
>
> This experience impressed on me the fact that effective pastoral care requires *accurate discernment*.[3]

The church's ministry of deliverance

A battle-ready church assumes the reality of an invisible, nonmaterial realm of existence. It recognizes the existence of spiritual beings and the interrelatedness of the physical and nonphysical realms.

For Luther, as we have seen, satanic powers were an earnest reality. He testified to the reality and awfulness of the devil's power, based on his own experience. Paul Althaus wrote:

It is not possible to try to understand [Luther's] theology on this point as a relic of the Middle Ages, however much he is in agreement with the traditional belief in devils and demons. He took the devil far more seriously than did the Middle Ages . . . that is, without question, because Luther recognized the nature of the lordship of God and Christ with a new clarity, and, as a further result, had a keen eye for the enemy and the depth and difficulty of the all-out war between God and opposing powers. Luther also returned to the viewpoint held by Jesus and by the early church. Luther's statements concerning the devil are closely and inseparably linked to the very core of his theology."[4]

The church of Luther's time reckoned with God's antagonist and the power of his demons. Sometimes the church lost sight of the victory already won over the powers of darkness by Jesus. Nonetheless, the church was aware that these powers should be taken seriously.

In modern times this has changed substantially. Among the educated today it is considered unsophisticated, a mark of ignorance, to reckon seriously with Satan and his demons. This has led to enormous superficiality of belief. Because we no longer recognize the extent of demonic power and the danger it poses, we are also no longer able to recognize the full dimension of the salvation that Christ gained for us. We see no need for spiritual warfare in the sense of Eph. 6:10-17. When it comes to fighting, we ignore the warning of Ephesians 6:12: we contend with flesh and blood; we fight other people instead of the powers of evil. We fight with the limited weapons of argumentation and with methods of manipulating other people in order to defend ourselves, or to win them over and keep them in line. Meanwhile, the powers of evil brazenly expand their sphere of influence. It is ironic that our culture, which has prided itself on being rid of primitive belief in evil spirits, should witness an unprecedented explosion of occult practices.

In Scripture, God has paved the way for a change that is now taking place. Increasing numbers of believers are recognizing that it is not naive to reckon with the devil and his powers. It is naive to deny them. We are beginning to sense that we will be able to win the spiritual battle of this age only when we recognize our real opponent. The church has a tremendous stake in the victory of Jesus over Satan and his demons. The Holy Spirit is waiting to bring Jesus' victory to practical reality in our lives.

Spiritual warfare is essential in the hour of temptation. This includes the ministry of deliverance from demonic oppression. We don't need a detailed doctrine of demons, an "ontology of the demonic," as it were. Undue fascination with the world of dark spirits is not wise. It is enough to know that demonic power is real and that it can be overcome in the name of Jesus.

The ministry of deliverance needs to be restored to the Western church. Our missionary task is hindered when we do not deal decisively with powers that hold people in bondage. Accompanying the ministry of deliverance is the gift of discernment of spirits (1 Cor. 12:10). Through the exercise of this gift the Holy Spirit will often reveal the nature or source of a problem. People may have become demonized through involvement in the occult, pagan religious rites, spiritualism, immorality, or mind-altering drugs. Demonic activity may be misdiagnosed as mental or emotional illness (or vice versa). Discernment is necessary. Where the problem is evil spirits, the first need is deliverance.

Demons may be dealt with in a variety of ways: for example, casting them out in the name of Jesus; overcoming them through declaring the power of Jesus' blood and cross; praying for inner healing or cleansing; participating in the sacraments; hearing God's Word; receiving the ministry of a loving and healing community; participating in praise and worship.

The ministry of deliverance, in which demons are directly encountered and driven out, is best exercised by experienced spiritual leaders and, when possible, by a team. Novices should not normally take on a deliverance ministry. Deliverance needs to be followed up with pastoral and personal care, and with teaching.

One charismatic Lutheran congregation that takes this ministry seriously has a pastor on staff who has a ministry of deliverance, and along with it a complementary ministry of counseling and pastoral care. As a result, many who are oppressed by demons, or wonder whether they are the target of demonic assault, seek and receive ministry. Several gifts of the Spirit may function in this kind of ministry: discernment of spirits, word of knowledge, word of wisdom, healings, speaking in tongues, interpretation of tongues.

Another aspect of spiritual warfare is the binding through prayer of demonic forces that control various sectors of society or affect individuals adversely. The Spirit guides the direction, focus, or manner of praying.

Scripture warns us that the devil will attack us. We are told to resist him firm in faith (1 Peter 5:8-9; James 4:7), to do battle with him (Eph. 4:27; 6:10-18), to overcome him by the blood of the Lamb and the word of our testimony, unmoved even by the threat of death (Rev. 12:10-11). Jesus promised us that the Spirit that dwells in us is stronger than the spirit that is loose in the world (1 John 4:4).

CHAPTER 52

THE CHURCH:
A FELLOWSHIP OF HOPE

In one of the oldest artistic representations of Jesus Christ, in the mausoleum of Galla Placidia in Ravenna, Christ is portrayed as a Roman general. His symbol of victory is the cross.

The Spirit's revelation of Christ is a revelation of victory, of triumph over the powers of darkness and the kingdom of this world. It is based on the concrete fact of Christ's victory over Satan in the atonement. It is being worked out in the world today through the Spirit, moving toward the final triumph at Christ's second coming.

The church under the cross is a victorious church. It has a Lord who is crucified and risen. As we are committed to following after the cross, we are also committed to follow after the resurrection. The two are inextricably linked. The mystery of this linking is not a contrivance of theology, but a reality of discipleship.

In many quarters of the church the message of hope is missing. The world over, many pastors and leaders communicate a message not of hope, but of discouragement and resignation. This is not New Testament faith. The church under Christ is not to give way to despair. It is called by the Spirit to a life of victorious hope, undeterred by present circumstances.

In the midst of an anxiety-ridden church the Holy Spirit is today calling men and women to a living hope (1 Peter 1:3). People who have been mired down in discouragment are giving testimony to this hope. Believers who have fallen into the habit of seeing themselves as losers are, in the power of the Holy Spirit, laying hold on the promises of the overcomer (1 John 5:4). Negative attitudes are giving place to positive faith, insecurity to confidence, and a defensive mentality to the assertion of Christ's victory, even in the midst of sorrow and seeming defeat.

Earl Kuester, a Baptist pastor in Gardena, California, began a healing ministry in his congregation, together with his wife. It brought great blessing to the congregation and to the surrounding community, but when his wife died of cancer, people feared that it would be the end of the healing ministry. The next Sunday night, however, he was at the altar of his church, praying for the sick. "My hope is in Christ," he said simply. This is hope that goes far beyond a new set of mental attitudes or a series of experiences. It is the fruit of faithful discipleship to the crucified and risen Lord, lived out in the power of the Holy Spirit.

The New Testament concept of hope

In the New Testament, *hope* is a technical term for Christians' ultimate expectation. Few things were as characteristic of the early church as its dynamic anticipation of the world to come. Conversely, few things today lie so distant from the mass of Western Christianity as this expectation.

In the center of Jesus' preaching was the sovereign authority of God, the fulfillment of which is still being awaited, but which was already beginning to break through in Jesus' words and deeds. The Beatitudes and the Lord's Prayer give clear teaching about the kingdom of God. Leonhard Goppelt wrote:

> The kingdom of God brings the comfort that eases all suffering, and the satisfaction that eases all hunger. . . . Consequently, the kingdom of God includes physical and spiritual healing; in the end, a new world, without want and suffering, a world of peace and justice. . . .
>
> How does this new thing come about? The kingdom comes through a work of God in humanity. . . . Consequently, the coming of the kingdom centers in God, and his personal intervention to establish the kingdom. . . .
>
> The first three petitions [of the Lord's Prayer] are interdependent: God's kingdom will come when God is recognized as God and his gracious will is done. Again, the focus is on God, the orientation strongly theocentric.[1]

The early church awaited the eventual coming of God's kingdom, when Jesus would come again in glory as the Son of man. His second coming, or *parousia,* does not mean his mere return, but rather his coming in majesty and power. The Aramaic-speaking early church prayed for the coming of Jesus as the fulfillment of God's eventual sovereignty: "*Maranatha*—our Lord, come!" This expectation finds expression even in the latest of the New Testament writings.

A hope that must be kept alive

The church did not preserve this hope. This failure is often explained by saying that the urgent expectation of Christ's return was a part of the old, apocalyptic worldview, which was refuted by a more sober historical awareness.

But in times of energetic church renewal, the expectation of the coming of Jesus springs alive again. The Holy Spirit inflames us with Jesus' own eagerness for the kingdom of God. This desire, that God will reveal himself as God of all, is not limited to an apocalyptic worldview.

The charismatic renewal as a whole has not lined up behind any particular prophetic or eschatological view in regard to Christ's second coming. There has been a certain downplaying of standard premillenialism by prominent teachers in the renewal, but even this is not a common theme. The focus is on the *kingdom* as such, not the events that may attend its coming. You frequently hear the assertion that we are living in the last days, but this is a call to discipleship, not a preamble to a Bible study on prophecy. Christian hope looks beyond the birth pangs of the kingdom to its glory, righteousness, and final victory.

The church is called to proclaim this joyful and glorious hope (Heb. 10:23; 1 Peter 3:15). All Christians are called to keep this hope in view so that they will not forget what they are called to be, and do, and become.

The history of the church confirms the truth spoken by the Lord in Matt. 24:48-51, that if the church forgets its hope, then it also neglects its holiness and its service. And Scripture warns that in so doing we not only forget our inheritance, we stand in danger of losing it.

Hope and holiness

Hope reminds the church of holiness. We belong to the Lord and not to ourselves (Rom. 14:7-8). We are not in this world for our own sake, but for the Lord's sake. Like the vessels in the old covenant temple service, we are elected and separated for holy use (1 Peter 2:9). It is this hope that helps the church live in this world without becoming like this world, but like the Lord (1 John 3:3).

The expectation of the parousia is a strong impulse toward holy living. "We know that when he appears we shall be like him, for we shall see him as he is. And every one who thus hopes in him purifies himself as he is pure (1 John 3:2-3; 2 Cor. 7:1); "Strive for . . . the holiness without which no one will see the Lord" (Heb. 12:14).

Hope and service

Hope reminds the church of its purpose and service. We are instruments by which God loves and serves the world (John 20:21), and through which he manifests his mercy and wisdom in heavenly places (Eph. 2:7; 3:10). When that hope has been obscured, the church has not loved, served, and suffered, but often has sought to rule in this world, entering into all sorts of unholy alliances with the world, and in the end become an instrument not of the Spirit but of the world. Until the last moment of the present age, this hope will remind the church of the purpose and service that the Lord sets before us.

Hope reminds the church of its stewardship. We will be called to give account of the grace that God has given us and the time in which to work, and to demonstrate that we did not, like the unfaithful steward, bury our talents (Matt. 25:14-30).

What kind of practical experience in the charismatic renewal has given fresh impetus to the eschatological hope? One recognizes such things as these:

- Through a living, Spirit-led involvement with the Word of God, people's lives are established more on the basis of the promises of Scripture than on the basis merely of human feelings and ideas.
- Through Spirit-wrought healings of emotional wounds, ingrained negative attitudes are overcome, and deliverance takes place.
- The gift of comfort or admonition (Rom. 12:8) comes to greater expression in a Spirit-equipped congregation. A person who teeters on the brink of despair is caught hold of by a brother or sister and is able to accept help.
- The fundamental confession that "Jesus is Lord" is particularly granted by the Spirit in the context of spiritual warfare, for example, in pastoral counseling dealing with the occult. Jesus shares his victory concretely with those who stand firm in discipleship, believing the promise that God will make them overcomers (Rom. 16:20; 12:21).
- Consistent, Spirit-prompted praise and worship of God teach one to focus attention more on the acts of God and less on one's own strengths or weaknesses. In personal and corporate life this brings encouragement (Heb. 12:2; 2 Cor. 4:1).

Hope and inheritance

Hope reminds the church of its inheritance. We are called to share in the glory of the kingdom of Christ and the victorious powers of the age to come. We look to the future, when that hope will be fully revealed. We shall reign together with Christ, as the Father has promised. That is our glorious hope.

But the Father has also called us to live already out of our inheritance. Already demonstrating the life of the kingdom, already manifesting the powers of the age to come, already discipling the nations unto Jesus—that is our impossible calling.

If we stood alone in the light of that glorious hope, faced with that impossible calling, we could only despair. But we hear again the word of the Lord, "Behold, I send the promise of my Father on you" (Luke 24:49).

And we are given the grace to say, "Welcome, Holy Spirit!"

COUNTRY-BY-COUNTRY OVERVIEW OF THE CHARISMATIC RENEWAL AMONG LUTHERANS

ITS BEGINNINGS IN THE UNITED STATES

In the summer and fall of 1961, small groups of Lutherans in scattered locations began to have what later came to be known as "charismatic experience."[1] These initial experiences were often sparked by ecumenical contacts, principally with Episcopalians. By mid-1962, Lutheran charismatics began to meet and correspond with one another.

The American Lutheran Church

Most of those affected at the outset were from the American Lutheran Church, and were located principally in Minnesota, Montana, Southern California, Illinois, and North Dakota. Herbert Mjorud, an ALC evangelist, became a prominent exponent of charismatic renewal and was instrumental in the initial spread of the movement. Other early participants who remained visible in the leadership of the movement include Larry Christenson, Dick and Betty Denny, James Hanson, Herbert Mjorud, Morris Vaagenes, and George Voeks.

The initial response in the ALC was one of cautious interest. A study commission was appointed to look into the matter of speaking in tongues. A team consisting of psychiatrist Paul Qualben, clinical psychologist John Kildahl, and New Testament theologian Lowell Satre visited Zion Lutheran Church in Glendive, Montana, and Trinity Lutheran Church in San Pedro,

California, where they interviewed and tested members who had experienced speaking in tongues. They found some convictions among those interviewed which they deemed un-Lutheran, such as equating "Spirit-filled" with speaking in tongues. On the other hand, they noted beneficial results in the personal lives and dedication of those who had entered into charismatic experience.[2] The study commission published a report in 1963 which discouraged speaking in tongues in public gatherings, but not in one's private devotions.[3]

In 1972, Paul Qualben reported on the commission's research in a seminar at Wartburg Seminary in Dubuque, Iowa. "We had two preconceptions when we went to these congregations," he said. "We expected to encounter people who were emotionally unstable, and we expected the phenomenon to be short-lived. We were wrong on both counts. The people we interviewed were a normal cross section of a Lutheran congregation, and today, ten years later, the movement is still growing."[4]

The Lutheran Church–Missouri Synod

In the mid-1960s some pastors of the Lutheran Church-Missouri Synod entered into similar experiences. These included Donald Pfotenhauer, Erwin Prange, Robert Heil, Rodney Lensch, Delbert Rossin, Herbert Mirly, Donald Matzat, and Theodore Jungkuntz.

The Commission on Theology and Church Relations produced two reports on the charismatic movement, one in 1972, another in 1977. The reports were generally cool toward the movement. They suggested that charismatic gifts were primarily for the apostolic age, though they did not disallow them.[5]

Nevertheless, the movement continued to grow in LCMS circles. LCMS congregations, such as Faith Lutheran Church in Geneva, Illinois, and Resurrection Lutheran Church in Charlotte, North Carolina, became prominently associated with the renewal and exerted considerable influence both inside and beyond the LCMS.

The Lutheran Church in America

The Lutheran Church in America had fewer participants in the renewal than the ALC or LCMS, but by the late 1960s prominent LCA pastors such as Paul Swedberg in Minneapolis and Glen Pearson in York, Pennsylvania, together with their congregations, were openly identified with charismatic renewal.

In 1974 the LCA produced a pastoral perspective on charismatic renewal that was generally more positive toward the movement than any previous Lutheran statement.

Growth

The growth of the movement in the United States during the 1960s was more widespread than most people realized. Even those involved in the movement were surprised when, with little publicity or fanfare, the first International Lutheran Conference on the Holy Spirit drew more than 9000 people to Minneapolis in 1972. This conference became an annual event and a focal point for renewal, with increasing attendance throughout the 1970s.

The movement grew significantly during the 1970s. By the middle of the decade it was conservatively estimated that about 10% of the Lutherans in the United States, clergy as well as laity, identified with the charismatic movement.[6] A relatively small number of Lutheran congregations—in 1975 fewer than 20, by 1986 about 80—could be described as "charismatic" in the sense of identifying visibly with this renewal and integrating the charismatic dimension into the total life of their church. A larger number of congregations, however, were significantly influenced by charismatic renewal. By the mid-1970s there was scarcely a Lutheran congregation in the country that did not have some members who were charismatic. Lutherans were the third-largest group represented when an ecumenical charismatic congress was held in Kansas City in 1977, drawing more than 50,000 people.

The leadership of the renewal in the United States has developed in clusters of regional leaders who meet annually, and in the International Lutheran Renewal Center located in St. Paul, Minnesota. The Center sponsors conferences, publications, leaders' meetings, congregational and community renewal events, and theological research. Larry Christenson has served as director of the Center, with Dick Denny, W. Dennis Pederson, and Delbert Rossin coordinating various aspects of the Center's ministry.

THE FEDERAL REPUBLIC OF GERMANY

In 1962 Arnold Bittlinger, director of evangelism for the Evangelical Church of the Palatinate in Germany, came into contact with the nascent charismatic movement during a study tour of the United States. While visiting in California, he met ALC pastor Larry Christenson and arranged for him to speak at a conference in Germany the following summer.

The conference was held in Enkenbach in August 1963, and it was attended by about 80 leaders from different churches, groups, and movements in Germany. A number of those in attendance had spiritual ties with the Brethren of the Common Life, a Lutheran group founded in 1905, whose spirituality included the practice of spiritual gifts. Other brotherhoods had similar experiences that helped prepare the ground for charismatic renewal. Spiritual gifts had played a significant part in the experience of the Evangelical Sisterhood of Mary, founded in Darmstadt in 1947, and the sisterhood's influence was already widespread by the early 1960s. Thus the setting in Germany was generally conducive to a positive hearing for the charismatic message. After this conference, charismatic experience began to spread into many groups and movements in German Protestantism.

In 1965 the first of a series of ecumenical conferences was held in Königstein near Frankfurt, under the theme "Church and Charisma." In 1968 the leaders who had been mainly responsible for these conferences founded a "Community for the Unity of Christians" at Schloss Craheim, in Bavaria. The original community included Arnold Bittlinger and Reiner-Friedemann Edel, Lutherans; Wilhard Becker and Siegfried Grossman, Baptists; and Eugen Mederlet, Roman Catholic. Schloss Craheim became a major center for charismatic renewal in Germany during most of the 1970s.

In 1976 the "Würzburg Theological Guidelines" were formulated by a group of Lutheran charismatic leaders to help pastors and congregations integrate charismatic renewal into the life of the local parish. In 1978 a coordinating committee was formed with the specific objective of fostering parish renewal, along charismatic lines, within the Evangelical (Lutheran) Church in Germany, with Hamburg pastor Wolfram Kopfermann as chairman. They sponsored annual parish-renewal conferences, sometimes working together with leaders of the Roman Catholic charismatic renewal. By 1983, regional conferences and leadership structures began to develop.

THE GERMAN DEMOCRATIC REPUBLIC (GDR)

Charismatic renewal in the GDR has occurred predominantly within the framework of the Lutheran folk church. It has also found expression in some other Protestant denominations, notably Methodists and Baptists, but these groups taken together make up less than one percent of the total population of the country; there is no organized Pentecostal church in the GDR.

Early renewal roots

In German pietism there was some experience of charismatic gifts. This had little direct influence on the present-day charismatic renewal, though the parallels are instructive.

In the 19th century, Christoph Blumhardt's congregation experienced revival accompanied by healings and exorcism. In his preaching Blumhardt kindled hope for a new Pentecost. By the turn of the century, regular Pentecost conferences were being held, with an emphasis on revival in the power of the Holy Spirit.

The experience of spiritual gifts, however, and especially speaking in tongues, was largely eliminated as a result of the Berlin Declaration of 1909. In this declaration Lutheran evangelicals wrote off the Pentecostal movement as demonic. This became standard teaching in many evangelical circles, and even today is a hindrance to the practice of charismatic gifts.

On the other hand, many teachings from the evangelical awakenings and the holiness movement in the English-speaking world were widely accepted in Germany, despite some elements of Pentecostal teaching. The writings of men such as Andrew Murray, R. A. Torrey, and Charles Finney received wide circulation.

The charismatic renewal found its most hospitable reception in the GDR through the *Volksmissionskreis Sachsen* (Evangelism Fellowship of Saxony), a fellowship of evangelical pastors and laymen.

Some evangelical Lutheran groups from West Germany also provided encouragement for the charismatic renewal in the GDR: the Brethren of the Common Life, the Evangelical Sisterhood of Mary, the Brotherhood of Christ, and the Jesus Brotherhood. The stewardship movement that began in the Lutheran church in the GDR after the Lutheran World Federation Assembly in Hannover in 1952, with its strong emphasis on lay participation, also helped create a climate hospitable to charismatic renewal.

In this rich spiritual soil, the message of charismatic renewal found friendly reception.

Early leadership in the charismatic renewal

The beginnings of charismatic renewal in the GDR are especially associated with four names and four centers of spiritual renewal: Bernhard Jansa, founder of the Julius Schniewindhaus retreat center with its large sisterhood, now led by Dieter Blischke; Gerhard Küttner, pastor in Bräunsdorf with its spiritual life retreats drawing people from the entire country; Erwin Pähl, pastor in Slate with its active retreat center; and Christoph Richter, pastor in Grosshartmannsdorf with its lay brotherhood and active youth ministry. Successors of these pioneers carried on the work of renewal.

The Volksmissionskreis Sachsen provided a source of spiritually awakened and responsible leadership when the charismatic movement began to spread: men with well-established ministries, like Hans Prehn, Lothar Köppe, Ewald Ehrler, and Gottfried Rebner became associated with the renewal in Saxony. Heinz Polzin in Weitenhagen, Friedrich Eichenberg in Stendal, and Paul Toaspern in Berlin became part of the growing network of charismatic leaders throughout the GDR.

Relationship to the church

The charismatic renewal in the GDR has focused primarily on parish renewal. Following the New Testament pattern, it seeks to build congregational life and prepare people for mission. It goes by the name of Spiritual Congregational Renewal, which indicates both its commitment to the church and its awareness that the church needs renewing. Renewal leaders have established official relationships with their Lutheran bishops, and in several places—Saxony and Thuringia, for example—bishops have taken a very positive attitude toward the renewal.

In 1983 the leadership of Spiritual Congregational Renewal issued a statement to all the churches, urging them to make room for the renewal to develop in a healthy way and to provide their spiritually awakened members with the necessary spiritual nourishment so that both inwardly and outwardly they remain faithful members of the church.

International and ecumenical contacts

The charismatic renewal in the GDR has been enriched by a variety of influences from outside the country. The writings of men such as Arnold Bittlinger, R. F. Edel, David Wilkerson, Dennis Bennett, and Larry Christenson received wide distribution. Several charismatic leaders (Edel, Christenson, Donald Pfotenhauer, Theodore Jungkuntz, Siegfried Grossman) had significant personal contact with pastors in the GDR. Christenson and Pfotenhauer had such contact on a fairly regular basis.

Some renewal leaders in the GDR were also able to attend conferences in other countries, such as the annual International Lutheran Conference on the Holy Spirit in Minneapolis or the ecumenical European conference in Strassbourg in 1982. Six GDR renewal leaders attended the strategic international Lutheran renewal leaders' meeting in Finland in 1981.

Theological work

Under the leadership of men such as Paul Toaspern and Gottfried Rebner, more sustained theological work among Lutherans has been carried on in the GDR than in any other country. The national renewal committee publishes an occasional theological newsletter. Some of the leaders, notably Toaspern and Christoph Richter, have also published theological and pastoral works under their own names.

In their retreats and conferences, particular weight is given to Bible study that strikes a balance between theological exposition and the personal or devotional use of Scripture. This has issued in a body of literature dealing with a number of charismatic themes, such as speaking in tongues, prophecy, healing, and discernment of spirits.

A particularly significant feature of the experience in the GDR has been the development of serious theological discussions between evangelicals and charismatics within the Lutheran church. This is especially noteworthy in light of the Berlin Declaration, which still has a strong hold on evangelical thinking in regard to anything that smacks of Pentecostalism. In 1981, after five years of theological dialog, they published *The Holy Spirit and Spiritual Gifts*. The report underscored many points of agreement and also stated points of disagreement.

The theological study commission of the evangelical church produced a report on the charismatic awakening in the GDR that was based on extensive firsthand material. Renewal centers were visited and a representative cross-section of participants in the renewal were interviewed in depth. The report posed two basic questions: (1) How can significant theological exchange take place between the church and the renewal movement? (2) To what degree is the charismatic renewal a challenge to the church and its theology? The report did not shy away from asking critical questions of the renewal, but the overall evaluation presented the renewal in a very positive light.

The development of a renewal leadership for the GDR

In 1977 a national Spiritual Congregational Renewal committee was formed. It encouraged a friendly theological exchange among the various groups and centers of spiritual renewal in the GDR, for mutual enrichment and any necessary correction. It helped establish regional renewal leadership. It served as an advisory group for the church, recommending policies that would facilitate a healthy integration of the renewal into the total life of the church.

The influence of the renewal

Charismatic renewal brought a fresh spiritual and theological impulse into the church. The person and work of the Holy Spirit has been taken up in theological discussion in a way not previously experienced. The number of church officials participating in serious discussion of charismatic renewal continues to grow. The discussion is not theoretical but is taking place with continued reference to what is actually happening.

The renewal has had an especially strong effect on youth. A district superintendent reported at a meeting of the World Council of Churches in Nairobi in 1975 that "the charismatic renewal among young people is the most encouraging phenomenon that we have seen in our Lutheran church."[7] The youth gatherings have been dynamic and unconventional. A spate of new songs has grown up in the renewal, and personal testimony has played a significant role in the spread of the movement. While there has been a strong emphasis on spiritual gifts, the cross has stood uncontested at the center of the proclamation. Despite the dynamism of the movement, a quiet and responsible spirit has prevailed; the experience of gifts and ministries of the Spirit are carefully weighed against the biblical norms of love and edification of the congregation.

Through the charismatic movement the renewal of congregational life has come to have a strong experiential dimension. Faith is no longer seen merely as head knowledge to which one assents: rather, it is a new life in Christ that includes the experience of freedom, joy, a sense of God's immediacy, personal communion with Jesus, and divine guidance in one's everyday life.

Those involved in the movement meet together out of a felt need to share their awakened faith with others of like mind; this has happened primarily in small house-groups, which continue to grow and spread out. Prayer stands at the center of these house-groups, with prayers of worship and adoration predominating. Answers to prayer are enthusiastically shared; there have been significant reports of healing through prayer. Prayer and singing in tongues occurs in a natural way and appears to convey a sense of being strengthened and helped in the Spirit.

The whole enterprise of parish renewal has been enlivened by a new sense of expectation in regard to traditional words and promises of Scripture. The theological paper *The Holy Spirit and Spiritual Gifts* states that "the working of the Holy Spirit is being experienced today exactly as it was in the days of the early church."

The work of the Holy Spirit presents a continuing challenge to the renewal itself and to the entire church.

NORWAY

The charismatic renewal in Norway can be traced back to several different sources. Some individuals had charismatic experience in their youth on the mission field, other people through visits abroad and through literature.

One of the sources of the interdenominational aspect of the charismatic renewal in Norway was the ministry of independent Pentecostal evangelist Aril Edvardsen. Through his magazine *Troens Bevis* he sought to spread the message of the charismatic renewal to the Scandinavian people. Beginning in the early 1970s, his big annual summer conferences attracted thousands of people, about half of them Lutherans.

In February 1970 two pastors from the Lutheran Church of Norway, Hans-Jacob Frøen and Hans Christian Lier, declared in a public meeting that they spoke in tongues. Both of these pastors became important exponents of the charismatic renewal in Norway.

Pastor Lier, who had visited Anglican charismatic circles, worked in the Oslo Inner Mission. He encouraged charismatic renewal in the Lutheran church. Serving as a seamen's pastor in the Lutheran church, Pastor Frøen established the Agape Foundation, which published the magazine *Dypere Liv (Deeper Life)*. The Agape Foundation spread charismatic renewal with an interdenominational emphasis, but mainly within the Lutheran church, in the 1970s. The foundation was dissolved in 1981 when Frøen retired.

In 1971 and 1972 three charismatic groups, inspired by the "Jesus Movement," were established in Norway: the Peace of God community in Oslo; Youth with a Mission, working nationwide; and Young Vision, working primarily on the west coast of Norway. During the 1970s these three groups became centers of charismatic renewal in Norway.

Youth with a Mission continued its evangelistic work with many full-time workers in the Lutheran church and its organizations. In 1980 the Peace of God community dissolved and reorganized into smaller groups. A little later some of the work of Young Vision also dissolved, but it continued to have influence through the large charismatic and evangelistic Jesus Festival every summer.

Almost from the outset, the charismatic renewal in Norway developed two somewhat distinct theological emphases. One group, represented by the Agape Foundation, was interdenominational with a measure of Pentecostal influence. The other group was more strongly Lutheran and was recruited largely from the evangelical Lutheran Student Movement. This group spread charismatic renewal in the Lutheran church and in some of the conservative evangelical organizations. A group of charismatic students was formed at the Free Faculty of Theology in Oslo.

An important event took place in 1977 in Oslo when a committee was organized by leaders within the Lutheran church and some of its organizations. They convened a "Holy Spirit Seminar" that was attended by about 1200 people. The same committee organized similar conferences in several major cities with good attendance. In the summer of 1980 the first nationwide Oasis Conference was held. This became an annual event with 5000-6000 participants.

In addition to the annual summer conference, the Oasis committee sponsored a special conference for pastors and other preachers in 1983; this too became an annual event. On initiative from local Lutheran charismatic groups throughout Norway, members of the Oasis committee conducted weekend renewal conferences. In 1985 Jens-Petter Jørgensen became the daily leader of Oasis.

Several of the committee members and speakers in Oasis have their roots in evangelical organizations. Many people found that Oasis provided a natural continuation of the spiritual ideals they had known as evangelicals. Even though Oasis conferences were openly identified with the charismatic renewal, evangelical bishops and other major speakers participated, openly stating that they were not charismatics themselves.

The theological profile of Oasis has been shaped by teaching, books, and cassettes that present it as a Lutheran confessional movement with a strong emphasis on repentance, holiness, the fullness of the Spirit, the gifts of the Spirit, worship, and power for witness and mission.

The Oasis committee purposely did not become another organization within the church. It aimed at fully integrating the charismatic dimension into local Christian communities, congregations, and prayer fellowships. In the Haugerud congregation in Oslo, which had been significantly influenced by the ministry of Anglican charismatic leader Michael Harper and his wife Jeanne, this kind of integration first began to take place. In a few other places, where pastors and preachers gave leadership, the renewal slowly gained ground.

The attitude toward Oasis on the part of the Lutheran church changed from opposition and criticism to a growing acceptance. Some charismatics in the Lutheran church did not fully identify with Oasis. They wanted to see a stronger emphasis on preaching faith, leading people into distinct charismatic experience, and a more definite charismatic identity in life and ministry.

In 1979 the Bishops' Meeting of the Lutheran church appointed a committee, headed by charismatic theologian Tormod Engelsviken, to produce a statement on the charismatic movement that could be presented to congregations. The report presented a positive evaluation of the renewal and encouraged congregations to welcome it. It won approval in the Bishops' Meeting and was published in 1981.

DENMARK

The initial breakthrough of the charismatic renewal in Denmark within the Lutheran church is closely associated with the activities of Dr. Michael Harry, who organized meetings in cooperation with the Full Gospel Businessmen's Fellowship International in the late 1960s. The first open charismatic meeting in a Lutheran church occurred in 1970 when Lutheran pastor A. E. Arentoft in Esbjerg and Michael Harry arranged a public meeting for Michael Harper in the N. F. S. Grundtvig House in Esbjerg. Pastor Arentoft was a Grundtvigian pastor who believed that the experience of the famous 19th-century Danish churchman included speaking in tongues.

The first major manifestation of the renewal within the Danish Lutheran church was at a meeting in Roskilde in 1975, arranged by Michael Harry and a group of Lutheran pastors. Tom Smail, a Presbyterian theologian from England, was invited to be the main speaker at this conference. It turned out to be a large and successful conference and was held again in 1976. By this time it was evident that the charismatic renewal was becoming a recognized reality in the Danish Lutheran church, even though its influence was small.

The charismatic renewal found its first structure in prayer groups, where people gathered for prayer, free worship, and Bible study. Most pastors and church authorities in Denmark looked condescendingly on charismatics or rejected them out of hand. Nevertheless, the prayer groups became a powerful tool of encouragement for those interested in renewal. They sponsored charismatic meetings and local conferences. They initiated Bible camps; the most well-known was the annual camp at Aalborg, with about 800 in attendance.

Some specialized activities and ministries have grown out of the charismatic renewal: mission centers such as Arken in Esbjerg with an effective work in street mission and broadcasting, and some aid centers for drug addicts and alcoholics such as Quo Vadis in Kolding and Shalom in Randers. As early as 1973, charismatic meetings near Sønderborg led to the founding of the deeper-life Asserballe Skov Bibelcenter. In 1981 a High School Kibbutz was founded in Vejen by charismatics.

In the mid-1970s, a small number of Lutheran pastors became involved in the renewal. In Jutland, until 1983, they gathered in the ØM Pastors' Conference under the leadership of Svend Boysen. From 1974-1982 a charismatic pastors group met in Copenhagen. In addition to Lutherans, this group included participants from some of the free churches (non-Lutheran) and the Catholic church. In 1981 charismatic pastors and lay people from Copenhagen and the rest of Zealand formed the Spirit and Life group to give leadership to the renewal in the Lutheran church.

By the mid-1980s only about 30, out of 1800, Lutheran pastors had been significantly influenced by the renewal. A number of prayer groups were scattered throughout the country. A few congregations, where the pastor was charismatic, were identified with the renewal: the Karlslunde Strandkirke near Copenhagen, with a markedly Pentecostal flavor; the Bethlehemkirke in Copenhagen, with a high-church orientation; churches in several towns of Jutland—Aalborg, Silkeborg, Give, and Sønderborg.

The charismatic renewal in Denmark began as an interconfessional movement. In the beginning there was close cooperation between charismatics from different denominations. This aspect of the renewal diminished, however, because of two factors. There were some cases of rebaptism that created a disturbance in Lutheran circles. But the primary factor was simply the church situation in Denmark: 94% of the population are members of the Lutheran church. Evangelizing their own church is a greater concern for Lutheran charismatics than building interconfessional relationships.

The Danish Lutheran church is a quasi-state church; it is part of the "establishment." On a typical Sunday, however, only two percent of the members attend worship services; a tiny minority of the people have personal faith. Basic Christian knowledge is declining rapidly in the society at large. The Lutheran church is spiritually weak and divided, suffering from a devastating pluralism in faith and life.

The general attitude toward charismatic renewal covers the spectrum from almost total deprecation to open and positive expectation. Both of these extremes are evidenced, for instance, among the bishops of the Lutheran church.

Due to the quasi-state-church situation, former revivals in Denmark created parachurch structures, generally known as "Inner Mission." Most spiritual life among Lutherans is concentrated in these groups. The attitude of Inner Mission groups toward the charismatic renewal has been generally negative, even though many charismatics have their spiritual roots in these groups.

Perhaps the most positive response to the renewal has been among some of the young people. A significant number of theological students at the Universities of Copenhagen and Aarhus, with roots in Pietism, have welcomed the charismatic renewal; they recognize baptism with the Holy Spirit and spiritual gifts as biblical, and as necessary for the immense task of evangelization. High school youth and young working people have also responded to the renewal emphasis. One sees among them a growing understanding and willingness to undertake radical Christian commitment.

These are small but significant signs of a coming spiritual springtime in Denmark, though a major breakthrough has not yet occurred.

SWEDEN

The culture of Sweden is deeply secularized. Although 95% of the population belong to the Lutheran church, most people profess a religion that expresses little or no experience of the living God. The presence of God living and acting among his people is a strange notion to most people, to say nothing of an experienced reality. Christianity has become little more than an ideology or pattern for moral behavior. Against this materialistic and technological culture the charismatic movement came as a counterculture, with strong youth participation protesting a dehumanized and despiritualized way of looking at life. For some, disappointment with a materialistic ideology created a longing for genuine spiritual experience that served as a waiting vessel for renewal.

Renewal in Stockholm

Early impulses for spiritual renewal came to Sweden through the Englishman Harry Greenwood, who visited Stockholm several times during the 1960s, and through Gösta Höök. By 1971 there were more than a hundred ecumenical prayer groups meeting in Stockholm. A general charismatic conference drew an overwhelming response. Lutherans and Pentecostals found themselves crowded to the doors. During the remainder of the 1970s, similar conferences were held in various parts of Sweden, creating a stimulus for the formation of many prayer groups and local charismatic meetings. Retired missionary bishop Helge Fosseus led the important Katarina conference in Stockholm in 1977.

Although the movement began as a protest against abstract, theoretical sermons and church services, without any call to personal involvement or commitment, it did not continue to exist on that basis. It soon led to renewal of Bible study, prayer, and active evangelistic work, with a vivid sense of the Holy Spirit's presence and working.

Renewal in the Gothenburg diocese

The charismatic renewal has had its most remarkable growth in the diocese of Gothenburg on the west coast of Sweden. There had been a revival in this area about a hundred years earlier. The lasting fruit of this revival has been high regard for the Word of God and comparatively widespread knowledge of Scripture. This legacy was like pieces of dry wood ready to be kindled. The growth of prayer groups, renewal weekends with hundreds of people in attendance, a new tone of adoration in worship, and training courses for pastors on the theme of spiritual renewal have been some marks of the renewal.

In 1972 a national ecumenical gathering was held in Gothenburg on the west coast of Sweden that again spawned many prayer groups. At this time the spontaneous youth awakening popularly known as the "Jesus People" served as an instrument for renewal. Some of the young people involved in this movement had been disillusioned when the radical social action promised by the 1968 World Council of Churches assembly in Uppsala ended up being mostly talk.

In the early 1970s, Bertil Gärtner, bishop of Gothenburg, gathered a group of pastors and lay people in his home for Bible studies on the Holy Spirit. Scripture passages dealing with the Holy Spirit, the baptism in the Holy Spirit, and the gifts and fruit of the Spirit were studied. The positive attitude of the bishop had a salutary effect on the spread of the renewal.

In 1974 Dr. Erik Ewalds from Finland held a one-day course on hospital chaplaincy that ended with a service of intercession for healing in the Maria

Church of Gothenburg. This was new to many in attendance, but a number of the pastors subsequently introduced similar services in their own parishes.

In 1974, prayer services that included prayer and the laying on of hands began to form throughout the diocese. By the early 1980s, groups had formed in 50 congregations. Renewal weekends began to be held regularly with hundreds of people in attendance. The worship had a strong accent on praise and adoration; the prayer life was obviously being deepened. There was also a greater readiness to share one's faith.

By the early 1980s, the renewal in Gothenburg had not reached many non-Christians. It was mainly a movement among church people.

Four visiting speakers from abroad had a particularly wholesome effect on the renewal in the Gothenburg diocese: Graham Pulkingham in 1976, Colin Urquhart in 1980, David Watson in 1982, and Morris Vaagenes in 1984. Each of these spoke at a three-day pastors' conference with a hundred pastors in attendance.

Campus Crusade for Christ inspired the churches in Gothenburg with a "Here's Life" campaign that drew many lay people into a deeper commitment. Renewal and evangelism flow from the same Spirit.

The renewal in the Gothenburg diocese has been particularly served by the Åh Stiftsgaard conference center. Renewal leadership has been channeled through several people. A renewal committee for the diocese has devoted itself to prayer and has given oversight to various aspects of the renewal. It publishes a quarterly newsletter that goes out to about a thousand people, and it has had major responsibility for the renewal weekends. It has sponsored several Scandinavian Leaders' Conferences, with 80-100 renewal leaders in attendance.

Another significant influence on the renewal has been the work of Anne S. White. Beginning in 1972 she held several schools on prayer counseling. A national committee was established to carry on this work.

Some charismatic literature has played an important role in fostering charismatic renewal in Sweden. The books of Dennis Bennett, Graham Pulkingham, Michael Harper, David Wilkerson, Michael Green, and David Watson have been widely read. Books on healing by Agnes Sanford, Anne S. White, and Francis MacNutt have also received wide distribution.

For the most part the renewal has found expression within the Lutheran state church. Many people have shared in the ministry; no one person or leader has dominated the scene. At one stage there was close fellowship with other denominations, but later the Lutherans turned more to developing the renewal within their own ranks.

FINLAND

Finland has often succeeded in warding off the rapid and direct impact of new impulses. Geographical, linguistic, and cultural circumstances obliged the charismatic renewal to adapt itself to some of the unique features of Finnish culture, such as Finland's location on the periphery of the Western cultural sphere, its language barrier, a critical attitude toward American influences, and the homogeneous nature of Finnish society.

Some impulses of charismatic renewal came to Finland in the 1960s through visiting speakers and literature, but it did not have a widespread impact. In the late 1970s, Nülo Yli-Vainio, a Pentecostal preacher, began holding extensive evangelistic and healing campaigns. About the same time, as one national magazine reported, "people began to fall down in the Lutheran churches also." More or less simultaneously, in Lutheran parishes around the country, people having no direct contact with each other began to experience in a new way the reality of the Lord through the Spirit. Pastors and laity alike were touched.

The media took an active interest in the renewal and did much to spread its influence. Michael Harry from Denmark, among others, visited Finland and helped provide a perspective on charismatic experiences through systematic Bible teaching.

The renewal found substantial access to the Lutheran parishes in Finland. Over the past 200 years there have been four major revivals in the Lutheran church of Finland, so spiritual renewal is not a new or strange thing to many Finnish Lutherans. Pentecostal and other non-Lutheran movements tend to form separate groupings, but the Lutheran church has generally held renewal movements within its own embrace. Except in certain pietist circles, Lutherans who were touched by the charismatic renewal experienced positive acceptance in the church.

In the initial phase of the movement, the interest both of the media and of the churches focused on some of its special doctrinal aspects, such as the work of the Holy Spirit, baptism in the Holy Spirit, speaking in tongues, prophecy, and Christian community. The movement was understood essentially as neo-Pentecostal. As the movement spread among Lutherans, some of the more obviously Pentecostal aspects of the renewal were modified or redirected. The experience of being "slain in the Spirit," in which a person falls down and lies still for a short time, has generally given way to confession and spiritual counseling at the altar. The gift of tongues, which has been widely characteristic of the movement elsewhere, was less conspicuous in the Finnish renewal. Surveys showed that only one in ten participants in Lutheran charismatic meetings had ever spoken in tongues.

Healing by prayer has been perhaps the most prominent feature of the Finnish charismatic renewal, and this has provoked the most public debate. On the one hand there has been a certain reluctance on the part of church leaders to venture into things that have not been part of traditional church practice. On the other hand, this has not prevented the Finnish people from streaming to large meetings where the healing power of Christ is both proclaimed and practiced.

In 1980, leaders of the Finnish charismatic movement initiated meetings with charismatic leaders from the other Scandinavian countries. Michael Harper from England and Larry Christenson from the United States were invited to participate in these meetings as resource people. Out of these meetings came the proposal for an international meeting of Lutheran charismatic leaders. The meeting was held outside Helsinki in the summer of 1981, with more than 100 people from 12 different countries in attendance.

One of the practical proposals to come out of that meeting was that an International Lutheran Charismatic Theological Consultation be undertaken, with the objective of preparing a theological and pastoral perspective on charismatic renewal for Lutherans. The present book is the fruit of that proposal.

EASTERN EUROPE

In most countries of eastern Europe, Lutherans are gathered together in tiny minority churches. While there have been some charismatic impulses, one can scarcely talk of a movement.

In Hungary there has been only the tiniest beginnings of charismatic renewal among Lutherans. Among Reformed and Roman Catholic people there has been somewhat more.

Poland is 95% Roman Catholic, and among them charismatic renewal has had a significant impact, especially through the Catholic "Oasis Movement." Among Lutherans the renewal is limited to individual believers or small local prayer groups.

In Czechoslovakia there are a number of Protestant churches, and in some localities there have been significant charismatic outbreaks. A small number of pastors have become actively involved in giving leadership to the renewal. Generally speaking, Lutherans have been less involved than other denominations.

In Rumania and Bulgaria the Orthodox church dominates the scene. The Lutheran church is small and carries on a German language tradition. It has had virtually no contact with the charismatic renewal.

Lutherans in Russia have had some contact with the charismatic renewal, chiefly through the influence of Baptists from Finland, whose spirituality includes the Pentecostal witness.

AUSTRALIA

Lutheran Renewal Australia (LRA) had its beginnings in the city of Adelaide, South Australia, in 1974, in a street outreach ministry known as Jacob's Ladder. The leader of this work was Lutheran pastor Doug Kuhl. Through this ministry bikers, drug addicts, and minor criminals were coming to faith in Jesus Christ. Soon the Jacob's Ladder Christian Community found that members of other Lutheran congregations wanted to join them in worship. Thus conservative Lutherans began to gather with those recently won from the street to worship God with enthusiasm and vigor. Praise and worship was the most notable feature of the early days of charismatic renewal in Australia.

Structure

In 1976 an interdenominational conference in Adelaide revealed the presence of a sizable number of charismatic Lutherans. A loosely structured steering committee was organized, with pastor Kuhl in the role of spiritual director until he moved to Sydney to take up other work. Regular day-long retreats were held in the Adelaide hills. Prayer groups began to form in some congregations, but structured activities focused on monthly meetings in Adelaide, the center of the Lutheran population. At this time the renewal among Lutherans was largely restricted to South Australia and parts of Victoria. In the late 1970s, small cells were formed in the rest of the Lutheran Church in Australia, and larger weekend conferences began to be held.

Encouragement from overseas

Larry Christenson was the first of a number of American Lutheran pastors to contribute to the ministry of Lutheran Renewal Australia when he spoke at conferences in 1978. Later other Lutheran pastors from America also ministered in Australia: Rodney Lensch, Morris Vaagenes, and W. Dennis Pederson in 1981; Rodney Lensch again in 1983, together with Jim Roberson and Walter Litke; and Larry Christenson again in 1985.

Lutherans in Australia profited greatly through the ministry of these visitors from America. In each case they made a significant impact on the growth of the renewal in Australia, breaking down barriers and dispelling misunderstanding.

Relationship to the Lutheran Church of Australia

The Lutheran Church of Australia is theologically conservative. For much of its history it has been isolated from outside influences. Church officials and some pastors and lay members became concerned about this new move-ment within the church. A number of meetings and position papers ensued. A statement was drawn up by the church's Commission on Theology and Inter-Church Relations. This was discussed with renewal leaders; some mod-ifications were made before it was adopted by the general church council in February 1977 under the title *The Lutheran Church of Australia and Lutheran Charismatic Renewal.* This helped lessen some tensions that had developed between church and renewal leaders. The official position of the church, however, was wary and at times openly hostile to the renewal.

Pastoral involvement

In its early years, Lutheran Renewal Australia was largely a lay-led move-ment. In the 1970s the number of pastors who were fully involved in char-ismatic renewal could be numbered on one hand.

In 1981 a National Lutheran Charismatic Conference was held in Adelaide with some 200 in attendance. A number of pastors became personally involved in the renewal, and as a result charismatic renewal began to emerge in a number of congregations. By the mid-1980s the renewal had spread in some measure to all corners of the Lutheran church. The numbers of those involved continued to grow, and national renewal leadership began to emerge.

ETHIOPIA

Inspired by Swedish and Finnish Pentecostal missions in the early 1960s, and sparked by Omahe Chacha, a visiting Kenyan evangelist, a strong Pen-tecostal-charismatic revival broke out in Addis Ababa in 1965. The initial outbreak was principally among university students. The revival spread rapidly to other urban and educational centers throughout the country.

All of the other Protestant churches in Ethiopia were touched. Individuals and groups in the Ethiopian Orthodox Church were also involved.

The revival led to the establishment of the independent Ethiopian Pente-costal Church, Mullu Wongel ("Full Gospel"), which suffered heavy per-secution during the last years of the reign of Emperor Haile Selassie. This church experienced a brief respite after the revolution in 1974; then the per-secution took up again under the Marxist regime. The government finally outlawed the church, driving it underground. Many of its members and leaders were thrown into prison, where they suffered harsh treatment and torture.

In the late 1960s, theological dialog was held between Pentecostal leaders and pastor Ezra Gebre Medhin of the large Mekane Yesus Lutheran Church in Addis Ababa. This resulted in a new measure of understanding between Lutherans and their Pentecostal neighbors. When Pentecostals began to be persecuted, many of them sought fellowship among the Lutherans. A large number of those who have had charismatic experience are now active in the Mekane Yesus church.

One feature of the charismatic renewal among Lutherans has been the formation of hundreds of youth choruses. They write words to indigenous Ethiopian meolodies and sing them all over the country.

In 1972 the officers of the Mekane Yesus church appointed Norwegian missionary theologian Tormod Engelsviken to investigate the charismatic renewal and report to the general assembly in 1973. His report, which concluded with a positive evaluation, was not too well received by the assembly. There were some understandable fears over the possibility of becoming too closely identified with a persecuted religious group.

In 1976 a consultation was called in Addis Ababa to discuss the charismatic renewal in the Lutheran congregations. The report of this consultation was positive toward the renewal, welcoming it in the church and giving guidelines for its integration.

Although there have been differing views of the charismatic renewal in the Mekane Yesus church, the renewal has been welcomed by some of the church's outstanding leaders, for instance, the former general secretary, Gudina Tumsa. Young people, especially, have been drawn into the renewal, with a resulting upsurge in praise and worship, Bible study, and evangelism.

Most of all, charismatically renewed people have shown a remarkable boldness and perseverance in the face of growing opposition, persecution, and torture.

All Christians in Ethiopia live under heavy pressure. Many have been imprisoned. They need the prayers and support of their Christian brothers and sisters all over the world.

TANZANIA

The Evangelical Lutheran Church in Tanzania was deeply influenced by the East African Revival that began in the 1940s. By the 1970s this had become a second-generation movement with some narrow, legalistic tendencies, though it was still a vital spiritual force.

Some of those who grew up in this revival have looked for fresh spiritual life from Pentecostal churches in Tanzania or through literature from the United States. Through such influences, a kind of incipient charismatic renewal came into the theological college in Makumira, where the Lutheran church trains its pastors.

Lutheran leaders have been somewhat wary of renewal movements. Among Christian students at Dar es Salaam University they witnessed a wilder sort of revival, unrelated to the charismatic movement, characterized by strong premillenial prophetic teaching, cessation from work, and rejection of all authority in the church.

Ecumenical and international contacts

In 1983, several Lutheran church leaders attended an ecumenical African spiritual renewal leaders' conference in neighboring Kenya. There they met leaders from other denominations, especially Anglicans, who testified to positive experience with the charismatic renewal. Lutheran charismatic leaders from the United States and Norway—Larry Christenson, W. Dennis Pederson, and Jens-Petter Jørgensen—were also present at the conference and participated in discussions with the Lutherans from Tanzania. Plans were laid for conferences that would offer teaching on charismatic renewal for Lutheran pastors in Tanzania.

In 1985 the International Lutheran Renewal Center was twice invited to send representatives to Tanzania. Larry Christenson, ILRC's director, together with Fred Hall, a layman from Trinity Lutheran Church in San Pedro, California, shared in Bible teaching and prayer ministry at two conferences and a series of evangelism rallies in the northern diocese of Tanzania.

In reporting on the pastors' and deacons' conference that he addressed, Christenson noted that "some of them had experienced charismatic gifts in their ministries—things like healing and exorcism—though for others this was unfamiliar territory." He observed that the Lutheran church in Tanzania is growing at the rate of about 11% a year, "though not without difficulties in the face of Islam and native African religions. Spiritual renewal is definitely under way. It needs only to be encouraged, expanded, and wisely shepherded."[8]

A "Lutheran Pentecost"

Later in the same year W. Dennis Pederson, ILRC's coordinator of international ministries, and Per Anderson, also a layman from Trinity Lutheran Church in San Pedro, participated in a week-long ecumenical pastors' conference in the beautiful northern part of Tanzania, on the foothills of Mt. Kilimanjaro. Michael Harper and a team of about a dozen Anglicans from England were also present. About 140 pastors attended, mostly Lutherans and Anglicans, with some Mennonites and Moravians. It was a significant group, with tremendous influence throughout most of Tanzania.

Per Anderson described the final session of the conference as a "Lutheran Pentecost." He wrote:

It was God's surprise, totally unexpected. Before the final talks the Lutheran bishop, Erasto Kweka, rose to speak to us. He was a regal sort of person, with real authority. He said, "We have a wonderful opportunity before us which we should not miss. We are going to ask Dennis Pederson and Michael Harper to pray for us after this last session that we all be filled with the Holy Spirit. You prepare your hearts!"

Dennis Pederson spoke on the fruit of the Spirit. He shared powerfully, humbly, and honestly from his own heart on the work of love that God does in us. The pastors were deeply touched. Up to that point there had been considerable teaching on the gifts of the Spirit, but the teaching on love finally convinced the hesitant and resistant. It was love that broke down the barriers in their hearts and made them ready to receive.

Michael Harper's message ended the session, and included a clear, balanced teaching on speaking in tongues—a live and troublesome issue in Tanzania. "Each gift has its place and its purpose," he said. "We need to humble our minds and learn how to move in the Spirit as we experience this gift."

After the talks came God's surprise. We did not expect that the Holy Spirit would fill the pastors as a whole group. Yet God did it. The presence of God was powerful in the room. Many were speaking in tongues to the Lord. Several prophecies came, then a vision. It was all very quiet. Nothing loud, dramatic, or flashy. Yet the Lord was there.

That evening thirty students at the teachers' college, where the conference was being held, said that they had seen a light "brighter than the sun, brighter than daylight" over the building where the pastors were meeting. These students did not participate in the conference and knew little of what was going on that morning. It was an interesting confirmation.

Because of the Corinthian-type problems in Tanzania in regard to some spiritual gifts, and because of the nature of the people, the Lord came to them in a way that they could accept and relate to. Does God call us to forsake all the characteristics of our tradition in order to receive his Spirit? Or does he work within the context of our individual and corporate personality? This whole event was so quiet and orderly that I was tempted to call it a "Lutheran Pentecost."[9]

PAKISTAN

The Church of Pakistan came into being when Anglicans, Methodists, Scot Presbyterians, and Lutherans united in 1970. Although individual members had experiences of receiving gifts of the Spirit, the charismatic renewal as such first came to Pakistan in October 1980.

The initial impulse came through two Anglicans, Jim Hunter and Awtar Singh. The bishop of Karachi, Arne Rudvin, a Lutheran from Norway, gave the renewal a positive reception. The leaders of the church in the Karachi and Hyderabad dioceses immediately spelled out ways that the renewal could be integrated into the life of the church.

Within a relatively short period of time more than half of the clergy and many of the missionaries in these two dioceses became actively involved in the renewal.

The renewal affected church life in two noticeable ways: (1) an emphasis on healing through prayer, including inner healing and exorcisms; (2) an emphasis on reconciliation between individuals and between groups.

The latter is extremely important in the Pakistani cultural environment, which is traditionally full of new and inherited enemies and unaccustomed to thinking in terms of forgiveness. Frequently reconciliation has turned out to be the first step or a precondition to healing. The result has been warm fellowships with many active lay people and a much greater openness toward Christians in other churches, especially Roman Catholics and Pentecostals.

MALAYSIA

In the late 1960s American missionaries returned from their furloughs in the United States having experienced personal renewal in the Holy Spirit. Some had come in contact with members of the Assemblies of God. They started prayer groups and meetings in the small Lutheran church.

Church leadership reacted negatively and stopped all open manifestations of the renewal. It continues only in private prayer groups.

LUTHERANS IN MINORITY SITUATIONS

In areas of the world where Lutherans are less concentrated, the renewal has tended to spread primarily by way of personal contact, among small groups, with less impact upon the institutional church: Brazil, Japan, Hong Kong, the Philippines, Taiwan, Singapore, Indonesia, New Guinea, India, France, Austria, South Africa, Nigeria, the Cameroons, Kenya, Latvia, Mexico, and Ecuador. Pastors and laymen from these areas have sometimes traveled to places where charismatic conferences and retreats were being held and have brought the impulse back to their own countries. In some countries, such as Austria, Brazil, Japan, France, and India, Lutheran renewal conferences or pastors' seminars have been held, often with a Lutheran charismatic from another country as speaker or resource person.

In the Lutheran state church of Iceland the renewal has had a noticeable impact among the youth associated with the congregation served by Pastor Halldor Grøndal; leaders from Youth with a Mission have been closely identified with this work.

Lutheran charismatics in Canada and the United States have been linked together primarily through an annual North American Lutheran Leaders' Conference, and through the annual International Lutheran Conference on the Holy Spirit held in Minneapolis.

Men such as Larry Christenson, Rodney Lensch, Charles Miller, Herbert Mjorud, W. Dennis Pederson, James Roberson, and Morris Vaagenes from

America; Arnold Bittlinger, R. F. Edel, and Wolfram Kopfermann from the Federal Republic of Germany; Paul Toaspern from the German Democratic Republic; Tormod Engelsviken and Jens-Petter Jørgensen from Norway; Seppo Löytty and Olli Valtonen from Finland; and Svend Boysen and Michael Harry from Denmark have traveled extensively, bringing the renewal message to Lutherans in other countries.

Generally speaking, within the short space of two decades, Lutherans had been significantly affected by the charismatic renewal in virtually every segment of their worldwide membership.

BACKGROUND AND MINISTRY OF PARTICIPANTS IN THE CONSULTATION

Jan Bjerregaard, cand. theol. from the University of Copenhagen; parish pastor in Hjørring, Denmark; member of the Charismatic Lutheran Pastors' Committee in western Denmark.

Svend Boysen, author and publisher of books on charismatic renewal; formerly parish pastor in Jutland; presently coordinator of Dialogue and Renewal, an international mission headquartered in Aarhus, Denmark.

Fredrik Brosché, doctor of theology from Uppsala University, Sweden, with dissertation on "Luther and Predestination"; formerly docent of theology at the University of Uppsala; presently chaplain in the diocese of Gothenburg.

Larry Christenson, parish pastor of Trinity Lutheran Church (ALC) in San Pedro, California, for 22 years; author of *The Charismatic Renewal Among Lutherans* (1976), *Speaking in Tongues* (1968), other books, and numerous articles on spiritual renewal; presently on the pastoral staff of North Heights Lutheran Church, St. Paul, Minnesota, and director of the International Lutheran Renewal Center.

Per Eckerdal, parish pastor in the Gothenburg diocese, Sweden.

Tormod Engelsviken, formerly missionary seminary instructor at the Mekane Yesus Seminary in Addis Ababa, Ethiopia; Ph.D. from Aquinas Institute in Dubuque, Iowa, with dissertation, "The Gift of the Spirit—An Analysis and Evaluation of the Charismatic Renewal from a Lutheran Theological Perspective (1981)"; author of several books and articles on the Charismatic renewal; presently senior lecturer in missiology at the Free Faculty of Theology in Oslo, Norway.

Helge Fosseus, formerly Lutheran missionary and bishop in southern Africa; during the 1970s, after his retirement, he coordinated a number of charismatic conferences in Stockholm.

Gerhard Grosse, parish pastor in Peggau, Austria.

Lorenz Hein, doctor of theology in church history; author of numerous scholarly theological articles; presently serving both as a parish pastor in Oldenburg, Holstein, and as professor of church history at the University of Kiel, Germany.

Bengt Holmberg, doctor of theology from Lund University, Sweden, with an interdisciplinary (exegesis/sociology) dissertation, "Paul and Power," 1978; formerly missionary seminary instructor in the Lutheran theological college at Makumira, Tanzania; served as assistant to the bishop for continuing education of church workers in the diocese of Gothenburg, Sweden; presently Docent in New Testament Exegesis at the University of Lund.

Jens-Petter Jørgensen, formerly Bible school teacher for eight years; on the Norwegian Inter-Varsity staff for three years; author of *Mulighetenes Gud* (1986) and other books on Christian living and renewal; presently daily leader of Oasis, an umbrella organization for Lutheran charismatic renewal in Norway.

Theodore Jungkuntz, doctor of theology from Erlangen University, Germany, with a dissertation dealing with the Lutheran church orders of the 16th century; formerly professor of theology at Valparaiso University in Indiana; presently serving as pastor of Cross and Resurrection Lutheran Church, a congregation associated with the Word of God ecumenical community in Ann Arbor, Michigan.

Gerhard Kelber, parish pastor in Schweinfurt, Germany; member of the coordination committee for Charismatic Congregational Renewal in Germany.

Wolfram Kopfermann, parish pastor in Hamburg, Germany; chairman of the coordination committee for Charismatic Congregational Renewal in the Protestant Churches of West Germany.

Kirsti Löytty, Th.M., teacher in divinity and missionary from Finland, formerly in Namibia; presently teaching in the Lutheran Theological College at Makumira, Tanzania.

Seppo Löytty, doctor of theology from Helsinki University, Finland; formerly missionary in Namibia as a teacher in theology; later Dean of the Cathedral in Mikkeli, Finland; five years as chairman of the working committee of Spiritual Renewal within the Lutheran Church in Finland; presently teaching systematic theology in the Lutheran Theological College at Makumira, Tanzania.

Ole Skjerbaek Madsen, author of a research project on eucharistic prayer in the Coptic Orthodox church and of several articles on spiritual renewal with special attention to liturgical questions; member of steering committee for the Danish branch of the Fellowship of St. Alban and St. Sergius; member of charismatic service committee for eastern Denmark; presently parish pastor at the Bethlehemskirken, Copenhagen.

Herbert Mirly, senior pastor of Resurrection Lutheran Church (LCMS), Charlotte, North Carolina, for 15 years; presently conducts seminars and counseling ministry for pastors and their families.

Per Mollerup, parish pastor in Boeslunde, Denmark.

Johan Østerhus, formerly university chaplain for Inter-Varsity Christian Fellowship in Norway; formerly committee member and arrangements chairman for the large Oasis Summer Conference in Norway; associate pastor at the Stromso church in Drammen, Norway.

W. Dennis Pederson, doctor of ministry from the Jesuit School of Theology in Berkeley, California; formerly administrative assistant to the governor of Minnesota; chairman of the Parish Renewal Council, a confederation of Protestant groups working for parish renewal in the United States; presently on the pastoral staff of North Heights Lutheran Church, St. Paul, Minnesota, and coordinator of international ministries for the International Lutheran Renewal Center.

Gottfried Rebner, chairman of the committee for Spiritual Congregational Renewal in the Lutheran Church in the German Democratic Republic; member of the steering committee of the Volksmissionskreis in Saxony; parish pastor in Lauter.

Arne Rudvin, bishop of the Karachi diocese in the United Church of Pakistan.

Asbjørn Simonnes, coordinator for a number of renewal events in Norway and Scandinavia; teacher of theology and philosophy at the teacher-training institute in Volda, Norway.

Per-Olof Söderpalm, formerly parish pastor in Gothenburg, Sweden; presently assistant to the bishop in the diocese of Gothenburg.

Carl Gustaf Stenbäck, formerly missionary to Malaysia; author of training manuals for evangelism; presently parish pastor in St. Lundby; leader of the Reference Group for Spiritual Renewal within the Church of Sweden and the equivalent group in the diocese of Gothenburg.

Paul Toaspern, doctor of theology and former parish pastor; author of numerous books and articles on the devotional life and spiritual renewal; presently *Hauptabteilungsleiter im Diakonischer Werk der Evangelischen Kirchen in der DDR; Geschäftsführer der "Arbeitsgemeinschaft Missionarische Dienste" in der DDR.*

Morris Vaagenes, doctor of ministry from Luther Northwestern Theological Seminary in St. Paul, Minnesota; additional studies in anthropology at the University of Minnesota and in French civilization at the Sorbonne University; presently senior pastor at North Heights Lutheran Church (ALC), St. Paul, Minnesota.

Geir Valle, Evangelist and District Superintendent of Mardan Deanery, Peshawar Diocese, Church of Pakistan; missionary from the Norwegian Missionary Society.

Arthur Vincent, doctor of ministry from Eden Seminary, St. Louis, Missouri; formerly professor of practical theology at Concordia Seminary, then at Christ Seminary (Seminex), St. Louis, Missouri; founder-director of Advancing Renewal Ministries.

Gunnar Weckström, parish pastor in the Lutheran Church in Finland.

In addition to the 31 participants in the consultation, nine other people contributed material, or read the manuscript at different stages of development, and offered helpful suggestions.

NOTES

Abbreviations for frequently cited works

A. Luther's Works

AE = *Luther's Works*. 55 vols. Jaroslav Pelikan and Helmut T. Lehmann, general editors. St. Louis: Concordia; Philadelphia: Fortress, 1955-1986. Example: vol. 12, p. 92 would be cited as AE 12, 92.

WA = *D. Martin Luthers Werke. Kritische Gesamtausgabe*. 61 vols. Weimar, 1883ff. Example: vol. 18, p. 606 would be cited as WA 18, 606.

WABr = *D. Martin Luthers Werke. Briefwechsel*. 18 vols. Weimar, 1930—

WADB = *D. Martin Luthers Werke. Deutsche Bibel*. 12 vols. Weimar, 1906-1961.

WATr = *D. Martin Luthers Werke. Tischreden*. 6 vols. Weimar, 1912-1921.

B. Lutheran Confessional Documents

AC = *The Augsburg Confession*

Apol. = *Apology of the Augsburg Confession*

SA = *Smalcald Articles*

Treatise = *Treatise on the Power and Primacy of the Pope*

SC = *Small Catechism*

LC = *Large Catechism*

FC = *Formula of Concord*

FC Epit. = Epitome of the *Formula of Concord*

FC SD = Solid Declaration of the *Formula of Concord*

Roman numerals refer to the major sections of a document. Where paragraph and page numbers are cited, they refer to the "Tappert Edition": *The Book of Concord*, trans. and ed. Theodore G. Tappert (Philadelphia: Fortress, 1959). Example: the Solid Declaration of the *Formula of Concord*, section XI, paragraph 76, pp. 628-629 would be cited as FC SD XI, 76 (pp. 628-629).

Chapter 1: The Scope of the Charismatic Renewal

1. Robert Whitaker, Presbyterian pastor and church historian, in a lecture to a group of pastors in San Pedro, California, March 1980. From notes by Larry Christenson.
2. Larry Christenson, *The Charismatic Renewal Among Lutherans* (Minneapolis: International Lutheran Renewal Center, 1976; rev. ed. 1985), p. 13.
3. Edward Fiske, "Pentecostals Gain Among Catholics," *The New York Times,* November 3, 1970.
4. Kenneth S. Kantzer, "The Charismatics Among Us," *Christianity Today,* February 11, 1980, p. 25.
5. Vinson Synan, *In the Latter Days* (Ann Arbor, Mich.: Servant, 1984), p. 141.
6. Whitaker, San Pedro lecture.
7. Tom Forrest, past director of the International Catholic Charismatic Renewal Office, in a report made at a meeting of representatives of the World Council of Churches and Anglican, Lutheran, and Roman Catholic charismatic leaders in England, September 1985. From notes by Larry Christenson
8. Synan, *In the Latter Days,* p. 144.

Chapter 2: The Questions and the Quest of the Charismatic Renewal

1. "Message of the Lutheran World Federation Fourth Assembly," two-page statement handed out to Assembly participants (July 1963), p. 1.
2. Private correspondence between Larry Christenson and a missionary of the American Lutheran Church, January-March 1985.
3. AC XX, 15 (p. 43).

Chapter 3: The Meaning of Charismatic Experience

1. See, for example, Carter Lindberg, *The Third Reformation? Charismatic Movements and the Lutheran Tradition* (Macon, Ga.: Mercer Univ., 1983). Lindberg sees Pietism defining "experience" primarily in terms of subjectivism and interiority (pp. 159ff.), and he lumps the charismatic renewal together with this tradition (see pp. 183, 187). See also Merton P. Strommen and others, *A Study of Generations* (Minneapolis: Augsburg, 1972), pp. 118-119. Strommen links religious experience exclusively to the categories of feeling and emotion. For example: "In the religious experience the effect is to 'know God,' to feel him. 'Knowing God' directly changes the person's feelings toward himself and other people."
2. See Mark D. McLean, "Toward a Pentecostal Hermeneutic," pp. 21-25, in *Toward a Pentecostal/Charismatic Theology of Baptism in the Holy Spirit,* ed. J. Rodman Williams, bound volume of papers from Fourteenth Annual Meeting of the Society for Pentecostal Studies (November 15-17, 1984). McLean articulates the more objective understanding of religious experience that is characteristic of the Pentecostal and charismatic movements, for example, "We have experienced the divine person directly acting in our lives, not only by internal renewal, but external experiences such as healings, not merely 'religiously sensitive reflections,' but as an infilling of the Holy SPIRIT . . . in language similar to that found in the naturalism of modernity, we proclaim that God acts and speaks today just as he did in biblical times."

Chapter 4: The Content of Charismatic Experience

1. Larry Christenson, *The Charismatic Renewal Among Lutherans* (Minneapolis: International Lutheran Renewal Center, 1976; rev. ed. 1985), pp. 22-23.
2. Arthur Richter, executive secretary of the Marburger Kreis, in a closing statement at a charismatic conference, Enkenbach, Germany, July 1963. Reported by Larry Christenson.

Chapter 5: The Effects of Charismatic Experience

1. Donald A. McGavran, "The Total Picture," *Christian Life,* October 1982, pp. 39-40. See also pp. 50-63, "Around the World."
2. This understanding, for example, lay behind the choice of a title for the World Council of Churches study, *The Church Is Charismatic,* according to Arnold Bittlinger, who edited the work.
3. Bengt Hoffman, *Luther and the Mystics* (Minneapolis: Augsburg, 1976), p. 221.
4. Morton Kelsey, *Encounter with God* (Minneapolis: Bethany, 1972), p. 144. James Kallas, *The Satanward View* (Philadelphia: Westminster, 1966), pp. 22-23.
5. See, for example, Theodore Jungkuntz, *Confirmation and the Charismata* (Lanham, Md.: University Press of America, 1983).
6. An illustration of effective social ministry in the charismatic renewal has been a work among the poor in Haiti that has gone out from Lutheran Church of the Master in Brooklyn Park, Minnesota. The congregation has provided relief supplies as well as a complex of buildings for a continuing work among the people; they have given both financial support and shorter or longer stints of volunteer service by members with a variety of gifts and skills. They have also involved other congregations in the work.

Chapter 6: The Threefold Task of the Charismatic Renewal

1. Kilian McDonnell, ed., *Presence, Power, Praise—Documents on the Charismatic Renewal,* vols. 1-3 (Collegeville, Minn.: The Liturgical Press, 1980). See the following articles: "Anointing and Healing," LCA/USA, 1962. "A Report on Glossolalia," ALC/USA, 1963. "Mühlheim Theses on Community and Charism," Lutheran Churches in Germany, 1963. "A Statement with Regard to Speaking in Tongues," ALC/USA, 1964. "Christian Faith and the Ministry of Healing," ALC/USA, 1965. "The Charismatic Movement and Lutheran Theology," LCMS/USA, 1972. "Guidelines," ALC/USA, 1973. "The Charismatic Movement in the Lutheran Church in America: A Pastoral Perspective," LCA/USA, 1974. "Policy Statement Regarding the Neo-Pentecostal Movement," LCMS/USA, 1975. "Theological Guidelines for the Charismatic Congregational Renewal in Protestant Churches," Evangelical (Lutheran) Church, Germany, 1976. "The Work of the Holy Spirit," Mekane Yesus Lutheran Church, Ethiopia, 1976. "Renewal in the Holy Spirit," United Evangelical Lutheran Church, Germany, 1976. "The Lutheran Church and the Charismatic Movement: Guidelines for Congregations and Pastors," LCMS/USA, 1977. "The Lutheran Church of Australia and Lutheran Charismatic Renewal," February 1977. "Report of the Lutheran Council in the United States," Lutheran Council, USA, 1978. "The Charismatic Movement in the German Democratic Republic," Lutheran Churches, East Germany, 1978. "Evangelical Spirituality," Evangelical (Lutheran) Church, Germany, 1979.

2. *Ibid.,* vol. 2, pp. 114-116.
3. *Ibid.,* vol. l, pp. 207-210.

Chapter 7: Biblical Interpretation in the Charismatic Renewal

1. In this book we have attempted to be sensitive to changes that are taking place in English usage in regard to words with a male or female connotation. In many places we have followed the growing tendency to replace generic use of male pronouns with inclusive phrases such as "he or she," "his or hers," or with a wider use of inclusive plurals. Where issues of theological substance are involved, we have weighed the question carefully. Sometimes a neutral reference is quite acceptable—for example, referring to the church as "it" rather than "she." In other instances, we let a noninclusive term stand. For example, we found no satisfying alternative to the generic use of *man* when we discussed "The Nature of God and the Nature of Man" in Chapter 30. The traditional use of male pronouns for references to God or the Holy Spirit is commonly followed in the charismatic renewal, and in this book.
2. Regin Prenter, *Spiritus Creator,* trans. John M. Jensen (Philadelphia: Fortress, 1953), pp. 208-209.
3. Bittlinger, a Lutheran, has authored several books, including *Gifts and Graces,* a study of 1 Corinthians 12–14 (Eerdmans, 1968), *Gifts and Ministries,* a study from Ephesians (Eerdmans, 1970), and *Epistle of Joy,* a study of Philippians (Bethany, 1975). Clark is a Roman Catholic layman whose book, *Man and Woman in Christ* (Servant, 1980), includes a major work of exegesis. Engelsviken's doctoral dissertation (see Appendix 2, pp. 375-376), includes more than 200 pages of biblical theology and exegesis which has been published in two books: *Aanden i Ordet* (Oslo: Lunde Forlag, 1977), and *Trent for å tjene* (Oslo: Norsk Forlag, 1985); Montague is a Roman Catholic biblical scholar with a number of scholarly articles to his credit.
4. See, for example, Kilian McDonnell, ed., *Presence, Power, Praise—Documents on the Charismatic Renewal,* vol. 2 (Collegeville, Minn.: Liturgical Press, 1980), p. 116. McDonnell describes Bob Mumford, one of the better known leaders in the charismatic renewal, as a "biblical teacher of real genius."
5. A lively discussion of the place and significance of speaking in tongues took place in May 1982 at a seminar of charismatic leaders in the United States. A wide divergence of interpretation and opinion was evident, despite the fact that these men had been meeting together annually for more than a decade, and had worked cooperatively on such projects as the large ecumenical charismatic conference in Kansas City in 1977. The charismatic renewal has not produced a monolithic or stereotyped interpretation even on something so identified with the movement as speaking in tongues, much less on a wider range of questions.
6. Lutheran theologian Bengt Hoffman has challenged the contemporary antipathy within the theological community toward the term *supernaturalism* in his book *Luther and the Mystics* (Minneapolis: Augsburg, 1976). In a talk at the Institute for Ecumenical and Cultural Research, Collegeville, Minnesota, in 1972, Morton Kelsey coined the term "radical orthodoxy" to express something along the same line. In a number of published works Kelsey has offered an alternative to an epistemology that rules out *a priori* the possibility of direct encounter with the divine. To express this line of thinking more directly as it relates to hermeneutics,

the term "biblical realism" has been used with some frequency in charismatic circles, which differs from a wooden literalism, on the one hand, and from a skeptical rationalism, on the other; the same term has been used to describe the exegetical method of the so-called Uppsala School in Sweden.

7. Morton Kelsey, *Encounter with God* (Minneapolis: Bethany, 1972), pp. 26-36.
8. Paul Althaus, *The Theology of Martin Luther,* trans. Robert C. Schultz (Philadelphia: Fortress, 1966), pp. 50-51.
9. Erich Seeberg, *Luthers Theologie in ihren Grundzügen* (Stuttgart: W. Kohlhammer Verlag, 1950), p. 141. Also Althaus, *Theology of Luther,* pp. 35, 74, 79-81.
10. AE 33, 26 (WA 18, 606 [*De servo arbitrio,* 1525]).
11. AE 34, 112 (WA 39/1, 47 [Thesis 49 from the disputation *"De fide"* of September 11, 1535]).
12. *Preface to the Old Testament,* 1523, WADB 8, p. 11.
13. *Ibid.*
14. Krister Stendahl, *The Bible and the Role of Women* (Philadelphia: Fortress, 1966), pp. 12-13.
15. C. S. Lewis, *Christian Reflections* (Grand Rapids: Eerdmans, 1971), pp. 152-166.
16. Vincent Taylor, *The Gospel According to St. Mark: The Greek Text with Introduction, Notes, and Indexes* (London: Macmillan, 1955), p. 327.
17. AE 34, 285-287 (WATr, no. 2425: "Quae faciunt theologum: 1) gratia spiritus 2) tentatio 3) experientia 4) occasio 5) seduta lectio 6) bonarum artium cognitio.")
18. John R. Stott, *The Baptism and Fullness of the Holy Spirit* (Downers Grove, Ill.: Inter-Varsity, 1964), p. 8.
19. Roger Stronstad, *The Charismatic Theology of St. Luke* (Peabody, Mass.: Hendrickson, 1984), pp. 5-9.
20. Gordon D. Fee, "Baptism in the Holy Spirit: the Issue of Separability and Sequence," p. 6, in *Toward a Pentecostal/Charismatic Theology of Baptism in the Holy Spirit,* ed. J. Rodman Williams, bound volume of papers from Fourteenth Annual Meeting of the Society for Pentecostal Studies (November 15-17, 1984).

Chapter 9: The Promise of the Spirit

1. Tormod Engelsviken (see Appendix 2, pp. 375-376) reports this from his experience in the Mekane Yesus Church in Ethiopia. A convert to Christianity from the *felashas* ("the black Jews") in Ethiopia stated, "We have not yet been baptized with the water of the Abyssinian church, but we have been baptized with the Holy Spirit in our inner man." Cf. Gustav Aren, *Evangelical Pioneers in Ethiopia* (Stockholm: EFS-forlaget, 1978), p. 245.
2. John R. Stott, *The Baptism and Fullness of the Holy Spirit* (Downers Grove, Ill.: Inter-Varsity, 1964), p. 8.
3. I. Howard Marshall, *Luke: Historian and Theologian,* Contemporary Evangelical Perspectives (Grand Rapids: Zondervan, 1970), p. 75.
4. Larry Christenson, "Receiving the Holy Spirit," *Practical Christianity* (Wheaton: Tyndale, 1987), pp. 63-65.
5. Roger Stronstad, " 'Filled With the Holy Spirit' Terminology in Luke-Acts," p. 21, in *Toward a Pentecostal/Charismatic Theology of Baptism in the Holy Spirit,* ed. J. Rodman Williams, bound volume of papers from Fourteenth Annual Meeting of the Society for Pentecostal Studies (November 15-17, 1984).

6. Fritz Rienecker, *Sprachlicher Schlüssel zum Griechischen Neuen Testament* (Giessen-Basel: Brunnen, 1952), p. 266.

Chapter 10: The Spirit and the Word

1. Emil Brunner, *The Misunderstanding of the Church,* trans. Harold Knight (London: Lutterworth, 1952), p. 52.
2. Harold D. Hunter, *Spirit-Baptism, A Pentecostal Alternative* (Lanham, Md.: University Press of America, 1983), p. 29.

Chapter 12: The Indwelling of the Spirit

1. E. C. Whitaker, *Documents of the Baptismal Liturgy* (London: SPCK, 1977), pp. 13-19. Cf. Gabriele Winkler, "Confirmation or Chrismation? A Study in Comparative Liturgy," *Worship,* 58/1, pp. 2-17. Also: J. D. C. Fisher, *Confirmation, Then and Now* (London: SPCK, 1978); Also Theodore Jungkuntz, *Confirmation and the Charismata* (Lanham, Md.: University Press of America, 1983), pp. 19-28.
2. Francis Sullivan, *Baptism in the Holy Spirit: A Catholic Interpretation of the Pentecostal Experience* (Rome: Gregorian Univ., 1974), pp. 52-53. Also, Jungkuntz, *Confirmation and Charismata.* pp. 33-35.

Chapter 15: Praying for the Spirit

1. In the Acts of Thomas, one of the apocryphal New Testament writings, oil is used instead of the laying on of hands as the physical expression of the expectant prayer for the gift of the Holy Spirit. In the Orthodox churches this act is called sealing, with a reference to 2 Cor. 1:22 and Eph. 1:13; 4:30. One cannot exclude this practice as a possible and correct interpretation of these texts because it is universally known. In the early church, as in the Eastern Orthodox churches, oil was used for sealing with the expectation of receiving the Holy Spirit. Oil is also used in Roman Catholic confirmation. These traditions suggest that the early Christian community knew of two outward actions combined with the prayer for the coming of the Holy Spirit: laying on of hands and sealing with oil. An outstanding witness of Western practice is found in the Apostolic Tradition of St. Hippolytus. See E. C. Whitaker, *Documents of the Baptismal Liturgy* (London: SPCK, 1977), pp. 13-19; also Theodore Jungkuntz, *Confirmation and the Charismata* (Lanham, Md.: University Press of America, 1983), pp. 22-23.

Chapter 16: Manifestations of the Spirit

1. David A. Dorman, "The Purpose of Empowerment in the Christian Life," pp. 3, 15, in *Toward a Pentecostal/Charismatic Theology of Baptism in the Holy Spirit,* ed. J. Rodman Williams, bound volume of papers from Fourteenth Annual Meeting of the Society for Pentecostal Studies (November 15-17, 1984).
2. Hans Dieter Betz, *Galatians.* Hermeneia—A Critical and Historical Commentary on the Bible (Philadelphia: Fortress, 1979). The author makes this comment in his commentary on Gal. 3:1-5.

Chapter 19: Solus Christus—Christ Alone

1. These criteria are most programmatically stated in Melanchthon's *Apology of the Augsburg Confession,* article IV (on Justification), but they are repeated and consistently applied throughout *The Book of Concord.* Melanchthon wrote:

   In this controversy the main doctrine of Christianity is involved; when it is properly understood, it illumines and magnifies the honor of Christ and brings to pious consciences the abundant consolation that they need. . . .Our opponents confuse this doctrine miserably, they obscure the glory and the blessings of Christ, and they rob pious consciences of the consolation offered them in Christ (Apol. IV, 2-3 [p. 107]; see also AC XXIV, 24-25, 30-32 [pp. 58-59]).

   Some have wondered whether the frequent appeal of the Lutheran Confessions to "conscience" and its struggle with "guilt" is still relevant in the 20th century, which appears to struggle more with the question of God's existence than with the problem of a guilty conscience. However, the important study by Ernest Becker, *The Denial of Death* (New York: Free Press, 1973), demonstrates how in our century guilt has merely gone underground, where, in the repressed form of an unconscious fear of death—the capitulation of the "self" to the mortality of the "body"—guilt still continues to control human behavior. Becker insisted that this guilt needs "God" as a basis for self-justification, even if only as illusion, if human personality is to be able to survive and develop.

2. Just as it is important to note the statement of these criteria in principle and the consistency with which they are repeated in *The Book of Concord,* it is equally important to note *how* they are actually applied. Here one must acknowledge that they are not used reductionistically, that is, in a fashion that asserts this "hermeneutical principle" at the expense of what might be called the "scriptural substance." From beginning to end, the Confessions make clear that normative doctrine is to be drawn from the fullness of canonical Holy Scriptures, which Scriptures in turn are to be interpreted in such a way that the hermeneutical criteria stated above are not contradicted but are rather promoted. (Apol. IV, 5 [p. 108]; FC SD, Rule and Norm [pp. 501-508]; FC SD III, 6 [p. 540]; FC SD V, 1 [p. 558]; AC XXVIII, 21-28 [pp. 84-85]). This assertion can be tested, for instance, by the manner in which the Confessions deal with a question such as "The Invocation of Saints" (Apol. XXI [pp. 229-236]; note references to Scripture, Word of God, promise, Gospel, command, example from Scripture, divinely instituted order) or with the issue of "Election" (FC SD XI [pp. 616-632]; note especially paragraphs 2-3 [p. 616] and 87-96 [pp. 631-632]). In both instances it becomes abundantly clear that the substance of the teaching is drawn from Holy Scripture and that the particular principles whereby it is interpreted are the scriptural and confessional criteria quoted above.

3. Luther summed it up well in his *Large Catechism,* where, after clarifying the distinction between the function of the Ten Commandments and the function of the Creed he wrote:

   For the present this is enough concerning the Creed to lay a foundation for the common people without overburdening them. After they understand the substance of it, they may on their own initiative learn more, relating to *these teachings of the Catechism* [that is, regarding the *Ten Commandments* and the *Creed*] *all that they learn in the Scriptures,* and thus advance and grow

richer in understanding. For as long as we live we shall have enough to preach
and learn on the subject of faith (LC II, 67-70 [p. 420; italics added].

Thereupon Luther proceeded to follow his own advice as in his catechisms he
summarized what Scripture teaches on prayer and the sacraments and interpreted
this according to the hermeneutical principle that honors Christ by proclaiming
salvation to sinners. Thus Luther did not think of his catechisms as limiting the
substance of what Lutherans should teach, but rather as establishing and illustrating
a *principle,* one which limits the applicable interpretation of the substance of Holy
Scripture to the enhancement of faith as it lives in the tension between law and
gospel.

4. Larry Christenson, *The Christian Family* (Minneapolis: Bethany, 1970). Theodore
Jungkuntz, "The Question of the Ordination of Women," *The Cresset,* December
1978, pp. 16-20; also "Trinitarian Ethics," *Center Journal,* vol. 1, no. 2 (Spring
1982), pp. 39-52.

5. "Although much that is good comes to us from men [Luther leaves open the
possibility of God's miraculous intervention], we receive it all from God through
his command and ordinance. . . . We receive our blessings not from them [that
is, God's creatures], but from God through them. Creatures are only the hands,
channels, and means through which God bestows all blessings. . . . Therefore,
this way of receiving good through God's creatures is not to be disdained, nor are
we arrogantly to seek other ways and means than God has commanded [for example, through prayer directed to the 'saints' (LC I, 11-15, p. 366)], for that
would be not receiving our blessings from God but seeking them from ourselves"
(LC I, 26-27 [p. 368]).

6. Luther wrote:

> In this sacrament [the Lord's Supper] he offers us all the treasure he brought
> from heaven for us, to which he most graciously invites us in other places,
> as when he says in Matt. 11:28, "Come to me, all who labor and are heavy-
> laden, and I will refresh you." . . . We must never regard the sacrament as
> a harmful thing from which we should flee, but as a pure, wholesome, sooth-
> ing medicine which aids and quickens us in both soul and body. For where
> the soul is healed, the body has benefited also. . . . Here in the sacrament
> you receive from Christ's lips the forgiveness of sins, which contains and
> conveys God's grace and Spirit with all his gifts, protection, defense, and
> power against death and the devil and all evils (LC V, 66-70 [p. 454]).

7. LC III, 114-118 (pp. 435-436).

8. The Lutheran Confessions teach as follows concerning free will: "We also declare
that to a *certain extent* reason has a free will. For in those matters which can be
comprehended by reason we have a free will. . . . Hearts which are without the
Holy Spirit are without fear of God, without faith, do not trust or believe that God
will hear them, that he forgives their sin, or that he will help them in their troubles;
therefore they are *without God*" (FC SD II, 31 [p. 527]; AC XVIII, 1-7 [pp. 39-
40; italics added].

9. The Formula teaches: "But even in wicked acts and works God's foreknowledge
operates in such a way that God sets a *limit and measure* for the evil which he
does not will—how far it is to go, how long it is to endure, and when and how
he will interfere with it and punish it. For the *Lord governs everything* in such a
way that it must redound to the glory of his divine name and the salvation of his

elect, and thereby the ungodly are confounded" (FC SD XI, 6 [p. 617]; also AC XIX, 1 [pp. 40-41; italics added]).
10. FC SD II, 65 (p. 534); AC XX, 27-34 (p. 45).

Chapter 20: Sola Gratia—Grace Alone
 1. SA III, VIII, 3-13 (pp. 312-313); also LC IV, 30-31 (p. 440).
 2. Apol. IV, 66-68 (p. 116); also AC V, 1-4 (p. 31).
 3. "It is God's will to call men to eternal salvation, to draw them to himself, convert them, beget them anew, and sanctify them through this means and no other way—namely, through his holy Word (when one hears it preached or reads it) and the sacraments (when they are used according to his Word)" (FC SD II, 50 [p. 531]).
 4. Apol. XIII, 13 (pp. 212-213); also FC Epit. VII, 20 (484); FC SD VII, 124 (p. 591).
 5. It is the difference between what has been called a "theocentric-evangelical" view and one which is basically "anthropocentric-nomistic" (Regin Prenter, *Spiritus Creator,* trans. John M. Jensen [Philadelphia: Fortress, 1953], pp. 252-254).
 6. FC SD XI, 76 (pp. 628-629); also FC SD II, 90 (p. 539). This meets the important concern registered by Avery Dulles and George A. Lindbeck in their contribution, "Bishops and the Ministry of the Gospel" in *Confessing One Faith: A Joint Commentary on the Augsburg Confession by Lutheran and Catholic Theologians,* eds. George Wolfgang Forell and James F. McCue (Minneapolis: Augsburg, 1982), p. 169, n. 44.
 7. SA III, IV (p. 310).
 8. Apol. IV, 73-74 (p. 117); FC SD III, 36 (p. 545); AC IV, 1 (p. 30).
 9. FC SD III, 41 (p. 546). For the intimate relationship between grace and faith see Apol. IV, 116 (p. 123); FC SD III, 43 (p. 547). It is of interest to note that the Confessions speak much more frequently of "faith alone" than they do of "grace alone."
10. SC II, 5 (p. 345); LC II, 34-37 (p. 415).
11. FC SD IV, 20 (p. 554); see also LC III, 8-9 (p. 421):

It is, of course, self-evident that in true conversion there *must* be a change, there *must* be new activities and emotions in the intellect, will, and heart, so that the heart learns to know sin, to fear the wrath of God, to turn from sin, to understand and accept the promise of grace in Christ, to have good spiritual thoughts, Christian intentions, and diligence, and to fight against the flesh, etc. For if none of these things takes place or exists, there is no true conversion (FC SD II, 70 [pp. 534-535]; also Apol. IV, 348-355 [pp. 160-161; italics added]).

See also Luther's strong words against the "Antinomians" and his distinction between "fine Easter preachers" and "very poor Pentecost preachers" (AE 41, pp. 113-115).
12. LC I, 311-312 (p. 407); LC II, 1-4 (p. 411), 67-69 (pp. 419-420); AC VI, 1 (p. 31); Apol XII, 143-145 (pp. 204-205); FC SD VI, 1-25 (pp. 563-568).
13. FC SD VI, 4 (p. 564); AC XX, 35-39 (p. 46).
14. LC I, 311 (p. 407); FC SD VI, 17-19 (pp. 566-567).
15. See the exchange between Theodore Jungkuntz and William Lazareth on this issue in "Confession and Congregation," *The Cresset. Occasional Paper: III,* ed. David G. Truemper (Valparaiso: Valparaiso Univ., 1978), pp. 12-15, 48-59.

Chapter 21: Sola Fides—Faith Alone

1. Apol. IV, 18 (p. 109).
2. Apol. IV, 46 (p. 113).
3. Larry Christenson, *The Gift of Tongues* (Minneapolis: Bethany, 1963), p. 9.
4. "Faith justifies solely for this reason and on this account, that as a means and instrument it embraces God's grace and the merit of Christ in the promise of the Gospel" (FC SD III, 43 [p. 547]; also FC SD III, 10 [p. 541]; Apol. IV, 116 [p. 123]). "We shall now set forth from the Word of God how man is converted to God, how and by what *means* (namely, the *oral Word* and the *holy sacraments*) the Holy Spirit wills to be efficacious in us by giving and working true repentance, faith, and *new spiritual power* and ability for good in our hearts, and how we are to relate ourselves to and use these means" (FC SD II, 48 [p. 530; italics added]).
5. FC SD II, 57, 60 (pp. 532-533).
6. For example, Edmund Schlink, *Theology of the Lutheran Confessions,* trans. Paul F. Koehneke and Herbert J. A. Bouman (Philadelphia: Fortress, 1961), pp. 96-98, 108.
7. FC SD II, 88 (p. 538).
8. FC SD II, 66 (p. 534).
9. Holsten Fagerberg, *A New Look at the Lutheran Confessions (1529-1537),* trans. Gene J. Lund (St. Louis: Concordia, 1972), pp. 155-161. See also Thomas A. Droege, *Self-Realization and Faith* (Chicago: Lutheran Education Association, 1978), pp. 35-49.
10. Apol. IV, 49 (p. 114).
11. Apol. IV, 44 (p. 113).
12. Apol. IV, 48, 50 (p. 114).
13. *Ibid.*
14. Fagerberg, *New Look at Lutheran Confessions,* pp. 125-129, where he discusses Melanchthon's understanding of the "affections" (= "emotion").
15. FC SD XI, 73 (p. 628).
16. FC SD XI, 74 (p. 628).
17. AE 24, 151.
18. AE 20, 222-223.
19. W. Dennis Pederson, *A Letter Home for Family and Friends from an Itinerant Renewal Teacher and Evangelist,* unpublished report, available through International Lutheran Renewal Center, pp. 16-17.
20. AE 21, p. 299; WA 7, p. 546.
21. AE 13, pp. 110-112; WA 4, p. 149; WA 40/3, pp. 542-545.
22. For further documentation of this position in *The Book of Concord* see Apol. IV, 275-276 (p. 148); LC III, 93-98 (p. 433); LC IV, 21 (p. 439); FC SD VIII, 27 (p. 596).

Chapter 22: Sola Scriptura—Scripture Alone

1. FC SD, Rule and Norm, 3 (pp. 503-504). Some contemporary Lutheran theologians reject the notion that Scripture is the "only source" of Christian teaching, thereby opening up the possibility of agreement with a Roman Catholic understanding of tradition. Distinctions are made between that which is antiscriptural and that which is unscriptural, with only the former posing a problem. An example

of the latter, the papal office, is understood as a development by way of "trajectory" from passages of Scripture which do in fact denote a "Petrine function." See *Exploring the Faith We Share,* eds. Glenn C. Stone and Charles LaFontaine (New York: Paulist, 1980), pp. 108, 119-122, 91, 96. See also *Confessing One Faith: A Joint Commentary on the Augsburg Confession by Lutheran* and *Catholic Theologians,* eds. George Wolfgang Forell and James F. McCue (Minneapolis: Augsburg, 1982), pp. 164-167 (Dulles and Lindbeck), and p. 196, n. 24 (Meyer and Schütte).

2. *Book of Concord,* Tappert edition, Index of Biblical References, p. 641.
3. FC SD III, 41 (p. 546).
4. Of the *Augsburg Confession* as such, Melanchthon could write:

> [It] is grounded clearly on the Holy Scriptures and [its teaching] is not contrary or opposed to that of the universal Christian church, or even to the Roman church (in so far as the latter's teaching is reflected in the Fathers) (AC Summary after Art. XXI [p. 47]; see also AC Conclusion, 5 [p. 95]).

And of "Church Usages" he wrote:

> With regard to church usages that have been established by men, it is taught among us that those usages are to be observed which may be observed without sin and which contribute to peace and good order in the church, among them being certain holy days, festivals, and the like. Yet we accompany these observances with instruction so that consciences may not be burdened by the notion that such things are necessary for salvation. Moreover it is taught that all ordinances and traditions instituted by men for the purpose of propitiating God and earning grace are contrary to the Gospel and the teaching about faith in Christ. Accordingly monastic vows and other traditions concerning distinctions of foods, days, etc., by which it is intended to earn grace and make satisfaction for sin, are useless and contrary to the Gospel (AC XV, 1-4 [pp. 36-37]).

5. Apol. XV (pp. 215-222). Such a contemporary issue is the necessity of a particular governmental structure of the church. See *Confessing One Faith,* pp. 164-167 (Dulles and Lindbeck).
6. This is opposed to a type of dispensationalism that arose in 17th-century Orthodoxy, which attempted to reserve the Pentecost command to evangelize the world to the apostles. With this reserve also went, of course, the need for Pentecostal power. See the article by Andrew S. Burgess on "Missions" and by Walter Holsten on "Missionary Activity" in *The Encyclopedia of the Lutheran Church,* ed. Julius Bodensieck (Minneapolis: Augsburg, 1965). Also John Warwick Montgomery, *In Defense of Martin Luther* (Milwaukee: Northwestern, 1970), pp. 159-169. Contemporary Lutherans fall more frequently into "semidispensationalism," affirming the Pentecostal command to evangelize but rejecting the need for the fullness of Pentecostal power.
7. FC Epit., Rule and Norm, 7 (p. 465).
8. SA III, VIII, 3-13 (pp. 312-313). Also AE 4, pp. 125-127; AE 24, pp. 365-367; AE 43, pp. 198; 201-202.
9. "The Lutheran Church and the Charismatic Movement: Guidelines for Congregations and Pastors" (A Report of the Commission on Theology and Church Relations of the Lutheran Church–Missouri Synod, April 1977) in *Presence, Power, Praise—Documents on the Charismatic Renewal,* ed. Kilian McDonnell, vol.

2 (Collegeville, Minn. Liturgical Press, 1980), pp. 311-314. But note again: SA III, VIII, 11-13 (p. 313). Precisely these important words are omitted when Luther is quoted by the authors of the aforementioned document.

10. Contemporary Lutheran/Catholic dialogue is carefully seeking to investigate the possibility and limits of continuing revelation. See *Confessing One Faith,* pp. 164-167 (Dulles and Lindbeck). Luther seemed to exercise this possibility with his strong emphasis on the value of *private* confession and absolution even "without a clear foundation in the Scripture." See Holsten Fagerberg, *A New Look at the Lutheran Confessions (1529-1537),* trans. Gene J. Lund (St. Louis: Concordia, 1972), pp. 247-248.

11. Regin Prenter, *Spiritus Creator,* trans. John M. Jensen (Philadelphia: Fortress, 1953), pp. 101-107, 168.

12. *Ibid.,* pp. 107-108, 124-127, 171, 294. See also Chapter 23 of the present book, pp. 123-135, where the important role of prayer in a Lutheran theology of the Spirit is specified.

Chapter 23: Four More *Alones*

1. LC III (pp. 420-436). The page distribution in the Tappert edition is as follows: Ten Commandments—45 pages, Creed—9 1/2 pages, Lord's Prayer—16 pages, Baptism—10 1/2 pages, Lord's Supper—10 pages, Confession—4 1/2 pages.

2. LC III, 30-32 (p. 424).

3. See Luther's emphasis on "earnest prayer" in connection with Baptism in AE 53, pp. 102-103. Also, the monograph by Martin E. Lehmann, *Luther and Prayer* (Milwaukee: Northwestern, 1985).

4. LC III, 25 (p. 423).

5. "The Lutheran Church and the Charismatic Movement: Guidelines for Congregations and Pastors" (A Report of the Commission on Theology and Church Relations of the Lutheran Church–Missouri Synod, April 1977) in *Presence, Power, Praise—Documents on the Charismatic Renewal,* ed. Kilian McDonnell, vol. 2 (Collegeville, Minn.: Liturgical Press, 1980), p. 312. But note Melanchthon's suggestion that prayer has a sacramental quality about it (Apol. XIII, 167 [p. 213]).

6. LC III, 8-9 (p. 421).

7. AE 53, pp. 102-103; AE 24, pp. 382-384.

8. AE 23, p. 183.

9. FC SD II, 50-54 (pp. 530-531).

10. Apol. IV 116 (p. 123); FC SD III, 10 (p. 541); III, 43 (p. 547).

11. LC III, 49-54 (pp. 426-427).

12. But note the qualification raised on p. 110 above, in the text preceding n. 4.

13. Luther wrote:

> [The church] is the mother that begets and bears every Christian through the Word of God. . . .Where Christ is not preached, there is no Holy Spirit to create, call, and gather the Christian church, and outside it no one can come to the Lord Christ. . . . Outside the Christian church (that is; where the Gospel is not) there is no forgiveness, and hence no holiness. Therefore, all who seek to merit holiness through their works rather than through the Gospel and the forgiveness of sin have expelled and separated themselves from the church (LC II, 42, 45, 56 [pp. 416, 418]; cf. Apol. IX, 2 [p. 178]).

14. SA III, IV (p. 310).
15. Richard Quebedeaux, *The New Charismatics* (New York: Doubleday, 1976), p. 189.
16. SA II, IV, 10 (p. 300); Melanchthon was not much kinder (Treat. 41 [pp. 327-328]).
17. SA III, Signatories (p. 316).
18. LC II, 49 (p. 417).
19. LC III, 53-54 (p. 427).
20. Treatise 67 (p. 331).
21. Edmund Schlink, *Theology of the Lutheran Confessions*, trans. Paul F. Koehneke and Herbert J. A. Bouman (Philadelphia: Muhlenberg, 1961), p. 308. Melanchthon described those who fill the pastoral office as "those who preside over the churches" and they do so in that they "preach the gospel, remit sins, administer the sacraments, and, in addition, exercise jurisdiction, that is, excommunicate those who are guilty of notorious crimes and absolve those who repent" (Treatise 60 [p. 330]).
22. Apol. VII-VIII, 14, 22, 29 (pp. 170, 172-173).
23. Apol. VII-VIII, 3 (p. 169).
24. Apol. VII-VIII, 18 (p. 171).
25. The *satis est* is subjected to a challenging interpretation in Meyer and Schutte's contribution to *Confessing One Faith: A Joint Commentary on the Augsburg Confession by Lutheran and Catholic Theologians*, eds. George Wolfgang Forell and James F. McCue (Minneapolis: Augsburg, 1982), pp. 184-188.
26. During a 1983 meeting of the "Parish Renewal Council," a grouping of leaders of charismatic fellowships from mainline Protestant denominations, the idea was voiced that "we are the children of David du Plessis." More than any other single person, du Plessis had conveyed to the historic denominations the conviction that the charismatic movement was meant to remain in, and bring renewal to, the churches.
27. Treatise 38 (pp. 326-327); FC SD, Rule and Norm, 15 (pp. 506-507); FC SD III, 6 (p. 540).
28. Note, however, how both Luther and Melanchthon stressed the "necessity" of Baptism—AC II, 2 (p. 29); IX, 1-3 (p. 33); Apol. IX, 1-3 (p. 178), LC IV 6 (p. 437). Luther, however, said only that Christ binds *us* to Baptism, not that Christ has limited *himself* to it. It is willful rejection of Baptism which jeopardizes one's salvation (LC IV, 31 [p. 440]). Also, see text preceding n. 4, p. 124, above.
29. FC SD III, 9, 13 (pp. 633-634).
30. When Lutherans speak of "covenant" they sometimes distinguish between unilateral and bilateral and between covenant and testament. The point of this is merely to emphasize that a covenant between God and man has a quality that distinguishes it from covenants between mere human beings. In a covenant with God, God remains sovereign and remains Savior. Man is never an equal party with God in the covenant, but can only be "graced" by God through the covenant, even though it calls for man's response of "faith" and "obedience." See Kenneth Hagen, "From Testament to Covenant in the Early Sixteenth Century," *The Sixteenth Century Journal*, vol. 3, no. 1 (April 1977), pp. 1-24.
31. SC IV, 10 (p. 349).
32. Apol. IV, 50 (p. 114); Apol. XIII, 18-23 (pp. 213-214); LC IV, 33 (p. 440).
33. LC IV, 34, 37, 73 (pp. 440, 441, 445); see also IV, 35-36 (p. 441).

34. LC IV, 53 (p. 443).
35. LC IV, 65-79 (pp. 445-446).
36. "To put it most simply, the power, effect, benefit, fruit, and purpose of Baptism is to save. . . . To be saved, we know, is nothing else than to be delivered from sin, death, and the devil and to enter the kingdom of Christ and live with him forever" (LC IV 24-25 [p. 439]). See also Luther's important word about "Easter preachers" and "Pentecost preachers" in his treatise *On the Councils and the Church* in AE 41, pp. 113-115.
37. See pp. 127-129 above.
38. See pp. 139-141 above.
39. FC SD XI, 72 (pp. 627-628).
40. LC IV, 77-78 (p. 446); see also FC SD II, 69 (p. 534). Biblical evidence is found in passages such as Rom. 11:29; 3:3-34; 2 Tim. 2:13; 1 Chron. 17:27, also in the simple but significant fact that there was no such thing as "recircumcision" but only repentance, conversion, and return to the everlasting covenant.
41. Larry Christenson, *The Charismatic Renewal Among Lutherans* (Minneapolis: International Lutheran Renewal Center 1976; rev. ed. 1985), p. 66.
42. See Theodore Jungkuntz, *Confirmation and the Charismata* (Lanham, Md.: University Press of America, 1983), p. 7.
43. Christenson, *Charismatic Renewal Among Lutherans,* p. 54.
44. AC XXIV, 1 (p. 56); Apol. XXIV, 35 (p. 256). See the considerable output of worship materials from Lutheran congregations involved in the charismatic renewal, for example, Resurrection Lutheran Church, Charlotte, North Carolina.
45. LC II, 36 (p. 415).
46. LC II, 67 (p. 420).
47. Paul Althaus, *The Theology of Martin Luther,* trans. Robert C. Schultz (Philadelphia: Fortress, 1966), pp. 25-34, 55-63.
48. Karl Lehmann and Horst George Pöhlmann even suggest that the Augsburg Confession itself and Western theology in general inadequately relate cross and resurrection. See their essay, "God, Jesus Christ, and the Return of Christ" in *Confessing One Faith,* p. 75. See also the conflicting statements regarding "cross" and "glory" in Frederick D. Bruner and William Hordern, *The Holy Spirit—Shy Member of the Trinity* (Minneapolis: Augsburg, 1984), pp. 51, 57, 66.

Chapter 24: The Source of Faith

1. Larry Christenson, *The Gift of Tongues* (Minneapolis: Bethany, 1963), p. 16.
2. *The Bethany Parallel Commentary on the New Testament* (Minneapolis: Bethany, 1983), p. 1135.
3. Johannes Hanselmann, "Brief an die Gemeinden," by the bishop of the Evangelical-Lutheran Church in Bavaria (February 1986), p. 6. It is interesting to see a Lutheran bishop cite this understanding of faith as the basis for his pastoral perspective on the charismatic renewal; it conditions his helpful consideration of charismatic phenomena with a particular emphasis on the Spirit's initiative: "Es muss uns immer wieder erstaunen, wie ganz und gar Glaube, Heiligung und Vollendung Wirkungen und Gaben des Heiligen Geistes sind. Glaube, Kirche und Reich Gottes sind eben keine menschlichen Möglichkeiten, sondern ausschliesslich Geschenk."
4. Martin Luther, *The Small Catechism, in Contemporary English* (Minneapolis: Augsburg; Philadelphia, Fortress, 1979), p. 14.

5. Lowell Erdahl, "Viewpoint," *The Lutheran Standard,* November 18, 1983, South-eastern Minnesota District Supplement.
6. Regin Prenter, *Spiritus Creator,* trans. John M. Jensen (Philadelphia: Fortress, 1953), pp. 60-61.
7. *Ibid.,* p. 61.
8. W. Dennis Pederson (see Appendix 2, p. 377), personal testimony.
9. Bertram Lee Wolff, trans., *Reformation Writings of Martin Luther,* vol. 2 (New York: Philosophical Library, 1956), p. 288.
10. The biblical meaning of *faith* is such a far cry from the common understanding of the word that the problem merits some patient analysis. According to Webster, when people use the word *faith* in a theological context, they mean "that trust in God and his promises as made through Christ by which man is justified or saved."

    The first word to notice is *trust.* According to the dictionary this implies an *instinctive,* unquestioning belief in and reliance on something or someone. (This is distinguished from confidence, which implies conscious trust because of good reasons, definite evidence, or past experience.)

    Instinctive, of course, is linked to the noun *instinct,* which has four basic meanings: an *inborn* response pattern (sociology, biology), an *innate* impulse or inclination, a *natural* aptitude, or a *natural* intuitive power.

    According to common understanding, therefore, *trust* implies a particular disposition arising out of a natural aptitude or inclination, that is, arising from *within* the individual.

    This innate disposition called trust is grammatically related to something or someone outside itself by the prepositions *in [to]* and *on.* The image evoked by these prepositions is that trust is something that "travels" from the person trusting and comes to rest in or on the one trusted: I am here, God is out there. I "put" my trust in[to] God. The common understanding of the word *trust,* therefore, carries with it a clear subject-object relationship. Man is the subject of trust; God, the object.

    Thus, according to common understanding, faith is rooted in a natural human capacity or disposition called *trust.* This is what the average person would agree to, whether explicitly or implicitly. For that, after all, is what language is—an agreement between people that a certain kind of sound passing over the lips shall have a certain assigned meaning. And people such as Webster, who make it their business to go around and collect the votes, as it were, tell us that people have agreed that when they give voice to the word *faith* they are talking about something that finds its root *in the person* who "has" the faith.

    But the definition goes further. Faith is defined not simply in terms of the innate disposition called trust. It is a trust that *accomplishes something:* it accomplishes man's justification. Put in its simplest form, the definition would read, "Faith is that trust which justifies."

    When this definition is brought to bear on the great teaching of the Reformation—justification by faith—it leads to absurdity. (The more precise formulation of the Reformation doctrine is "justification by grace through faith," though it is also said, as in Apol. IV, 69, p. 116, that "faith justifies.") For if we say that man is justified by faith, according to common understanding we are in effect telling people, "Man is justified by a trust that justifies." But this is merely a tautology, like saying, "Dirt is removed by a detergent that removes"; it only raises the question, What kind of trust is a "justifying trust"? To which we can only answer, from the definition, "A justifying trust is one that has man for its subject and God for its object." Or, simply, a justifying trust is the trust *of* man *in* God. Thus our justification is seen to rest on something that we have by nature, something we can summon up from within ourselves. *When we speak of faith, the average person understands us to be speaking about something that should come from within ourselves.*

11. Martin Luther, *Commentary on Galatians,* ed. Philip Watson (Westwood, N.J.: Fleming H. Revell, n.d.), p. 343.
12. Martin Luther, *The Precious and Sacred Writings of Martin Luther,* ed. John Nicholas Lenker, vol. 4 (Minneapolis: Lutherans in All Lands Co., 1904), reprinted under the title "Justification by Faith" in *The Protestant Pulpit* (Nashville: Abingdon-Cokesbury, 1974), p. 15.

Chapter 25: The Effects of Faith

1. "Pastor Hermae, Visiones 1–4," *Die Vision, Erfahrungsformen und Bilderwelt,* ed. Ernst Benz (Stuttgart: Ernst Klett, 1969), p. 213.
2. Kilian McDonnell, ed., *Presence, Power, Praise—Documents on the Charismatic Renewal,* vol. 1 (Collegeville, Minn.: Liturgical Press, 1980), p. 563. See the 17 articles in vols. 1 and 2 produced by Lutheran church bodies.
3. Larry Christenson, "God Is Speaking—Are You Listening?" *International Lutheran Renewal,* no. 49 (December 1983), p. 2.
4. This stands out with special clarity in the form often given to Jesus' pronouncements. Jesus began many of his statements with the Aramaic word *Amen,* usually translated as "verily" or "truly." This word is not uncommon in the Old Testament and could be translated, "It is certain, it stands fast, it is true, it is so!" In Jewish usage and in later primitive Christian worship, it was consistently employed as a conclusion to prayer or a liturgical response. Jesus, however, used it to introduce and intensify his own words. In other words, when he said, "Amen, I say to you," Jesus was declaring beforehand the truth and authority of the words he was about to utter (cf. Mark 11:23; 10:15; Luke 18:17; Matt. 5:26; 13:17; 18:3,13,18). In John's gospel the expression, always doubled, occurs 25 times. Jesus' use of the *Amen* formula is "the only objective parallel to the prophetic formula 'Thus says the Lord.' It gives expression to his authority and power." See Joachim Jeremias, *Neutestamentliche Theologie,* Part One: Die Verkündigung Jesu (Gütersloh: Gütersloher Verlagshaus Gerd Mohn, 1971), p. 45. See also Helmut Thielicke, *I Believe: The Christian's Creed* (Philadelphia: Fortress, 1968), pp. 79-80.
5. "Spiritus sanctus non est Scepticus, nec dubia aut opiniones in cordibus nostris scripsit, sed assertiones ipsa vita et omni experientia certiores et firmiores" (WA 18, p. 605; De servo arbitrio, 1525; AE 33, p. 24).
6. Krister Stendahl, "The New Testament Evidence," in *The Charismatic Movement,* ed. Michael P. Hamilton (Grand Rapids: Eerdmans, 1975), p. 56.
7. Fredrik Brosché (see Appendix 2, p. 375), in a lecture at the International Institute on Church Renewal, St. Paul, Minnesota, August 10, 1984.
8. David Dorpat, "Hindrances to Faith," *International Lutheran Renewal,* no. 57 (August 1984), pp. 1-2.

Chapter 26: The Importance of the Biblical Worldview

1. Merton P. Strommen and others, *A Study of Generations* (Minneapolis: Augsburg, 1972), p. 111.
2. *Webster's New Collegiate Dictionary* (Springfield, Mass.: G. & C. Merriam, 1949), pp. 560, 977.
3. James Kallas, *The Satanward View* (Philadelphia: Westminster, 1966), p. 13.
4. Hans Werner Bartsch, ed., *Kerygma and Myth* (London: SPCK, 1953), p. 69.
5. Rudolf Bultmann, *Jesus Christ and Mythology* (New York: Charles Scribner's Sons, 1958), pp. 37-38, 36.
6. Some works that we have found helpful in addressing the question of the Western *Weltanschauung* are: Morton Kelsey, *Encounter with God* (Minneapolis: Bethany, 1972); C. G. Jung, *Modern Man in Search of a Soul* (New York: Harcourt Brace, 1933); Ben Johnson, "The Authority of the Bible: Its World View," *Trinity Seminary Review,* vol. 2, no. 2, pp. 6-8; Kallas, *Satanward View;* Mark D. McLean, "Toward a Pentecostal Hermeneutic," pp. 1-31, in *Toward a Pentecostal/Charismatic Theology of Baptism in the Holy Spirit* ed. J. Rodman Williams, bound volume of papers from Fourteenth Annual Meeting of the Society for Pentecostal Studies (November 15-17, 1984).
7. Johnson, "Authority of Bible: Its World View," p. 2.
8. *Ibid.*
9. *Ibid.,* p. 3.
10. *Ibid.*
11. Morton Kelsey, *Christianity and Psychology* (Minneapolis: Augsburg, 1986), p. 76.

Chapter 27: The Secular Worldview under Scrutiny

1. Morton Kelsey, *Encounter with God* (Minneapolis: Bethany, 1972), pp. 64-65.
2. *Ibid.,* pp. 62-90.
3. *Ibid.,* p. 73.
4. Garret Vanderkooi, "Evolution as a Scientific Theory," *Christianity Today,* vol. 15, no. 16 (May 7, 1971), p. 13.
5. M. Stanton Evans, ed., *National Review Bulletin* (February 25, 1972), p. 30.
6. Pierre Teilhard de Chardin, *The Vision of the Past* (New York: Harper & Row, 1966), p. 95.
7. *Ibid.,* pp. 169, 246, 142.
8. *Ibid.,* p. 130.
9. Kelsey, *Encounter with God,* pp. 95-96.
10. John Magee, *Reality and Prayer* (New York: Harper and Brothers, 1957), p. 73.
11. Rudolf Bultmann, *Jesus Christ and Mythology* (New York: Scribner's, 1958), p. 15.
12. C. G. Jung, *Modern Man in Search of a Soul* (New York: Harcourt Brace, 1933), p. 130.
13. *Ibid.,* pp. 127-128.
14. Kelsey, *Encounter with God,* pp. 63-64. It should be noted that while Plato's epistemology has a structural similarity to that of the Bible, in that it allows for the category of revelation, the *source* of revelation is altogether different from that in the Bible, where revelation is by the Word of the Lord. Further, the early

church, in its battle with gnosticism, took issue with the cosmological aspects of Neoplatonism.

15. Emil Brunner, *The Misunderstanding of the Church* (London: Lutterworth, 1952), pp. 49-53.
16. Bengt Hoffman, *Luther and the Mystics* (Minneapolis: Augsburg, 1976), p. 221.
17. Kelsey, *Encounter with God,* p. 144.
18. *Ibid.,* pp. 156-161.
19. *Ibid.,* p. 155.
20. *Ibid.,* p. 35. Kelsey, writing in 1972, made this observation in relation to Pentecostals. The same would apply to charismatics.
21. Robert J. L. Burrows, "Americans Get Religion in the New Age," *Christianity Today,* May 16, 1986, p. 17.
22. *Ibid.,* pp. 18, 23.
23. Donald G. Bloesch, *The Battle for the Trinity: The Debate over Inclusive God-Language* (Ann Arbor, Mich.: Servant, 1985), p. 12.
24. Burrows, "Americans Get Religion in New Age," p. 23.

Chapter 28: The Biblical Worldview and the Proclamation of the Gospel

1. Donald McGavran, "The Total Picture," *Christian Life,* October 1982, p. 40.
2. *Ibid.* (The statement by Kraft is inserted by the editor as a boxed item in the article by McGavran.)
3. Ben Johnson, "The Authority of the Bible: Its World View," *Trinity Seminary Review,* vol. 2, no. 2, pp. 6-8.
4. Morton Kelsey, "Spiritual Beings," unpublished paper, p. 2.

Chapter 29: The Effects of Theological Tradition on Renewal

1. Martin Luther, *The Small Catechism in Contemporary English* (Minneapolis: Augsburg; Philadelphia: Fortress, 1979), pp. 14-15.
2. Kilian McDonnell, ed., *Presence, Power, Praise—Documents on the Charismatic Renewal,* vol. 1. See, for example, "A Report on Glossolalia," pp. 58, 62; "A Statement with Regard to Speaking in Tongues," p. 111. Note, however, a measured encouragement to seek spiritual gifts in "Mühlheim Theses on Community and Charism," pp. 104, 107.
3. Williston Walker, *A History of the Christian Church* (New York: Scribner's, 1959), pp. 444-445.
4. Wayne Wood, *The Lutheran Charismatic Movement in the United States,* unpublished D.Min. dissertation (Divinity School of Vanderbilt University, 1983), p. 14.
5. George Aiken Taylor, *A Sober Faith* (New York: Macmillan, 1953), p. 67.

Chapter 30: The Nature of God and the Nature of Man

1. Johannes Hanselmann, "Brief an die Gemeinden," by the Landesbischof of the Evangelical-Lutheran Church in Bavaria (February 1986), p. 5.
2. Johannes Hanselmann, commentary on his "Brief an die Gemeinden," in private correspondence with Larry Christenson.
3. Essays from this consultation are published in *The Holy Spirit in the Life of the Church,* ed. Paul Opsahl (Minneapolis: Augsburg, 1978).

4. Warren Quanbeck, in discussion at one of the sessions of the dialog referred to in the previous note. From notes by Larry Christenson.

Chapter 31: Justification and Sanctification

1. See, for example, Eric Gritsch, "Lutheranism and Born Againism," *Academy,* vol. 40, nos. 1 & 2 (1984), p. 25; and the response by Theodore Jungkuntz, "The Charismatic Renewal in Light of the Reformation," vol. 40, nos. 3 & 4 (1984), pp. 110-121. The relationship between justification and sanctification was taken up during an extended floor discussion at a National Lutheran Charismatic Leaders' Conference in Ann Arbor, Michigan, in 1972. One of the participants shared his personal testimony of being baptized in the Holy Spirit. Asked to comment on the testimony theologically, one of the speakers at the conference, Lutheran theologian William Lazareth, said, "I would call that a dramatic instance of sanctification." This has been the basic framework in which Lutheran charismatics have dealt with charismatic experience—as an aspect of sanctification.
2. Regin Prenter, *Spiritus Creator,* trans. John M. Jensen (Philadelphia: Fortress, 1953), p. 95.
3. Martin Luther, *Preface to Romans,* 1522 (AE 35, 370-371; WADB 7, 9ff.) Spener cited the place in Luther's Preface that begins with the words, "Faith is not a human delusion or dream, as some think it is. . ." in *Pia Desideria,* rev. ed., ed. Erich Beyreuther (Giessen/Basel: Brunnen, 1975), p. 38. See also Lorenz Hein, "Philipp Jacob Spener, ein Theologe des Heiligen Geistes und Prophet der Kirche," *Festgabe für Peter Meinhold,* ed. Lorenz Hein (Wiesbaden: Franz Steiner, 1977), pp. 103-126. Also Karlfried Froelich, "Charismatic Manifestations and the Lutheran Incarnational Stance," *The Holy Spirit in the Life of the Church,* ed. Paul Opsahl (Minneapolis: Augsburg, 1978), pp. 136-157.
4. Carter Lindberg, *The Third Reformation?—Charismatic Movements and the Lutheran Tradition* (Macon, Ga.: Mercer Univ., 1983), pp. 96, 97, 102.
5. *Ibid.,* p. 79.
6. *Ibid.,* p. 115.
7. Larry Christenson, *Back to Square One* (Minneapolis: Bethany, 1979), pp. 88-89.
8. Philip Gehlhar, "Are Charismatic Lutherans Confused in Their Understanding of Salvation by Grace through Faith?" Summary of a Survey of Lutheran Congregations with Charismatic Pastors. Available from St. Luke's Lutheran Church, Westminster, California. The report states, in part:

In 1972 Augsburg Publishing House published Merton Strommen's *A Study of Generations,* a report on a two-year study of 5000 Lutherans and their beliefs and attitudes.

The most shocking part of the study was the revelation that the Lutherans, whose denomination prides itself in its clear distinction between law and gospel and emphasis on justification by grace through faith as its central teaching, were more oriented toward law than gospel, more toward works than toward grace. In spite of the church's continued emphasis on true teaching of salvation through grace the study found a "law-oriented misbelief system."

[In our study] we selected 15 questions from *A Study of Generations.* Nine of these related to the concept of law and gospel or justification by faith. We added to that list a question as to whether the respondent was confirmed as a Lutheran and two other questions. One of these questions asked, "Have you personally received the gift of tongues?'' The other was, "The gifts of the Spirit like prophecy, healing, and tongues are for today (Yes/No)?''

The first of these two questions was meant to determine to what extent the respondent had entered into a charismatic experience. While we realize that many consider themselves charismatic even though they have not received the gift of tongues specifically, we asked this question because it gives a clear indication of information we seek, and because we have found that the non-charismatic usually bases his discernment of a charismatic on whether or not a person uses the gift of tongues. The second question was to determine the extent of the openness towards the gifts of the Spirit. So when the results were tabulated, there were three categories, the charismatic, the ones open to charismatic gifts, and the anticharismatic who did not believe the gifts were for today or who doubted their validity.

The surveys were taken in six Lutheran congregations in various parts of the United States in 1979.

The analysis of the survey was to determine three major items:

1. Is there a difference in belief or attitude in the areas of law and gospel or justification by faith among Lutherans who have had a charismatic experience? If so, is that difference positive, negative, and to what degree?

2. Does the charismatic experience of the pastor help him to communicate the gospel message to his people, even to those who do not personally participate in the charismatic gifts?

3. When a person is closed or unbelieving in the presence of the charismatic gifts, does that rejection influence his attitude or belief in the areas of justification by faith? Is he *more* or is he *less* receptive to the gospel?

The results of the survey were rather startling:

1. Charismatic Lutherans are much more conservative in their approach to the Scripture and Christian doctrine than their non- or anticharismatic counterparts.

2. Charismatic Lutherans hold a sharper distinction between law and gospel, and a stronger belief in salvation by grace than other Lutherans. The extent of this difference is especially noteworthy (between 30 and 40 percent difference).

3. There are some Lutherans in churches with a charismatic pastor who reject or doubt the validity of the "charismatic gifts." These persons show only a slight improvement in understanding of salvation by grace by comparison with the "average" Lutherans who responded to the Strommen study.

The results of this survey should lay to rest the concerns of Lutheran leaders that a participation in a charismatic experience would lead to a loss of the pure gospel of salvation by grace. Rather it clarifies the believer's understanding of salvation and strengthens his faith.

These figures also point to a resistance to the gifts of the Spirit as a resistance to the gospel itself.

9. Christenson, *Back to Square One,* pp. 89-91.
10. See, for example, the tendency to see Pentecostal/charismatic teaching on the infilling of the Holy Spirit as compromising Christ's sufficiency in regard to justification/regeneration/ conversion in such writers as Frederick D. Bruner, *A Theology of the Holy Spirit* (Grand Rapids: Eerdmans, 1971), pp. 261-284; James D.

G. Dunn, *Baptism in the Holy Spirit* (Philadelphia: Westminster, 1970), p. 95; Richard A. Jensen, *Touched by the Spirit* (Minneapolis: Augsburg, 1975), pp. 61-62; Lindberg, *The Third Reformation?* pp. 260-263. Lindberg states categorically that "A reading of Larry Christenson's major writings nowhere reveals a discussion of the theological motif of justification" (p. 235), but he ignores two of Christenson's books in which the theme of justification is dealt with several times: *The Renewed Mind* (Minneapolis: Bethany, 1974) and *Back to Square One* (Minneapolis: Bethany, 1979). See pp. 186-188, in the present book.
11. Lindberg, *The Third Reformation?* p. 306.
12. Statement by an official of the Lutheran Church–Missouri Synod in private conversation with Larry Christenson.
13. Delbert Rossin, in a message given at the Southern California Lutheran Conference on the Holy Spirit, 1980. Here Rossin uses the term *salvation* according to its commonly understood meaning of obtaining forgiveness and the promise of heaven, which is narrower, of course, than we often find in Luther; for example, see SC VI, 6, p. 352; see also Prenter, *Spiritus Creator*, p. 244. In any case, there is much that God has given in Christ (1 Cor. 3:21-23) that believers do not regularly appropriate.

Chapter 32: The Theology of the Cross

1. Regin Prenter, *Spiritus Creator*, trans. John M. Jensen (Philadelphia: Fortress, 1953), p. 111.
2. AE 31, 53. See also Theodore Jungkuntz, "Secularization Theology, Charismatic Renewal, and Luther's Theology of the Cross," *Concordia Theological Monthly*, vol. 62, no. 11 (January 1971), pp. 5-24.
3. Discussion at a meeting of men involved in monthly prayer ministry service at Trinity Lutheran Church, San Pedro, California, in the late 1970s. Reported by Larry Christenson.
4. William Hordern, *The Holy Spirit—Shy Member of the Trinity* (Minneapolis: Augsburg, 1984), pp. 66-70.
5. Merton P. Strommen and others, *A Study of Generations* (Minneapolis: Augsburg, 1972), pp. 125-129. This study presents an interesting example of the common tendency to link a theology of the cross or a theology of glory with certain kinds of outward actions, rather than with a concrete response to the Holy Spirit in a given situation. The authors attempted to determine how widely their study group lived a "gospel-oriented life" by presenting them with hypothetical problems and asking them to choose between alternative solutions that were pegged by the researchers as "democratic," "humanistic," "authoritarian," and "gospel." Living under the cross cannot be reduced to living by a principle, not even a "gospel principle." It can only be done in the Holy Spirit. If the Spirit calls for a "democratic" or an "authoritarian" response in a given situation, then that precisely describes a theology of the cross, a gospel-oriented life, in that situation.
6. AE 54, 476.
7. Bob Mumford, "Singing in the Rain," Tape MR 144 (Mobile, Ala.: Recommended Tapes, 1984).
8. AE 41, 113-115.
9. An International Lutheran Charismatic Renewal Leaders' Conference was held near Helsinki, Finland, in the summer of 1981 (see the Introduction to this book).

The Lutheran archbishop of Finland, Mikko Juva, together with Carl Mau, executive secretary of the Lutheran World Federation, visited the conference one
evening. During a coffee hour following, the need for a responsible theological
and pastoral perspective on charismatic renewal in the Lutheran church was discussed at some length. Out of this conference a planning committee was formed
to put together the International Lutheran Charismatic Theological Consultation
that is responsible for the present book.
10. Paul Anderson, "The Nature of Grace," *Loaves and Fishes,* no. 153 (San Pedro,
California: Trinity Lutheran Church, April/May 1982), p. 3. Cf. LC, 68-69 (pp.
1-3, 420).

Chapter 33: The Kingdom and the Church

1. John Bright, *The Kingdom of God* (Nashville: Abingdon, 1953), p. 217.
2. *Ibid.,* p. 236.
3. Bob Mumford, "Focus on the Throne," Tape TM 70 (Mobile, Ala.: New Wine
Tape of the Month, August 1983).
4. Arnold Bittlinger, *Erneuerung in Kirche und Gesellschaft,* no. 7 (1980), p. 25.
(This excerpt translated by William Sims.) Bittlinger cites comments of Philip
Potter on the relationship between the World Council of Churches and the charismatic renewal, in a consultation held March 8-13, 1980, in Geneva.

Chapter 34: Baptism

1. AE 34, 337.
2. Larry Christenson, *The Charismatic Renewal Among Lutherans* (Minneapolis: International Lutheran Renewal Center, 1976; rev. ed. 1985), p. 57.
3. *Ibid.,* p. 61.
4. *Ibid.,* p. 62.
5. Paul Anderson, "Baptism," unpublished paper presented to the faculty of Luther
Theological Seminary, St. Paul, Minnesota, 1972. See also Christenson, *Charismatic Renewal Among Lutherans,* pp. 61-62.
6. See, for example, note 1 to Chapter 15, above; also *Gudstjänstordning för Svenska
Kyrkan* (1982), p. 12, where it is suggested that the pastor, and, if possible,
relatives and assistants, lay their hands on the child's head and pray silently, after
which the pastor says, "God of life, fill [name of child] with your Spirit."
7. Reported by Pastor Herbert Mirly (see Appendix 2, p. 377).
8. "Order of Confirmation," *Service Book and Hymnal* (Minneapolis: Augsburg,
1958), p. 246. See also Theodore Jungkuntz, *Confirmation and the Charismata*
(Lanham, Md.: University Press of America, 1983).

Chapter 35: God's Fatherly Provision

1. Albrecht Fürst Castell, in private conversation with Larry Christenson.
2. Mark D. McLean, "Toward a Pentecostal Hermeneutic," pp. 24-27, in *Toward a
Pentecostal/Charismatic Theology of Baptism in the Holy Spirit,* ed. J. Rodman
Williams, bound volume of papers from Fourteenth Annual Meeting of the Society
for Pentecostal Studies (November 15-17, 1984). McLean argues that "the uni-
vocal use of the words 'speak' and 'act' imputed to scripture by biblical interpreters,

from orthodox to neo-liberal, in the vast majority of the cases is a violation of the text." He contends that biblical phrases such as "God spoke" cannot be univocally interpreted to mean that God spoke in an audible voice. His point is that the Spirit's mode of "speaking" in the Bible is essentially the same as people experience today. So also Luther: see the emphasis he gives to Shem as God's "voice" (AE 12, 231, 249-250, 358).

3. WABr 11, no. 4120, pp. 111-112.
4. WA 9, 98. Luther: the true theology "est sapientia experimentalis et non doctrinalis" (Randbemerkungen zu Tauler, 1516).
5. Wayne Wood, *The Lutheran Charismatic Movement in the United States,* unpublished D.Min. dissertation (Divinity School of Vanderbilt University, 1983), p. 2.
6. Williston Walker, *A History of the Christian Church* (New York: Scribner's, 1959), p. 445.
7. Reported by Larry Christenson in a letter to the constituency of the International Lutheran Renewal Center, November 27, 1985.
8. Peter Meinhold, *Geschichte der kirchlichen Historiographie,* vol. 1 (Freiburg/ Munich: Karl Alber, 1967), p. 212.

Chapter 36: Truth and Authority

1. Philip Jacob Spener, *Pia Desideria,* ed. Theodore G. Tappert (Philadelphia: Fortress, 1964), p. 87.
2. Marie E. Richard, *Philipp Jakob Spener and His Work: Augustus Hermann Francke and His Work* (Philadelphia: Lutheran Publication Society, 1897), pp. 108-109.
3. Larry Christenson, *Back to Square One* (Minneapolis: Bethany, 1979), p. 73.
4. Kilian McDonnell, ed., *Presence, Power, Praise—Documents on the Charismatic Renewal,* vol. 2 (Collegeville, Minn.: Liturgical Press, 1980), p. 269.
5. *Ibid.,* p. 138.
6. Ralph Martin, talk given at the 1980 Notre Dame National Charismatic Conference.
7. Ole Skjerbaek Madsen, "The Authority of Scripture," *Ånd og Liv* (December 1982), pp. 5-6.
8. Larry Christenson, personal correspondence with John MacArthur, November 15, 1979, in regard to MacArthur's article in *Moody Monthly* (November 1979), p. 38.
9. Bertil Gärtner, Lutheran bishop of Gothenburg, Sweden, in a workshop of *Acts 86,* an all-European ecumenical charismatic conference held in Birmingham, England, July 23-27, 1986.
10. In ecumenical settings this may be muted in favor of an emphasis on the authority of Scripture, a position held in common with Protestants, and Protestants may erroneously conclude that Catholics change their views on the place of tradition when they become charismatic. Kevin Ranaghan, then chairman of the National Service Committee of the Catholic Charismatic Renewal in the United States, speaking to an annual seminar of charismatic leaders in St. Louis, Missouri, in May of 1982, pointed out that Catholic teaching on the place of tradition is accepted as normative by Catholic charismatics.
11. In an ecumenical discussion group in May 1977 in Jerusalem, Derek Prince noted that the kind of solutions to ecclesiological questions that the Catholic Church had come to as it faced certain problems were very similar to the kind of solutions that he and those associated with him (Don Basham, Ern Baxter, Bob Mumford,

Charles Simpson) were coming to in present circumstances, and this gave him a fresh appreciation for the place of Christian tradition.

12. In a charismatic leaders' seminar in May of 1982, Jon Braun, a bishop in the Evangelical Orthodox Church, offered the opinion that tradition, which he defined as the consensus of the church through the ages, was the necessary counterpoise to any current theology. "Without it," he said, "you simply turn the church over to the exegetes of each generation."

13. John Poole, "How Shepherds Relate in a Local Body," Cassette KC 106 (Mobile, Ala.: Christian Growth Ministries, 1975).

14. Larry Christenson, "That the World May Know," Cassette KC 110 (Mobile, Ala.: Christian Growth Ministries, 1975).

Chapter 37: Confirming the Word

1. Peter Meinhold, *Studien zu Ignatius von Antiochien* (Wiesbaden: Franz Steiner, 1979), p. 9. See the letters of Ignatius of Antioch: Polycarp 2, 2; Philadelphians 7, 1; Trallians 4, 1; Ephesians 20, 1.

2. Ignatius, Letter to the Ephesians 20, 2.

3. Ernst Benz, *Die Vision, Erfahrungsformen und Bilderwelt* (Stuttgart: Ernst Klett, 1969), p. 420, n. 8. See also "Sokrates," Historia Ecclesiastica VIII, Migne *PG* 67, 692.

4. Ignatius, Letter to the Romans 4, 1.

5. Hans Von Campenhausen, *Ecclesiastical Authority and Spiritual Power in the Church of the First Three Centuries,* trans J. A. Baker (Stanford: Stanford Univ., 1969), p. 178.

6. Donald A. McGavran, "The Total Picture," *Christian Life,* October 1982, pp. 39-40. See this entire issue, in which the course, "Signs and Wonders and Church Growth" at Fuller Seminary, Pasadena, California, is covered in depth from biblical, historical, theological, and practical perspectives.

7. Helge Fosseus (see Appendix 2, p. 376) supplied this story from his experience as a missionary bishop in southern Africa.

8. Ernest Hemingway, *For Whom the Bell Tolls* (New York: Scribner's, 1940, 1968), p. 15.

9. Karlfried Froehlich, "Charismatic Manifestations and the Lutheran Incarnational Stance," *The Holy Spirit in the Life of the Church,* ed. Paul Opsahl (Minneapolis: Augsburg, 1978), pp. 141, 149-150.

Chapter 38: The Power of the Indwelling Christ

1. Kilian McDonnell, in open forum at theological conference in Rome, May 19, 1975.

2. Harold D. Hunter, *Spirit-Baptism, A Pentecostal Alternative* (Lanham, Md.: University Press of America, 1983), p. 193. See also the author's rationale for "charismatic work of the Spirit" as a helpful technical term, p. 29.

3. See "The Holy Spirit in the Charismatic Life and Renewal of the Church Today in Evangelization Report," *Let the Earth Hear His Voice,* International Congress on World Evangelization at Lausanne, Official Reference Volume, ed. J. D. Douglas (Minneapolis: World Wide Publications, 1975), pp. 1150-1153. See also doctoral dissertation of Tormod Engelsviken (see Appendix 2, pp. 375-376); also

Kilian McDonnell, ed., "Theological and Pastoral Orientations on the Catholic Charismatic Renewal: Malines Document I" in *Presence, Power, Praise—Documents on the Charismatic Renewal,* vol. 3 (Collegeville, Minn.: Liturgical Press, 1980), pp. 13-69; also Larry Christenson, *The Charismatic Renewal Among Lutherans* (Minneapolis: International Lutheran Renewal Center, 1976; rev. ed. 1985).

4. The following summary is supplied to amplify some of the historical antecedents in Lutheranism that relate to the present theological inquiry:

Negative experiences with the left wing of the Reformation, especially with Thomas Müntzer and his Anabaptist "Kingdom of Zion," which ended with the Münster revolution on June 25, 1535, were a shock to Lutheranism that has lasted to the present day. These experiences fostered a view of spiritual awakenings as a threat to the church.

From the time of Luther down to the present, the epithet *Schwärmer* ("spiritualist," "enthusiast," "fanatic") has been hurled more or less indiscriminately at any who may lay claim to spiritual experience. Even though this name-calling is a perverse caricature of Luther's position, it has had a chilling effect on renewal movements among Lutherans.

While that shock has remained a decisive factor in the history of Lutheranism, it has never been quite forgotten that the reformer himself had his own perceptions of the spiritual dimension of the church sharpened through the insights of the mystic Johann Tauler. Among Luther's followers, Andreas Osiander, known as the reformer of Nuremberg, later active in East Prussia, warned strongly against separating justification and sanctification. The new birth and sanctification are central themes of his theology. His theology of "essential" justification, while bordering on a confusion of law and gospel, stresses the harmony of sound doctrine and living faith. ["Est itaque huius mediatoris officium, ut nobis deum propitium reddat, nos autem iustificet, ut deo oboedientes et bene placentes in iustitia et sanctitate vera omnino simis irreprehensibiles" (Osiander, *De unico mediatore Jesu Christo et iustificatione fidei, 1551*). Cf. Lorenz Hein, "Francesco Stancaro," *Kyrios VII* (1967), p. 144.] Nominal Christianity was deeply troubling to him. He could speak of spiritual gifts and go along with Luther in saying that the fruits of genuine faith have nothing to do with works-righteousness.

Johann Arndt (1555–1621) sought to bring the deepest insights of medieval mysticism into harmony with Lutheran confessional writings. Arndt was from Saxony, and after 1611 was, from his position in Celle, general superintendent of the Lutheran church in the principality of Lüneburg. His activity released the first great wave of revival in the area of Celle-Hermannsburg. [Walter Nigg, *Heimliche Weisheit: Mystiker des 16. bis 19. Jahrhunderts* (Olten and Freiburg im Breisgau: Walter, 1975), p. 127.] Arndt's "Four [later, Six] Books of True Christianity" have been universally effective devotional materials through the centuries, especially in North America. [Book 1: 1606; Four Books, 1610.]

With a great variety of expression, Arndt taught that the Christian participates in a supernatural life that is worked in him by the risen Christ. Arndt was a biblical scholar, but he preferred to use symbolical and allegorical interpretations of the Scripture to shed light on his spiritual experiences. "Everything," he emphasized, "depends on the rebirth and renewal of an individual." [*Vier Bücher vom wahren Christentum,* I, 6, ed. Baensch, p. 23.] What the Bible teaches outwardly "must happen in people spiritually, by faith. In spirit and in faith I must feel the reality of which the Scriptures speak." [*Ibid.*] With the help of his spiritual understanding of the Scriptures, he was able to bring the Bible to life. In the tradition of the great mystics, Arndt proclaimed: "As Christ was bodily conceived and born of Mary by her faith through the Holy Spirit, so must He be conceived and born in me and in me grow and increase." [*Ibid.*, p. 24] Thus understood, earnest discipleship does not cramp one's life, but rather expresses the indwelling life of Christ.

In the depths of his heart, Arndt himself had tasted and felt a real communion with the heavenly world. He was concerned with bringing people to awareness of their souls as the centers of their beings, so that they might give themselves over to the Physician of all physicians for total healing. Angrily Arndt cried out: "Oh, who today takes his soul in earnest!" [*Ibid.*, p. 135, n. 92.] Arndt had no time for "churchly dilettantism" in a Christendom embattled by the world and sin. [*Ibid.*, p. 138.] "Bring Christ's teaching into life!" became his watchword.

Arndt and his friends also exercised spiritual gifts. He laid special emphasis on the charism of prayer. Prayer is a suprarational work and no mere human activity In some mysterious way, one who prays participates in shaping events in the world. He described prayer in tongues as a "prayer of feeling," a prayer that makes it possible, in a way no mere words can, to express the thanks due the Creator and Redeemer. [*Ibid.*] For Arndt, "internal" Christianity was not in opposition to the external church, but rather the prerequisite for its being what its Founder intended, the salt of the earth (Matt. 5:13).

Philip Jacob Spener (1635–1705), the "father of Pietism," was deeply impressed as a youth by a devotional volume, written by the Scottish preacher Lewis Bayly and entitled *Practice of Piety*, which appeared in its 23rd edition in 1636.

Besides this, Luther's writings, above all, had aroused Spener's interest. Spener's goal was a spiritually renewed Lutheranism. In 1675 he published a collection of Arndt's sermons, the so-called "Arndsche Postille" [*Geistliche Erklärung der evangelischen Texte durchs ganze Jahr . . .*, 1615. Frequently reprinted.] Spener added a prolog to the publication, which soon appeared separately under the title *Pia Desideria* (A Longing for Piety). It became a type of blueprint for Pietism, calling for spiritual renewal in the church.

Spener and then Augustus Hermann Francke (1663-1727), who subsequently became chief spokesman for Pietism, created a tidal wave of influence in their day—an influence which is still being felt in the Lutheran church. They both desired to be orthodox Lutherans who, however, placed strong emphasis on the doctrine of sanctification. One prominent Lutheran historian believes they were the inspiration for John Wesley's major emphasis on sanctification, which would put them in the line of influence that helped shape the Pentecostal and charismatic movements. [Philip Jacob Spener, *Pia Desideria*, ed. Theodore G. Tappert (Philadelphia: Fortress, 1964), p. 24.]

As chief pastor in Frankfurt am Main, court preacher in Saxony, and prior in Berlin, Spener served the cause of renewal in the Lutheran church and exerted great influence far beyond Germany's borders. In *Pia Desideria* he stressed that pastors, first of all, must experience spiritual renewal. [*Pia Desideria oder herzliches Verlangen nach gottgefälliger Besserung der wahren Evangelischen Kirchen . . .," 1676.*] He saw that the temporal order was weak because political ambition had eclipsed interest in the church. He respected the scholarly pursuits of theologians as long as true faith, in Luther's sense of being a gift of the Holy Spirit, was not neglected. [See note 3, Chapter 31, above.]

Spener and Francke emphasized that ministers need to be practical and pious in their everyday life. "Study without piety is worthless," Spener wrote. [*Pia Desideria,* pp. 103-105.] He placed the blame for the ungodly German Lutheran minister, "who grows in learning and declines in morals," squarely at the feet of the seminary professors, who should make their schools "workshops of the Holy Spirit rather than places of . . . ambition, tippling, carousing, and brawling." [*Ibid.,* p. 112.] All seminarians should be professionally guided into the devotional life "because theology is practical discipline and does not consist only of knowledge and study . . . the mere accumulation and imparting of information." Students should be guided into the right professional books [Augustus Hermann Francke, *Of Useful Preaching: A Guide to the Reading and Study of the Holy Scriptures* (Philadelphia: David Hogan, 1823), pp. 112ff.] and into a revolutionary seminar on practical spiritual growth with a peer influence model. [Spener, *Pia Desideria,* p. 113]

Spiritual parallels between the charismatic renewal and Pietism are to some extent universal; one could cite similar parallels with other renewal movements in the history of the church. However, there are also historical links between the two movements. The influence of Lutheran Pietism moved beyond Lutheranism through the Moravian missionary movement. The leader of the Moravian movement, Count von Zinzendorf, was a graduate of the Pietist seminary in Halle. The Moravians had a profound influence on John and Charles Wesley. The Methodist revival of John Wesley and the Holiness Movement which grew out of it in America were the predecessors of the modern-day Pentecostal and charismatic movements. [Vinson Synan, *The Holiness-Pentecostal Movement in the United States* (Grand Rapids: Eerdmans, 1971), pp. 217-223.]

In this entire line of development, the issue of personal religious experience and spiritual growth is written large. John Wesley's heart was "strangely warmed" as Luther's *Preface to Romans* was being read at a meeting in Aldersgate in 1738. Wesley came to believe, however, that Luther stopped short of considering the believer's new life. "Who wrote more ably than Martin Luther on justification by faith alone? And who was more ignorant of the doctrine of sanctification, or most confused in his conception of it." [*The Works of John Wesley,* vol. 7 (Grand Rapids: Zondervan, n.d., reprint of London: 1872 edition), p. 204. A more recent echo of this charge comes from a Lutheran charismatic leader who claims that Lutherans have too often missed the message of the regenerating power of the Holy Spirit by reading the Bible through Lutheran eyeglasses: Hans-Jacob Frøen, "What is Baptism in the Holy Spirit?" in *Jesus, Where Are You Taking Us?* ed. Norris Wogen (Carol Stream, Ill.: Creation House, 1973). Cf. also George M. Marsden, *Fundamentalism and American Culture* (Oxford: Oxford Univ., 1980), pp. 73ff.]

Wesley proclaimed and longed for the fullness of Christian experience, of entire sanctification and the indwelling of the Holy Spirit. For Wesley, Christian perfection is directly linked to Pentecostal reality. Thus the twofold sequence of salvation history—resurrection and the sending of the Spirit—is also a paradigm for the individual believer's personal experience of salvation.

5. Larry Christenson, *What About Baptism?* (Minneapolis: Augsburg, 1986), pp. 19-20.

6. Note Jaroslav Pelikan's maxim as quoted by Richard John Neuhaus in *The Religion and Society Report,* vol. 3, no. 4 (April 1986), p. 1: "Tradition is the living faith of the dead, traditionalism is the dead faith of the living."

Chapter 39: Holiness

1. Gregory the Great (504-604), Dialog 2, c. 35. See Ernst Benz, ed., *Die Vision, Erfahrungsformen und Bilderwelt* (Stuttgart: Ernst Klett, 1969), p. 504, n. 1.
2. Offhand remark on Tauler (WA 9, 98). Luther worked through the basic elements of Tauler's mysticism when he edited *Theologia Germanica* in 1516 and a second edition in 1518 (WA 1). See Bengt Hoffman, *Luther and the Mystics* (Minneapolis: Augsburg, 1976), pp. 93-94.
3. WA 9, 98ff. Luther, marginal notes to Tauler, 1516: "theologie autem propria de spirituali nativitate verbi incarnati; habet 'unum necessarium' et 'optimam partem.' " Also, "theologia mystica est sapientia experimentalis et non doctrinalis."
4. Cf. Luther's sermon on John 9 from 1518 (WA 1, 267-273). See also Ernst Wilhelm Kohls, *Luther oder Erasmus* (Basel: Friedrich Reichardt, 1972), p. 88.
5. See Adolf Köberle, *The Quest for Holiness* (Minneapolis: Augsburg, 1938), pp. 84-136.

Chapter 40: Training in Discipleship

1. See Stephen Clark, *Unordained Elders and Renewal Communities* (New York: Paulist, 1976), chap. 5.

Chapter 41: Manifesting Spiritual Gifts

1. "The Charismatic Movement and Lutheran Theology" (A Report of the Commission on Theology and Church Relations of the Lutheran Church–Missouri Synod, January 1972) in *Presence, Power, Praise—Documents on the Charismatic Renewal,* ed. Kilian McDonnell, vol. 1 (Collegeville, Minn.: Liturgical Press, 1980), pp. 345-347.
2. Morton Kelsey, *Encounter with God* (Minneapolis: Bethany, 1972), pp. 30, 247 (n. 3). See also Martin Luther, *Luthers Evangelien-Auslegung, ein Kommentar zu den vier Evangelien,* ed. Chr. G. Eberle (Stuttgart: Verlag der Evangelischen Bücherstiftung, 1877), p. 1308. In commenting on Mark 16:17-18, Luther allows that the signs mentioned here may be done by any Christian: "Wenn ein Christenmensch ist, der den Glauben hat, der soll Gewalt haben, diese nachfolgende Zeichen (und nicht diese allein) zu thun, und sollen ihm folgen, wie Christus Joh. 14, 12, vgl. Matth. 10, 8. Ps. 91, 13. sagt; denn ein Christenmensch hat gleiche Gewalt mit Christo, ist eine Gemeinde und sitzt mit Ihm in gesamten Lehen. Wenn ich glaubig bin, so kann ichs thun und steht in meiner Gewalt; denn der Glaube gibt mir so viel, dass mir nichts unmöglich ist, *wenn es vonnöthen ist*" [italics added]. With this last phrase Luther slipped into a dispensational stance, effectively limiting expectation of supernatural signs; thus he went on to say, "Sintemal aber das Evangelium nun ausgebreitet ist, ist es nicht vonnöthen, Zeichen zu thun wie zu der Apostel Zeiten." However, his respect for the plain sense of Scripture returned in his closing paragraph, despite a dispensational tag: "Wenn es aber die Noth erfordern würde, und sie das Evangelium ängsten und drängen wollten, so

müssten wir wahrlich dran und müssten auch Zeichen thun, ehe wir das Evangelium uns liessen schmäen und unterdrücken. Aber ich hoffe, es werde nicht vonnöthen sein." See also John Calvin, *Commentary on the Epistle of Paul the Apostle to the Romans,* trans. and ed. John Owen (Grand Rapids: Eerdmans, 1955), p. 460. In commenting on the list of *charismata* in Romans 12, Calvin made a distinction between the "miraculous graces by which Christ *at first* rendered illustrious his gospel" and the "ordinary gifts, such as were to *continue perpetually in the Church*" [italics added].

3. The dispensationalist argument is challenged by Theodore Jungkuntz with a theology of the cross in the review of a book by Douglas Judisch. See "The Canon, the Charismata, and the Cross: An Evaluation of Claims to Charismatic Gifts," *The Cresset,* vol. 42, no. 91 (September, 1978), pp. 25-29.
4. Justin Martyr, Dialogus cum Tryphone Judaeo, c. 88 (Migne SG 6, 685).
5. Irenaeus, Adv. haereses V, 6, 1 (Migne SG 7, 1137).
6. Origen, Contra Celsum I, 46; VII, 8 (Migne SG 11, 745; 1432).
7. Epiphanius, Haereses 48, 13, 1.
8. Bernd Moeller, *Geschichte des Christentums* (Göttingen: Vandenhoeck & Ruprecht, 1965), p. 59.
9. Cf. G. Ruhbach, "Das Charisma-Verständnis des Neuen Testaments," *Monatsschrift für Pastoraltheologie* (October 1964), p. 409. See also Kilian McDonnell, *The Baptism with the Holy Spirit as an Ecumenical Problem* (Notre Dame, Ind.: Charismatic Renewal Services, 1972), p. 44.
10. *Ibid.* (McDonnell).
11. Cf. *Reallexikon für Antike u. Christentum,* XI, ed. Th. Klauser XI (see n. 9), pp. 386-441.
12. H. Bacht, "Antonius und Pachomius: Von der Anachorese zum Conobitentum," *Studia Anselmiana, 38* (Rome: Athenäum, 1956), p. 66.
13. One of the desert fathers, Apa Matthew, healed a girl by commanding an evil spirit to leave her. The spirit complained because it was tormented by the command. Apa Matthew's healing power was known throughout the region. Cf. W. C. Till, *Koptische Heiligen und Martyrerlegenden II* (Rome: Orientalia Christiana Analecta, 1935-36), pp. 13-14. See also *Historia Monachorum in Aegypto [Mönche im frühchristlichen Aegypten],* trans. Suso Frank OFM (Düsseldorf: Patmos, 1967), pp. 54-58 (Abbas Or), 88-91 (Patermuthius), 104 (Johannes).
14. Constitutiones Apostolorum VIII, 1.
15. *Ibid.*
16. *Ibid.*
17. Reinhold Seeberg, *Lehrbuch der Dogmengeschichte,* vol. 1, no. 4 (Basel: Benno Schwabe & Co. Verlag), p. 329, n. 28.

Chapter 42: The Gift of Prophecy

1. Gesenius, *Hebrew and Chaldee Lexicon of the Old Testament Scriptures,* trans. Samuel P. Tregelles (Grand Rapids: Eerdmans, 1954), p. 528.
2. Larry Christenson, *The Charismatic Renewal Among Lutherans* (Minneapolis: International Lutheran Renewal Center, 1976; rev. ed. 1985), pp. 107-111.
3. Joachim Jeremias, *Neutestamentliche Theologie. Part One: Die Verkündigung Jesu* (Gütersloh: Gütersloher Verlagshaus Gerd Mohn, 2nd ed., 1973), p. 82.

4. Eduard Schweizer, article on "Pneuma," etc., *Theologisches Wörterbuch zum Neuen Testament*, vol. 6, ed. Gerhard Friedrich Kittel (Stuttgart: W. Kohlhammer, 1960), p. 406.

5. Ernst Benz, ed., *Die Vision, Erfahrungsformen und Bilderwelt* (Stuttgart: Ernst Klett, 1969), p. 549, n. 1—revelationes 1, 1, 30).

6. *Ibid.*, p. 549.

7. Wayne Wood, *The Lutheran Charismatic Movement in the United States*, unpublished D.Min. dissertation (Divinity School of Vanderbilt University, 1983), p. 3.

8. Dale W. Brown, *Understanding Pietism* (Grand Rapids: Eerdmans, 1978), p. 106.

9. Bruce Yokum, *Prophecy* (Ann Arbor, Mich.: Servant, 1976), p. 22.

10. Demos Shakarian, *The Happiest People on Earth* (Old Tappan, N.J.: Chosen, 1975), p. 19-22. In 1853 an illiterate, 11-year-old Russian boy, Efim, received a vision of charts and a message in beautiful handwriting. The map and the words that he laboriously copied for seven days warned the Christians to flee Russian Armenia and cross the Atlantic Ocean to America. A group of them heeded the prophecy and escaped the persecution that followed.

Chapter 43: The Gift of Tongues

1. Luther P. Gerlach and Virginia H. Hine, *People, Power, Change—Movements of Social Transformation* (Indianapolis, Ind.: Bobbs-Merrill, 1970), pp. 120, 125, 188. See also their article in *Journal for the Scientific Study of Religion*, vol. 7, no. 1 (Spring 1968).

2. Larry Christenson, *The Charismatic Renewal Among Lutherans* (Minneapolis: International Lutheran Renewal Center, 1976; rev. ed. 1985), pp. 17, 21, 23, 24, 25, 31. See also Larry Christenson, *Speaking in Tongues and Its Significance for the Church* (Minneapolis: Bethany, 1968), pp. 13-14, 27-28, 76-79. Erwin Prange, *The Gift Is Already Yours* (Plainfield, New Jersey: Logos, 1973), p. 53.

3. Gerhard Kittel, ed., *Theological Dictionary of the New Testament*, vol. 1 (Grand Rapids: 1964), pp. 719ff. Also William F. Arndt and Wilbur Gingrich, *A Greek-English Lexicon of the New Testament and Other Early Christian Literature* (Chicago: Univ. of Chicago, 1957), p. 161. While the term *glossa* literally means the tongue, as an organ of speech, both Kittel and Bauer indicate that *en glossais lalein* (speaking in tongues) is used as a technical term in the New Testament for a spiritually or religiously effected utterance, for a peculiar language, that is, a "language of the Spirit." In the German edition, Kittel invented a Greek-German term, *Glossenreden*, to convey the sense of a technical term. In Germany the term *Zungenreden* carries with it a strongly negative Pentecostal connotation. Arnold Bittlinger and others have offered alternatives such as *Sprachenreden* or *Sprachengebet*.

4. Christenson, *Speaking in Tongues*, p. 24.

5. Eddie Ensley, *Sounds of Wonder* (New York: Paulist, 1977), chap. 7. The author makes a case for a connection between glossolalia and jubilation, even though it is not specifically so stated in the church fathers. Descriptions of jubilation show marked similarities to present-day descriptions of tongues. St. Augustine of Hippo: "Where speech does not suffice. . .they break into singing on vowel sounds, that through this means the feeling of the soul may be expressed, words failing to explain the heart's conceptions" (*Sounds of Wonder*, p. 8). St. John Chrysostom: "Though men and women, young and old, are different, when they sing hymns,

their voices are influenced by the Holy Spirit in such a way that the melody sounds as if sung by one voice. . .for when we sing the angels blend their voices with ours and we blend our voices with theirs" (*Sounds of Wonder*, p. 13).

6. Ernst Adolph Rossteuscher, *Der Aufbau der Kirche Christi auf den ursprünglichen Grundlagen: Eine geschichtliche Darstellung seiner Anfänge* (Siegen: Hermann Neier Nachf., 1871, reprinted 1969), p. 258. The author noted that the occurrence of tongues in a Presbyterian congregation in London in the 1830s led the pastor, Edward Irving, to this particular estimate of tongues: "The unknown utterance [in tongues] is for us a prevenient sign that the words addressed to our understanding are a message from God, a prophecy in the power of the Spirit, an utterance impelled by the Holy Ghost, and not the utterance of an enlightened and pious human intellect." See Larry Christenson, "Pentecostalism's Forgotten Forerunner," *Aspects of Pentecostal-Charismatic Origins*, ed. Vinson Synan (Plainfield, N.J.: Logos, 1975), pp. 15-37; and *A Message to the Charismatic Movement* (Minneapolis: Bethany, 1972). Christenson draws significant parallels between the history and spirituality of the Catholic Apostolic Church, sometimes called Irvingism, and the present-day Pentecostal/charismatic movement, which is all the more remarkable in that there was no historical link between the two.

7. Ole Skjerbaek Madsen (see Appendix 2, p. 377), personal testimony.

8. Arthur Adams Lovekin, *Glossolalia; a Critical Study of Alleged Origins, the New Testament and the Early Church* (Sewanee, Tenn.: American Theological Library Association Microtext Project, 1962), p. 61.

9. Risto Santala, *Armolahjoista armon tasolta* (Helsinki: Karas-Sana Oy, 1978), pp. 80-89. In this Finnish publication Santala reports linguistic analysis of a recording of several glossolalia utterances that Larry Christenson recorded one morning in 1963 during his private devotions, at the request of a research team from the American Lutheran Church that was visiting his congregation in San Pedro, California. Santala, a longtime missionary in Israel, heard the recording some years later during a lecture by psychiatrist Paul Qualben, a member of the research team that had visited Christenson's congregation. He determined that the utterances were a mixture of Hebrew and Aramaic. His transcription and translation of the utterances were a hymn of praise cast in Old Testament bridal imagery. His initial report read:

"In the beginning of January 1976 there was a lecture dealing with the phenomenon of glossolalia at Concordia Theological Seminary, Springfield, Illinois. The speaker, M.D. Paul A. Qualben, has both theological and psychological training and he presented the results and conclusions which he had made in his field study among charismatics. The topic was handled scientifically and with reverence showing an uncommonly unbiased attitude. According to Dr. Qualben there are two kinds of tongue speaking in the New Testament. The first type could be called *xenolalia:* God speaks to the congregation in a real language as it was in the beginning of Acts. The second type is represented in 1 Corinthians, where the believer speaks unknown tongues, *glossolalia,* to God. According to the lecture, however, 'linguists that have analysed many tapes of persons speaking in tongues have not found that any of them represent a known language or dialect.'

"Dr. Qualben gave some prerecorded examples of tongue speaking—among them a beautiful liturgical chant. I was astonished and I asked to get an additional copy of the tape. After a couple of days I heard again the same chant together with my wife in our guest room. We understood straight away the message, and after having heard the chant several times, every single word became familiar. After some days I sent a long letter to Dr. Qualben with a detailed linguistic and theological analysis. And here is the main part of the letter with some minor changes:

"The chant shows all the signs of well spoken old Hebrew with Aramaic addenda. And since I've been preaching and teaching more than ten years in modern Hebrew in Jerusalem and since I've also been used to medieval RASHI-Hebrew and Talmudic texts, I felt that it would be good to notify you of the treasure which you have in your hands.

"The musical wonder of the chant: The song is probably in the Hypodorian mode, with A as the reciting tone, similar to Gregorian chant though its roots are pre-Gregorian monophonic plainsong. This type of singing traces back to the first Christian hymns and the ancient Temple service. The song has all the signs of professional musical work. The whole song is well balanced beginning with 'clivis' and then with 'virga subtripunctum' followed by three beautiful phrases of 'podatus' coming back to 'virga subtripunctum' and closing with a peaceful 'podatus.'

"The text is interesting and based mainly on Numbers 6:24, "The LORD bless thee." The holy name of God which is never pronounced by a religious Jew is however departed to two synonyms of God, *El* and *Jah*—theologically a very interesting solution. The word "to bless" is repeated six times and always in strictly correct grammatical form (*jevarechech, jevarechech, va-verech, ve-jevarech, va-avarech,* and *avarech*). The Hebrew equivalent in Numbers sounds *jevarechecha,* but as the object in this blessing is the "bride," in Aramaic *kaleea* and in Hebrew *kalah,* even the object here is in feminine form. This is already a masterwork. The word *Jah,* God, repeats six times; the Aramaic word *kaleea,* bride, is in our song five times; the word *shomeea,* to hear, twice; *hoshea,* to save, twice; *iish,* the Man, twice; and so forth. The grammar follows the Hebrew rules but the spiritual concepts are inclined to sound in their Aramaic forms—which is typical of some rabbinic texts.

"The sentences are long and built with grammar. The pronunciation is of highest professional quality and has no American features whatsoever. In fact, I have been studying singing about eight years with a well known Jewish professor who also taught some Jewish cantors, and I must admit that this man glides over the words very distinctly and smoothly, which is a sign of high professional skill.

"The song is divided into almost equal sections having typical Hebrew rhymes. Twice an 'a'-sound is added to words where it does not seem necessary, in order to fit the rhyme, but this is sometimes typical in Hebrew poetry. And in addition: the chant also stands the test of linguistic rhythm in the Hebrew language. Every single word has the stress properly on the correct syllable.

"It is rather difficult to hear a living language, especially old rarely spoken Semitic dialects, where the expressions have been preserved only in a written form. And now we are opening a riddle the opposite way, from a spoken tongue to a written form. The pronounciation varies throughout the centuries—our chant however is not too difficult in its linguistic structure. It translates [literally] as follows—

" '. . . may the Lord God bless thee./ O Man of His, O Man "Thou art as He," bless the bride./ That God shaketh thee, thus He hears and blesses the bride./ Be still, thus, and he will bless the bride as if in heaven/ in order to save, and God reveals His full power./ Thou hast made the Exalted One as if cursed by God and I shall bless the bride./ The light of God your Messiah becomes wonderful./ He answers, thus he saves./ I shall bless the bride with strong latter rain, thus He hears./ Raise.' The last word corresponds presumably with the Latin 'sursum corda,' 'lift up your hearts.'

"We meet in our chant profound musical expertness, good Hebrew pronunciation, old poetical type of language with pure rhymes, a clear biblical message which follows beautifully the nature of the music—and most important of all, a clear Christian gospel of Him, who became cursed instead of us. This heavenly Man ['Thou art as He,' in the chant, is a name-identification similar to Jesus' 'Before Abraham was, I AM' in John 8:58], the Messiah and the Light of God, is going to bless the bride with the 'latter rain as if in heaven.' Our chant shows the lowliness and humiliation of Christ in such a way that I am inclined to think that it is a real case of *xenolalia* given by the Holy Spirit."

10. Hubert Kirchner, and others, eds., *Charismatische Erneuerung und Kirche* (Berlin: Evangelische Verlagsanstalt, 1983), p. 58. (Excerpt translated by Larry Christenson).

11. "Charisma on the Rise," *Time*, June 14, 1968, p. 64.

12. Larry Christenson, *Speaking in Tongues*, p. 18.

13. Krister Stendahl, "Gossolalia—the New Testament Evidence," in *Paul Among Jews and Gentiles, and Other Essays* (Philadelphia: Fortress, 1976), p. 111. Stendahl cites his own and other scholarly opinion that interprets Rom. 8:26 as a reference to glossolalia.

14. Christenson, *Speaking in Tongues*, p. 19.

15. Sharon E. Mumper, "Where in the World Is the Church Growing," *Christianity Today*, July 11, 1986, p. 21.

16. Kilian McDonnell, ed., *Presence, Power, Praise—Documents on the Charismatic Renewal*, vol. 1 (Collegeville, Minn.: Liturgical Press, 1980), p. 100.

17. Paul Qualben, a psychiatrist who participated in a field study of glossolalia for the American Lutheran Church in 1963, said in a lecture at Wartburg Theological Seminary, Dubuque, Iowa, April 1972, that initially they expected to encounter people who were emotionally unbalanced, but that in fact this did not prove to be true; the people that they interviewed and tested were a cross section of ordinary Lutheran congregations. Reported by Larry Christenson.

18. Arthur Lovekin, *Glossolalia*, p. 40. The occurrence of speaking in tongues in non- or pre-Christian settings is frequently alluded to as accepted wisdom. Lovekin, however, does a thorough study of the sources and concludes that "there is no well documented instance of phenomena similar to apostolic glossolalia in either the preceding or contemporary pagan, or Jewish religions. The only similarity is a quality of ecstasy noted in prophecy which is present in the experience of the glossolalist. But this is not of equal degree because the ecstatic prophet has to lose consciousness; and this is nowhere to be found in apostolic glossolalia. In no case of ecstatic prophecy is the prophet ever portrayed as being able to interpret his own unintelligible speech. The apostolic experience of glossolalia must be interpreted as something new." See also Morton Kelsey, *Tongue Speaking* (New York: Crossroad, 1964; rev. ed. 1981), pp. 138-145. Kelsey, also relying on firsthand study of sources, comes to the same conclusion as Lovekin: "There is nothing to be found in either Hebrew or Greek antecedents comparable to the experience described by Paul's letters and the Book of Acts as speaking in tongues" (p. 141). Independently of one another, both Lovekin and Kelsey credit Coynbeare's article

in the *Encyclopaedia Brittanica* [11th ed., vol. 27 (New York: 1911), pp. 9ff.] with contributing to widespread misunderstanding at this point.

19. McDonnell, *Presence, Power, Praise,* vol. 1. See, for example, the comment by Bishop James Pike that speaking in tongues "would seem to run counter to the Anglican tradition" (p. 100); and the observation of a study commission of the American Lutheran Church that "speaking in tongues is not Lutheran" appeared to be a commonly voiced (but, in the view of the commission, unhelpful) attitude among Lutherans (p. 58).

20. *Ibid.,* pp. 101, 111.

21. *Ibid.,* p. 61.

22. Emil Brunner, *The Misunderstanding of the Church* (London: Lutterworth, 1952), p. 52.

23. Stendahl, "Glossolalia—New Testament Evidence," p. 124. Note his remark: "It is not a question of whether glossolalia is a theologically proper phenomenon— of course it is. It is rather a question of how this phenomenon can be a force to the benefit of the whole church. It is in that sense that *Paul's vision and perspective strike me as unsurpassed both in wisdom and vitality"* [italics added].

24. McDonnell, *Presence, Power, Praise,* vol. 1, pp. 102, 111, 63.

25. Christenson, *Speaking in Tongues,* p. 54. This is generally true in other mainline churches as well; see, for example, Barbara A. Pursey, "Charismatic Myths," *Acts 29,* Newsletter of the Episcopal Renewal Ministries, vol. 3, no. 5 (1985), p. 8.

26. Kenneth S. Kantzer, "The Charismatics Among Us," *Christianity Today,* February 22, 1980, pp. 25-27. David Barrett, author of *The World Christian Encyclopedia,* in a lecture to a group of charismatic leaders at Glencoe, Missouri, May 7, 1986, said that out of 44 million people in the United States who designate themselves as "charismatic," only six million (about 14%) speak in tongues.

27. Christenson, *Charismatic Renewal Among Lutherans,* p. 24.

28. Stephen B. Clark, *Baptized in the Spirit and Spiritual Gifts* (Ann Arbor, Mich.: Servant, 1976), p. 38.

29. Stendahl, "Glossolalia—New Testament Evidence," p. 121. Note his remark: "As I read Paul it seems to me crystal clear that if the Presbyterians and Episcopalians and Lutherans, and all the 'proper' Christians, including the Catholics, did not consciously or unconsciously suppress such phenomenon as glossolalia, and if other denominations did not especially encourage them, then the gifts of the Spirit—including glossolalia—would belong to the common register of Christian experience."

30. Christenson, *Speaking in Tongues,* p. 7.

31. The following comment from a charismatic Lutheran layman (August 12, 1986) is typical of the kind of complaints that charismatic leaders encounter almost constantly: "The perennial question is, 'Why is it that when a Lutheran becomes "alive in Christ" the average Lutheran pastor cannot relate to that person but instead "pours on the tradition" to keep us "pure Lutheran"—and sometimes dead?" Private correspondence, Larry Christenson.

32. Larry Christenson, "The Pastoral Ministry in Relation to the Charismatic Move- ment" in *Towards a Mutual Understanding of Neo-Pentecostalism,* eds. Walter Wietzke and Jack Hustad (Minneapolis: Augsburg, 1973), pp. 31-34.

Chapter 44: Gifts of Healings

1. Martin E. Marty, *Health and Medicine in the Lutheran Tradition* (New York: Crossroad, 1983), pp. 86-88.
2. Morton T. Kelsey, "The Healing Ministry Within the Church," *Journal of Religion and Health,* vol. 9, no. 2 (April 1970), p. 115. See also some of Luther's own statements expressing his belief in healing, for example, the letter to Pastor Severin Schulze, above, p. 209 (WABr 11, no. 4120), pp. 111-112), and his comment on overcoming sickness through faith and prayer (AE 54, 453-454).
3. Johann Christoph Blumhardt, *Seelsorge* (Munich and Hamburg: Siebenstern, 1949), pp. 42-44. See also the brief biographical sketch of the author, noting his emphasis on healing and exorcism, facing the title page.
4. See, for example, the book by Peder Olsen, *Healing Through Prayer,* trans. John Jensen (Minneapolis: Augsburg, 1962).
5. Richard G. Hutcheson Jr., *Mainline Churches and the Evangelicals* (Atlanta: John Knox, 1981), pp. 82-97.
6. William Vaswig, *I Prayed, He Answered* (Minneapolis: Augsburg, 1977), pp. 28-38.
7. John Wimber, "Zip to 3000 in 5 Years," *Christian Life,* October 1982, pp. 18-23.
8. John Wimber, in a message at Acts 86, an all-European ecumenical charismatic conference, on July 24, 1986, said that "failures" outnumber healings in his ministry.
9. In private conversation with Larry and Nordis Christenson.
10 In private conversation with Larry Christenson, 1959.
11. In private conversation with Larry Christenson, 1960.
12. Robert Whitaker. Personal testimony shared on several occasions.
13. See Agnes Sanford, "The Healing of the Emotions," (chap. 11) in *The Healing Light* (St. Paul: Macalaster Park, 1947), pp. 120-129.
14. Arthur Richter, executive secretary of the Marburger Kreis (the German expression of the Oxford Group Movement), frequently made this observation when sharing the long and rich experience of the Marburger Kreis with the practice of private confession.
15. Don H. Gross, *The Case for Spiritual Healing* (New York: Thomas Nelson, 1958), p. 78.
16. In Scripture we find times when healing or deliverance is attributed to the faith of the afflicted person: Matt. 9:22; Mark 10:52; Acts 14:9. This is not always the case, however: see Mark 2:5, where Jesus responded to the faith of friends of the sick person. It is an unwise and dangerous practice indiscriminately to lay responsibility for healing faith on the ill person.
17. Ignatius of Antioch, Epistle to the Ephesians 20, 2.

Chapter 45: The Church: Workshop of the Spirit

1. Emil Brunner, *Dogmatik III: Die christliche Lehre von der Kirche, vom Glauben und von der Vollendung* (Zürich: Theologischer Verlag Zürich, 1960) pp. 57ff.
2. Edmund Schlink, *Der kommende Christus und die kirchlichen Traditionen: Beiträge zum Gespräch zwischen den getrennten Kirchen* (Göttingen: Vandenhoeck & Ruprecht, 1961), p. 164. (Excerpt translated by William Sims.)
3. See sequence in the *Augsburg Confession* from IV to V.

4. Edmund Schlink, *Der kommende Christus und kirchlichen Traditionen*, pp. 161ff. (Excerpt translated by William Sims.)
5. Kilian McDonnell, "Towards a Critique of the Churches and Charismatic Renewal," *One in Christ*, vol. 16, no. 4, p. 331.

Chapter 46: The Church: Institution and Free Movements

1. In the mid-1980s, three Lutheran bodies in the United States engaged in discussions aimed at forming a new Lutheran church. The three bodies were the American Lutheran Church (ALC), the Association of Evangelical Lutheran Churches (AELC), and the Lutheran Church in America (LCA).
2. Larry Johnson, ed., *Institutions and Movements: Two Structures within One Church*, unpublished paper prepared on behalf of the Affiliation of Lutheran Movements for discussion with members of the Commission for a New Lutheran Church, p. 4. The discussion was held April 5, 1984, at Luther Northwestern Theological Seminary, St. Paul, Minnesota.
3. See Ralph Winter, "The Two Structures of God's Redemptive Mission," *Missiology: An International Review*, January 1974, p. 124.
4. 1 Clement 57.
5. Irenaeus, Adv. Haereses III, 3, 1-2.
6. Berthold Altaner, *Patrologie* (Freiburg im Breisgau: Herder, 1955), pp. 37-40. Cf. Adv. haer., III, XXIV, 1, and II, XXXII, 4.
7. Didache XI, 8.
8. *Ibid.*, X, 7.
9. *Ibid.*, XI, 12.
10. Berthold Altaner, *Patrologie*, p. 235.
11. In the history of the development of the papacy, the basic position "papa a nemine iudicatur" was first promulgated in the year 502 by Eunodius, the bishop of Pavia, during the see of Pope Symmachus (498-514). Later, through the "corpus iuris canonici," this position became an established ingredient of the "ius divinum" understanding of canon law ("nemo iudicabit primam sedem"; Decretum Gratiani—promulgated in the 12th century—causa IX, questio 3, canon 10).
12. Franz Anton Staudenmaier, *Der Pragmatismus der Geistesgaben oder das Wirken des göttlichen Geistes im Menschen und in der Menschheit* (Tübingen: Heinrich Laupp, 1835), p. 23.
13. Winter, "Two Structures of God's Redemptive Mission," pp. 126-127.
14. Johnson, *Institutions and Movements*, p. 7.
15. *Ibid.*, p. 13.
16. Kilian McDonnell, ed., *Presence, Power, Praise—Documents on the Charismatic Renewal*, vol. 1 (Collegeville, Minn. Liturgical Press, 1980). The documents in this volume cover the period from 1960-1974. In considerable degree the documents produced by Protestant churches during this period represent attempts to respond to a new phenomenon that is perceived as a threat to peace and order. "The Charismatic Movement and Lutheran Theology," from the Lutheran Church–Missouri Synod, in 1972, traces a brief history of the renewal and observes, "It has touched nearly every Protestant denomination in our country as well as in many foreign countries. In spite of warnings by denominational leaders and even the removal of pastors from their charges, the movement seems to increase in influence" (pp. 324-325).

17. From 1972–1984, Lutheran charismatic leaders made numerous overtures to Lutheran church officials to visit the International Lutheran Conference on the Holy Spirit, held annually in Minneapolis, Minnesota. Several responded and brought greetings or participated in forums, but the majority of invitations were declined. The churches appeared to feel more comfortable in the role of observer. Dr. Martin Lieske, a district president of the Lutheran Church–Missouri Synod, was quoted as saying that he had sent observers to report on "the theological implications" of the Holy Spirit conference (Herb Strentz, "Lutheran meeting on Holy Spirit has non-Lutheran side," *Minneapolis Tribune,* August 11, 1973).

18. In 1984 Wayne Weissenbuehler, a bishop of the American Lutheran Church, taught the morning Bible studies at the International Lutheran Conference on the Holy Spirit, as well as participating in an open forum with Lowell Erdahl and Darold Beekmann, two other bishops of the American Lutheran Church. This was announced as a "first" and was warmly received.

19. In conversation with some Lutheran charismatic leaders in 1983, David Preus, presiding bishop of the American Lutheran Church, said that he had received criticism from various quarters when he spoke out about what he perceived to be a rise of antinomianism in the church, but had received no encouragement from the charismatics, whom he had thought would have stood with him on this issue. Morris Vaagenes, responding on behalf of the charismatics, acknowledged that charismatics had generally neglected this kind of communication with church officials.

20. Merton P. Strommen, and others, *A Study of Generations* (Minneapolis: Augsburg, 1972), p. 150.

21. Richard G. Hutcheson Jr., *Mainline Churches and the Evangelicals* (Atlanta: John Knox, 1981), pp. 105-106.

Chapter 47: The Church: An Ordered Body

1. Richard G. Hutcheson Jr., *Mainline Churches and the Evangelicals* (Atlanta: John Knox, 1981), p. 174.

2. Kilian McDonnell, in an open forum at the 1975 Assembly of the World Council of Churches in Nairobi. Reported by Larry Christenson.

3. In 1984 a group of Lutheran pastors and theologians representing both free movements and institutional structures in American Lutheranism met and formed a group which they called *Friends for Biblical Lutheranism.* Participating in this group were two leaders in the Lutheran charismatic renewal, Larry Christenson and Paul Swedberg. The statement of faith which this group developed includes a reference to biblical standards not only for doctrine and ethical conduct, but also in regard to church *structure:*

> We confess Jesus Christ as Lord and Savior and accept all the canonical books of the Old and New Testament as the inspired Word of God. The Word of God is the sacred Scriptures, the eternally true, written record and witness of God's revelation centering in Jesus Christ and proclaiming both Law and Gospel.
>
> The Scriptures are the source, the authoritative norm, and the ultimate inspiration and judge of the Church's proclamation, teaching, *structure,* and conduct [italics added].

4. Herbert Mirly, talk given at Lutheran Charismatic Regional Leaders' Meeting, Onamia, Minnesota, March 1983.
5. "1975 Annual Report," Trinity Lutheran Church, San Pedro, California, pp. 16-18.

Chapter 48: The Church: A Worshiping Community

1. Philip Schaff, *History of the Christian Church,* vol. 1 (New York: Scribner's, 1882-1910), pp. 230-231. The author pointed out that "the glossolalia [speaking in tongues] on the Day of Pentecost was, as in all cases where it is mentioned, *an act of worship and adoration,* not an act of teaching and instruction, which followed afterwards in the sermon of Peter. The Pentecostal glossolalia was the *same* as that in the household of Cornelius in Caesarea after his conversion, which may be called a Gentile Pentecost, as that of the twelve disciples of John the Baptist at Ephesus, where it appears in connection with prophecy, and as that in the Christian congregation at Corinth" [italics added].
2. Merlin Carothers, *Prison to Praise* (Plainfield, N.J.: Logos, 1969). The author's first title sold five million copies and was followed by nine other books, all built around the basic theme of praise. Lutheran charismatics have taken issue with some theological aspects in these books, but it is nevertheless evident that the author struck on a theme that had been widely neglected.
3. Paul Anderson, "Finding the Balance in Worship," *Loaves and Fishes,* no. 183 (Trinity Lutheran Church, San Pedro, California: May/June 1986), pp. 6-7.
4. The Lutheran bishop of Oulu (Lapland), in Finland, Olavi Rimpiläinen, made this observation in a conversation with Larry Christenson in 1982. He had just recently published an article on early Christian liturgies, and was interested that Christenson's congregation in San Pedro, California, without any knowledge of this practice in the early church, had opened up their liturgy for charismatic expressions at exactly the same points: following the reading of Scripture, and during the distribution of Holy Communion.
5. Luther, *Deutsche Messe,* 1526 (AE 53, 64; WA 19, 75).
6. Ern Baxter, "The Power of a Superior Passion," *New Wine Tape of the Month,* WT 104 (Mobile, Ala.: Integrity Communications, 1986).
7. Krister Stendahl, "Glossolalia—the New Testament Evidence," *Paul Among Jews and Gentiles, and Other Essays* (Philadelphia: Fortress, 1976), p. 111. Stendahl cites his own and other scholarly opinion that interprets Rom. 8:26 as a reference to glossolalia.
8. Martin E. Lehmann, *Luther and Prayer* (Milwaukee: Northwestern, 1985), p. 133.
9. *Ibid.,* p. 143.
10. Ole Skjerbaek Madsen (see Appendix 2, p. 377) observed that the general prayer in the communion service of their congregation (Bethlehemskirken, Copenhagen) took on added vitality when specific intercessions for members of the congregation were incorporated, for example, "for Julianna, that her legs be healed and that she be delivered from the bondage of fear, we cry unto you." They usually have 10-15 such petitions, which have been brought to the attention of the pastor or deacons the week previous. Answers to prayer are reported to the congregation. This is an example of a widely used liturgical form that is readily adaptable to

free expression and that could also include charismatic gifts such as prophecy, tongues and interpretation, word of knowledge, discernment of spirits.

11. Wayne Wood, *The Lutheran Charismatic Movement in the United States,* unpublished D.Min. dissertation (Divinity School of Vanderbilt University, 1983), p. 12.

Chapter 49: The Church: A Missionary Community

1. Philipp Jakob Spener, *Pia Desideria,* rev. ed., ed. Erich Beyreuther (Giessem/Basel: Brunnen, 1975), p. 53. In considering the renewal of the Lutheran church in his day, Spener said, "Der Heilige Geist ist heutzutage nicht säumiger und unvermögender als in den Tagen der Urchristenheit."
2. "Lutheran Evangelism a Joke," *The Lutheran,* September 17, 1986, p. 40.
3. Jim Roberson, "Radical Evangelism! What Is It?" *International Lutheran Renewal,* no. 85 (Dec. 1986), p. 1.
4. David Barrett, "Annual Statistical Table on Global Mission," *International Bulletin of Missionary Research,* vol. 10, no. 1 (January 1986), pp. 22-23.
5. Derek Prince, "Update #35," (Derek Prince Publications: Fort Lauderdale, Fla., 1985), cassette tape.
6. *Christian Life,* vol. 44, No. 6 (October 1982), pp. 10, 18, 64.

Chapter 50: The Church: A Servant

1. This example provided by Per-Olaf Söderpalm (see Appendix 2, p. 377).
2. For further information on Müntzer see: Eric Gritsch, *Reformer Without a Church* (Philadelphia: Fortress, 1967); Hans-Jürgen Goertz, *Innere und Aeussere Ordnung in der Theologie Thomas Müntzers* (Leiden: Brill, 1967); Hans Hillerbrand, "Thomas Muentzer's Last Tract Against Martin Luther," *Mennonite Quarterly Review,* no. 38 (1964), pp. 2-36; Carter Lindberg, "Theology and Politics: Luther the Radical and Muntzer the Reactionary," *Encounter* no. 37 (1976), pp. 356-371; idem., "Conflicting Models of Ministry: Luther, Karlstadt and Muentzer," *Concordia Theological Quarterly,* no. 41 (1977), pp. 35-50; Gordon Rupp, *Patterns of Reformation* (Philadelphia: Fortress, 1969).
3. Joachim Jeremias, *Neutestamentliche Theologie. Part 1: Die Verkündigung Jesu* (Gütersloh: Gütersloher Verlagshaus Gerd Mohn, 1973), p. 229.

Chapter 51: The Church: A Battle-Ready Community

1. Leonhard Goppelt, *Theologie des Neuen Testaments: Part 1: Jesu Wirken in seiner theologischen Bedeutung,* ed. Jürgen Roloff (Göttingen: Vandenhoeck & Ruprecht, 1975), p. 126.
2. Joachim Jeremias, *Neutestamentliche Theologie: Part 1: Die Verkündigung Jesu* (Gütersloh: Gütersloher Verlagshaus Gerd Mohn, 1971), p. 98.
3. Ole Skjerbaek Madsen (see Appendix 2, p. 377) supplied this example from his pastoral ministry.
4. Paul Althaus, *The Theology of Martin Luther,* trans. Robert C. Schultz (Philadelphia: Fortress, 1966), p. 161.

Chapter 52: The Church: A Fellowship of Hope

1. Leonhard Goppelt, *Theologie des Neuen Testaments: Part 1: Jesu Wirken in seiner theologischen Bedeutung,* ed. Jürgen Roloff (Göttingen: Vandenhoeck & Ruprecht, 1975), p. 119. (Excerpt translated by William Sims.)

Appendix 1: Country-by-Country Overview of the Charismatic Renewal among Lutherans

1. Erling Jorstad, *Bold in the Spirit* (Minneapolis: Augsburg, 1974), pp. 22-32.
2. Kilian McDonnell, ed., *Presence, Power, Praise—Documents on the Charismatic Renewal,* vol. 1 (Collegeville, Minn.: Liturgical Press, 1980), p. 55.
3. *Ibid.,* p. 162.
4. Paul Qualben, lecture at Wartburg Theological Seminary, Dubuque, Iowa, March 1972. From notes by Larry Christenson.
5. "The Charismatic Movement and Lutheran Theology (A Report of the Commission on Theology and Church Relations of the Lutheran Church–Missouri Synod, January 1972, in *Presence, Power, Praise—Documents on the Charismatic Renewal,* vol. 1, pp. 345-347.
6. Merton P. Strommen, and others, *A Study of Generations* (Minneapolis: Augsburg, 1972), p. 119.
7. Reported by Larry Christenson, from an open forum on charismatic renewal at the Nairobi Conference of the World Conference of Churches in 1975.
8. Larry Christenson, "Christianity in East Africa: In the Midst of Problems— Power!" *International Lutheran Renewal,* no. 72 (November 1985), p. 3.
9. Per Anderson, " 'Lutheran Pentecost' in Tanzania," *International Lutheran Renewal,* no. 75 (February 1986).

INDEX OF BIBLICAL PASSAGES CITED

2:16,6	150	14:16	317, 266	2:16	74
3:16	94, 324	14:16-17	269	2:20	75, 90, 185
4–6	245	14:18	269	3:1-5	61, 90
4:20	116, 169, 197, 219	14:18-19	266	3:2	60, 74
		14:22	267	3:3-5	197
6:11	79, 92, 203	14:24-25	257	3:5	99, 116
6:19	94, 316	14:25	261	3:5,14	74
7:7	244	14:26	289, 326	3:8	91
9:25	238	14:26-33	121	3:14	91
10–11	133	14:27	269	3:23-29	131
10:16-17	319	14:28	269, 266	3:26-27	80
11:4-16	321	14:29	255	3:27	78, 203
11:23-25	286	14:31,5	245	4:6	74
11:23-30	245	14:32	263	4:19	200
11:25	130	14:37	259	5:16-18	91, 93
11:26	286	14:39	257, 270	5:16-25	93
11:26-32	319	15:3-11	146	5:18	90
12	37, 244	15:10	210, 238	5:22	93
12–14	106, 133	15:24-28	341	5:22-23	132, 221
12:3	65, 246, 255	15:26	279	5:25	93, 194
12:4-6	245	15:50	191		
12:4-11	132, 248, 341	15:51-58	257	**Ephesians**	
12:7	246, 336			1:4	234
12:7,11	288	**2 Corinthians**		1:7	58, 146
12:7-11	121	1:11	321	1:13	58, 75, 87, 384
12:8-11	100	1:21-22	116, 384		
12:9	107, 283	1:22	75, 87	1:13-14	116
12:10	25, 252, 255, 265, 346	3:2	232	1:14	75
		3:5	73, 92	1:16-23	321
12:10,28	257	3:12-18	194	1:17-19	66
12:12	245	3:17	245	1:20-23	342
12:13	60, 202, 211	3:17-18	93	1:22-23	262, 340
12:14-26	245	3:18	235	2:1-3	180
12:27	262	4:1	350	2:4-10	180
12:28	257, 262, 273	4:5	25	2:6	341
12:31	93, 246, 248, 255	4:7	92	2:7	350
		4:18	49	2:8	65, 139
13	246	5:5	75	2:8-9	131
13:1-3	246	5:14-15	65	2:10	186, 189
13:3	194	5:16	181	2:11-22	128
13:9	252, 259	5:17	75, 107, 285	2:12	130
13:13	93	5:17	182	2:20	257, 262
14:1	32, 246, 248, 255, 257, 271	5:19	257	3:5	65, 257, 262
		6:10	93	3:10	350
14:2	265, 267-268	7:1	349	3:14-19	115
14:2,4,16,28	266	10:3-6	341	4:1-3,13	129
14:3	257, 260	10:4	340	4:8,11-12	127
14:4	269, 266	10:12	210	4:11	248, 257, 262
14:5	271	12:9-10	92	4:11-12	246
14:5,13,27	266	12:12	100	4:12	248
14:10-11	267	13:7	321	4:15-16	128, 246
14:13	246, 269			4:27	346
14:14	266	**Galatians**		4:30	94, 384
14:15	269	1:6-9	129	5:5	241
		2:15-21	90		

INDEX OF NAMES AND SUBJECTS

References to *charismatic renewal* in the index are abbreviated as "CR." References to *charismatic* are abbreviated as "c."